SOCIAL AND ECONOMIC STUDIES OF
POST-WAR FRANCE

Prepared under the auspices of the

COLUMBIA UNIVERSITY COUNCIL FOR RESEARCH
IN THE SOCIAL SCIENCES

EDITED BY

CARLTON J. H. HAYES

PROFESSOR OF HISTORY IN COLUMBIA UNIVERSITY

VOLUME I

THE PUBLIC FINANCES OF POST-WAR FRANCE

BY

ROBERT MURRAY HAIG

THE PUBLIC FINANCES OF POST-WAR FRANCE

BY

ROBERT MURRAY HAIG

PROFESSOR, SCHOOL OF BUSINESS
COLUMBIA UNIVERSITY

with the assistance of

CARL S. SHOUP, ALEXANDER WERTH
and
NATHALIE MOLODOVSKY

New York
COLUMBIA UNIVERSITY PRESS
1929

Published 1929

PRINTED IN THE UNITED STATES OF AMERICA
BY THE PLIMPTON PRESS · NORWOOD · MASS.

EDITOR'S PREFACE

THIS volume is the first of a series of *Social and Economic Studies of Post-War France*, sponsored by the Columbia University Council for Research in the Social Sciences and published by the Columbia University Press. The series aims to present a survey of such facts in French public life as have had important bearing on the great economic crisis through which France has passed since the conclusion of the World War.

France is by no means the only nation which has been tested by the war and tried by multitudinous problems of post-war reconstruction. In different ways and in varying degrees all the belligerents — and most neutrals — have had to cope with difficulties which the greatest war in human annals created for the entire world. But, of all the nations, France is perhaps the most suitable field for intensive study of post-war phenomena. France, in proportion to her area and population, bore greater burdens in the World War and suffered graver losses from it than any other nation. Her post-war difficulties, therefore, have been particularly acute. On the other hand, her post-war history has been characterized by no cataclysm, by no striking revolution, by not even a serious threat of revolution. France has not fallen under a Bolshevist dictatorship, like Russia, or under a Fascist dictatorship, like Italy; she has not startled the world by the suddenness of an heroic return to solvency, like England, or of a desperate drop into bankruptcy, like Germany, or by the emergence of any vast new wealth, like the United States. Rather, she has seemed to drift along, as an opportunist, living from day to day and from hand to mouth, and very haltingly, but in the end quite surely, regaining her political poise and regaining her economic equilibrium. In other words, there is nothing really sensational in the outward course of French history of the post-war decade; and for this reason France lends herself peculiarly to scientific study.

In any event, France would invite and merit special attention. She is, in many respects, the most civilized country in the world; and anyone who would seek the effects of the war upon civilization should find them *par excellence* in France. She is, too, an "old" country with an "old" independence, a Great Power with a wide range of interests and activities, which, rightly or wrongly, render her story more abidingly instructive and appealing to the general public than the story of any newer or lesser Power. She is, moreover, a "victor" from the last war and a leader in the present League of Nations, and there is natural curiosity to know something of the price that has been paid for military victory and pacific leadership.

To Americans, France possesses an eternal attraction. The attraction is largely sentimental, to be sure. It is not based on any absolute community of interests. Indeed, the actual contrasts between France and the United States are glaring and are certainly greater than those between England and the United States. Yet the very strangeness of the French scene has a romantic charm for the American; and when he recalls what he has been taught in his own schools concerning Lafayette and Rochambeau and the parallel rise of democracy in New World and Old, he is tempted to feel that he can (or should) know France better than any other European country, better even than England. And most American scholars, having a more thorough knowledge of French than of any other foreign language, are better equipped to study France than any other country of Continental Europe.

Work upon the present series of *Social and Economic Studies of Post-War France* was begun in the winter of 1925–1926. Funds for its prosecution were made available by grants from the Laura Spelman Rockefeller Memorial to the Columbia University Council for Research in the Social Sciences, and the organization of the work was entrusted by the latter to a committee consisting of Professors William F. Ogburn, Robert M. Haig, Lindsay Rogers, Wesley C. Mitchell, and Carlton J. H. Hayes (as chairman).

From start to finish the work has enjoyed the constant patronage and counsel of President Nicholas Murray Butler, and considerable assistance from the Trustees of Columbia University. It was at Dr. Butler's suggestion and with letters of introduction provided by him that the chairman of the committee went to France in January, 1926, and explained to high officials of the French Republic and to prominent scholars in French Universities precisely what was contemplated: the collection and publication of authentic data on social and economic developments in France since 1918, without purpose of determining France's "capacity" to discharge her foreign debts or of serving the ends of American tariff policy, but merely as a coöperative undertaking of a private group of American scholars devoted exclusively to an objective study of phenomena of general interest and significance. The cordial, even enthusiastic, response from French scholars and officials must be ascribed primarily to the confidence which they have long reposed in the character and judgment of Dr. Butler. It was through Dr. Butler's good offices, moreover, that the numerous staff, which conducted the ensuing investigations, were commodiously quartered for three years at 173 Boulevard Saint-Germain, Paris, in rooms assigned by the Centre Européen de la Dotation Carnegie (the European Centre of the Carnegie Endowment for International Peace) and by the American University Union in Europe. Repeatedly, as the work progressed, a word or letter from Dr. Butler proved an open sesame to French documents or French offices.

The Trustees of Columbia University have liberally fostered this, as well as a very large number of other scholarly researches, by relieving professors from teaching and enabling them to go abroad and devote themselves entirely to study, and by providing accommodations and stenographical assistance for the completion of the work in America. It is the Trustees who, by means of generous financial appropriations to the Columbia University Press, have made possible the final publication of the present series.

The staff, which was engaged on the work from 1926 to 1929, numbered about fifty. The principal members, the "directors of departments," were mainly supplied by the Faculties of Columbia University — Professors Hayes, Haig, Moon, Ogburn, and Lindsay Rogers; but the University of Missouri kindly furnished the services of Professor James Harvey Rogers, and the Brookwood Labor College those of Professor David J. Saposs, while from the Social Science Research Council came two Research Fellows, Dr. Jaffé and Mr. Evans, who collaborated respectively with Professors Ogburn and Saposs. To these principals were attached the research-assistants whose names are mentioned in the prefaces to the several volumes in this series, and also a corps of clerks and stenographers. All worked with zeal and in splendid coöperation. And in this connection it is only fair to state that the American scholars who participated in the enterprise did so at very considerable personal sacrifice of time and money and that they received (and will receive) absolutely no financial compensation beyond their regular academic salaries.

Every member of the staff did a large part of the work in France. The work involved a vast deal of traveling across the ocean and throughout the country, a vast number of personal conferences with Frenchmen in all walks of life, and the use of a vast quantity of documents, books, pamphlets, magazines, and newspapers. It could not have been done in the relatively short period allotted to it, had not the staff been favored with many helpful words of advice and letters of introduction from that great-hearted American Ambassador whom Frenchmen loved, the late Myron T. Herrick, and from Dr. Earle B. Babcock, the Associate Director of the Dotation Carnegie in Paris, from Dr. Horatio N. Krans, the Associate Director of the American University Union in Europe, and from Dr. James T. Shotwell, Director of the Division of Economics and History of the Carnegie Endowment. Indeed, the French volumes in the last-named's monumental series on *The Economic and Social History of the World War* (Yale University Press, New Haven; and Les Presses Universitaires, Paris) supplied much of the background and some of the models for the present investigation. In last analysis, however, the staff could not have brought its work to satisfactory completion, had it not been the beneficiary of the utmost cordiality and coöperation on the part of the highest French officials, such as MM. Poincaré, Briand, Herriot, and Painlevé, and of French scholars, publicists, bankers, ecclesiastics, labor leaders, and teachers, too numerous to mention here by name. Some measure of the staff's obligation to these is indicated in the prefaces to the several volumes of the series.

The results of the staff's investigations have been written up largely in America during the past year and are embodied in the seven volumes herewith presented to the public. The first volume, by Professor Robert Murray Haig, with the assistance of Messrs. Carl S. Shoup, Alexander Werth, and Mlle. Nathalie Molodovsky, is basic to the whole series. It tells the story of what happened to French public finance from 1918 to 1928: the accumulation of state indebtedness, and the various attempts of a succession of Governments, by means of borrowings, economies, and taxation, to support colossal national budgets. It is the most accurate, up-to-date, and comprehensive survey of French debt-questions and taxation-questions now available.

The second volume, by Professor James Harvey Rogers, with the assistance of Messrs. August Maffry and Robert E. Landman, shows in detail how the process of inflation, taking its rise in the disordered state of public finances, was carried, through the media of the banks, into the realm of private finance, until by 1926 it had wrought a veritable revolution in the prices of French commodities and in the costs of French living. This volume contains a reliable analysis of the whole French banking-system and a fully documented critique of the phenomena of inflation.

The third volume, by Professors William F. Ogburn and William Jaffé, outlines the whole post-war economic development of France and points out with a wealth of statistical data how national production in factory and field has been affected by all manner of post-war occurrences: the reconstruction of the devastated areas, the reannexation of Alsace-Lorraine, the formation of cartels, the process of monetary inflation. It presents specific studies not only of French agriculture but of such key-industries as metallurgy, machinery, electricity, textiles, and chemicals.

The fourth volume, by Professor David J. Saposs and Mr. A. D. Meurig Evans, deals with the French post-war labor movement, how it is organized, how it functions, how it has responded to the industrial development of the country and reacted to the fiscal and other policies of the national government. This volume is complementary to the third, and does for French labor what that of Professors Ogburn and Jaffé does for French industry. It is, moreover, the only available account of the recent history and present status of Socialism, Communism, and trade-unionism in France.

The first four volumes, it will be noted, are directly economic in content or implication. The other three are only indirectly economic; they treat chiefly of political and psychological matters, which, however, have conditioned in France, as elsewhere, the economic and social trends of post-war development.

The first of these last three volumes — the fifth in the series — is that of the chairman of the directing committee and editor of the series, on *France: A Nation of Patriots.* It presupposes that the French nation has withstood, with little murmuring and certainly without political revolution, the test of the World War, the trials of post-war inflation, and the tribulations of profound economic readjustment, mainly because its members are supremely devoted to France — because they have an intensely patriotic psychology. The volume undertakes, therefore, to probe the foundations of this psychology and to isolate the factors which mold and modify it. It describes the rôle of the State, the schools, the army, the churches, the press, radio, and cinema, national societies and national ceremonies; it discusses the contemporary situation in Alsace-Lorraine; and it deals with regional and international propaganda in France. This volume obviously belongs to *Social and Economic Studies of Post-War France;* but it may also be read in connection with the series of *Studies in the Making of Citizens* which Professor Charles E. Merriam of the University of Chicago is directing and editing on the parallel methods employed by other countries for the patriotic training of their citizens.

The sixth volume in the present series, that of Professor Lindsay Rogers, tells the story of French post-war politics. It explains the structure and especially the functioning of a government which has had to grapple with the most troublesome economic and social problems and yet at the same time has kept itself free from either socialist or reactionary dictatorship and has stubbornly adhered to parliamentary and republican traditions. The volume affords an authoritative commentary on contemporary French government and politics.

Finally, in the seventh volume, Professor Parker Thomas Moon analyzes the foreign and colonial policies of France in the period since the war, tracing the interplay of popular sentiment, politics, government finance, and economic interests in the realm of international relations. The French attitude, or attitudes, toward reparations and war debts, disarmament and security, colonies and tariffs; the French military action in Syria and Morocco, in the Rhineland and the Ruhr; the significance, for France, of the Locarno Pact and the Pact of Paris; the new system of French alliances; the rôle of France in the League of Nations — together with various other features of French diplomacy — are brought into relationship with the primary objectives of French foreign policy, as well as with the political and economic problems of post-war France.

The whole series of *Social and Economic Studies of Post-War France* represents a coöperative effort of historians, economists and political scientists to record in permanent form certain fleeting but highly significant events in the life of a great nation. Whatever merits the series as a whole may possess must be attributed, in first instance, to the Laura Spelman Rockefeller Memorial and to Columbia University, to both of which the Editor, in behalf of his colleagues, would again express gratitude, and, in last instance, to the members of the staff themselves, to whose arduous labor and earnest coöperation the Editor is proud to testify. The Editor would also acknowledge, with sincere thanks, the constant enlightened aid of his Editorial Assistant, Miss Vera Mikol, and, last, but by no means least, the uniform helpfulness of Mr. Frederick Coykendall and his associates in the direction of the Columbia University Press.

CARLTON J. H. HAYES

COLUMBIA UNIVERSITY
in the City of New York
July 14, 1929

AUTHOR'S PREFACE

THE present volume represents an attempt to describe the public finances of France in an objective spirit. Every effort has been made to avoid even the appearance of prescribing remedies. To record what the French did and to attempt to discover why they did it were found to be tasks more than sufficiently engaging in themselves. The French are not lacking in technical competence in matters of public finance. They are perhaps justified in feeling that they have already received a surfeit of gratuitous advice from abroad. Realizing that he cannot hope to discuss French finance with the precision and clarity of an Allix, or with the fluency and eloquence of a Jèze, the writer will be content if it proves that his sojourn in the gloomy offices of the Ministry of Finance has made recent French financial history more comprehensible particularly to American readers than it has been before.

Any alien who ventures to write about French public finance essays a rôle as perilous as that of Blondin crossing Niagara Falls on a tight rope. At every step he assumes strange and unusual risks and the chances of making errors and missteps are so great that if he succeeds in avoiding them it is as by a miracle. Balancing himself precariously with a copy of Allix's *Traité élémentaire* in one hand and with a letter from President Nicholas Murray Butler to M. Poincaré in the other, the writer has stepped boldly forth. Time after time, as some hypothesis regarding the true meaning of an account has failed or some figure has proved untrustworthy, he has been sickeningly conscious of slipping and swaying and even as the manuscript goes to press, his heart is not free from grave misgiving.

This feeling of apprehension and uncertainty rests partly upon the complicated character of the French financial system, but more largely upon the serious difficulties encountered because of lack of published data and because of the inaccuracy of such data as have been published. For example, when an investigator attempts to learn what the public expenditures of France have been during recent years, he discovers that at present nobody, not even the French Treasury itself, knows the facts.[1] Moreover, in all probability, no one will be able to tell the full story for another decade, if indeed then. The aggregate figures of expenditures which have been published are only rough approximations. Detailed information can be secured for credits opened, but not only are there important expenditures without regular budgetary authorization but there are also various balances of unutilized credits. The current monthly statements of expenditures, published in the *Journal Officiel*, are practically useless for the purposes of arriving at dependable aggregates. They show, by ministries, the credits opened and the expenditures ordered (*dépenses ordonnancées*), but even if the investigator carefully allocates and adds to the proper account the data for the various budget years which appear after the date when they are technically closed, he then finds that the figures are untrustworthy. This is because of the fact that important expenditures do not pass through the technical process of "*ordonnancement*" before payment but are covered by general orders at the time of the final closing of the accounts. Consequently before any investigator can secure definitive figures of expenditures he must have available that remarkable and admirable annual document known as the *Compte Général de l'Administration des Finances*.

While the writer was in France a volume of the *Compte Général* appeared. It covered the operations of the year 1916! The accounts for the years since 1916 are in such a state of confusion that several officials, high in the service of the Ministry of Finance, frankly described as well-nigh hopeless the task of completing in the traditional form this series of beautifully arranged and carefully articulated annual reports. If and when the complete series does finally become available, perhaps in another ten years, it will probably develop that the skein has proved to be too tangled to be straightened out and has had to be arbitrarily cut and knotted at numerous points.

Items of huge amounts[2] are still floating about in the records.

[1] See pp. 413-443.

[2] See below, pp. 220 and 333.

No one knows to what year's accounts these drifting derelicts will ultimately be attached. In any case, a table of expenditures based on figures thus far made public will probably bear little resemblance to the definitive tables which may finally be offered. Moreover, until the ultimate disposition of these derelicts is determined, it seems futile to devote effort to the discussion of the extent to which the budgets of the various years under review were out of balance.

Aside from the long delay in the publication of the *Comptes Généraux,* attributable to the demoralized state of the accounts, another serious obstacle is encountered in the fact that the French, as a matter of general policy, are not favorably disposed toward publicity. Public finance in France still carries a pronounced tinge of the occult. To a much greater extent than in England or America, it is considered a black art beyond the ken of the ordinary citizen. The public are asked to pay the taxes and to subscribe to loans in staggering amounts, but they are asked not to be inquisitive but rather to wait with patience and confidence while, behind the screen, the high priests perform their financial miracles.

There is some evidence that the French themselves are beginning to question the wisdom of this policy. Often it was with obviously sincere regret and not merely with polite excuses that information was refused at the Ministry of Finance. Especially among the younger men in the public service there was the feeling that the facts should be more freely available. Again in the *Inventaire* and the *Report of the Committee of Experts,*[3] the policy of secrecy is condemned as injuring the position of the Treasury by bringing about a condition of suspicion and distrust.

Incidentally it is here, at the door of this policy of secrecy, that much of the blame is to be placed for the misunderstanding and lack of sympathy which exist in America in respect of the French financial situation. In this respect France has unwittingly been her own worst enemy.

The blame, however, is partly our own. The rôle of a creditor nation in international public finance is new and strange to us.

[3] See *Inventaire,* pp. 1, 2; *Report of the Committee of Experts,* pp. 5, 18.

We naturally carry into this new relationship the same attitude which we are accustomed to assume in private commercial transactions. If a private debtor is unable to meet his obligations and pleads for leniency, we are accustomed to demand that he lay all his cards on the table; that he permit us to make our own appraisal of his assets and liabilities, to determine for ourselves the limits within which he shall be held to account and to dictate the scope and character of his private expenditures. In such a situation we demand and expect complete frankness and abject humility. If we receive these, we are likely to be generous. If we do not receive them, we feel that we are being imposed upon and that we are under no obligation whatsoever to make concessions. The fact is, of course, that our formula for dealing with a private bankrupt is quite inapplicable in the case of the French Republic. But the French policy of meager publicity has contributed materially to the growth of the impression, widely current in America, that we have not been dealt with in a proper spirit.

In the course of the analysis, instances have been encountered in which the French have exercised considerable ingenuity in the selection of the facts they chose to emphasize and those they chose to repress. It is not difficult to understand why this should have been done. One sympathizes with them in their effort to brighten a dark picture. In such cases particular care has been taken in this book to state frankly and fully all the available facts. To the writer this has seemed the only possible course to follow. He was given considerable data not hitherto made public. He was not asked to regard as confidential any of the information furnished him. He has withheld nothing. He realizes that in France this may possibly be interpreted as unfriendliness. Except for the case of the acknowledged falsifying of the accounts of the Bank of France during the early months of 1925, he has found no evidence of any deliberate misstatement of fact whatsoever. It does appear very clearly, however, that France has upon occasion not been entirely innocent of what may be described as financial pretentiousness. As an example, the situation during 1927 may be cited, when great emphasis was placed upon the reductions in the debt to the Bank of France and little said of the growth of that even more embarrassing liability, the deposits with the Treasury.[4]

It is not the intention here to pass upon the question as to whether, on the whole, France has been unwise not to be more frank. She has had many irons in the fire, including reparations, the protection of her exchange rate, and the political problems of reconciling her people to the effects of inflation. Whatever its other effects, however, the policy of scanty publicity has certainly complicated the task of writing a history of the financial development of France.

Scarcely less serious than the fragmentary and complicated character of the accounts, is the obstacle encountered in the carelessness with which the published statistics are prepared and printed. It is indeed discouraging, after it has been determined that a certain account is available and after it has been learned what the figures are supposed to represent, to discover that the statistics themselves are often undependable because of arithmetical and typographical errors. Yet it is almost literally true that before it is safe to transcribe a single item from a French financial document, a superficial audit must be made and the footings checked to locate possible discrepancies. The situation may be made clear by a few specific illustrations selected from the many which might be cited.

In a single statement of expenditures for the budget year 1923, no less than five errors were found.[5] In this statement, for example, the total credits opened were stated in both the official publications, the *Journal Officiel* and the *Bulletin de Statistique et de Législation Comparée,* as totalling 25,881,492,059.74 francs. The sum of the individual items in the table came to exactly one billion[6] francs more than this. The officials in the Ministry of Finance were unaware of the discrepancy until it was called to their attention, although it had stood in the printed records for a period of

[4] See pp. 246–253.

[5] Statement as of March 31, 1924, *Bulletin de Statistique,* April, 1924, p. 728 *et seq.*

[6] The word "billion" is used in this volume in the American sense for a thousand millions, equivalent to the French *milliard.* The English use the word to indicate a million million.

three years. After several hours of cross-checking they concluded that the true figure is 26,881,492,059.74 francs.

In a statement of public expenditures printed in the *Bulletin de Statistique* for August, 1926, it was impossible for a long time to find any relationship at all between the printed footings and the actual aggregates arrived at by adding together the individual items. Finally it was discovered that nearly half of the figures published as relating to the budget-year 1925 were really 1926 figures and had been transferred bodily to the 1925 table by mistake.

The officials at the Ministry of Finance gave the writer what they said to be an official statement of the capital amount of the public debt at the close of each year during the war and post-war period. Such data had been published for only scattered years. Checking the figures given in the statement against such published statistics as were available, it was found that the statement of the Ministry of Finance gave the amount of the internal debt (floating debt excluded) for the year 1918 as 97,779 million francs, whereas both the budget *projet* for 1920 (page 162 *et seq.*) and the *Annuaire de Statistique* (1926, page 157) gave the figure as 67,779 million francs, a difference of exactly 30 billions. When the discrepancy was called to the attention of the officials, they at first stated that the stenographer had probably made an error in copying the data. But upon investigation they reported that the figure in their table was correct and that the published figure was really 30 billions too low!

Each month the Ministry of Finance publishes a statement of collections which includes a table with this heading: "*Situation d'apurement des rôles concernant les contributions directes et les taxes assimilées des exercices 1914 à 1919 et des rôles émis pour les impôts sur les revenus pendant les exercices 1914*[7] *à 1922.*" It was possible to reconcile the data presented in this table with those published elsewhere only on the assumption that this title was incorrect and that "1919" should really read "1922." This was pointed out to the heads of the two bureaus in the Ministry of Finance most directly concerned. Both of them agreed that

[7] It may be observed that this date is also an error. It should be 1916.

1922 rather than 1919 was the correct date. But the error had been repeated monthly for 18 months.[8] Moreover, it continues to be published incorrectly in the latest available monthly statement, printed six months after the error had been called to the attention of the officials.

An error of one billion francs was discovered in the debt statistics of the *départements* in 1923.[9] The seven-billion-franc discrepancy in the statistics of the *Bons de la Défense Nationale* for 1920 is described elsewhere.[10]

Such instances could be multiplied almost indefinitely, but enough have been cited to explain the trepidation with which this manuscript is offered to the reader. The statistics are believed to be more dependable than those which have hitherto appeared. Certainly pains have been taken to check them. However, the writer must be pictured as passing them on with the same shrug of the shoulder which accompanied the delivery of some of the data to him.

The various complications and difficulties encountered have materially affected the scope and character of this book. The original plan, for example, called for a somewhat elaborate analysis and appraisal of the results of the financial policy adopted by the French. However, this portion of the project had to be greatly curtailed because of the time consumed in gathering the fundamental data bearing upon the immediate financial effects. This explanation is urged in partial extenuation of the character of the treatment.

It is suggested that the reader who has only a general interest in the problem of French public finance will probably find in Part One a treatment which is sufficiently elaborate for his purposes. The remaining sections of the book are addressed primarily to those who have a special or technical interest in the subjects discussed. It is hoped that the rather detailed descriptive data

8 The correct date appeared once during this period, in the *Bulletin de Statistique* for July, 1926.

9 *Situation financière des Départements en 1923*, p. 57. The "réalisations effectuées" are shown as 1,853,268,933.03 francs. The true figure is one billion greater.

10 See p. 229.

presented in these sections may prove helpful in acquainting American students with the more important particulars of the French financial situation. It is hoped also that they may be of assistance to that future worker who, in the fullness of time, may undertake the task of writing a truly definitive financial history of this interesting period.

To those who have aided in the present study, the writer makes his grateful acknowledgments. The contributions of his research assistants, Mr. Shoup and Mr. Werth, have been very substantial. Under great pressure of time and under circumstances which were often difficult and trying, they have labored with intelligence and devotion. The writer is also deeply indebted to the numerous officials in the Ministry of Finance to whom he has referred for enlightenment on the many puzzling questions which arose during the progress of the study. He hesitates to select names for particular mention, but he cannot refrain from expressing in specific fashion his gratitude to M. Léon Araud, *Chef de Bureau au Ministère des Finances,* who so often and so graciously responded to his calls for aid. Thanks are also extended to the various business men who took a kindly interest in the study and particularly to Mr. W. E. Seatree, of Price, Waterhouse & Co., who coöperated by making the elaborate computations of French taxes payable in certain assumed cases. Finally the writer wishes to record his appreciation of the assistance of Mlle. Nathalie Molodovsky, whose aid at all stages of the work has been so valuable as to justify the recognition given her on the title-page of the book.

ROBERT MURRAY HAIG

SCHOOL OF BUSINESS,
COLUMBIA UNIVERSITY,
February 29, 1928.

CONTENTS

DIAGRAMS

TABLES

PART ONE

THE DEVELOPMENT OF FRENCH FINANCIAL POLICY SINCE THE WAR

CHAPTER I

THE PRE-WAR STRUGGLE FOR TAX REFORM

An exhaustive history of the evolution of France's financial policy since the war is not attempted in the pages which follow. These chapters merely sketch briefly what now appear to have been the important steps in the development of that policy. The story is a fascinating one of an evolution from indifference to easy confidence, later to growing doubt, distrust, and confusion, followed by disillusionment, fear, and wild panic, culminating finally in a reaction, in the course of which France pulled herself together and with startling abruptness laid the basis for the recovery now (1928) in progress.

In America the feeling regarding French war and post-war finance is predominantly one of frank disapproval and disappointment. The prevalent opinion of even well-informed and intelligent people is that the record is damning in the extreme. In particular it is felt that the taxation policy has been unforgivably weak and vacillating. According to the analysis generally accepted, the French, confronted with a great financial problem, showed an incapacity to tax themselves with the courage and resourcefulness displayed by the English and Americans. If the French have suffered or are suffering, it is the result of their own folly, and sympathy is wasted upon them.

As a foreigner gains a familiarity with the background of French public finance, as he reads the public documents of the period and studies the character of the financial problem as it presented itself from time to time to the successive ministers of finance, he finds himself questioning the correctness of the current diagnosis and the justice of the unqualified condemnation so commonly meted out to France. He becomes more and more impressed by the inevitableness of the process. It is not difficult to find much to criticize as he views the occurrences in the light of subsequent events, but, as he comes to understand the character of the options available as the various crises arose, he is inclined to wonder whether, under similar circumstances, the decisions of his own leaders would have been much different, and whether French policy was really the grotesque monstrosity which many consider it.

To be wise, a financial policy must fit its environment. If it is to work, it must be suited to the character, the customs, and the capacity of the people. The plain fact is that the entire background of public finance in France is different from that in England or in the United States. While no one can study the finances of France without being stirred to admiration by the technical competence of the financial leaders and by the skill displayed in elaborating and administering that marvelously complicated financial mechanism, the French budget, it is nevertheless a fact that, in their general attitude toward the public fisc, the French are many decades behind England and America. Thus the French have scarcely begun to develop the conception of the State as a convenient device for accomplishing specific ends approved by a democratic people, fully aware of the costs involved and willing and eager to pay the bills. In this respect, the French are backward.

The reasons for this backwardness are manifold and cannot be elaborated here. Many of them are deeply rooted in history and tradition. However, if one is to understand why the French have behaved as they have during the recent past, it is important that these fundamental differences of background be recognized. In passing critical judgment as to the wisdom of French financial policy, these differences must be given weight. When this is done, a large portion of the blame is shifted from the present-day leaders to those remote historical circumstances which have made the French what they are.

In this monograph these remote circumstances cannot be reviewed. Indeed, the happenings of even the pre-war and war periods must be discussed within the scope of a few pages. However, since many of the recent changes in the French tax system are but steps in a new development begun just before the war, the reader must be asked to take a hasty glance at the situation as it stood in 1907 and to trace the evolution from that date.

Between 1907 and 1914 the story centers in the political war waged in France over the reform of the system of direct taxes.[1] On the one side were the partisans of the old system, based on the principles of proportionality, impersonality, and the determination of tax liability by "external signs." The other side advocated personal taxation, progressive taxation and precision in the determination of taxable income. The first task will be to show what was the nature of the system of direct taxation that had existed in France since the days of the Great Revolution, why the system, in spite of successive changes, had become technically antiquated, and why progressive opinion in France favored its suppression.

THE OLD FRENCH DIRECT TAX SYSTEM

It should be made clear at the very outset that the so-called direct taxes about which the struggle waged formed a relatively insignificant part of the French revenue system. For every franc raised by such taxes, three or four francs were raised by taxes which in this country would be described as indirect.[2] Customs

[1] The phrase, "direct taxes," is used to describe that portion of the French taxes which are assessed on the basis of "rôles." It should be noted that in France the phrase covers certain taxes which in England and America are usually described as indirect. See p. 325.

[2] In 1907, a typical year, the state revenue from the taxes which were the subject of the attention of the reformers amounted to 676 million francs, as follows (figures in millions of francs):

Direct taxes and "taxes assimilées"	575
Taxes on the income from securities	101
	676

The "taxes assimilées," it should be noted, contain many taxes which in this country would be described as indirect. The other state taxes may be grouped as follows:

Registration taxes (including inheritance taxes)	646
Customs duties	509
Sugar taxes	156
Stamp and Bourse taxes	215
Miscellaneous indirect taxes	602
	2128

In addition, the gross receipts from the sales of monopolies amounted to 865 million francs, and there were certain tax items under "miscellaneous receipts." The duties alone were almost as productive as the direct taxes. The great bulk of French taxes levied for the support of both the central and local governments were frankly designed to spread the burden as widely as possible and to raise the money as quietly as possible. The responsible financiers showed little eagerness to make the populace "tax-conscious." They did not seek to impose an economic check upon public expenditures through the submission of a definite bill for a definite project or policy. Many little indirect taxes, carefully concealed in the enveloping drapery of the prices, were greatly preferred to few heavy direct taxes which, naked and unadorned, had to be billed to the people.

Again, the French exhibited a distinct preference for old taxes. "When I consider the French tax system," remarked one ancient senator to the writer, "I am impressed with the truth of the Italian saying: 'One walks easily in an old shoe.'" That an old tax is a painless tax seems to have been generally accepted as true almost without limitations. A new tax, simply because of its newness, was under a great initial handicap. When the war broke out, France had only old shoes in her wardrobe.

Four state taxes, known as the *Quatre Vieilles Contributions*, formed the backbone of the French direct tax system before the war. They were a tax on income from real estate, a tax on doors and windows, a tax on business and certain liberal professions, and a tax on presumptive income, measured mainly by the amount of rental paid (*impôt foncier, impôt sur les portes et fenêtres, patente, personnelle-mobilière*). Only one of these exists to-day — the *impôt foncier*, and that in greatly modified form. The *patente* and the *mobilière* are used only to furnish local revenues, and the door-and-window tax has been abolished altogether.

The *Quatre Vieilles* had become highly conventionalized and very unequal. One of the main causes of this, though perhaps not the fundamental one, was the opportunity for abuse which lay in the method used in imposing the taxes. All but the business tax

---

figures for direct taxes and "taxes assimilées" are from *Bulletin de Statistique et de Législation Comparée*, 1908, Vol. 63, p. 213, and are for "rôles émis" as of Feb. 1, 1908. The other figures are from *Doc. Parl.*, 1908, *Chambre, Sess. Ord.*, Doc. No. 1709, p. 365.

(*patente*) were "apportioned" (*impôts de répartition*) in much the same manner as, in New York, the direct state tax on property is apportioned among the counties and levied against the local assessments of property. Not the rate of the tax, but the total amount to be collected by it, was fixed in advance each year by Parliament. This amount (*contingent*) was then divided and subdivided among the local tax districts. It was the faulty distribution of the *contingent* that made the *système de répartition* an agent of fiscal inequality. In addition to the prevalent American vice of competitive local undervaluation, the French, in the course of the decades, developed many others. As a result, the effective rate of the tax on income from real estate, for instance, is reported to have varied in 1887 from less than 1 per cent to more than 40 per cent, depending on the locality in which it was levied.[3] The same abuses could be found in the distribution of the *contingents* of the door-and-window and the *mobilière* taxes. Even Paul Leroy-Beaulieu, that violent antagonist of the reform of the French system of direct taxation, wrote of the *mobilière* tax: "If one examines how this tax is divided by communes, one encounters facts that suffice to condemn it without appeal."[4] A parliamentary commission, which inquired into the subject in 1894, stated that only 2,340 districts out of 36,040 assessed the *personnelle-mobilière* on house rent, the apportionment in the other cases being based on the taxpayers' local reputation and often determined by the political views of the commissioners or by their personal dislikes.[5]

From the standpoint of the liberals of the time, the objection to the *Quatre Vieilles* was directed even more to the economic conceptions on which they were based than to their lack of success in expressing those conceptions. Designed to distribute taxes roughly in proportion to income, through the use of various "external signs," the system failed woefully to accomplish its purpose. But its purpose after all was merely a tax in *proportion* to income. A reform of the direct taxes which would have resulted

[3] Allix, *Traité élémentaire de Science des Finances*, p. 495.

[4] Quoted in *Renoult Report, Doc. Parl.*, 1907, *Chambre, Sess. Ord.*, Doc. No. 1053, p. 540.

[5] *Ibid.*

in nothing more than a proportional tax, however accurately assessed, would not have satisfied the radicals at the beginning of this century. With the growth of large incomes a *progressive* income tax had become in their eyes the true basis of democratic taxation.

A large number of taxpayers were terrified at the prospect of a fiscal reform. The old taxes, despite their manifold disadvantages, were convenient in many ways, and the French public had become thoroughly accustomed to them. For one thing, they involved a minimum of interference with the taxpayer's private affairs. Often a *contribuable,* who was quite willing to tell the *contrôleur* how much rent he paid or how many workers he employed, was entirely unwilling to tell how much money he was making. The system also saved time; the assessments were made almost automatically — normally only once in several years — and the taxpayer seldom entered into any discussion with the *contrôleur*. Even if the *système de répartition* was unjust to many, they did not protest too violently, for the rates were generally moderate.

But whatever the virtues of the *Quatre Vieilles* from the standpoint of many taxpayers, there was another factor that sooner or later would have necessitated their reform. It was the State's need for revenue. The *Quatre Vieilles* were extremely inelastic and consequently, with the constant growth of the state budget, insufficiently productive. The "external signs" often did not vary with changes in wealth or income. The inequalities of the *système de répartition,* tolerable so long as the taxes were low, became unbearable when rates were substantially raised.[6] Under the circumstances large increases in the old direct taxes were out of the question. At the same time the state budget was steadily growing during the first decade of this century by 100 millions

[6] In this connection an interesting calculation has been made by M. Bodin in his pamphlet, "*Nos anciens Impôts ont-ils fait faillite?*" quoted by Allix and Lecerclé, *L'Impôt sur le Revenu,* Vol. I, p. 138. Taking some pre-war assessment figures of the *personnelle-mobilière* and multiplying them by 13 — i.e., roughly the coefficient by which the yield of direct taxation has risen in France since 1913 — he found that the rate of the tax would vary from 9.77 per cent to 273.5 per cent of the post-war house rent of the taxpayers.

or more every year. Indirect taxes were already numerous and high. Thus, from the standpoint of both "radical democracy" and the French Treasury, a fiscal reform had become, if not indispensable, at least very desirable. From time to time numerous income-tax bills had been presented to Parliament, but all had been abandoned. By 1907, however, the time of reform had come; and this time, at last, the matter was taken up seriously.

The Caillaux Income-Tax Proposal of 1907

It was in February, 1907, that M. Caillaux, the Minister of Finance in the Clemenceau Cabinet, announced to the Chamber of Deputies, amid cheers on the Left and Extreme Left, that he had submitted a *projet* for the suppression of the old direct taxes and for the creation of a new income tax. This *projet* is of great interest, because it foreshadows, almost in its entirety, the present French system of direct taxation.

Description of the Caillaux Proposal.—In the *Exposé des Motifs* which he read to the Chamber,[7] M. Caillaux charged that the indirect taxes weighed more heavily on the less well-to-do classes than on the wealthy ones and really constituted inversely progressive taxes. He pointed out that throughout almost all the civilized world the justice of the principle of progressive taxation had been recognized and adopted in some form or other; that France was the only one among the great nations which had not taken part in that evolution. Her system of direct taxation, based largely on forgotten theories and abandoned traditions, was, he insisted, antiquated and incoherent.

The Finance Minister then proceeded to explain the relative merits of the Prussian *Einkommensteuer* and the English income tax and expressed the belief that he had succeeded in combining in his *projet* the advantages of both.[8] His suggestion called for a set of schedule taxes on various elements of income and for a supplementary progressive tax on total income.

The proposed schedule taxes, patterned after the English model, corresponded roughly to the present normal taxes of the

[7] *Doc. Parl.*, 1907, *Chambre, Sess. Ord.*, Doc. No. 737, pp. 1–18.

[8] Caillaux's first income-tax *projet* of 1900 was based on the Prussian law.

American income tax. Total income was to be ascertained by adding together the incomes disclosed in the basic schedules, with certain adjustments, and progressive rates, corresponding to the American surtaxes, applied to the aggregate.

The device of schedules gives great flexibility to an income-tax system. It invites variations among the schedules in rates and allowances and in methods of administration. M. Caillaux recognized the demand for an "ability" tax by proposing a progressive surtax. He utilized the schedules to recognize the demand for discrimination in favor of "earned" income, as well as to facilitate the administration of the tax.

In the first place, the various schedules were grouped into three classes for differentiation with respect to rate. The heaviest rate, 4 per cent, was to apply to income from capital, *viz.*, to those schedules which included the income from land, houses and securities. The lowest rate, 3 per cent, was to apply to labor income, *viz.*, to those schedules which included income from salaries and wages and from professional fees. Finally, 3½ per cent was to be applied to mixed income, arising from both capital and labor, *viz.*, to those schedules which included income from business and agricultural[5] undertakings.

In addition to this rate differentiation, there were to be allowed considerable initial exemptions in most schedules — and particularly in the two agricultural schedules.

The proposed development of the plan of schedules involved the suppression of three old taxes — the *personnelle-mobilière*, the *portes-et-fenêtres*, and the *patente*.

M. Caillaux expected the proposed new system to yield substantially the same amount in the aggregate as the old, but to shift some of the taxes then borne by agriculture to the security-owning class. This relief to agriculture had stood at the head of the program of the parties of the Left in the 1906 Chamber. The tax on the land was to be cut about one-half and this amount recouped, with a little more besides, from the security owners.

Such an increase in the yield from the securities taxes was

[5] The differentiation between agricultural land rent and agricultural profits in French tax law may be of particular interest to American readers.

possible because, under the existing system, a large part of this intangible wealth was legally exempt — principally the French *rentes,* foreign government bonds, and foreign private securities not under the *abonné* system.[10] French investors were noted for their fondness for securities of foreign governments, and, as to the *non-abonné* private issues, the Senate Finance Commission estimated in 1913 that 40 billion francs of such securities were held in France.[11] The coupons of such securities could be cashed abroad, and the French fiscal authorities had practically no means of controlling them. The same trouble, indeed, exists to-day.

The justice of suppressing the privileged position of holders of foreign securities could scarcely be denied, but over the question of taxing French *rentes* lengthy battles were to be fought. Such taxation was regarded by many as a breach of contract, since these securities had been guaranteed immunity by the old act of *Vendémiaire An VI* (September, 1797), and by subsequent declarations made by numerous finance ministers. The Senate Commission, to which the income-tax bill was submitted in 1909, "intended to respect those solemn engagements," and on this point Caillaux's opponents were to have their own way.[12]

Not only was the amount of the tax on land to be decreased but the equity of the tax was to be improved by suppressing entirely the *système de répartition* and by substituting a new appraisal, so that the proposed new rate of 4 per cent [13] would apply to fresh estimates of rentals and not to the obsolete data shown by the old *cadastre.*[14] No effective opposition developed to the proposal for a revision of the land appraisal. The work was begun in 1908 and the results were destined to furnish the basis

[10] A system of tax control for foreign corporations.

[11] *Aimond Report, Doc. Parl.,* 1913, *Sénat, Sess. Extraord.,* Doc. No. 438, p. 62. It has been estimated that at the outbreak of the war between 13 and 14 billion francs had been invested in Russian governmental and industrial securities. (Germain Martin, *Les Finances publiques de la France et la Fortune privée,* 1925, p. 41.)

[12] *Aimond Report, loc. cit.,* p. 62.

[13] The average rate under the old plan was probably about 6 per cent but, because of the inaccuracies of the "cadastre," varied widely. See p. 7.

[14] Caillaux proposed a revision of the appraisals each 20 years. The "cadastre" is the evaluation of the land made for direct tax purposes.

for the change in the method of assessing the land tax which was finally made in 1914.[15]

It is important to note the extent to which M. Caillaux proposed to abandon estimates and external signs and to determine the real net income. Chief reliance was still to be placed on estimating the income, rather than on determining it exactly, but the methods to be used were a substantial advance over the old system.

For the real-estate, business-profits and agricultural-profits schedules, the income was to be estimated. For the first, the tax was to be based on the revised cadastral estimate of income (one-fifth of the income to be deducted as an allowance for depreciation and other charges). Business incomes were to be determined by the tax *contrôleur* and a special control commission, who

> will have to consider, in the first place . . . the pieces of information which can be gathered from the visible working conditions of each business. To this information they will further have to add facts derived from sale of businesses and from inheritance documents, information collected at railway stations regarding goods dispatched and received, and information collected by the indirect taxes administration. . . .[16]

Further, the taxpayer was to produce a written declaration regarding the various visible aspects of his business activity, and the *contrôleur* had the right to visit the business during working hours to check up on these. As to agricultural profits, they were to be considered, arbitrarily, as equal to the rental value of the land.

For the securities, wages, and non-commercial schedules, actual income was to be taxed. Security incomes were to be taxed at the source, wages and salaries were to be declared by the employer, and reliance was necessarily placed on the taxpayer's honesty in self-assessment for the third schedule.

The Caillaux *projet* was considered at the time to be a revolutionary proposal, but, as can be seen from the above de-

[15] Act of March 29, 1914. This same act established the new method of taxing foreign securities. See p. 21.

[16] *Doc. Parl.*, 1907, *Chambre, Sess. Ord.*, Doc. No. 737, p. 9.

scription, considerable respect was shown for the sacredness of the taxpayer's private affairs. The habit of taxing on a *forfaitaire* or estimated base had not been completely shaken off, and it has persisted in some of the schedules up to the present day. Nevertheless, the word "inquisition" was at the height of its vogue in 1907, and was repeated without end by the numerous critics of Caillaux's plan.

The capstone of Caillaux's income tax was formed by an *impôt complémentaire* (supplementary tax), levied on the sum total of the various schedule incomes. Its rate was progressive, mounting to 4 per cent of the total income on those incomes above 100,000 francs. Incomes under 5,000 francs were to be exempt. The tax was strictly a personal one (corporations being exempt), levied on the family as a unit.

Impression Created by the Caillaux Proposal. — The Caillaux bill produced a tremendous stir in France, and for several years a violent struggle raged between the partisans of the new and the old system, a struggle which, in the light of subsequent events, seems rather amusing in the extravagance of the hopes and fears displayed by the partisans. The question of revenue entered little into those discussions; what mattered was the principle involved. The Radicals and Socialists were delighted with the *projet* not so much for what it intended to achieve immediately as for the attractive vistas of "anti-capitalist" legislation it opened up. Shortly after Caillaux's announcement in the Chamber, Jean Jaurès spoke in Lyons as follows:

> The income tax *projet* is not a fiscal measure, for it will furnish new means of action to the workers; the question it raises takes the form of a symbol around which democracy and socialism will fight the battle against the reactionary forces; it is the seed from which a gigantic tree will grow.[17]

And a few days later, speaking before the Renoult Commission, Jaurès said:

> When, at last, exact accounts of capitalist and *bourgeois* incomes are drawn up, it will be possible to estimate more closely what sacrifices may

[17] *Le Temps*, Feb. 11, 1907.

be asked from the owning and privileged classes for supporting, in the interest of the laboring classes, the works of social solidarity.[18]

This was the blessing bestowed on the proposed reform by its extremist partisans; a form of approbation which could more easily displease than please the author of the *projet,* because the opposition naturally used as its strongest argument the joy the *projet* had occasioned among the " revolutionary elements." On the "*bourgeois*" side there was Paul Leroy-Beaulieu, the celebrated economist, influential editor of *L'Économiste Français:*

Many thanks [wrote Leroy-Beaulieu, after reading Jaurés's triumphant prophecy], many thanks for the prediction; it is most reassuring. We, for our part, believe that a tax of that kind would poison the whole life of a democracy; it would undermine confidence everywhere, and cause capital to flee; it would reduce our credit establishments to a subordinate and limited rôle; it would mean the beginning of a life-and-death struggle between the fiscal administration and the taxpayers. Both parties would feel very ill, and France even more ill. We hope that this fifteenth or twentieth *projet* of a progressive income tax, with its general inquisition, will share the fate of its predecessors.[19]

It is characteristic that both sides used the word " democracy " in support of their own views. Particularly strong objections were raised against the general income tax and the exemption of incomes under 5,000 francs, because this would divide taxpayers into two classes — those who paid the tax and those who, without paying it, collaborated in its establishment.[20] Leroy-Beaulieu even went so far as to maintain that the progressive tax was, strictly speaking, illegal, because in a democracy the only legal taxes were those paid by everybody, or nearly everybody, and a parliamentary majority could not legally create a tax which hit hard only a very small fraction of the taxpayers. The great principle of democratic taxation was that the taxpayer taxed himself.[21] The other important objection was that raised against the control commission, and a great newspaper went so far as to label the proposed system a " régime of terror and espionage." [22]

18 *Le Matin,* Feb. 16, 1907.
19 *L'Économiste Français,* Feb. 16, 1907.
20 *Renoult Report, Doc. Parl.,* 1907, *Chambre. Sess. Ord.,* Doc. No. 1053, p. 541.
21 *Économiste Français,* Feb. 23, 1907.
22 *Renoult Report, loc. cit.,* p. 541.

THE RENOULT REPORT AND ACTION BY THE CHAMBER, 1907–1909

The Caillaux *projet* was referred in due course to the Finance Commission of the Chamber, headed by Renoult. Thus was begun a legislative history which was destined to drag along through seven years before any substantial portion of the plan became law. Some of this history is highly significant.

Renoult's report, presented in June, 1907, is in some respects more radical — more socialistic, as the Senate Commission said afterwards — than Caillaux's bill, and clearly illustrates the desire of the extreme Left to place the main burden of the fiscal reform on the rich.

On the question of assessment, however, the Finance Commission of the Chamber was more conservative than Caillaux, largely, no doubt, on account of the protests that the bill had provoked on many sides. One of the most important amendments introduced into Caillaux's *projet* for this reason by the Commission related to the taxation of business profits. The French chambers of commerce had protested violently against the "inquisitorial and vexing" method of assessment and the "even deeper inquisition" that would accompany every matter of dispute.[23] The Commission therefore reverted to a system of assessment known as "normal productivity" which, though they did not admit it, was similar to that used for the old *patente*.

Beside a number of other minor changes proposed by the "Socialist" Commission, further concessions were made, despite Caillaux's warnings,[24] to labor incomes, which the Commission extended to include agricultural profits, reducing the tax rate here from 3.5 to 3 per cent. The worker and the farmer were to pay the minimum rate, and the *Renoult Report* frankly admitted that of a total number of 5,700,000 farmers, only 230,000 would pay the tax under the agricultural-profits schedule, if the Commission's recommendations were to be accepted. The tax would then completely spare small-scale agriculture, "touch only gently" the medium-scale, and but moderately the large-scale. The initial

[23] See p. 13. [24] Against favoritism.

exemptions were increased by the Commission in the case of all labor incomes; wage earners (the Commission stated) would in most cases pay nothing.

The loss occasioned by these new concessions to the "workers" was to be compensated for by an increase in the progressive general income tax.[25] On this point the Commission was firm. They completely agreed with Jaurès's views on the subject and described the tax as

> a corrective, intended for straightening out the inequalities in the burden of indirect taxation, and for reaching, in particular, the taxpayers enjoying a surplus, while leaving alone those earning only the necessaries of life or a little more. . . . Its aim is to develop at the expense of other direct and indirect taxes in order to become some day the principal fiscal instrument of the democratic régime.[26]

This was clearly, as Jaurès had described it in more picturesque terms, the seed from which the gigantic tree was to grow.[27] On this point no compromise was possible for the Commission, for the issue had been made definitely a political one.

For nearly two years (July 2, 1907 to March 9, 1909) the Chamber devoted a considerable part of its time to the discussion of Caillaux's *projet* and the Commission's report. Two important modifications were made during this period. The estimated yield of the new taxes was raised, and a new method of determining taxable profits under the business schedule was introduced.

The latter change took the form of a proposal to tax the trader or the industrialist on his average income for the three years preceding. The taxpayer was to declare his income, instead of having it arbitrarily fixed according to external signs.

To understand the subsequent fate of the reform, it must be remembered that throughout the debate in the Chamber, the more conservative parties protested violently and often, if not against the reform as a whole, at least against many of its clauses. It is therefore not safe to conclude that the adoption on March 9, 1909, of the *projet* by 407 deputies against 166, indicated a true

[25] Rates proposed by Caillaux: 0.28 to 4; by the Commission: 0.15 to 5.
[26] *Renoult Report, loc. cit.*, p. 539.
[27] See p. 13.

measure of the progressive spirit among the large majority of the Chamber. It was not simply a struggle between a "progressive Chamber" and a "reactionary Senate." A large number of deputies, while acknowledging the usefulness of many of its principles, were strongly opposed to the bill as a whole, and voted for it "conditionally," i.e., with the understanding that the Senate, whose wisdom they trusted, would smooth off many of its rough edges and ultimately put the bill into a more moderate and generally more acceptable form.[28]

The Reform Proposals in the Senate, 1909–1914

Such were the circumstances under which the bill was sent to the Senate and consigned to a Commission headed by M. Émile Aimond. The final report of this Commission was destined not to appear until November 27, 1913, i.e., nearly five years after the voting of the *projet* by the Chamber. As the years passed, the Chamber became convinced that the delay in the Senate Commission was caused not so much by eagerness for thoroughness as by hostility to the principle of progressive taxation. At last it took steps to force the Senate's hand.

Pressure from the Chamber in the 1913 Finance Bill.—The course of action adopted by the Chamber early in 1913 consisted of the insertion of a clause in the finance bill (following the proposals made by MM. Renard and Malvy), which in its final form was to read as follows:

[28] An expression of this attitude is to be found in the numerous speeches of M. Theodore Reinach early in 1909. "As soon as the abstract idea of justice," he said on one occasion, "which is at the root of the *projet*, found itself in conflict with political considerations, it was justice that capitulated." "The original *projet* of M. Caillaux," he said, "kept within fairly moderate terms. It was afterwards that all the schedules were invaded and curtailed by the extension of exemptions at the base. . . ." Nevertheless he welcomed and admired the general principles of the bill and concluded by saying that "the Senate would be equally ill-advised in rejecting wholesale the work of the Chamber, as it would be in ratifying it wholesale." Quoted in *Aimond Report, loc. cit.*, pp. 33–35. On an earlier occasion Caillaux himself had stated that 263 deputies had declared themselves partisans of the *projet*, 150 had agreed to the reformation of the direct taxes, and 166 were definitely hostile to it. See Chapter I in Caillaux's *Impôt sur le Revenu* (Paris, Berger-Levrault, 1910).

Beginning on January 1, 1915, the tax on unimproved real estate (*propriétés non-bâties*) shall be transformed into a proportional tax (*impôt de quotité*) calculated on four-fifths of the rental value of such property as determined by the valuation made in compliance with the act of December 31, 1907.[29]

Beginning at the same date the taxes on doors and windows and the *personnelle-mobilière* shall be suppressed and replaced by a general and progressive tax on income.

Before the said date the necessary legislative measures shall be taken to cover the diminution in receipts resulting from the coming into force of the two foregoing paragraphs.[30]

The transformation of the real-estate tax was adopted unanimously by the Chamber; the substitution of the income tax was voted by a large majority [31] in spite of the fact that Jaurès and many others objected to its limitations. To Jaurès it amounted to no less than a triumph by the Senate. To him it meant the abandonment of the Caillaux bill over which the Chamber had labored so long and so patiently.

It would be [he wrote in February, 1913] under the pretext of forcing the hand of the Senate, the most incredible renunciation and obliteration by the Chamber of bills it had itself voted. . . . The great income tax bill, voted with such great care [*péniblement*] would now be reduced to nullity by the Chamber itself.[32]

Others, remembering the way in which the door-and-window tax had been " theoretically " abolished twenty years before, feared that the Renard-Malvy clause would prove equally futile. This clause, they felt, practically surrendered the only true basis of the Caillaux reform, *viz.*, the schedule taxes, and they thought that the general income tax would prove quite ineffective without that solid basis.

For all that, the authors of the clause ably defended their position.

29 See pp. 11, 21.

30 Law of July 30, 1913, " portant fixation du budget pour l'exercice 1913," art. 3.

31 *Débats, Chambre, Sess. Ord.*, Feb. 21, 1913, pp. 509, 510.

32 Quoted by M. Klotz, Minister of Finance. *Ibid.*, p. 477.

It is sufficient [said M. Renard on February 20, 1913] to look at the present position of the reform as it stands before Parliament, to be convinced that many long years will elapse before the two houses come to an agreement on any definite text. . . . Under the circumstances we will simply have to face the alternatives . . . of either accomplishing at once a partial reform promised during many past years to millions of agriculturists, which will only be a just amendment for a piece of injustice nearly a century old, or else to postpone it and merely keep it as a pledge of a general reform of which the date of realization escapes entirely our power of foresight.[33]

The Aimond Report, 1913. — The Senate accepted the compromise, preferring to acquiesce rather than face an indefinite delay in the passage of the 1913 finance bill. The Senate took this step, committing itself to action on the tax on unimproved real estate and the general income tax, before it received the report of its Finance Commission on the Caillaux *projet.* When Aimond submitted his report in November, 1913, it became apparent that the Commission regarded the original Caillaux *projet* as having been definitely abandoned.[34] The report practically ignored the suggestions for a series of schedule taxes and devoted itself to the elaboration of the narrow program called for by the Renard-Malvy clause, *viz.*, the reform of the tax on unimproved real estate and the introduction of the general progressive income tax, in substitution for the door-and-window tax and the *personnelle-mobilière.*

On one important point the Chamber and Senate fully agreed. The farmer was to be relieved of a large part of his fiscal burden, and this was to be placed on the shoulders of those holders of stocks and bonds whose income had so far escaped taxation altogether. Measures were to be taken to tax at 4 per cent the coupons of foreign government bonds cashed by anyone residing in France. The taxation of French and foreign private securities was to be altered but slightly.

The general income-tax proposal sent to the Senate from the Chamber suffered considerable modification at the hands of the Senate Commission. The most serious question was:

[33] *Ibid.*, pp. 466, 467.

[34] *Aimond Report, loc. cit.*, p. 35 *et seq.*

How was the tax to be assessed? At this point the Senate was anxious not to infringe upon the traditions of the French taxpayer. This meant that there should be a minimum of spying on the part of the authorities into the taxpayer's private affairs.[35]

Alternatives were suggested for assessment, *viz.*, a declaration by the taxpayer which was to be checked and corrected by a tax commission, or an administrative evaluation based on visible signs of wealth. The rate, as in the original Caillaux proposal, was progressive up to 4 per cent. The chief interest in this proposal is that it reveals the strong influences which were at work to keep the old *Quatre Vieilles* method of assessment in the new taxes. Many of these influences were from outside of Parliament, and, indeed, they did not stop at mere modification of the reform. Two powerful "middle-class" leagues, carrying on for many years a violent pamphlet and newspaper campaign against the income tax, called it the "suicide of the Republic."[36]

The New Taxes on Land and Securities of March, 1914

The first real fruits of the pre-war struggle for tax reform appeared in the act of March 29, 1914, which addressed itself to the tax on unimproved realty, together with the adjustment of the tax on securities. While it is true that the Chamber was not

[35] The Senate was convinced that "inquisition" amounted to a break in a national tradition. As M. Ribot, the future manager of French war finance, explained to M. Caillaux in February, 1914: "The declaration, as it is practiced in other countries, has never been very popular in France. If one looks for reasons, one may perhaps find them in the recollections of the Old Régime, when the administration of taxes was so often tyrannical, hateful and oppressive. But what makes declaration so terrifying to people, is that they are not certain to find a body of sufficiently independent officials . . . to carry the full burden in applying such a system." "In England," he continued, "there is a body of income-tax commissioners who enjoy to such an extent the general confidence of the people, and are so independent in their origin and especially through the atmosphere that surrounds them [*Très bien! Très bien!*], and by the customs of that great country of England, that nobody ever doubts their impartiality. Could the same be said of France? Could one soon hope to have the same here?"—*Débats, Sénat*, 1914, *Sess. Ord.*, Feb. 17, p. 169.

[36] Kergall, *Le Suicide de la République, l'Impôt sur le Revenu* (Paris, Fédération des Contribuables, *circa* 1910). A typical pamphlet of the time.

entirely satisfied, it reluctantly accepted the portion of the loaf the Senate offered.

This act instituted the "*impôt de quotité*" on unimproved real-estate values at the rate of 4 per cent on four-fifths of the rental value as determined by the valuation under the act of December 31, 1907,[37] and reduced the burden of agriculture under this head from about 115 million francs to 65 millions. On the other hand, the transmission tax on all securities was raised, and there was instituted a system for taxing the revenue from foreign securities, aimed logically at foreign government bonds, which had not been so taxed hitherto.[38]

The Emergency General Income Tax of July, 1914

A few months later a second hesitating step was taken in the direction of tax reform. This law established a general progressive income tax, but it was a curious, misshapen product very remotely and tenuously connected with the Caillaux *projet* and the Renard-Malvy clause. Its final introduction was destined to be postponed by the outbreak of the war.

While the Senate was still leisurely discussing the proposal of Aimond for a general income tax in substitution for the door-and-window and *personnelle-mobilière* taxes, as called for under the Renard-Malvy compromise, an emergency arose which required speedy action which would increase the tax revenue. The 1913 fiscal year was about to close with an alarming deficit of

[37] See pp. 11, 18.

[38] The income from the "non-abonné" foreign securities was taxed at 4 per cent. The tax was to be withheld by the banker, money-changer or any other person effecting in France the payment of any interest coupons, dividend checks or other proceeds. Any such dealer had to register his occupation at the local "bureau d'enregistrement" and enter in a special book ("bordereau") all sums withheld by him. On the other hand, any owner of foreign securities domiciled in France who cashed his coupons, etc., abroad had to present his security for a stamp tax each year of 4 per cent of the income for the coming year. Heavy penalties for non-compliance were imposed. (*Loi du 29 mars, 1914*, arts. 34, 35 and 37.) The tax on the income from houses was raised from 3.20 to 4 per cent. The estimated additional yield due to this act was 97 millions from securities and 11 millions from houses.

over 450 million francs.[39] Moreover, M. Dumont was unable to balance the budget for 1914. The expenditure foreseen in the general budget exceeded the "normal" receipts by nearly 800 millions. This did not include the "special" war budget and the expenditure on Morocco, two items which amounted together to over a billion francs.[40] The special expenditure could be met partly out of "exceptional resources," i.e., borrowing; but something drastic had to be done about the general budget. Jaurès, like Caillaux and many others, proclaimed that "at the present time the budget is becoming more and more inseparable from the fiscal reform." [41]

The Government took matters into its own hands and, without waiting for the Senate to act on the measure before it, introduced a new bill into the Chamber on March 26, 1914.[42] It came up for discussion in May before that Radical Chamber which was to continue in existence throughout the war period.

As M. Clémentel explained in his report of July 7, 1914, the new income-tax proposal was not to be confused with the tax as voted by the Chamber of 1909. It was an exceptional financial measure, not to supersede the *portes-et-fenêtres* and the *personnelle-mobilière*. The present tax was merely a kind of supertax which was to bear part of the national defense expenditure.[43] Large initial exemptions were allowed, 5,000 francs being entirely free from tax, and generous allowances were made for children and dependents. The maximum rate was only 2 per cent.

Declaration was not compulsory, but those who made voluntary declaration enjoyed preferential treatment, because in the case of disputes, such persons were to act as defendants and the authorities were to introduce the proof. Any person who had not made a declaration and had been consequently taxed on an estimated basis by the authorities, had to act as plaintiff in a dispute,

[39] Dumont's 1914 budget *projet*, *Doc. Parl.*, 1913, *Chambre, Sess. Extra.*, Doc. No. 3123, p. 1.

[40] Figures cited by Deputy Dubois in *Débats, Chambre, Sess. Ord.*, Feb. 27, 1914, p. 1167.

[41] *Ibid.*, p. 1169 *et seq.*

[42] *L'Économiste Européen*, 1914, Vol. 45, p. 390.

[43] *Doc. Parl.*, 1914, *Chambre, Sess. Ord.*, Doc. No. 277, p. 1985.

and it was he, and not the authorities, who would produce the evidence showing the assessment to be incorrect.

On July 7 the Senate voted the tax in place of the one its Commission had proposed earlier in the year (the two were similar in many respects). It was returned to the Chamber, slightly modified, and was finally voted July 15, not without much criticism to the effect that it had been prepared in a great hurry and would prove a practical failure. However, a large number of deputies who had voted for it were not greatly concerned with the immediate practical aspect of the reform. It had set a precedent. For the first time in French history the principle of a progressive income tax had been recognized by Parliament and this, to many, promised a brighter outlook for the future.

A fortnight later Germany declared war.

It is clear, then, that the outbreak of the war found France financially unprepared. Her revenue system, with its highly elaborated indirect taxes and its entirely antiquated direct taxes, was inadequate to meet even the relatively insignificant pre-war demands. When war was declared England had immediately available a well seasoned income tax and supertax administered by an admirable civil service. When the need came, it was necessary only to increase rates. Moreover, she could utilize the materials immediately at hand to establish an effective excess-profits duty. In America, it has been customary to emphasize the lack of financial preparedness. But how much more fortunate was America than France! America, when she entered the war, at least had an income tax actually established and one which had passed through the fire of three successive annual assessments. France, torn by factional strife, had managed with difficulty to secure a fresh appraisal of land rentals, destined soon to be rendered obsolete by impending economic changes. She had recast somewhat her tax on securities. She had, also, only a few days before the opening of hostilities, written on the statute book a general income tax. However, this untried and hastily drafted law hung virtually in mid-air, without the structure of supporting schedule taxes necessary for its effective enforcement and with such slight provision for its administration that its actual imposition had to be temporarily abandoned. Immediately, the rank and file of the civil service was riddled by the call to the colors, and the energies of the leaders were diverted to pressing military problems. The man who was to head the Ministry of Finance, M. Ribot, had been prominent in the struggle against the reform of the direct taxes and carried with him to his task of war finance some of the prejudice and bitterness engendered by that struggle. Such was the financial equipment as France rushed to repel the German invasion in August, 1914.

CHAPTER II

FINANCIAL HISTORY DURING THE WAR YEARS

MEASURED by the standards of those who believe in heavy taxation to meet the costs of war, among whom most Englishmen and Americans are numbered, the French revenue system made a very dismal record during the period of hostilities. The following figures represent the total yield of the French state taxes [1] for these years:

	Billions of paper francs	*Billions of pre-war francs*
1913	4.1	4.1
1914	3.4	3.4
1915	3.3	2.4
1916	4.1	2.2
1917	5.7	2.2
1918	7.0	2.1

During 1914 and 1915, the taxes actually decreased. Even in 1918 the yield was not double what it had been in 1913. Moreover, these figures are in paper francs and by 1918 inflation had proceeded to a point where the paper franc had less than one-third of the purchasing power of the pre-war franc. In terms of pre-war francs the 1918 collections were only about half as great as the 1913 collections.

During the five years, 1914–1918, the French spent approximately five borrowed francs for every franc from revenue receipts. The revenues in 1914, although not half large enough to meet the total expenditures, did nevertheless suffice to meet the total cost of the civil service, the total debt service and a small part of the military expenses. In 1915, they were insufficient to meet even civil service and debt charges. By 1918 the civil services alone demanded more than the total collections.[2]

[1] From Table 59, p. 396. For local revenues, see p. 377.

[2] These statements are based in part on the following figures (in billions of paper francs) from the *Inventaire de la Situation financière de la France, présenté par M. Clémentel, Ministre des Finances,* 1924, *Doc. Parl.,* No. 441, pp. 17–18:

The Period of Inertia, 1914–1915

Behind these bare figures there was more activity than might be inferred. Even so poor a showing was not achieved without the exertion of considerable pressure by a radical Chamber of Deputies upon a conservative Minister of Finance. At the outbreak of the war, M. Ribot, a man of unquestioned patriotism and high personal prestige, but clearly out of sympathy with the financial philosophy of the Chamber, was placed at the helm of French finance. Influenced by various considerations, among which uncertainty regarding the length of the conflict, preoccupation with immediate military problems, and distrust of the financial wisdom of the radicals were all doubtless important, the Government decided to wage war without the aid of Parliament. Thus it was that not until toward the end of 1915 did Ribot find himself in the position of being compelled to defend a policy of complete inertia before a Chamber of Deputies which clamored for taxes and for taxes of a type which were anything but palatable to this ancient foe of the direct-tax reform.

Year	Revenues	Expenditure					
		Civil services	Public debt	Military expenses	"Recoverable" expenditure	Special accounts	Total
1914	4.2	2.–	1.4	6.5	0.4	0.1	10.4
1915	4.1	2.5	1.8	14.7	1.9	1.2	22.1
1916	4.9	2.8	3.3	23.9	2.9	3.9	36.8
1917	6.2	4.1	4.8	28.6	4.1	3.–	44.6
1918	6.8	5.4	7.–	36.1	6.–	2.1	56.6
Total	26.2	16.8	18.3	109.8	15.3	10.3	170.5

For a discussion of the limitations upon their accuracy, see p. 413. It will be noted that the revenue figures differ somewhat from the figures compiled by the writer, and presented on p. 400. A comparison of these figures with the statistics of annual net borrowings, p. 185, shows that in paper francs the tax collections (see p. 400), during the period 1914–1918, were 23.4 billions while the borrowings were 128.1 billions. In pre-war francs the tax collections were 12.1 billions and the borrowings 60.6 billions.

THE IMPOSITION OF THE GENERAL INCOME TAX, DECEMBER, 1915

The spirit of the Chamber and the attitude of the Minister of Finance are clearly shown in the debates of December 16, 1915. The radicals in the Chamber insisted upon the immediate application of the general income tax of July, 1914,[3] the introduction of which had been postponed.[4] In an address, punctuated by caustic interruptions from unsympathetic deputies, Ribot attempted to explain why the income tax had not been imposed and why he opposed its imposition now.[5]

He pointed out that at the beginning everybody thought the war would be of short duration. This was the first reason why financial reforms had been put off until "after the war." Nobody believed at the time that it could last for seventeen months. How much longer would it last? No one knew; it was simply necessary to hold out. Those with the greatest tenacity and perseverance would be the victors. They had spent and were spending largely, perhaps extravagantly ("*Très bien! Très bien!*"), but it was impossible to reef the sails when the ship was in full course. At the beginning they had been spending 1,700 million francs a month; they were now spending 2,500. The manufacture of munitions was immense. How were these expenses to be met? By borrowing. There was no country in the world which could dream of meeting such expenditure by taxation. England had increased her taxes, and had shown a noble example of economy and courage. . . .

M. JEAN LONGUET. — She has doubled the income tax.

M. RAFFIN-DUGENS. — Yes, and we haven't one at all.

M. RIBOT. — True, we have no income tax, but nothing is more difficult in time of war than to improvise taxes; nothing is more difficult, and also, in most cases, more delusive. You say England has doubled her taxes? And yet the deficit she anticipates in the current year amounts to 35 or 36 billion francs. It is on loans that England lives, just as do all the nations engaged in this struggle. But we cannot compare ourselves to England. That would be a great error and a

[3] See p. 21.

[4] By an act of December 26, 1914.

[5] *Débats, Chambre, Sess. Ord.*, December 16, 1915, p. 2136 *et seq.*

great delusion. England is not, like us, invaded. England is working [" *Très bien! Très bien!* "] and one of her ministers was able to tell Parliament the other day that during the war her income was greater than during peace. . . . England pays her taxes. In France — and I pay homage to the country that makes a great effort to pay its taxes — a notable improvement is shown in the tax receipts; the financial patriotism is on a level with the military patriotism.[6]

Ribot contended that, considering the invaded provinces and the profound economic disturbances in industry and business, tax collections were good.[7] Generally, the country was in a very bad state; the people were, with a few exceptions, poorer. There were, of course, some who were making big profits out of the war, and these, the Finance Minister thought, ought to be taxed accordingly. He promised shortly to submit to Parliament a bill for the taxation of exceptional war profits. But the decision to tax "profiteers" was due largely to motives of a moral order. By introducing such a tax, he said,

we shall respond to a general feeling in public opinion, and also fall in with the true interests of those who have made the profits, because they themselves will understand that they owe this sacrifice to the country, and that an honor is being done them in asking for that sacrifice.[8]

But the radicals were not content to be put off with a promise to "honor" the profiteers with a war-profits tax. They wanted the income tax and did not hesitate to charge that the opposition to its introduction was a survival of the old fight of the pre-war period. One Socialist, M. Bedouce, even went so far as to suggest that if France had had an income tax before the war, she would not have been invaded, and that Germany's great strength was due largely to her income tax.[9]

[6] *Débats, loc. cit.*, p. 2136.

[7] The *Inventaire*, p. 18, estimated that the invasion of the ten départements in the north and east diminished the tax base about one-fifth.

[8] *Débats, loc. cit.*, p. 2137.

[9] "If the up-to-date fiscal mechanism, for which we had asked so often, had been given to the country a few years earlier, [Socialist cheers] our frontier would perhaps have remained unviolated. Who knows if it was not the income tax which permitted Germany to win the battle of Charleroi? Who knows if the carefully studied, scientifically prepared military equipment which — I shall not

The Budget Commission of the Chamber, by a large majority and without party distinctions, now recommended the early introduction of the general income tax. This met with opposition from the Finance Minister. He thought it was not the right time. A half or a third of the inspectors of direct taxes were in the army. Should they be recalled? But even if that were done, there was a moral objection which it would be difficult to overcome. How many citizens were now in the trenches facing the enemy! Could these people be asked to make declarations, and if so, how could such declarations be controlled? How could one have "official talks" with them which were indispensable for a sound functioning of the income tax? He begged the Chamber not to be rash.

"Whatever you decide," he concluded, "it will still be borrowing to which we must principally have recourse." [10] Those who loaned their money to the Government were patriots, they were to be admired almost as greatly as the men in the trenches. Was it any fairer to tax them than it was to tax the men at the front? M. Paul Beauregard, a conservative deputy, probably revealed much of the Finance Minister's private feelings in the matter when he said: "Once you have asked this wonderful France to supply the funds for the loan, you have appealed to all there is. Will you reward yesterday's subscribers by threatening them to-day with a more or less disquieting tax which cannot fail to make them uneasy?" [11]

Such pleas carried little weight with the Chamber, however. It decided that the time had arrived to introduce the general income tax and, by the act of December 29, 1915, directed that the law of 1914 should go into force in 1916.

So ended the period of complete inactivity and began a period of real effort to increase revenues. Events now moved rapidly.

---

say, broke — but amazed even the heroism of our soldiers, and nearly stole the victory from them — who knows if this powerful equipment had not been realized thanks to the income tax which had given Germany all the necessary resources at the time she was conceiving this monstrous attack upon us which has disconcerted the civilized world?" — *Débats, loc. cit.*, p. 2139.

[10] *Débats, loc. cit.*, p. 2137.

[11] *Débats, loc. cit.*, p. 2151.

In this new period, Ribot dropped the rôle of obstructionist. He even became a friend of the income tax. As early as the middle of 1916, it was seen that his private convictions on the subject had altered and he gracefully recommended that the rate of the tax be increased from two to five per cent.[12]

The War-Profits Tax, July, 1916

Ribot's suggestion regarding a war-profits tax has already been noted. The Chamber had been unwilling to accept a tax on war profits in place of the income tax. But this did not mean that it would oppose a war-profits tax in addition to the income tax. Such a tax was inaugurated July 1, 1916.[13] It applied to two kinds of war gains: "exceptional" profits made by those who were not regularly in business but who had contracted to furnish supplies to the Government (excepting agriculturalists selling their crops); and "excess" profits made by business men in any line above their "normal" profits. Both pre-war earnings and invested capital were used in determining "normal" profits. Such profits were considered to be the average made during the three years prior to August 1, 1914, unless the resulting figures were below 5,000 francs or less than six per cent on the capital invested. The rate of fifty per cent fixed at this time was soon to be increased. Both self-assessment and administrative evaluation (*d'office*) were employed.

When it is considered that this tax was established practically simultaneously with the income tax and that French commercial accounting is notoriously inadequate, it will be granted that the outlook for its success was not promising. When, in addition, one realizes that inflation had already robbed the franc of nearly half its pre-war value and was soon to go very much further, rendering grotesque both the pre-war and invested capital standards, it is obvious that the French war-profits tax was doomed to de-

[12] In his *projet* for "crédits provisoires" for the third semester of 1916, cited in *Aimond Report, Doc. Parl.*, 1916, *Sénat, Sess. Ord.*, Doc. No. 470, pp. 619–620.

[13] For a more detailed description, see p. 327.

velop all the shortcomings of the British and American laws and many special ones of its own besides.

General Increases in Tax Rates, December, 1916

About the same time, Ribot presented a plan for increasing the rates of a number of the taxes already in existence.

Looking back on that period a few months later M. Aimond, the *Rapporteur* of the Senate Commission, described the situation as follows: [14]

> Until May, 1916, the Government had regarded it as unnecessary to increase the existing taxes or to create any new ones. Since the beginning of the war it had proposed nothing but the tax on war profits and the modification of the *patente* for those who furnish supplies to the Government; now, however, it thought that the moment had come for modifying the financial policy which could be defended on certain grounds, but which the Finance Commissions of Parliament had strongly criticized on several occasions. The Government therefore incorporated in the bill for provisional credits for the third quarter of 1916 some important fiscal proposals, explaining in the following terms the general motives which had dictated their choice: "Our first preoccupation was to keep a just balance between the taxes weighing on wealth . . . and those extending over the mass of the population proportionately to their needs as well as their abilities. We have carefully avoided striking necessities and increasing the burden which puts a restraint on the development of transactions [i.e., registration fees, etc.] . . . We have also endeavored to proceed by increasing existing taxes rather than by creating new ones. The taxes which in war time are most productive are those to which the country is accustomed and the collection of which does not give rise to difficulties and errors inseparable from the introduction of any new fiscal measures."

The Government had proposed to double the rates of the land taxes, the *personnelle-mobilière* and the *patente,* and to raise the income-tax rate. The Chamber Commission rejected the appeal to the old direct taxes, and concentrated its attention on the general income tax, with the result that when the new tax provisions were finally passed at the end of the year, the most important single item in point of yield was the modification of this new mem-

[14] *Aimond Report, loc. cit.*, p. 619.

ber of the French fiscal family. The exemption limit was lowered, and the steepness of the progression increased, a ten per cent rate applying to that part of a taxpayer's income above 150,000 francs.

The Government had likewise proposed more taxation on securities, and on spirits, wines, beer, sugar, and tobacco. It obtained practically what it wanted here, and more too, for taxes were also laid on theatres, patent medicines and food products from the colonies. The postal, telegraph and telephone rates were also raised. The Chamber apparently consented to these indirect tax increases upon the promise of the Senate to help along the side-tracked schedule taxes.[15]

This was not all, for the war-profits taxes were raised to sixty per cent, a new *taxe exceptionnelle de guerre* was created (really an addition to the general income tax, striking men subject to mobilization who had the good fortune not to be called into actual military service) and several of the *taxes assimilées* were increased.[16]

The Completion of the Income Tax Reform, July, 1917

These rate changes of December, 1916, promised to yield additional revenue of nearly 600 million francs. But by this time so much money had been borrowed that the increase in the annual debt service alone amounted to no less than 2500 million francs. Faced with this situation Parliament decided to create further taxes. At the end of 1916 the Senate Commission declared that, not content with the act of December 30, it was anticipating at an early date the creation of an entirely new, well coördinated system of schedule income taxes, by which important additional resources could be obtained for the State in an equitable way. This did not mean an exclusive concentration on direct taxes. "We must," said the Commission, "endeavor to maintain a suitable equilibrium between the two great categories of taxes. . . . It is evident that we must also use largely the indirect taxes on non-indispensable articles of consumption, as it is entirely im-

[15] Jèze, *Les Finances de Guerre de la France, la Politique financière du Gouvernement pendant les Années 1915 et 1916*, pp. 63–64.

[16] Law of December 30, 1916.

possible to find billions of francs by merely increasing the taxes striking the taxpayers directly." [17]

This program was followed out. During 1917 attention was almost exclusively devoted to direct taxes, and the great reform of July 31 was passed, whereas nearly all fiscal legislation in 1918 was devoted to the increased yield from indirect taxation.

The act of July 31, 1917, completed the present system of French income taxation by creating the last four schedules of the Caillaux *projet* of 1907,[18] the fate of which, owing to the opposition of the Senate, had been left undecided at the outbreak of the war. It will be recalled [19] that only a partial reform had been secured before the war — the transformation of the tax on unimproved real estate into an *impôt de quotité,* a stricter fiscal régime for security incomes, and the assent to the principle of a general income tax. But three of the *Vieilles* were still in force, and the system was a hybrid. No satisfactory results could be expected from the general income tax until it could be based on a set of schedules, the assessment of which rested on actual incomes and not on elements of an arbitrary and uncertain nature.

Whether or not it was a good thing to put through in the midst of war time what M. Jèze called "the greatest fiscal reform since the French Revolution" [20] is a question that can be and has been disputed. For years afterward, *L'Économiste Français* went on protesting against it, pointing out, beside many other objections, the administrative difficulties that such a reform had involved during war time. That, of course, was undeniable, but it was by no means an argument that those responsible for the reform had overlooked. The finance commissions saw ahead more clearly than did the opponents of the reform. They realized that the measures would prove to be of the highest importance in solving the many financial difficulties that France would have to face immediately after the war. Large revenues would have to be raised by means of taxation, and under the inelastic and unjust system of the *Vieilles,* nothing would be more difficult.

[17] *Aimond Report, loc. cit.,* p. 623.

[18] See p. 10.

[19] See p. 20.

[20] *Revue de Science et de Législation Financière,* 1917, p. 448.

It is of interest that the Senate, which had so obstinately opposed the reform before the war, now declared itself its supporter, and even M. Ribot finally decided that the best he could do for the welfare of France was to give the commission his coöperation. In speaking to M. Caillaux shortly before the final adoption of the reform, he showed a fine spirit of conciliation in view of the common end that had to be achieved:

> We had once been much divided, and were engaged in discussions of "school" and doctrine. Since the war I have felt as much as anybody — I do not wish to say more than anybody — that we must reach our aim and leave aside all minor differences. I have been to the Senate and have asked that the elaboration and discussion of this income tax be resumed.[21]

The system of schedule taxes, as adopted by the act of July 31, 1917, is, on the whole, identical to that proposed in the original *projet* of 1907 except for some important changes in rates and an essential innovation regarding the method of assessment in the commercial and industrial schedule.

It will be remembered [22] that the administrative assessment of business profits, as proposed in 1907, was eventually replaced, in the course of the Chamber's debates, by a system of declaration. The latter method had seemed, on grounds of history and "national tradition," particularly objectionable to the Senate, and it was this clause which was largely responsible for the upper Chamber's apprehensive feelings toward the reform as a whole. In order to hasten matters, Caillaux himself, early in 1914, had made to the Senate Commission an entirely new proposal — an ingenious method eliminating all the objections of both the earlier proposals, and now gladly adopted by Parliament. All taxpayers coming under the commercial and industrial schedule, with the exception of corporations, which were already obliged to remit their balance-sheets to the registration administration, could choose between two different modes of assessment. Either they presented their accounts to the direct tax administration, in which case they were taxed on their actual net profits, or, if they were

[21] *Débats, Chambre,* July 17, 1917, p. 1827.

[22] See p. 22.

unwilling to admit the authorities to the privacy of their business, they were taxed on such profits as their particular business should produce normally. The determination of such " normal " profits was no longer made in the manner proposed by the Renoult Commission,[23] but by applying a certain coefficient to the gross receipts of the taxpayers (*chiffre d'affaires*), and it was only this figure that was to be declared. No embarrassing questions were to be put to the taxpayer by the controller; no books were to be examined except those showing the gross receipts during the taxable year. To determine this relation between gross and net was a delicate piece of work. The Chamber Commission rejected the Government's suggestion to let the controllers do it, and decided that a special Commission, representing all the parties involved — the administration, industry, and retail and wholesale trade — should be formed which would carefully calculate the coefficients to be applied to the figure of gross receipts in the various types of industry and trade. To lend further elasticity to the system each business should have a maximum and minimum coefficient between which two figures the controller could then use his own discretion. This system, though abolished in 1926, had obvious advantages at a time when the French taxpayer still shuddered at the word " inquisition," and the possibility of serious injustice was eliminated by the fact that a taxpayer whose business had suffered a loss, or whose profits were decidedly below " normal," had the alternative of the first method – that of direct declaration. On the other hand, the inevitable effect of the arrangement was to favor those taxpayers whose profits were unusually large.

The rate was fixed at four and one-half per cent of the profits (which happens to be the peace-time rate of the New York state tax on corporations) but the fraction up to 1,500 francs was taxed at one-quarter, and that between 1,500 and 5,000 francs at one-half this rate.

Besides this regular tax on business incomes, the act of July 31, 1917, provided for a light tax on turnover (not to be confused with the later *chiffre d'affaires* tax created in 1920) whereby all

[23] See p. 15.

retail businesses with an annual turnover of over a million francs were taxed as follows:

0.1 per cent on portion of turnover	between	1	and	2 millions
0.2 " " " " " "	"	2	"	10 "
0.3 " " " " " "	"	10	"	100 "
0.4 " " " " " "	"	100	"	200 "
0.5 " " " " " "	over	200 millions		

This was to strike chiefly the big stores in Paris, and its object, apart from revenue, was to favor the small retailers who were said to be suffering badly from the competition of the *grands magasins*. It also illustrates a dislike of the French legislator for large-scale capitalism.

The schedule taxes on salaries and wages, and on professional and other non-commercial income, were levied on actual income. In the case of the former, the employers were to supply the necessary information. Self-assessment was relied upon in the latter, and here evasion was comparatively easy. True, the taxpayer ran the risk of being assessed arbitrarily by the administration (*d'office*), with a fifty per cent increase in the tax rate, if no agreement on his supposed income could be reached between the authorities and himself, but if he declared a fairly plausible figure he might succeed in concealing a substantial part of his income, as the information at the disposal of the authorities went little beyond "external signs." The rate was 3.75 per cent in both schedules, but considerable initial exemptions were allowed in the wages schedule, so that a wage earner who was paid, for instance, 5,000 francs a year might owe only 37.50 francs tax.

For the fourth schedule — agricultural profit — no attempt was made to ascertain the actual net income. Such profits were arbitrarily presumed to equal one-half the rental value of the land. The rate was 3.75 per cent, and here, too, initial exemptions were allowed.

Further, by this 1917 act, there were incorporated under the division of security incomes (*valeurs mobilières*) created on March 29, 1914, the incomes from personal loans, deposits and guarantee funds (*créances, dépôts et cautionnements*). The same act raised the rate of the real-estate tax from four to five per cent, and that of the general income tax from ten to twelve and one-half per cent, the method of calculation remaining the same as before.

This act of July 31, 1917, was passed in the midst of the war period with comparatively little opposition or disturbance. Irrespective of convictions regarding principles, an effective income tax had become a financial necessity.

The Thierry Sales Tax Proposal, June, 1917

The transformation of the system of direct taxes just described was carried to completion while M. Thierry was Minister of Finance, although he was not primarily responsible for it. However, apparently Thierry does deserve the credit for originating the sales tax, an honor commonly given to Klotz who succeeded him in September, 1917. Thierry's plan of June, 1917, was in reality the basis of Klotz's later *projet,* which was to become part of the finance act of 1918 (act of December 31, 1917).

What was needed above all in 1917 and 1918 was ready cash. The debt service was increasing month by month, and something had to be done. The moral arguments that underlay the creation of new taxes were not much more than the sugar coating of the pill. Direct or indirect, their creation was above all due to the urgent need of money. That was why Thierry proposed to raise the war-profits tax to a maximum of eighty per cent on that portion of profits over 500,000 francs. The English allies had done it, and there was a strong opinion in the country that war profits ought to pay the largest tribute to the real necessities of the budget.[24]

But there was an even more important and far more productive tax that Thierry had proposed, one which later was to become one of the most important elements of the French system. Although its real justification was fiscal need, Thierry advanced other reasons for its creation.[25]

> One is imperiously driven to examine the taxation of expenditure. The ideal solution in this matter would be the creation of a state tax

[24] *Doc. Parl.*, 1917, *Chambre, Sess. Ord.*, Doc. No. 3452, p. 865.

[25] *Ibid.*, pp. 865–866.

on all individual expenditure. Such a tax would present obvious advantages: it would escape the reproach of non-proportionality made against indirect taxes. . . . It would also conform to the special necessities of a time which demands from the country the highest degree of thrift and restraint; besides, it would be favored by the general rise in the price level, which, modifying the scale of values, would reduce the relative importance of such fiscal changes.

The proposed tax was to consist of three separate items: [26] a regular turnover tax to be paid by every kind of trader — both retail and wholesale — at the rate of one-tenth of one per cent, a five per cent tax on all individual retail purchases of a non-indispensable character and a ten per cent tax on the purchases of luxury goods. The meaning of "luxury goods" will be defined in due course. Thierry stated that, as distinct from indirect taxes such a system would not be inversely progressive, but actually progressive, on account of the exemptions given to articles of primary necessity.

The "Taxe de Luxe," the Tax on Payments, and Other Legislation, December, 1917

The new Minister, M. Klotz, did not quite agree. He thought the cumulative effect of such levies would weigh too heavily on the individual purchaser. He therefore limited the tax to two items only — a small stamp duty on retail purchases over 10 francs, and an ad valorem tax of ten per cent on the purchase at retail of *de luxe* goods which would be specially defined as such. These two measures were incorporated in the act of December 31, 1917. The 20-centimes tax per 100 francs or fraction of 100 francs of retail purchases was compulsory on all sales above 10 francs where a receipt was given, and compulsory in any case where the purchase figure was above 150 francs.

A few months after the enforcement of the *taxe de luxe* the London *Economist* wrote:

Considerable opposition has already been raised in connection with the operation of the *taxe de luxe* of ten per cent imposed on all transactions above a certain value in a large number of categories of goods.

[26] *Ibid.*, pp. 877–878.

What is objected to is not so much the tax itself, but the manner in which it is levied.[27] Trade associations complain that the tax is practically killing the trade in the higher-priced goods. The Lyons Chamber of Commerce urges the Government to replace the tax levied on the customer by an increase in the amount of the *patente*. It is argued that customers would raise no objections to paying the tax indirectly in the form of an increase in the price of the goods, but in its present incidence it is universally believed that the tax will prove unworkable.[28]

As early as June, 1918, a bill was submitted to the Chamber by three deputies proposing the abrogation of the tax and its replacement by a new impost of two per cent on the total turnover of all traders and manufacturers.[29] A year later, March, 1919, the Chamber did pass a bill abolishing the *de luxe* tax, but the Senate refused to concur.

In August, 1918, again, the *Economist* wrote:

> No tax has been imposed of recent years which has proved so undoubtedly unpalatable to the public. . . . Paris depends very largely for its commercial existence on " luxury " trades. The influence . . . is plainly visible in [its] effect upon the daily habits of the population. In view of the heavy tax now applied on all restaurant meals which cost more than 5 francs, a substantial number of people who formerly habitually dined out have now taken to having their evening meal at home.[30]

In addition to the above taxes, a few more tax burdens were imposed by the act of December 31, 1917. War profits became taxable up to the limit of eighty per cent (as had been already suggested by Thierry), certain changes were made regarding the taxation of gifts and legacies and the fixed stamp tax on receipts for non-commercial payments was made proportional, with a low rate. The total yield of the reform was estimated at 980 millions, 800 millions being expected from the taxes on luxury sales, commercial payments, and civil payments.

27 " Dresses under 250 francs are exempt of tax; but on a dress of 255 francs the purchaser has to pay an additional 25.50 francs as a luxury tax. It is argued that if the tax is retained it should only be levied on that part of the price above which an article ceases to be a necessity and becomes a luxury." *Economist*, May 18, 1918.

28 *Ibid.*, May 18, 1918.

29 *Doc. Parl.*, 1918, *Chambre, Sess. Ord.*, Doc. No. 4730, p. 754.

30 August 17, 1918.

Further Increases in Rates, June, 1918

After passing early in 1918 two minor laws — one increasing the price of tobacco and the other creating " measures directed against fiscal frauds " (the principal one prohibiting any private person to open without official authorization the safe or safe-deposit box of a deceased person), Parliament voted on June 29, 1918, the most important fiscal reform of the year, and thereby sanctioned the last considerable effort at increased taxation made by the Government during war time.

Indirect taxation was called on to bear most of the burden in this final war-time appeal to the taxpayer. The taxes on wines and spirits were once more raised, a gross receipts tax was levied on the railroads, sugar was tapped for more revenue, and a number of other items in the indirect stamp and registration taxes brought the estimate of the total new yield to about 750 millions.[31]

The rest of the new revenue was to come from the general income tax, which was once more modified. The highest rate, applying to that portion of the income above 550,000 francs, was now by this law increased to twenty per cent. Somewhat offsetting this were initial exemptions and reductions of the tax, for family charges, large enough to reduce the final tax considerably. M. Milliès-Lacroix, *Rapporteur* of the Senate's Finance Commission, thought that these modifications would allow the tax to be more clearly and easily established, sparing the average income while striking more heavily the large ones.[32]

Contemporary Comment

Whether the choice of taxes which had been increased and created by the act of June, 1918, and by those preceding it was well made or not, was a disputed question.

With the departure of M. Ribot from the Ministry of Finance, early in 1917 [wrote M. Jèze], it seems that a new fiscal policy has come to the top. It is certain that the policy of fiscal inertia has been aban-

[31] *Marin Report, Doc. Parl.*, 1918, *Chambre, Sess. Ord., Doc.* No. 4767, pp. 799–804.

[32] *Débats, Sénat, Sess. Ord.*, June 13, 1918, p. 457.

doned. As for the nature of the new taxes, however, the change has not been very tangible. This policy has expressed itself, on the one hand, by the increase in the taxes on gifts and legacies (December 31, 1917), by the measures against fiscal frauds in matters of inheritance (April 18, 1918), and by the increase in the rate of the general income tax (June 29, 1918), but on the other hand, there has been a real avalanche of taxes on consumption, the most important of which, though by no means the only ones, are the tax of two-tenths of one per cent on payments and the ten per cent tax on *de luxe* purchases.[33]

M. Klotz, though accused of giving preference to indirect taxation, thought his system entirely satisfactory. He estimated the yield of the direct (income) taxes at 1,829 million francs, or 22 per cent of the total, the direct "capital" taxes (i.e., registration, stamp, etc.) at 1,852 millions, or 23 per cent, and indirect taxes (including tax on payments) at 4,527 millions, or 55 per cent. "This calculation," he said, "suffices to show that there is a normal, equitable, reasonable distribution between the direct and the indirect burden. . . . One cannot therefore call ours a lame system; its equilibrium seems, on the contrary, harmonious."[34]

Whatever the merits of these arguments, it is certain that the last two years of the war showed a great difference from the first two with regard to financial policy. Not that the fiscal troubles were solved by any means; the vast problem of war liquidation and reconstruction lay ahead; but it is true that a serious effort had been made to adopt measures sufficient to enable France to meet during and after the war the normal and permanent charges of her budget.

To have doubled the amount of her tax collections seemed at the time something of an achievement. But already inflation had in fact robbed these efforts of any net effect. At the cost of considerable exertion, France had doubled her forward pace. But even so, the treadmill of inflation was by this time carrying her backward at a still faster rate.

[33] *Revue de Science et de Législation Financières*, 1918, p. 403.

[34] *Débats, Sénat, Sess. Ord.*, June 13, 1918, p. 463. The analysis presented on p. 403 indicates that the result of the tax legislation during the war was to increase sharply those taxes which were designed so as to be weighted against the rich.

CHAPTER III

POST-ARMISTICE APATHY

It is clear from the preceding chapter that the Frenchman, in his capacity as a taxpayer, contributed nothing toward the costs of the war while hostilities were in progress. It was in his capacity as a bondholder that he made his financial contribution and it was a very large one. The collapse of Germany found him with his pockets full of *Bons de la Défense Nationale*. These, he felt, perhaps foolishly, were infinitely to be preferred to tax receipts. But in fact the problem of war finance had merely been postponed. It was now necessary to decide who should pay the deferred bill represented by these quantities of *bons*. It also remained to determine who should pay for restoring the damaged properties in the devastated region.

"Germany Will Pay"

The answers to these questions seemed quite obvious to practically all Frenchmen at the time of the Armistice. Who had won the war anyway? The financial implications of victory had been impressed upon the French at the close of the Franco-Prussian War. Now the shoe was on the other foot. Germany was defeated and Germany would have to pay. With victory, the financial problem had become Germany's problem. To France remained only the bother of making out the bill.

The financial history of post-war France is essentially the story of the gradual disillusionment of the French. Almost immediately it became apparent that there would be a delay in drawing up the accounts and in auditing the bill. In the meantime, those sections of France which were physically unharmed would, acting on behalf of Germany, proceed to restore the region which had been shattered by the war, the costs to be added to Germany's bill. But ultimately Germany would pay all. However, as time went on, it began to be whispered that Germany either could not or would not pay, in anything approaching the proportions called for in the bill. To the Frenchman with his pocket full of *Bons de la Défense Nationale,* such a whisper brought terror. This was because he realized that if Germany did not pay the bill, his *bons* would be transformed automatically into something closely resembling worthless tax receipts. As a taxpayer he would have to take up his loss as a bondholder. For practically every thousand francs the Germans did not pay he, as a taxpayer, would have to pass a thousand-franc note from one trousers pocket to the other, and then, as a bond-holder, tear up one of his thousand-franc *bons,* replacing it with his tax receipt. Thus to commit financial hara-kiri was certainly not his conception of the rôle of a conqueror. Had he defeated the Germans only to be robbed by them? " Germany must pay " became the slogan of French financial policy not merely because of a hatred of Germany and of a desire to punish her, but also because the individual Frenchman became sickeningly conscious that, if Germany did not pay, his personal fortunes were ruined.

Viewed in retrospect, with a knowledge of the slight extent to which Germany was destined to contribute to the liquidation of French war and reconstruction costs, the character of the political problem of the period becomes clear. The people of France had to be reconciled to poverty. They had to be brought to the realization that instead of being affluent they were well-nigh ruined. Every one holding a claim payable in francs had to have his estimates regarding his economic position punctured and deflated. He had to be persuaded that he was, after all, fortunate if he succeeded in securing payment at a discount of about four-fifths. France now has political stability because this task has at last been accomplished. During the process of its accomplishment, she passed through an inferno.

General Survey of Financial Results of the Post-War Period

Before turning to a detailed description of the financial measures adopted during these years, it will conduce to clarity to present certain summary figures.

Tax Collections. — Consider first the tax collections [1] of the State for the post-war years, which were as follows:

	Billions of paper francs	*Billions of pre-war francs*
1913	4.1	4.1
1919	10.0	2.8
1920	18.3	3.6
1921	17.8	5.2
1922	20.8	6.4
1923	20.9	5.0
1924	25.4	5.2
1925	29.8	5.4
1926	38.1	5.4
1927	43.7	7.0

In paper francs the showing is remarkable. France collected 10 billion francs during the first year of the post-war period. Important changes were made in the tax system in 1920, including the establishment of the famous sales or " turnover " tax. With this revamped system in force, the annual collections during the next four years, 1920–23, were more than doubled. This was the period of international conferences, devoted to attempts to secure payments from Germany. By 1924, the hope that Germany would solve completely France's financial problem had been largely dissipated. New tax measures, sponsored by the harassed finance ministers who paraded through the Louvre during the years after Poincaré's fall in 1924, whipped up the collections from 20 billions to almost twice that amount — in paper francs. In 1927 France collected nearly 44 billion francs, more than 10 times the

[1] These figures, which are comparable with those for the war period presented on p. 25, are drawn from Table 59, p. 396. For local revenues, see p. 377.

collections in 1913 and more than 4 times the collections in 1919.

Deflated, however, the story is not impressive. In francs of equivalent purchasing power, the 10 billions of taxes collected in 1919 are found to have been worth much less than the 4 billions collected in 1913. Not until 1921 did France tax herself as heavily, judged by this test, as before the war. Even the sum of 44 billions, wrung from the country by Poincaré in 1927, was really considerably less than double the pre-war tax burden. If one adds together the deflated tax collections for these 14 years, 1914–1927, and strikes an average, he reaches the remarkable conclusion that the average annual tax collections for the entire war and post-war period were 4.15 billion francs. This figure is substantially identical with the 4.07 billions collected during 1913. It is obvious that, to date, tax collections in France have contributed almost nothing to war costs or the costs of reconstruction.

Annual Net Borrowings. — The French statistics of expenditures are so faulty that it is vain to attempt at this time to construct a table of annual deficits.[2] The general situation may be shown, however, with the aid of Treasury statistics of net borrowings. The expenditures of France during these years were such that it was necessary to supplement the tax collections by borrowing, year by year, the following amounts: [3]

	Billions of paper francs	*Billions of pre-war francs*[4]
1913	0.1	0.1
1914	6.3	6.2
1915	20.3	14.5
1916	29.2	15.5
1917	35.1	13.4
1918	37.2	11.0

[2] See pp. 413–433.

[3] From Tables 1 and 4, pp. 185, 190, 191.

[4] These figures represent the purchasing power of the borrowings as the paper francs were received by the Treasury, year by year.

	Billions of paper francs	*Billions of pre-war francs*
1919	48.7	13.7
1920	37.7	7.4
1921	24.9	7.2
1922	17.4	5.3
1923	15.8	3.8
1924	6.8	1.4
1925	4.4	0.8
1926	1.5	0.2

In view of the fact that, as has been shown above, the tax collections contributed practically nothing toward the extraordinary expenses of the war and of reconstruction, it is possible to approximate the money cost of the war by aggregating this table of net borrowings. Thus calculated, this cost came to slightly more than 100 billions of pre-war francs.

Aggregate Outstanding Debt. — The effect of these annual net borrowings can be traced in the following figures of the outstanding debt of France at the end of each year in billions of paper francs: [5]

	Domestic	*Foreign*	*Total*
1913	32.6	0	32.6
1914	39.4	0.1	39.5
1915	59.4	2.9	62.4
1916	80.2	8.8	89.0
1917	107.1	21.6	128.7
1918	144.3	29.0	173.3
1919	185.6	67.1	252.7
1920	219.2	105.1	324.3
1921	241.4	84.0	325.4
1922	254.4	98.0	352.4
1923	275.3	140.9	416.2
1924	285.5	142.9	428.4
1925	291.6	213.9	505.4
1926	291.8	205.3	497.1
1927	297.3	210.8	508.1

[5] From Table 3, p. 188. No adjustments have been made in this or in the following tables to force the totals into precise agreement with the sum of the individual items. Each individual figure is rounded off to the nearest tenth of one per cent.

The above figures for the foreign debt vary widely from year to year because the debt is expressed in paper francs of fluctuating value. As a matter of fact, foreign borrowing on a large scale ceased when America withdrew her treasury support in 1921.

Part Played by Loans from America. — The manner in which America stepped into England's place as France's foreign financial supporter in 1917 is clearly shown by the following table in which the foreign borrowings of the French Treasury are presented (in billions) year by year, the dollars, pounds, etc., having been translated into francs at the average exchange rate of the year: [6]

	From America	From Great Britain	From Other Countries	Total [7]
1914	.5	0.	0.	.5
1915	1.8	.8	.1	2.8
1916	1.6	7.0	.2	8.8
1917	7.5	4.0	.4	11.9
1918	5.4	1.6	1.7	8.7
Total	16.4	13.4	2.4	32.2
1919	9.3	1.8	.3	11.3
1920	3.3	.2	.1	3.6
1921	1.4	0.	0.	1.5
1922	0.	0.	0.	0.
1923	0.	0.	0.	0.
1924	0.	.4	0.	.4
1925	0.	.3	0.	.3
1926	0.	0.	1.1	1.1
Total	14.0	2.6	1.5	18.1
Grand Total [7]	30.5	16.0	3.9	50.4

Taxes and Borrowings Combined. — By consolidating the annual tax collections, shown on pages 396–397 and 400, with the annual net borrowings, shown on page 185, the results shown in Diagram I are obtained.

This diagram presents the clearest general picture it is possible to give at the present time of the finances of France for this period. The combination of the taxes and the borrowings yields

[6] From Table 4, pp. 190–191.

[7] See p. 190, footnote b.

a result which will doubtless be found to approximate very closely the total expenditures of France, deflated, for these years.

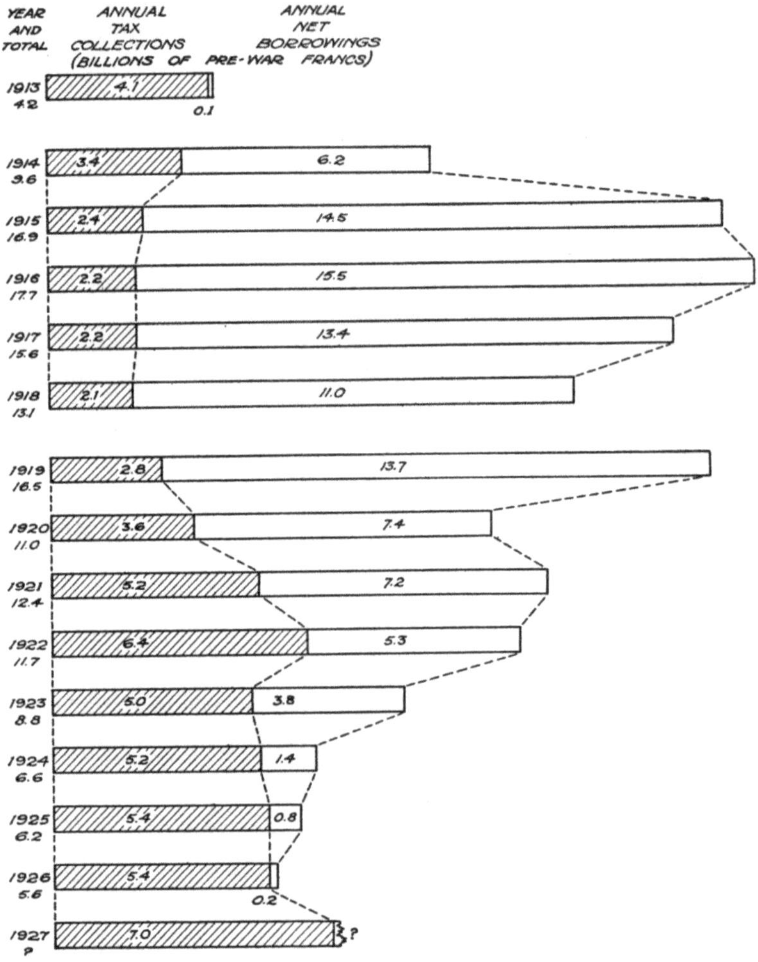

DIAGRAM I

Annual State Tax Collections and Net Borrowings, 1913–1927
(In pre-war francs)

Particular attention is called to the following points: (1) The high level of expenditures during the years immediately following the Armistice. The average annual expenditure during the war years was 14.6 billions. Expenditure was maintained on a level almost as high as this (12.9 billions) for four years after the war. More was spent in 1919 than in either 1917 or 1918.

(2) The rapid and steady decline after 1919 in borrowings as a financial resource. France borrowed as long as she could. She curtailed her program of expenditures in the devastated region and increased her taxes only when she could borrow no more. The foreign sources of loans practically dried up in 1921. The domestic sources began to dwindle the same year, and by 1924 produced only driblets.

(3) The early date at which the peak in expenditures was reached. The diagram shows that 1916 was the year of greatest expenditure. This was the year during which Great Britain made her most substantial contribution to the French Treasury. If one ignores foreign borrowings, the figures show that France reached her peak of domestic effort one year earlier, 1915. The heavy dependence on loans clearly made it possible for France to bring her full economic power to bear with a mimimum of delay. This time element should not be forgotten in criticizing France's financial policy. She could not wait for taxes. Moreover, having once resorted to loans and inflation, she found it much more difficult to impose taxes when later she sought to do so, because inflation itself had impaired the productivity of the revenue system.

Prices and Exchange. — The financial operations reflected in the preceding tables were accompanied by changes in the wholesale price level and in the dollar exchange in Paris as shown in the table on page 50.

As is well known, exchange rates were much more completely controlled than were prices. The movements in the two series following the Armistice are particularly interesting. A Frenchman even after the Armistice could see the franc quoted in dollars or pounds at approximately its par rate. So long as this was true, he could think of the franc as a franc, even though the price level had more than trebled. This price derangement could be dismissed as a temporary phenomenon, inconvenient but probably not fundamentally significant. However, when the exchange

WHOLESALE PRICE LEVEL AND DOLLAR EXCHANGE

	WHOLESALE PRICE INDEX [8] (Base 1913 = 100)	DOLLAR EXCHANGE IN PARIS [9] (Par = 5.18)
December, 1914	110.5	5.17
" 1915	163.2	5.85
" 1916	203.5	5.84
" 1917	304.3	5.70
" 1918	352.8	5.45
December, 1919	422.7	10.52
" 1920	434.8	17.04
" 1921	325.7	12.40
" 1922	361.9	13.74
" 1923	458.6	19.59
" 1924	507.2	18.56
" 1925	632.4	26.90
" 1926	626.5	25.25

rates began to rocket skyward, to join the price level, alarm seemed to be justified. Here was the opportunity for the political leader who would loudly proclaim that France was financially sound, that Germany would pay, and that the only trouble with the franc was that it was being attacked by wicked foreign speculators.

THE REËSTABLISHMENT OF BUDGETARY PROCEDURE

The French budget system [10] is a marvelously refined mechanism which, however admirably it may function on the smooth speedway of peace, is certainly not well adapted to operate on the rutted road of war. Quite sensibly the French abandoned it when, shortly after the outbreak of the hostilities, the going became rough.

In 1915, 1916 and 1917, France had no budget. In its place a system of *crédits trimestriels* was established, whereby Parliament simply granted authority to make expenditures, without attempting to specify with precision the sources from which the

[8] From Table 73, p. 448. [9] From Table 74, p. 449. [10] See p. 312.

money was to come. The Treasury would have to find the money. As has been seen, it did so by borrowing in one form or another.[11] All the regular " civil " expenditure was thrown in with the special war expenditure and all covered by the quarterly credits.

The Conception of the " Ordinary " Budget. — In 1917, when it resorted to fresh taxation, the French Government took the first step toward a return to the normal budgetary procedure. It proposed an " ordinary " or civil budget, which was not to include " exceptional " expenditure, met by borrowing, but which was to separate the " permanent " items of expenditure from the non-permanent and relate these permanent expenditures to ordinary receipts.

The conception of this ordinary budget is well stated in M. Klotz's *exposé* of the budget bill for 1919.[12] In it the Finance Minister explained that he had been led to classify the expenditure of France during the war in the following manner:

In the first place, the war had made it necessary for the State, in the interests of national defense, to perform such functions as in normal times were performed by private individuals. These functions included the manufacture of various war materials, the supply of foodstuffs, etc. The expenditure that such functions involved could not be confused with the permanent expenditure of the State, and had no place in an ordinary budget. For the most part they brought counterbalancing receipts, and should constitute separate Treasury accounts, which, when necessary, could be fed by special credits. M. Klotz was quite aware of the dangers that the existence of such accounts could involve in the way of deficits, and realized that they should be subject to the strictest possible control.

The second category included those expenses which, without any counterpart of revenue, had been determined by the military,

[11] Theoretically the French Treasury is supposed to have no sources of revenue. It is supposed to act merely as " banker " for the budget, advancing funds which it borrows, and being repaid from the budgets. Actually, however, the Treasury during the post-war period did develop certain tax revenues, quite independent of the budgets.

[12] *Doc. Parl.*, 1918, *Chambre, Sess. Ord.*, Doc. No. 5005, p. 1137 *et seq.*

social and economic necessities of war time. Their nature was such that no valuations as to their amount could be made in advance for any length of time, and their size was vastly greater than any amounts that could possibly be supplied by the taxpayer. They were essentially temporary in their nature, and it would be wrong, he said, to meet them out of permanent resources. All things considered, it was therefore better to let the quarterly credits take care of such expenditure, the resources of these provisional credits being supplied by borrowing. The total of such credits could then, at the end of the year, be converted by a special act into definitive credits.

Finally, there was a third group of expenses the stability and permanence of which made it possible to include them in the "ordinary" budget. Such expenses should be strictly counterbalanced by normal resources.

It seems to us [said M. Klotz] that this classification of our total financial transactions answers, so far as the exceptional circumstances through which we pass permit it, the essential need of order and clarity which more than ever should dominate our financial methods. . . .

In this system . . . the ordinary budget of the civil services plays a part of primary importance. By including from year to year, within its framework, the increased charges resulting from the growth of the public debt, the increased pension list and the growth of administrative expenses caused by the rise in prices and war conditions, and by creating, when necessary, renewable resources for the purpose of balancing such charges, we will make use of the only method which will allow us to keep unimpaired our financial power and to start on a solid and stable basis the epoch of economic development that lies before us.[13]

The "Ordinary" Budgets of 1918 *and* 1919. — The difficulties that lay in the way of normal budgeting both in 1918 and 1919 were, however, enormous. It was not until the 1918 budget had been largely remoulded as a consequence of the large interest due on the new *rentes* (four per cent, perpetual, 1917,[14] estimated by Klotz at 346 millions) and the passage of the series of new fiscal measures described on pages 38–41 that it was finally adopted with a delay of six months. The expenditure, estimated

[13] *Doc. Parl., loc. cit.*, p. 1138.

[14] See p. 264.

at 8,009 millions, left an apparent surplus of 48 millions. Although M. Klotz called this a "highly satisfactory result,"[15] it must be recognized that it was possible to show a surplus only because no provision was made for the inevitable increase of the debt service during the period covered by the budget, and because the assumption was made that all military expenditure was "abnormal," an assumption which many a peace-time finance minister wishes were a valid one! It is curious to hear M. Klotz state that "it goes without saying that the expenses incurred by the Ministries of War, Munitions and Marines and the military expenditure of the Ministry of Colonies must be classed within the extraordinary budget."[16]

The same criticisms may be brought against the 1919 budget. Its original draft, contemplating 8,932 millions of receipts and 8,927 millions of expenditure, was submitted to Parliament before the Armistice, on September 24, 1918. With the Armistice, the issue of the immensely successful *rentes* (four per cent, perpetual, 1918)[17] and the absence of any new fiscal legislation to meet the increased debt service, the conditions were drastically changed. The new *rentes* demanded an additional sum for service of 1,060 millions, and the war being at an end, some important changes could be expected in the yield of the various taxes. The tax on payments had shown itself far less productive than had been anticipated, and the estimate of its yield was reduced by 450 millions. On the other hand, with demobilization in progress, an increase in the yield (estimated at 115 millions) could be expected from direct taxes. This, however, still left a considerable deficit as against the increased debt service, and the gap in the "ordinary" budget had to be filled by a very "extraordinary" bit of revenue, *viz.*, 2 billions resulting from the liquidation of war stock.[18]

[15] *Doc. Parl.*, *loc. cit.*, p. 1139.

[16] *Idem.*

[17] See p. 264.

[18] Klotz had suggested (*Doc. Parl.*, 1919, *Chambre*, *Sess. Ord.*, Doc. No. 5551, p. 89), that the proceeds of the liquidation of war stock should be carried to the credit of a special Treasury account. It was the Budget Commission which disagreed, and desired this source of revenue to be classed under State Domains, in the ordinary budget.

Thus by the middle of 1919 France already had an "ordinary" budget with credits to the extent of 10.4 billion francs (of which 6.5 billion francs were for debt service) and a revenue estimated at 10.7 billions (which included 2 billions from the liquidation of war stock). This was the largest budget that France had yet had, but even so it did not by any means answer the real needs of the moment. M. Klotz himself had no illusions on this point.

Even if it is not necessary [he said] to have recourse to new fiscal measures for the purpose of balancing the 1919 budget, one must guard oneself against thinking that an equilibrium has been arrived at between the burden that we must carry in the future and the normal and permanent revenue to be expected from taxation. To let such an opinion take root would mean preparing for the country a cruel disappointment. . . . The shape of the 1919 budget is only a transitory one. If the expenditure is covered by already existing sources of revenue, it is only because it counts on temporary receipts derived from the liquidation of war stock. Further, it only includes a very small part of the war pensions and no provision at all for the inevitable increase in the public debt during 1919.[19]

Waiting for the Treaty of Peace

As to the immediate future, the Minister was not willing to make any commitments. The Peace Treaty had not yet been signed. He thought it would be useless to try to make any arrangements for the future equilibrium of the budget while the problems submitted to the Peace Conference were still unsettled. Regardless of the amounts receivable from the Central Powers under the treaty, however, M. Klotz thought it would be necessary to impose new financial sacrifices on France, and to undertake a wide administrative reorganization.

But as we have already stated before Chamber and Senate, we shall refrain from making such an appeal to the French taxpayer so long as the enemy's debt is not fixed. Yet, we are certain in advance that our country which has shown during the war so many proofs of its spirit of sacrifice, will bravely make the financial effort asked from it, if only it knows that everything has been done to obtain from our oppressors the maximum of just reparations to which it is entitled.[20]

[19] *Doc. Parl.*, 1919, *Chambre*, *Sess. Ord.*, Doc. No. 6029, p. 1221.

[20] *Idem.*

These were the reasons, or perhaps the excuses, why no fiscal effort of any kind (except an increase in the price of tobacco and some customs rates) was made during the year 1919. It was, indeed, not until the last days of the year that M. Klotz was ready to give to Parliament and to the country a complete exposition of both the financial situation of France and of the program he intended to pursue in the near future.

CHAPTER IV

THE TAX REFORM OF 1920

M. KLOTZ, who was destined almost immediately to relinquish his portfolio as Finance Minister, delivered his speech on the financial situation on December 29, 1919.[1] It is a document of considerable importance because it represents the first serious attempt, after the Armistice, to analyze the position of France not only in strictly financial terms but also in terms of the broad economic and psychological phenomena which played so large a rôle in these post-war years.

As has been seen, 1919 had been a year of inactivity in the field of taxation. On the other hand it had been a year of enormous activity in the field of the public debt, the net borrowings amounting to the staggering total of 48.7 billions of paper francs, the high-water mark of the era under study.

THE KLOTZ ANALYSIS, DECEMBER, 1919

The total expenditures since the outbreak of the war, M. Klotz estimated at approximately 200 billion paper francs, a figure which appears to be substantially accurate. The public debt, incurred to meet war costs, he placed at about 186 billion paper francs, which was apparently an understatement.

Despite these large figures, M. Klotz — together with a very large number of his countrymen — was optimistic as to the financial position of France. He realized that one of the primary needs was the consolidation of the floating debt; but that did not make him nervous. France, he said, had shown both during and after the war that the State was enjoying the full confidence of the people. The internal debt was vastly greater than the foreign

[1] *Débats*, 1919, *Chambre, Sess. Extraord.*, p. 5399 *et seq.* The figures used by Klotz were published in the *Journal Officiel* for December 26, 1919, and related to the preceding October 31.

debt, and not only were the *Bons de la Défense Nationale* an extremely popular short-time investment, but also the big consolidation loans — and above all the 1918 *rentes* — had proved enormously successful. "One may say," said M. Klotz, "that by its subscriptions the country has manifested its wealth, its thrift and its confidence in the final victory. So it will continue in the future." The possibility of a "confidence" crisis was therefore considered to be out of the question; the bondholder had as yet shown no sign of weariness or discouragement, despite a drop in the value of the franc. Provided the right measures were adopted for improving the budgetary situation — and only now was it becoming possible to begin that task — France would rapidly enough recover her economic strength after the terrible years of suffering and waste.

As to the budget, M. Klotz pointed out that France was leaving a realm of uncertainty to enter a realm of precision and solidity. What had been the position so far? Since 1918, budgets had been established, but the "normal" revenue had been insufficient to meet even the civil service expenditure. The total credits voted in 1919 had amounted to 41.2 billions; of this amount about three-quarters had been destined for exceptional expenditure, and as for the remaining 10.4 billions of "civil service" expenditure, only about 8.5 billions had been met out of "ordinary" revenue.

But even the deficit of 1.9 billions was far from giving the correct idea of the real budgetary requirements of the country. At least a part of the military expenditure would have to be inscribed in the "ordinary" budget; the interest charge of the floating debt was increasing enormously month after month and a considerable increase had to be anticipated for 1920 in the salaries and wages of government officials; funds were necessary for effecting technical improvements in the state monopolies. Billions of francs would be asked from the Minister of Finance. M. Klotz prophesied that if the budget were to be fed out of normal and permanent resources, it would be between three and four times the size of the pre-war budget, i.e., somewhere between 15 and 20 billion francs. In addition to the "ordinary" budget, there were still three important classes of exceptional expenditure which would have to be met. One included the military and civil expenditure resulting directly from war conditions, demobilization, etc.; another included such reconstruction work (outside the devastated regions proper) as had been necessitated by the new requirements of peace time; thirdly, there was the expenditure eventually to be covered by reparations from Germany. France had already acted as banker for Germany, "advancing" 25 billions for such expenditure. This was, of course, unfortunate, but the capital outlay needed by the devastated provinces could not be stretched over the period of the German payments.

To meet the increase in ordinary expenditure [said M. Klotz] we have at present nothing to show except a careful calculation of the normal increments in the existing taxes. A state cannot support itself, unless its subjects support it. This country which, at a time of agony, in the midst of anxiety and tears, had accepted over 3 million francs in new taxes, despite her devastated provinces and the hecatomb of her sons, will not give way on the morrow of peace.

M. Uhry: — The rich must be made to pay.

On Center and Right: — Germany must be made to pay.

M. Klotz: — I shall give satisfaction to both sides . . . only it is not the rich who shall pay first; the first to pay shall be the enemy. (*Loud cheers.*)

But so far as the ordinary budget was concerned, this question of Germany's payment was only subsidiary. It was no more than one of three moral conditions which were necessary for putting the French taxpayer in a good mood. These conditions, according to M. Klotz, were the following: (1) profiteers must be taxed, (2) strict economy must be practiced to preserve the confidence and respect of foreign countries, and (3) Germany must pay, because every concession made to her would be to the detriment of the French taxpayer and for the benefit of the German taxpayer. Having received these three assurances, the Frenchman will then pay his taxes. He will be able to do it, considering the present value of the franc. A billion to-day is not equal to a pre-war billion, and since everything has "gone up," it is only natural that taxes should follow suit.

Oh, I know well [said M. Klotz] that the taxpayer will discuss the means of balancing the budget. You will also discuss them, gentlemen. . . . No tax is perfect. Generally, what seems a good tax, is the one paid by the neighbor. . . . In the present state of affairs there must, regardless of school doctrines, be created both direct and indirect taxes.

The mere increase in the quantity of taxation was not, however, sufficient. The quality must also be given attention. As already mentioned, the creation of the schedule taxes and the general income tax in the midst of the war had been criticized as untimely, partly on account of the serious disorganization of the financial administration during this time. The yield of the income taxes and the tax on war profits had been poor. It was not to be wondered at. The new fiscal laws were complicated and the application of some of them required detailed legal commentaries. The tax on war profits confronted the French administration with problems and methods of investigation to which it was quite unaccustomed. Yet it was just at a time when so many new elements had been brought into the work of the tax inspector that the fiscal administrative bodies were reduced to a skeleton. The inspectors who had returned from the army and who, before the war, had known nothing of the present taxes, could hardly be expected to be of great service at once. They were forced to study their jobs all over again. All this was bound to affect the tax yield. Besides, the various moratoria granted during the war had to some extent demoralized the taxpayer, and on the other hand it was perhaps only natural that a certain amount of indulgence was shown in the treatment of the demobilized.

Owing to such abnormal conditions there had also been a great delay in thousands of tax assessments, as well as collections, which naturally involved a considerable accumulation of bad debts. Therefore it was one of the urgent needs of the moment not only to create new taxes, but also to restore and bring up to date the efficiency of the fiscal administration.

Klotz's Fiscal Program

Following M. Clemenceau's unsuccessful candidacy in the presidential elections in January, 1920, his cabinet resigned and was succeeded by a cabinet with M. Millerand as Premier and M. François-Marsal, the "banker-minister," as Minister of Finance. A few days before the resignation of the Clemenceau Cabinet, M. Klotz fulfilled his promise given on December 29 to submit to Parliament his outline of financial policy. This outline took the form of two closely connected bills, one being the budget *projet* for 1920[2] and the other a bill for the creation of new fiscal resources.

The 1920 Budget Projet.[3] — The former is concerned with the budgetary position as a whole, and the main interest of this paper consists in the fact that here for the first time, officially, there is clearly formulated the conception of the "special account" (later called "budget") of "recoverable" expenditure. The budget is divided into several sections, as follows, the figures being in millions of paper francs:

	Expenditure	*Revenue*
"Ordinary" budget.......	17,861.	17,884.
"Extraordinary" budget...	7,568.	3,000.
"Recoverable" expenditure special account.........	22,089.	......
	47,518.	20,884.

The revenue figure of the "ordinary" or civil budget, including as it did 2 billions of "exceptional" revenue, was about 8 billions higher than the corresponding figure in the "ordinary" budget of 1919. This difference was to be met out of the new taxation which M. Klotz, in his bill for the "new fiscal measures," submitted to Parliament together with the budget. The

[2] *Doc. Parl.*, 1920, *Chambre, Sess. Ord.*, Doc. No. 168, p. 57 *et seq.*

[3] One of the causes of deficits in the early post-war budgets was that they were presented to Parliament and voted with considerable delay. The 1920 budget, which should have been voted by December 31, 1919, was only presented on January 13, 1920, and was not voted until the end of July.

difference between the totals of revenue and expenditure as given above was to be met from loans.[4]

Proposed New Fiscal Measures.[5] — This bill was the basis of the most important post-war reform in French taxation — the act of June 25, 1920. It differed in numerous respects, however, from the shape it was finally to take, and these differences revealed the lines along which the struggle regarding fiscal policy was to take place in the years to come.

Klotz proposed (1) to raise a large majority of existing tax rates, and (2) to create several new taxes, including the all-important turnover tax (*taxe sur le chiffre d'affaires*). Most of the new revenue to come from old taxes was to be drawn from higher indirect taxes, such as those on liquor, sugar, and imported colonial products, from higher registration taxes (including the inheritance tax), and from increased postal, telegraph and telephone rates. The rest was to come largely from increases all along the line in the income taxes.

As to revenue from new taxes, Klotz relied chiefly on an addition to the war-profits tax in the form of an additional supertax on war "enrichment," along with two interesting levies on increment value, and above all, on the new turnover tax.

In view of the importance which the movement for a capital levy later developed, it is of interest to outline briefly Klotz's two proposed levies on increment value. The first was designed to tax, on a progressive scale, all "increases in wealth" between January 1, 1914, and December 31, 1919, the tax to be payable in five yearly installments. "Normal thrift" and agriculture, "the efforts of which had sustained the nation," would be spared. The extreme difficulty of securing the double inventory of wealth which would be required is obvious.

The second increment-tax proposal was for a special tax on increments in the value of business concerns and real estate as determined by the comparison of the purchase price and the sales price, the time limit between the two being 25 years. M. Klotz

[4] *Doc. Parl., loc. cit.*, pp. 58, 59.

[5] *Doc. Parl.*, 1920, *Chambre, Sess. Ord.*, Doc. No. 166, p. 1 *et seq.*

argued that the benefit of any increment which was not directly due to the owner's own efforts, but had been caused by some local improvements or a growth of population in the particular locality should be partly repaid to the community.

It is clear that Klotz depended upon indirect taxation to fill most of the 8.5-billion gap in the " ordinary " budget — the turnover tax alone was to supply over 4 billions. The modifications of the income taxes (including the one on revenue from securities) were to give only about seven-tenths of a billion.

EVOLUTION OF TAX PROPOSALS IN THE LEGISLATURE

It must be borne in mind that the fiscal measures proposed by Klotz were for the purpose of showing a balance in the 1920 " ordinary " budget. The budget year was now already under way, but six months were to pass before agreement could be reached regarding the character of the new taxes.

Changes Proposed by François-Marsal, January, 1920. — On succeeding M. Klotz at the Ministry of Finance, M. François-Marsal introduced some radical changes in his predecessor's bill. He seemed to have a special affection for the proposed new turnover tax, but the retroactive business supertax he considered impracticable and almost immoral. He said, for example, that companies who, trusting in the existing laws, had distributed dividends, would have to claim back a part of these from the shareholders, which, from a practical standpoint, would seem impossible. He thought it would be better from every point of view to extend the application of the war-profits tax for another year, i.e., until the end of 1920, and that the yield from that additional period would indeed be greater than from the revision proposed by M. Klotz.

The increment-tax proposal pleased him no better.

> From certain standpoints, of course [he said], and in a few individual cases, such a tax would seem equitable, but taken as a whole, one cannot fail to realize the very weighty objections it arouses. . . . One of the most serious criticisms that can be put forward is that it places in

a privileged position the very people who have shown themselves most wasteful. Those who have economized and saved, who have restrained their expenditure and consumption at a time when the country needed such restraint, would be hit with a heavy tax, while those who have spent lavishly would remain untouched. . . .

Besides, the assessment and then the collection would present insuperable difficulties. The double valuation of property in 1914 and 1919 would be an almost impossible task. The events during the past six years had unsettled numerous families and transformed in many cases the composition of the family estate. Such a tax, the Finance Minister thought, "would give rise, without the slightest doubt, to a movement of general dissatisfaction throughout the country." [6]

While discarding on the one side these taxes on acquired wealth and slightly modifying the taxation of successions and salary incomes, he proposed, on the other hand, to raise the tax on turnover from 1 per cent, as planned by M. Klotz, to 1.5 per cent. Certain classes of business activity were to be exempt, the most prominent of these being the sale of bread and certain public transport organizations. The latter item shows that M. François-Marsal intended that the turnover tax should be passed on to the consumer. "How could one increase, for instance, by 1.5 per cent the price of tickets on the Paris *Métro* or on the urban tramway lines?" [7] As to M. Klotz's proposals on the other direct and indirect taxes, these were left unchanged by his successor. The whole scheme, however, led to a long series of discussions and compromises between the Minister and the parliamentary finance commissions before the *projet* in its general form was voted on June 25, 1920.

Report of Commission of Chamber, March, 1920.—The Finance Commission of the Chamber, headed by MM. Dumont, Bokanowski, and De Lasteyrie, rejected most of the modifications that M. François-Marsal had introduced in the bill, and

[6] Letter to the President of the Chamber Finance Committee. *Doc. Parl.*, 1920, *Sess. Ord.*, Doc. No. 376, p. 315.

[7] *Doc. Parl., loc. cit.*, p. 315.

adhered, on the whole, to M. Klotz's original text. The Finance Commission of the Senate, on the other hand, supported M. François-Marsal's point of view. The delay in the voting of a bill labelled " urgent " at the beginning of its journey was most unfortunate and had a serious effect on the equilibrium of the 1920 budget. In their first report of March 23 the Chamber Commission warned the deputies not to hold up the bill longer than necessary. " We must ask the Chamber," they wrote, " for an exceptional effort of diligence, brevity and fiscal courage. Every day elapsed since the first of January represents a loss in revenue of 24 millions. Every hour of useless talk will cost a million." [8]

It is interesting to note that, even at this early date, the Commission was earnestly seeking to impress the seriousness of the situation upon the many people in France who were picturing to themselves a financial millenium. Indeed, the *exposé* of the Chamber Commission suggests a feeling of disillusionment, and indicates deep apprehension as to the trustworthiness of the " Germany will pay " motto which had been at the root of M. Klotz's optimism.

Fiscal courage [they said] means above all that the deputies vote and the country pays, as soon as possible, the indispensable taxes. So long as we have not reëstablished the equilibrium between our permanent expenditure and our normal revenue, we shall not have accomplished what the peace has prescribed as a necessity, and what our allies and associates regard as our duty.

Of course, it has taken France many long months to convince herself that it is a duty to make a heavy levy on her labor and her savings. The victim of an unjust attack, invaded, exhausted by four years of heroic resistance and by the death of innumerable young men, with her wealthiest provinces devastated, yet victorious in the end, she thought for a long time that those who had wanted the war, who had conducted it barbarously and had been defeated, would also pay for it. In this the Treaty of Versailles had disillusioned her.

As for German payments, " the Allies and associates have given their word that France, mangled and victorious, would be paid

[8] *Rapport Dumont, Bokanowski et de Lasteyrie. Doc. Parl.*, 1920, *Chambre, Sess. Ord.*, Doc. No. 589, p. 209.

by Germany. England, the United States, Japan, Italy, have all pledged their honor. . . . Not a cent of the 8.5 billions of taxes is to be used to pay for Germany." And further, "if the Allies do not leave us to pay for what Germany owes, our Treasury will not have any serious difficulties during the coming years, provided, however, that we reëstablish immediately the equilibrium of our ordinary budget by means of unavoidable taxes and the necessary economies." The "if" is already ominous, and indicated that the hopes of financial rehabilitation were based by the Finance Commission on the one and only condition that Germany *would pay.*

While realizing the necessity for increasing taxation, the Commission drew back from François-Marsal's proposal to raise so much of the money by indirect taxes. It again lowered the rate of the proposed turnover tax to one per cent. It changed the income-tax rates so as to produce 600 millions more than Klotz had suggested. It kept Klotz's additional war-profits tax and one of his proposed increment value taxes. In this form the proposal went to the Chamber.

There was another way out, of course, and that was an attempt at a capital levy, advocated by the Socialists. But the Chamber Commission feared it, on grounds of both doctrine and technique.

> Some people [they said] may consider at first sight the proposals of the Government and the Commission as mediocre and insufficiently daring in view of the seriousness of the present position. . . . Two hundred billions of debt! Shall one carry such a burden during a hundred years? Why not levy immediately on everybody's capital the sums necessary to repay it, or a great part of it? After studying it, we have, however, rejected the tax on capital. . . . Germany has had a "distress" tax on capital which has proved a lamentable failure.

Important technical difficulties lay in the way. The tax would involve an endless amount of disorder and injustice, and

> to determine the capital value of French fortunes and assess on such fortunes a progressive tax, it is necessary to imagine that all movable and immovable property owned by Frenchmen should immediately and

simultaneously change hands. But if all property were thrown into the market at the same time, its value would fall to nil.[9]

The Proposal before the Senate Commission. — The Chamber adopted the main points of its Commission's plan, sent the bill to the Senate Commission, and then the battle started in earnest. François-Marsal, with his extra half of one per cent on the turnover tax, and his rejection of the addition to the war-profits tax, gave the Senate Commission far more peace of mind than did the lower house. Also, the Senate Commission made the situation even more embarrassing by discovering that 8.5 billions was not enough after all — nearly 10 billions should be raised by new taxes to balance the ordinary budget. So it again raised the rate of the proposed turnover tax to 1.5 per cent, intimating that its chief value lay in the fact that it was the tax "by which it seems easiest to secure very large resources." [10] It was counted on for 6.3 billion francs. The Commission also decided to ask for small increases in the yields of the income taxes and the liquor taxes.

The Position of the Chamber. — The Chamber Commission still stood by its one per cent rate on the turnover tax, however, and, as to the need of an additional 10 billions instead of 8.5 billions, it declared that: "While paying full tribute to the ideas of financial prudence which have dictated the vote of the Senate and while sharing entirely its anxiety to see the equilibrium of our budget restored, we have estimated that the fiscal measures demanded by the Upper Chamber are not necessary in the present circumstances and might throw too heavy a burden upon the country." [11] They argued that neither M. Klotz nor M. François-Marsal had demanded more than 8.5 billions and suggested in veiled language that the Senate should mind its own business. True, they admitted that they were equally concerned about the delay in the voting of the 1920 budget, which meant a considerable loss to the Treasury. They pointed out that conditions were not yet normal. The 1920 budget was one of transition. It was

[9] *Doc. Parl., loc. cit.*, p. 210.
[10] *Doc. Parl.*, 1920, *Sénat, Sess. Ord.*, Doc. No. 201, p. 66.
[11] *Doc. Parl.*, 1920, *Sess. Ord.*, Doc. No. 1032, p. 1632.

the first budget presented to Parliament since the signing of the Peace Treaty, etc. They expressed the hope that subsequent budgets would be voted promptly. All of which meant that once more a little borrowed money would do no harm.

The Chamber had its way, in the main, for the new resources bill, as finally passed, levied the turnover tax at one per cent, with an additional 0.1 per cent to help out local finances. The addition to the war-profits tax, however, and both the increment taxes which Klotz had proposed, never got over the hurdles.

The Budget of 1920

The budget bill of 1920 had meanwhile been following the new resources bill along the stormy path that led from the Finance Minister to the Chamber and to the Senate, and it was voted on July 31. It showed the following balances (figures in millions of francs): [12]

	Expenditure	*Revenue*
"Ordinary" budget.....	21,761	21,770
"Extraordinary" budget	5,420	5,425 (loans)
"Recoverable" budget..	20,751	.....
	47,932	27,195

The ordinary budget was made to balance. This, however, was an illusion, if one takes as a criterion the formula of "ordinary expenditure supplied by permanent resources." Of the 22 billions of expenditure only some 13 came out of "permanent" resources, and even these were not based on the regular system of estimating the yield on the basis of the penultimate year. A special item entitled "*Prélèvement sur les plus-values fiscales de l'exercice 1920,*" and amounting to 1.5 billion francs, was added to the estimated yield of the taxes. Moreover, the liquidation of war stocks was fixed at nearly 3 billions, and the war-profits tax at the exaggerated figure of 4 billions. These three items constituted the "exceptional" resources. As for expenditures, anything even slightly "exceptional" was not included in the ordinary budget, but carried into the "extraordinary" one. The

[12] *Journal Officiel, Lois et Décrets,* Aug. 1, 1920, pp. 10967,–82,–88,–89, 11002.

question presented itself, how long these "exceptional" resources to meet ordinary expenditure would last, and also how far the full scope of the ordinary expenditure was really indicated in the budget estimates. Time was to show that for 1920 the ordinary budget alone was burdened with supplementary credits which raised the expenditure figure from 21.8 billions to 23.2 billions.[13]

It would be unfair, however, to overstress the lopsidedness of the 1920 budget. The expenses ran all through the year, while the great tax increases did not take effect until the middle of the year. It was particularly unfortunate, from a finance minister's point of view, that the Chamber and the Senate had spent so much time in disagreeing about methods of taxation, for the net result of the argument was to cut the annual yield of the taxes below what either Klotz or François-Marsal had thought necessary. According to the estimate given by M. François-Marsal in his budget bill for 1921,[14] the annual yield of the tax reform of June 25 was no more than 7,331 millions. The compromise between Chamber and Senate had thus, unfortunately, been on the wrong side — both parties ultimately agreed to the partial *rejection* of their own proposals: the Chamber, to the rejection of the exceptional taxes on war wealth; the Senate, to the suppression of the extra half per cent of the turnover tax.

The Revised Tax System

In the confusing figures of estimated yield, budget deficits, and "ordinary" versus "extraordinary" items, one is apt to overlook the importance of the radical change that had been effected in the structure of the tax system. For the first time since the war had started, something like a definitive effort was made to establish taxes lucrative enough to meet permanent budgetary charges, and the income taxes showed themselves (at least to those in power) incapable of meeting the test. The call once more

[13] *Cf.* de Lasteyrie's *projet* for 1923 budget (*Doc. Parl.*, 1922, *Chambre, Sess. Ord.*, Doc. No. 4220, pp. 11, 15, 21 of the *projet*).

[14] *Projet* for 1921 budget, pp. 19–21 of the *projet* (*Doc. Parl.*, 1920, *Chambre, Sess. Ord.*, Doc. No. 1523).

went out for indirect taxes, and the result was a tax system vastly different from that to which the reforms of 1914 and 1917 had seemed to point. The *Quatre Vieilles*, it is true, had largely disappeared, but in their place, so to speak, came the turnover tax. It was destined to grow in importance as France's financial troubles developed, until in 1927 it was covering about one-fifth of all the charges of a completely balanced budget.

The tax was simple in its conception; the rate was levied on gross receipts from all sales and commissions on sales in the ordinary course of industry or commerce, excepting agricultural products direct from the farm, sales for export, railroad and some other public utility receipts, and other minor exemptions. It was not intended to be a business tax; rather, it was levied as a tax on expenditure, with the expectation that it would be passed on to the consumer of the finished product. The *taxe de luxe* of ten per cent on retail sales of luxury articles and on receipts of *de luxe* hotels, restaurants, etc., was kept without vital changes and made an integral part of the turnover tax.

Other indirect taxes were increased by the same law, notably those on liquor; and many of the registration and stamp duties, including the inheritance tax, were raised.

The opportunity to touch up the income taxes was not lost; rates were raised, methods of assessment (in the agricultural-profits tax) slightly changed, and new complications devised to exempt income burdened by family charges.

Speaking of this act of June 25, and the finance act of 1920, M. Jèze thought that these measures had "considerably cleared the horizon." [15] Others thought it had definitely brought about fair weather. During the three and a half years that followed, France did not cease to applaud the "fiscal courage" that the voting of those acts had manifested. The French believed that the tax reform of 1920 was the last and utmost sacrifice that could be expected from them. This mistaken belief was so strong that it took years to shatter it.

[15] *Revue de Science et de Législation Financières*, 1920, p. 615.

CHAPTER V

INFLATION FOR RECONSTRUCTION, 1921–1923

By adopting the tax reform of 1920, the French considered that they had made the final adjustment in the revenue system to meet their post-war financial problem. It was anomalous, they felt, that even this sacrifice should be required of a victorious people. But the financing of the war had brought about a condition of inflation which presumably would soon be corrected but which in the meantime involved an increase of taxes. The yield of the new taxation should suffice to meet the situation, for the German reparations would certainly support the expenditure being made to restore the devastated regions as well as the service of the foreign debt. It was not generally recognized at the time that the Treasury was already in the midst of a second cycle of borrowing which, with the collapse of the hopes for receiving huge reparations from Germany, was to sweep France into virtual bankruptcy and require new taxation compared with which the 1920 schedules would seem moderate.

Some conception of the proportions of the task of reconstruction which France was facing at this juncture may be gained from a statement in the 1928 *projet* [1] that the total war-damages expenditure during the seven years, 1920–1926, exceeded 100 billion francs. Nearly two-thirds of this represented capital payments for war damages to private property. Such payments during the four years immediately under review, 1920–1923, aggregated more than 47 billions. The bulk of this money came from the series of eight *Crédit National* loans which were floated as rapidly as the market would absorb them, beginning in December, 1919, and continuing, at higher and higher rates of interest, until the disastrous issue of January, 1924.

It will be recalled that M. François-Marsal's budget for 1920, voted on July 31 of that year, divided the budgetary expenditure

[1] P. 185. See below, pp. 297–303.

of France into two distinct parts. One was the French *budget général*, subdivided into the "ordinary" and the "extraordinary" budgets; the other, the German budget of recoverable expenditure. The tax reform of June 25, 1920, was the necessary condition for the realization of that scheme. With the aid of the revenues thus provided, the French budget of "ordinary" expenditure was to be fed entirely out of "permanent" and "ordinary" revenue. The French "extraordinary" budget was to carry on its revenue side only "exceptional" receipts of a temporary nature, including loans when necessary. As the "exceptional" expenditure of the French budget was largely in the nature of capital outlay for various kinds of post-war reconstruction work, it was considered legitimate that such expenditure should partly be met out of borrowing.

The much more formidable German budget included not only the regular capital outlay for the purpose of reconstructing the devastated regions but also considerable sums for the payment of certain classes of war pensions and war indemnities. Yet this budget was, provisionally, to draw all its resources from internal loans.

THE 1921 BUDGET — MORE TAXATION "UNTHINKABLE"

The budget for 1921,[2] presented by M. François-Marsal the day after the long-delayed 1920 budget was voted, indicated no special change in financial policy. Taxes were not yielding enough to cover permanent charges, but neither the Finance Minister nor the Chambers would consider a serious increase in the tax burden.

To M. François-Marsal this had seemed quite out of the question:

> Could one think [he wrote in the *projet*] of raising the revenue by making a new appeal to the taxpayer? The Government has considered that the answer could only be in the negative. An unprecedented fiscal effort, a sacrifice, one might say, without an equal, has been asked from the country and courageously consented to by it. . . . The additional

[2] *Doc. Parl.*, 1920, *Chambre, Sess. Ord.*, Doc. No. 1523, p. 2253 *et seq.*

burden imposed upon the country since the beginning of the war amounts to the sum of 11 billion francs. . . .[3] Reduced in numbers as they are, could the French taxpayers, whose burdens were already considered heavy before the war, and have since been increased by 11 billions, support a further burden without collapsing? An excess of taxation undermines the base and leads to evasion, and is apt to weaken, if not paralyze, the economic activity of a country. Such consequences are particularly to be feared in our position. France is a country that has been sorely tested, that has suffered enormous losses, and whose productive capacity is diminished; if it wishes to rise again, it must reconstruct its capital and intensify its production.[4]

In other words, it was better to patch up the hole in the 1921 budget with borrowing than with increased taxation.

When, four months later, the budget was finally voted on April 30, 1921, the "ordinary" budget showed a microscopic balance, with expenditures of 23,263 millions and revenue of 23,303 millions. The "extraordinary" budget called for expenditures of 3,236 millions, all of which was to come from loans. It has already been shown [5] that during the year 1921 the total net borrowings were to amount to no less than 24.9 billion francs, considerably more than the total revenue budgeted.

The 1922 Budget

M. Doumer, Finance Minister in the Briand Cabinet of 1921-1922, adopted a much sterner attitude than M. François-Marsal had done, and his budget *projet* for 1922 [6] is a piece of violent criticism directed against the policy that had hitherto been pursued.

Doumer's Indictment. — The keynote of M. Doumer's attitude is struck in the opening sentence of his *exposé des motifs:* "By the time the financial year of 1922 is opened, three years will have elapsed since the end of the war." It was high time

[3] He made no mention of the fact that the depreciation in the value of the franc had more than offset this increase.

[4] *Loc. cit.*, pp. 2255, 2257.

[5] See p. 46.

[6] *Doc. Parl.*, 1921, *Chambre, Sess. Ord.*, Doc. No. 3068, p. 2274 *et seq.*

to put the house in order. "If the French budgets must for a long time feel the effects of the war and bear the heavy burdens it has left, it is nevertheless necessary that these budgets be no longer war budgets, that is, budgets of ruin and disorder. . . . The State ought to stop at once living on loans. It must break once and for all with methods which were justified by the war, but, which, if continued much longer in peace time, would lead the country to a catastrophe." While it was still early to start amortizing the debt, it was imperative to stop at once its increase, and to consolidate it as fast as possible.

"But in order to enable the State to stop borrowing, the first necessity is that its budget be made to balance, that the annual expenditure, reduced to a minimum, be strictly adjusted to the resources supplied by the taxpayer." [7]

He insisted on the immediate closing of the special Treasury accounts,[8] and also suggested that the budget of recoverable expenditure should more literally become a *budget*, in which German payments should offset the corresponding expenditure, while other expenditure should be discounted against the proper pledges and guarantees.

M. Doumer pointed out that a healthy budget was not simply in the interests of the State:

> It is inevitable [he said] that the uncertainty of the morrow, weighing as it does on public affairs, should create repercussions in private affairs. The industrialist and the business man . . . may hesitate to commit themselves to long-term undertakings. And even the *rentiers* are seeing, not without apprehension, how the State is constantly appealing for credit. They are begining to fear the eventual depreciation of their holdings to which they had subscribed during the war, at a time when the fate of the country could seem uncertain; whereas in reality they should naturally benefit by the prestige attached to the loans of a victorious nation. . . .
>
> In a budget of 25 billions, over 12 billions are employed for debt service. Half of our expenditure is therefore used for covering liabilities relating to the past. Of our permanent revenue, estimated at present at 20 billions, we have only some 7 billions with which to meet our present liabilities. We have therefore arrived at that paradoxical posi-

[7] *Ibid.*, p. 2274.

[8] See p. 414.

tion in which, as our budgets increase, the amount of revenue for the upkeep of the public services diminishes. If one does not take care, the State, having mortgaged all its revenue with its creditors, will be deprived of its means of living.[9]

He emphasized the fact that the real salvation of France lay in the reëstablishment of her budget, and that it would be a sign of disastrous weakness not to ask for a new sacrifice from the taxpayer with that vital object in view. That, however, was not all. Economy on a large scale would also need to be exercised.

The clearest and simplest notions of our financial law are constantly lost sight of owing to that carelessness which is the result of either ignorance or flippancy. One scarcely knows which. No one seems to know any more what is meant by a credit; even the most scrupulous services consider themselves the rightful owners of the credits opened to them. If any saving is made in the course of the financial year on the original estimates, no attempt is made to let the Treasury benefit by it, but one looks for a new way of spending it, which is easily found.[10]

All this wasteful spending, he said, a psychological effect of the war, could be easily avoided if all revenue and expenditure could be incorporated in a single self-contained budget, as this would eliminate all possibility of shifting, in doubtful cases, a number of expenses from the ordinary to the extraordinary budget or to some Treasury account.[11] The revenue and expenditure of M. Doumer's *projet* before taking into account increases in taxation were as follows (in millions of paper francs): [12]

	Expenditure	*Revenue*
"Ordinary" budget.......	23,180	19,401
"Extraordinary" budget..	1,752	3,050
	24,932	22,451

Increase in Turnover Tax Proposed. — M. Doumer meant to meet this deficit of 2.5 billions by increased taxation, but the

[9] *Doc. Parl., loc. cit.*, p. 2275.

[10] *Idem.*

[11] The control over expenditure was subsequently increased to a considerable degree by the new regulations incorporated in the act of August 10, 1922.

[12] *Doc. Parl., loc. cit.*, pp. 2278, 2281.

tax selected by this former champion of the income tax was, curiously enough, the turnover tax, and this is the reason he assigned:

> In spite of the temporary miscalculation, due at once to optimistic estimates and also to the economic crisis through which we are at present passing, this tax commends itself by the very qualities which had determined the legislator of 1920 to make it one of the pillars of our fiscal reconstruction. It is the most widely spread of all our taxes, and the burden it imposes on the taxpayer is extremely diffused, as it becomes assimilated with the cost price and the working expenses. Its influence on the sale price to the consumer, if noticeable, is not overwhelming. At a time when the purchasing power of money is so unstable . . . the incidence of the tax loses itself in the general fluctuation of the various economic factors.[13]

M. Doumer proposed to raise the state rate from 1 to 2 per cent, though he later cut his suggestion to 1.5 per cent.[14]

Opposition immediately developed. It was expressed by M. Maurice Bokanowski,[15] on behalf of the Finance Commission of the Chamber. The reasons agreed well with M. Doumer's own theoretical views on the subject. The year 1921 was not, economically, a period of inflation, but a time of heavily falling prices. The Commission considered that for this reason the yield of 5.6 billions expected by the Finance Minister from the 2 per cent tax would not be obtained. "It has seemed obvious to the Commission that the worst possible time for increasing the tax was one when business transactions were made difficult by the economic crisis, when the power of demand was greatly weakened, and when in more than one branch of industry and trade the profits obtained represented no more than 1 or 1.5 per cent of their gross receipts."[16] In some cases, where certain articles passed through a long series of processes of production before reaching the consumer, the tax on turnover was equivalent to as much as 7.7 or 8.8 per cent of the purchase price of the article.

The Commission argued — and here they brought up a question of primary importance — that it was useless, particularly

[13] *Ibid.*, p. 2282.

[14] *Doc. Parl.*, 1921, *Chambre, Sess. Ord.*, p. 2456.

[15] *Idem.*

[16] *Idem.*

in a time of business crisis, to "demand new sacrifices from the taxpayer so long as the already existing taxes are not giving a full yield. . . ." "It is certain," said the Commission, "that the French taxpayer is carrying a heavy burden, and it is necessary to let him get accustomed to the taxes already levied upon him by the law of June 25, 1920." [17]

Counter-Proposal of Administrative Reform. — Throughout 1922 and 1923 the policy of the Finance Commission of the Chamber lay in its endeavor to improve the yield of existing taxation, by reducing evasion, whereas that of the successive Governments — of M. Briand at first, of M. Poincaré afterwards — consisted rather in a number of attempts to cover budget deficits by increasing the rates of the old taxes.

Fraud and evasion were certainly rampant, particularly in the *impôt général*,[18] but also in many other taxes. To what was it due? Partly, of course, to the still imperfect organization of the financial departments of the Government, but mainly to the attitude of numerous taxpayers with regard to their fiscal duty. A disastrous influence was being exerted on the taxpayer by a powerful press campaign against the income tax:

> If among the natural guides of public opinion [the Finance Commission wrote] [19] some had a clearer conception of the responsibility that their influence places upon them, and instead of setting the people against the Treasury and defending fiscal evasion in a more or less disguised way, they made it clear to everybody that the fiscal duty in peace time is the exact equivalent of the military duty in war time, there would be very few Frenchmen tempted to shun their obligations towards the country. . . . If public opinion were educated on this point instead of being systematically deformed, every citizen would understand that it is no more humiliating for a free man to submit his accounts to the fiscal control than it is for him to pass a test of military fitness before a *conseil de revision*.

The newspaper propaganda had indeed given many people the idea that the progressive income tax had proved a failure

[17] *Doc. Parl.*, 1921, *Chambre, Sess. Ord.*, p. 2457.
[18] *Doc. Parl.*, 1921, *Chambre, Sess. Ord.*, Doc. No. 2743, p. 1708.
[19] *Doc. Parl.*, 1921, *Chambre, Sess. Ord.*, Doc. No. 3160, p. 2454.

and that sooner or later there would be a return to the system of the *Quatre Vieilles*. This, the Finance Commission pointed out, was entirely out of the question and they gave all the necessary arguments to show the utter impossibility of a return to the old system. They were nevertheless quite aware of the fact that there was in France "a conviction widely spread among a part of the public by misleading press campaigns, that the present fiscal system was only a temporary one, and that by crippling its results through a tenacious ill-will one would quicken its disappearance." [20]

> Parliament [the Commission continued], in voting the act of June 25, 1920, which represented an unprecedented fiscal effort, was entitled to expect from the Government an appropriate recasting of the financial services. The necessary effort has, however, not been made. During the course of the past financial years some brutal facts have shown that in the present state of affairs, the collection of taxes is still handled in an inadequate and defective way. . . . Many take advantage of such conditions [the Commission concluded] by not declaring what they should, out of fear — so they say — of paying for their neighbor as well and thus being dupes.[21]

Balance by Treasury Paper. — At length, on December 31, 1921, the general budget for 1922 [22] was passed, showing among its exceptional resources 1,320 millions in Treasury paper. This, compared with the two preceding budgets, marked a notable improvement, especially if one considers that on the question of suppressing the "extraordinary" budget, it was M. Doumer who had his way.[23] Moreover, with the 1922 budget there was assimilated the hitherto independent budget of Alsace and Lorraine. But in spite of everything, the net borrowings for the year 1922 amounted to 17.4 billion francs.

[20] *Idem.*

[21] *Idem.*

[22] Revenue, 24,702,059,912 francs; expenditures, 24,687,958,948 francs.

[23] The Budget Commission had apparently agreed with a deputy's opinion that "it is premature in the present conditions to wish to suppress the extraordinary budget which, after the War of 1870, was not only maintained until 1891, but actually disappeared nominally at that date only to give way to a loan in the ordinary budget." *Doc. Parl.*, 1921, *Chambre, Sess. Ord.*, Doc. No. 3160, p. 2457.

The 1923 Budget

The year 1922 passed in a state of comparative stability. Early in the year, as a result of M. Briand's foreign policy at the Cannes Conference, his Cabinet fell, and M. Poincaré, the new Prime Minister, appointed to the highly responsible post of Finance Minister a young deputy, the Count Charles de Lasteyrie, who was destined to be christened "*le comte déficitaire.*"[24] It was he, the Senate Finance Commission hinted, who propounded the maxims that "budgets with a deficit are sometimes the best" and that "economies interfere with the regular progress of public services."[25]

Proposal to Balance by Borrowing. — The charge of the public debt during 1922 continued to increase at a rapid rate, and tax collections were far from keeping pace with such increase. The interest on reconstruction loans issued after January 1 was carried to the debit of the extraordinary budget. Even so, owing to the economic crisis of the time, the revenue estimates of M. de Lasteyrie's "sincere" 1923 budget bill, presented to the Chamber on March 31, 1922, fell below the estimates of the preceding years, particularly as to the turnover tax.[26] Besides, the "exceptional" revenue from the liquidation of war stock and the war-profits tax which had formed such important items in the earlier budgets, were bound to shrink as time went on; they showed a diminution in the 1923 budget bill, as compared with the preceding budget, of nearly 2.5 billions. While on the other hand some improvement could be expected from the direct taxes, the administrative management of which was gradually improving, the budget bill for 1923 showed, all things considered, a deficit of 3.9 billions. Borrowing was to fill the gap. The deficit was not due, according to M. de Lasteyrie, to excessive spending, but to an insufficient revenue.

"The losses in revenue," he stated, "amount, as compared

24 Léon Daudet, *L'Agonie du Régime* (1925), p. 137.

25 *Doc. Parl.*, 1924, *Sénat, Sess. Ord.*, Doc. No. 1601, p. 127.

26 *Projet de budget* for 1923, p. 99 of the *projet* (*Doc. Parl.*, 1922, *Chambre, Sess Ord.*, Doc. No. 4220).

to the estimates of 1922, to 4,096 millions. Our receipts at present are diminishing more rapidly than our expenditure. . . . What makes this budgetary crisis particularly serious is not only the fact of the deficit but also the difficulty of finding at present any ordinary means of covering it." [27]

The obvious thing was to increase taxation. M. de Lasteyrie, however, rejected this solution.

In the present economic situation, confronted as we are by a persistent business crisis, to ask the country for an additional fiscal sacrifice would mean, we are convinced, discouraging initiative, compromising the chances of the coming economic restoration and perhaps leading to ruin numerous enterprises which have great trouble to meet their general working expenses.[28]

Since the Armistice, France has made an unheard-of effort, one without precedent in history, to bandage her wounds and to rise from the ruins; she has not hesitated to quadruple her taxes to meet the burdens that the war had left her. In spite of the economic crisis which has continued during the past two years, she would have succeeded, through her fiscal effort of 1920, in achieving the equilibrium of her budgets. Why have the hopes of the time been frustrated? Why do we see before us a deficit of nearly four billions? It is because Germany has not executed the Versailles Treaty, it is because her obligations to the fulfilment of which we were entitled, have not been met.

Before demanding new sacrifices from the French people, it is the duty of the Government to make use of all the means in its power of forcing Germany to make good all the ruin and destruction she has caused.[29]

M. de Lasteyrie expressed the hope that the London agreement would shortly give the desired results. But assuming that Germany were suddenly to begin to pay, this would only solve the question of how to avoid a further increase in the internal debt. As for the ordinary budget, deprived as it was of the "exceptional" revenue of the liquidation years, there would still remain this deficit of 4 billions. As taxation would not be increased, what other remedy was there? This was M. de Lasteyrie's answer:

"We have every hope of being able, three or four years hence, to balance our ordinary budget by means of the taxes existing at

[27] *Ibid.*, p. 102. [28] *Ibid.*, p. 103. [29] *Ibid.*, p. 118.

present. If our hope does not come true, it is obvious that one should then not hesitate to ask for further sacrifices; such a request we do not, however, think possible at present." [30]

The Budget Bill in Parliament. — Fifteen months were to elapse between the first presentation of this budget to Parliament early in 1922 and June 30, 1923, date of the final compromise.

The deficit of nearly 4 billions announced in the *projet* by M. de Lasteyrie produced a bad impression on both houses. Although neither the Senate nor the Chamber did anything drastic and fundamental to eliminate the deficit, they finally did succeed by various means, some of them questionable, in showing on paper a budget in which the item "*Prélèvement sur ressources d'emprunt*" amounted to no more than 400 million francs. The size of the voted budget was, at the same time, over 250 millions larger than its original estimates.

The solutions proposed on various sides in Parliament for eliminating or at least reducing the deficit, were numerous and of considerable interest. The solution proposed by the Senate Commission was to transfer nearly the whole deficit of the budget — some 3.6 billions — to the budget of recoverable expenditure. Considering that M. de Lasteyrie himself had explained in his budget bill that this amount was equivalent to the interest France was paying on money borrowed prior to January 1, 1922, "in place of Germany," for various reparation needs, the Senate Commission thought it only logical that this interest charge should be carried to the debit of the "German" budget.[31] The Chamber Commission, probably not quite so confident as the Senate in the immediate results of the Ruhr occupation, rejected this proposal and merely suggested that the debt charge in the general budget, paid "on behalf of Germany," should be specified accordingly. In any case, for the time being, the interest on the "German debt" would have to be paid by France, and neither of these proposals amounted to any more than a

[30] *Projet de budget* for 1923, p. 99 of the *projet* (*Doc. Parl.*, 1922, *Chambre, Sess. Ord.*, Doc. No. 4220).

[31] *Doc. Parl.*, 1923, *Chambre, Sess. Ord.*, Doc. No. 6244, p. 1336.

jeu d'écritures which could, whatever its moral impulse, deceive nobody in its financial aspect.[32]

Much more important were the lengthy discussions in Parliament and the numerous proposals made with regard to two other possible solutions of the problem.

The principal advocate of the improved methods of tax control was M. Bokanowski, the *Rapporteur* of the budget in the Chamber. What the policy of the Finance Minister himself was, is difficult to say. He wavered between his original plan of tolerating a deficit in the budget, and a desire to improve the technical side of taxation, without, however, making any serious proposals on the subject — and ended with the conviction that an increase in tax rates would perhaps be the best solution.

The "Revolt" against the Income Tax. — The position, on the whole, was particularly unfortunate in one respect. Many French politicians who some years previously had "agreed" to give the so widely advocated income tax a chance, now broke out in something like open rebellion against it. M. Vincent Auriol, the Socialist, quoted a speech which the Finance Minister himself had made at a banquet given in his honor by the Paris Chamber of Commerce, in which he had apparently declared himself in favor of returning to a system of taxation by external signs, something like the *Quatre Vieilles*.[33] M. de Lasteyrie's denial of the allegation was none too vehement. "I consider it impossible," he said, "to give up the income tax in the present circumstances." [34] At the same time, he advocated the renewed use of external signs in the assessment of various income-tax schedules.[35] The more whole-hearted supporters of the new

[32] *Ibid.*, pp. 1336–7.

[33] *Débats*, 1922, *Chambre, Sess. Extraord.*, Oct. 26, p. 2844.

[34] *Ibid.*, p. 2848.

[35] *Ibid.*, p. 2849. A year later, at the Paris Chamber of Commerce again, he was to say: "What, in my opinion, we ought to do, is to accommodate our new tax system to the manners and traditions of the country; to suppress as much as possible the contact between the fiscal administration and the taxpayers, and to have recourse, wherever conditions permit it, to the use of external signs of acquired wealth and the employment of automatic assessment bases (forfaitaires)." — Speech at Paris Chamber of Commerce, October 5, 1923. (Quoted by Germain-Martin, in *Les Finances publiques de la France et la Fortune privée*, p. 247.)

system did not cease to complain of the unfair attitude of many people in France towards it. M. Charles Dumont in the Chamber gave this significant retort to a deputy who had tried to condemn the income-tax system:

I deeply regret that some of your political friends do not hesitate to say: "We have voted the income tax, but at bottom, we remain its opponents." They have no right to say that, because the income tax has become the keystone of our fiscal structure. So long as there are still such mental reservations, so long as it still remains possible to orate, not here, but in other circles, against the income tax, the tax will be unable to enter not only into the mentality, but also into the morals of the French taxpayer.[36]

Others again, while accepting on principle the income tax, complained that its distribution among the various classes of the population, and particularly between the agricultural and the business class, was disproportionate and unjust. Before the 1914 reform it was the rural deputies who had complained of this unfair treatment of their electors; in 1923 — a time when the material results of the income-tax reform were beginning to be felt — it was the deputies representing the business classes who came to realize that the income-tax reform had shifted from country to town a burden larger even than had been anticipated. Deputy Artaud (*Entente Républicaine*) stated that, of the population of France, 70 per cent (53 per cent agriculture and 17 per cent manual labor) "paid nothing." [37]

[36] *Débats*, 1922, *Chambre, Sess. Extraord.*, Nov. 9, p. 3030. There was also another aspect of the tax yield problem. It was contended in many quarters — so M. de Lasteyrie said — that many of the imperfections of the French financial system not only regarding tax collections, but also Treasury accountancy generally, were due to a very bad state of disorganization in the administrative services. This was, of course, true to some extent, but there is nevertheless no doubt, to judge by results, that the administration was steadily improving. If there were still some shortcomings, these were inevitable. "Do you forget," said M. de Lasteyrie, "that our Treasury transactions have risen since 1914 from 5 to 50 billion francs per annum? . . . and that for an accumulation of work of this kind we are forced to appeal, to a large extent, to a new staff, devoid of experience at the beginning? Do you forget that out of every 2000 Treasury and tax officials 1200 have had less than two years' service? . . . For all that we have arrived at results showing considerable progress. Our current revenue and expenditure transactions are becoming centralized, just as before the war." — *Débats*, 1922, *Chambre, Sess. Extraord.*, Nov. 13, p. 3078.

[37] *Ibid.*, Oct. 24, 1922, p. 2796.

M. de Lasteyrie himself confirmed this by relating a personal experience in an agricultural district in France: "I asked my neighbor, who was the local tax collector: 'How many people pay the general income tax in your district?' He answered: '*Monsieur le Ministre,* there is only one person, and that is myself.'"[38]

All these statements agreed well with M. de Lasteyrie's own maxim that taxes must not be increased until the existing ones gave a full yield, and that any increase in rates would only put an added premium on tax evasion. Among the moderate parties there were, indeed, remarkably few politicians who ventured to suggest that the existing rates were still fairly low, and that the budget question could be solved, without considerable injury to anybody, if the rates were slightly raised. M. de Lasteyrie's maxim was obviously highly moral, but it was one that could not help the budget out at a moment's notice. The few deputies who ventured to suggest increased taxation nevertheless felt that their audience was hostile and they spoke as though they were propounding a dangerous heresy.[39]

M. de Lasteyrie's Conversion to Taxation. — After nine months of wrangling, the Finance Minister became suddenly impressed by the advantages of a program of increased taxation. On January 11, 1923, he addressed a letter to the Finance Commission of the Chamber containing a proposal to raise (with a few exceptions) the whole bulk of the French taxes by a *double décime,* i.e., 20 per cent. "Believing," he said, "that the future increment in the yield of taxes would cover the deficit, and still

[38] *Ibid.,* Nov. 13, 1922, p. 3079.

[39] M. Landry (Action Républicaine): "The general feeling in France is that the fiscal sacrifice agreed to cannot be surpassed. Such a feeling has always existed. . . . I, for my part, consider such a feeling as unfounded, and I wish to fight it at the risk of making myself unpopular, which I do not fear. . . . Various kinds of securities issued in France in 1919 amounted to 35 billions, in 1920 to 45 billions, in 1921 to 39 billions. . . . Every year French investors lend the State for the needs of public finance a considerable number of billions. It would be possible for a part of these billions to be brought to the Treasury in another form — *viz.,* by way of taxation." ("Trés bien! Trés bien!" on Left and Extreme Left.) *Débats, loc. cit.,* Oct. 24, 1922, pp. 2808–9.

hoping that during 1923 the burdens of the Treasury would be alleviated by German payments in accordance with the Peace Treaty, the Government has considered it possible to have temporary recourse to a loan in order to balance the ordinary budget. During the discussions of the budget several speakers, and not the least important . . . , have requested the Government to demand from the country the indispensable sacrifice." The Minister referred then to the unsatisfactory end of the Paris Conference [40] and to the Ruhr occupation which he thought was the only means of reaching a favorable solution to the problem of reparations. But as such a solution could not immediately be obtained, he considered it necessary to ask the country for an additional sacrifice in order to balance the 1923 budget. The 20 per cent increase, however, was to apply during one year only and had to be regarded as an exceptional measure. He said the Government was convinced that the existing system contained large potentialities of an increased yield of taxation, but that the process of perfecting the methods of assessment and collection would be lengthy, extending over a number of years.[41]

Balance by Adjustment of Estimates. — The Minister's sudden change of mind was commented on, not without a certain amount of irony, by the *Rapporteur* of the Chamber Commission, M. Bokanowski.[42] He noted with satisfaction that the controversy as to the necessity of achieving that equilibrium had ceased, and that everybody — Government, Chamber Commission and Senate Commission — was now in full agreement that it was necessary to balance the budget. The question was now not whether, but how this equilibrium should be achieved.

He did not consider the *double décime* a satisfactory solution. "It is, of course, unnecessary to recall the reception that was unanimously given both in the country and in Parliament to the Government's proposal. One can state, without being contradicted, that it has not found a single protagonist, that the Gov-

[40] The conference of the prime ministers was held in Paris, January 3–4, 1923.

[41] *Doc. Parl.*, 1923, *Chambre, Sess. Ord.*, Doc. No. 5432, pp. 8–10.

[42] *Doc. Parl.*, 1923, *Chambre, Sess. Ord.*, Doc. No. 5545, p. 305.

ernment itself had soon made it clear that it had no intention of throwing the weight of its high authority into the discussion, that it did not consider the *double décime* as the only possible and admissible solution of the problem . . ." [43] Evidently M. de Lasteyrie, in view of the " unanimous " outcry against his proposals was easily persuaded that he had made a blunder, and one thing, at least, must have become quite obvious to him — that he had been inconsistent. This fact is also clearly suggested by M. Bokanowski when, in his criticism of the *double décime,* he used as his main argument practically the very words that had so often been uttered by the Finance Minister himself. " There is the conviction," he said, " shared by the whole Chamber without distinction of opinion and party, that it is impossible to continue demanding sacrifices from the same taxpayers over and over again before efficacious measures are taken to stamp out fraud which persists particularly in the case of the general income tax and inheritance duties." [44]

Moreover, the *double décime,* simple as its enforcement appeared on the surface, was not so simple in practice as it seemed. How could one possibly raise by 20 per cent (M. Bokanowski asked) inheritance taxes which in some cases already attained 80 per cent? The turnover tax was in many cases a snowball the dimensions of which, at its final stage, were already quite large enough. He also thought that an all-round increase by 20 per cent of the customs tariff had many grave objections — it might lead to serious friction with foreign countries.

M. Bokanowski turned from new taxes to more stringent collection of the old — especially the general income tax, as concerned revenue from securities. What measures could be applied to suppress tax evasion here? There were three types of " information at source " in view. One was the compulsory registration of all securities, i.e., the suppression of bearer stock. But this also would mean the suppression of a valuable " instrument of credit," and therefore seemed to M. Bokanowski, from the business standpoint, a reactionary and undesirable solution. The second system was that of the *bordereau de coupons,* already

[43] *Ibid.*, p. 306. [44] *Idem.*

proposed by the Government in March, 1922, a system whereby all banks and other establishments would be compelled to keep a complete record, to be communicated by them to the administration, of all dividends paid and coupons cashed to customers. This method seemed to the *Rapporteur* as one involving too much work both for the banks and the tax authorities. What he therefore proposed was the system of the *carnet de coupons* (coupon book) which he himself had already described and recommended.[45] This was a booklet bearing its holder's name and address and " viséd " by the inspector of direct taxes of the district where the holder was resident. No coupons could be cashed for him unless he produced the *carnet*, in which the bank entered the amount paid and the date of payment. The *carnet* could also be deposited with the bank. At the time of declaring his income for the *impôt général*, the holder of the *carnet* had to present it to the tax inspector.

M. Bokanowski realized that the formalities it involved for even the smallest bondholder were open to criticism, but thought it would be worth while, as the yearly declaration for the *impôt général* would at least be freed from much of the superfluous discussion with the authorities that usually accompanied them. Further, some government bonds — particularly the short-term *Bons de la Défense Nationale* were not subject to the *impôt général*, and strict control would make effective the preferential position which these bonds already theoretically held.[46]

The Government did not support M. Bokanowski's scheme, which also met with violent criticism in business circles.[47] It was pointed out that fraud would still remain possible, because false names could be put on the *carnet*, and also several *carnets* could be obtained without great difficulty by unscrupulous persons. Besides, what was to be done if the holder had the misfortune to lose his *carnet?* It was also argued that the penal measures that M. Bokanowski had proposed to prevent the export of capital for avoiding the *carnet* would prove ineffective. Fur-

[45] *Débats*, 1922, *Chambre, Sess. Extraord.*, Nov. 13, pp. 3088–9.

[46] *Doc. Parl., loc. cit.*, pp. 306–7.

[47] Allix and Lecerclé, *L'Impôt sur le Revenu* (1926), Vol. II, p. 192.

ther there had to be considered the administrative difficulties of seriously examining the *carnets* of which the number would probably reach about 15 millions. As will be seen later, the Government, while rejecting the *carnet*, intended to try out its own system — which, administratively, was even more difficult — *viz.*, the *bordereau de coupons*. This was, however, not to be instituted until March, 1924. This particular attempt to check tax evasion has been presented here in detail, for it is important as illustrating the difficulty of enforcing the new laws as long as the taxpayer refused to coöperate.

As far as the 1923 budget deficit was concerned, then, the Commission had rejected the Government's solution, and the Government that of the Commission.

It was ultimately the Senate Commission which, in March 1923, discovered a way out. It suggested breaking away from the traditional method of estimating the yield of taxation on the basis of the penultimate year, and by estimating it directly instead. The formal budgetary rules were, in truth, rather ridiculous during such hectic times as these. The idea was suggested to them by the fact that the tax yield during the last few months of 1922 had seemed to indicate that the economic crisis of the two preceding years was coming to an end, and this impression was strongly confirmed by the further improvement shown in the returns of the first two months of 1923.

While criticising this method from certain standpoints, the Government and the Chamber Commission nevertheless found it too attractive to be resisted. In March the Commission was therefore already able, after some " rectifications " had been proposed by the Government itself, to present a newly-balanced budget bill wherein the original deficit of 3,900 millions was reduced to 1,430 millions. The Senate, still determined to transfer a part of the debt charge into the " German " budget, actually substituted for this deficit a surplus of nearly 900 millions! [48] After much discussion it was finally agreed, on the

[48] A chronicle of the successive modifications undergone by the budget bill of 1923 is given in M. Bokanowski's final report of June 27, 1923. (*Doc. Parl.*, 1923, *Chambre, Sess. Ord.*, Doc. No. 6244, p. 1330 *et seq.*)

one hand, to adopt the new system of evaluation, and also a number of economy measures the Senate had proposed, but, on the other hand, to reject, as artificial and meaningless, the transfer of a considerable part of the debt charge to the budget of "recoverable" expenditure. There also had to be taken into account an additional *recette d'ordre* of 500 millions and a few minor tax modifications. As a final result the budget was balanced with the original deficit reduced from nearly 4 billions to only 400 millions.

But this year was to witness still further progress on "the road to ruin." In 1923 the net borrowings amounted to 15.8 billion francs.

CHAPTER VI

THE DOUBLE DÉCIME, 1924

HALF of the year had already elapsed when the 1923 budget was finally passed. Since the 1924 budget was now pressing for attention, Parliament attempted to solve the problem by the simple device of the ditto mark, and the 1923 budget, with certain exceptions, was declared applicable to the 1924 fiscal year.[1] However, a final solution was not to be reached so easily. Before the year was well begun, the new budget was being retroactively modified by the important act of March 22, 1924.

By this time the stage was arranged for exciting events to come. As has been shown,[2] the net borrowings for 1920, 1921 and 1922 amounted to no less than 80 billion francs and during 1923 the Treasury continued its calls upon the people to absorb issues of huge amounts.[3] In February, 1923, the sixth loan of the *Crédit National* produced 3 billions.[4] In March and April, an issue of *Bons du Tresor* produced more than 10 billions.[5] At the end of June short-term Treasury paper was outstanding to the amount of 58.9 billions, while the borrowings at the Bank of France stood at 23.1 billions, the legal maximum being only 24.[6]

COLLAPSE OF THE BORROWING POLICY

At this juncture the patient investors began to show distinct signs of disquietude. The prevailing policy of "trick" balances could continue only so long as new loanable funds were available in large amounts and only so long as the holders of short-time paper evinced a willingness to allow the Treasury to retain use of their money.

[1] By the closing article (No. 213) of the 1923 budget law, published in the *Bulletin de Statistique* for July, 1923.

[2] See pp. 45–46.

[3] See p. 191.

[4] See p. 265.

[5] See p. 265.

[6] See pp. 206, 209

The conviction began to grow that the policy in the Ruhr was not to prove a financial success. The effects are apparent in the quotations of both *rentes* and exchange. The 5 per cents of 1915–16, for example, which had been quoted at a premium above their emission price as late as October, 1920, were depreciated approximately 10 per cent at the beginning of 1923, 12.5 per cent by the middle of the year and nearly 20 per cent by December.[7] Exchange, which had been remarkably strong during the early months of 1922, slumped badly. In April, 1922, 10.82 francs would buy a dollar. In January, 1923, 15.57 francs were required; in June, 16.32 and in December, 19.59.[8] Prices, which in 1922 had averaged 327 as compared with the 1913 base reached 459 by the end of 1923.[9]

In July, 1923, the seventh loan of the *Crédit National*, offered to yield 6.17 per cent, produced only about 2 billions and an issue of *Bons du Tresor*, priced to yield about 7.5 per cent, brought in slightly over 6 billions.[10] But the end was recognized to be at hand when in January, 1924, the eighth loan of the *Crédit National*, yielding 6.29 per cent, was a flat failure, producing only 1.6 billions. The lenders had served notice that they had no further funds for reconstruction. The Government was forced to face the situation and, except for a small issue of *Bons du Tresor* in the fall of 1924 [11] and the ill-fated Caillaux guaranteed loan of 1925, withdrew from the long-term domestic market. Not until the fall of 1926, after the general house-cleaning under Poincaré, was it possible to make another appeal to the domestic buyers of long-term bonds.

In their capacity as investors, the French had become skeptical regarding the prospect of collecting huge sums from Germany. However, speaking as taxpayers, they still insisted upon debating the question. Moreover, in the latter capacity, they greatly de-

[7] Quotations from *L'Économiste Français* for last day reported in last number for each month.

[8] See p. 449.

[9] See p. 448.

[10] See p. 265.

[11] See p. 265. A small loan was also secured in the United States in November, 1924.

sired not to complicate the issue by giving evidence of either ability or willingness to assume the burden which was rightfully the enemy's to bear. Early in 1924 the people plainly said: "No more loans." But at the same time they created an impossible situation for the leaders by chanting: "No more taxes." They were now convinced that the odds were against Germany's paying and this determined their policy as investors. They were disappointed and angry because of the change in the odds and this determined their policy as taxpayers. The result was two years of political chaos.

Poincaré Insists on the Double Décime

Although many people, including M. Poincaré himself, were inclined to ascribe the rapid decline of the franc to the criminal machinations of the international financiers, the failure of the eighth *Crédit National* loan of January 2, 1924, was recognized as a critical episode. A fortnight later, on January 17, Poincaré and de Lasteyrie proposed once more,[12] and this time in earnest, the measure which was to lead to such violent discussions and to such far-reaching political results — *viz.*, the all-round increase by a *double décime* of the existing taxes, besides "other measures of a financial order."[13] They remarked that since they had last (a year before) proposed the *double décime* the general position of the country had considerably improved, the general budget had been balanced, and the tax yield during 1923 had shown important progress. The only problem that had not been properly solved was that of the "recoverable" budget.

Up to the present, loans have been practically the only means of feeding that budget. For want of German payments, we were compelled to borrow during the course of the past financial years even for the purpose of paying the interest on earlier loans. This policy, though legitimate in principle, cannot however be continued much longer without giving rise to such criticism as would undermine the credit of the State and the results already achieved on our way towards financial reconstruction. The country has enough common sense and real cour-

[12] See p. 83.

[13] *Doc. Parl.*, 1924, *Chambre, Sess. Ord.*, Doc. No. 6972, p. 137 *et seq.*

age, when it clearly sees danger, to make at the right moment the necessary resolutions. It will understand that the question is a vital one. . . .[14]

They stated that the measures proposed did not imply in the future a more slack handling of the German problem, but that, on the contrary, the French position would be all the stronger if the Germans were to realize more clearly the financial soundness of France.

The bill contained the following proposals: (1) Economy " cuts " amounting to 1 billion francs, to be effected in successive stages by means of ministerial decrees. (2) An all-round increase (with a few exceptions) of all taxes by 20 per cent. (3) The institution of a *carnet de coupons* (this proposal was ultimately discarded, and the act of March 22, 1924, prescribed the *bordereau de coupons* instead). (4) The introduction of more stringent punitive measures in matters of fraud and evasion. (5) The creation of an independent pensions fund, and a few other minor measures.

The Bokanowski Report

The real significance of Poincaré's and de Lasteyrie's sensational bill with its laconic *exposé* was explained more clearly in Bokanowski's report that was presented to Parliament a few days later.[15]

In the first place, he tried to make it quite clear that the monetary trouble had no connection with the *general* budget. The equilibrium of that budget could be regarded as a definite attainment, even allowing for the gradual disappearance of " exceptional resources " (war-profits tax, liquidation of war-stocks, etc.) because the yield of taxation was constantly improving. The reproach that France had been inflating her currency was also unfounded. Since 1921 the Treasury had actually reduced its debt to the Bank of France. The economic position and the trade balance of France were also favorable. What then was causing doubt and anxiety to the holders of francs? This, and this only

[14] *Doc. Parl.*, 1924, *Chambre, Sess. Ord.*, Doc. No. 6972, pp. 137–138 *et seq.*
[15] *Doc. Parl.*, 1924, *Chambre, Sess. Ord.*, Doc. No. 6980, p. 151 *et seq.*

was the cause — the existence of the "German" budget, the expenditure of which was entirely met out of borrowing, without any German payments to improve the position.

The *Rapporteur* quoted an interesting document — an *avis* issued by the Strasbourg Chamber of Commerce which summarized rather well the monetary problem:

> Considering that the loans to which the State has recourse at present for the purpose of feeding the budget of recoverable expenditure, while not, naturally, constituting inflation in themselves, create nevertheless the danger of inflation in the future in case the State were unable to meet at any given moment, with means at its disposal, all repayment claims;
>
> And that in order to restore confidence among the holders of francs it would no longer be desirable to resort exclusively to borrowing for the purpose of restoring the devastated regions; and considering that it is preferable for the French taxpayers to make a further monetary sacrifice than to see their wealth gradually dwindle away as a result of the fall of the franc;
>
> The Strasbourg Chamber of Commerce . . . gives the following opinion:
>
> It is necessary that the Government should, above all, continue its firm policy with regard to Germany, and that it should continue, by every possible means, the recovery of the debt that that country owes to France. . . .
>
> But it is also important that France should balance without delay not only — as she has already done — her ordinary budget, but also her special "recoverable" budget, and that she should balance it not by means of borrowing, but by means of taxes which would strike all taxpayers without exception in accordance with their capacities.[16]

The principal danger of the German or "recoverable" budget lay in the fact that it included not only expenses for capital outlay but also a number of recurring expenses. It has been noted that the interest on the debt contracted "on behalf of Germany" before January 1, 1922, had been incorporated in the general budget. This interest amounted to about 3.6 billions. On the other hand, the interest on loans of the same nature issued since that date had been inscribed among the credits of the German budget. The total of that interest charge amounted, according

[16] *Ibid.*, p. 154.

to M. Bokanowski, to 4.13 billion francs. This amount would now have to be transferred to the general budget, as well as an annuity of 1.75 billions payable for war pensions, 158 millions for *Pupilles de la Nation* (war orphans) and 25 millions payable to the national office of war invalids (*Office National des Mutilés*), a total of exactly 6,063,134,000 francs.[17]

The remaining expenditure of the German budget of about 7.5 billions was non-recurring, as it merely constituted capital outlay on reconstruction, and the *Rapporteur* stated that expenditure of that kind would come to an end in 1926. These expenses should still remain outside the general budget and M. Bokanowski thought that "nobody could object to the discrimination between permanent charges and expenses made once and for all."[18]

The *Rapporteur* estimated that the new financial measures contained in the Government's *projet* represented an annual yield of 6,234 millions while the recurring expenses of the special budget (now to be added to the general budget) amounted to 6,063 millions, leaving a surplus of 171 millions.

Thus, in the presence of a disturbing monetary situation, the Finance Commission of the Chamber which only a year before had so summarily dismissed de Lasteyrie's proposal to add a *double décime* to the existing tax rates, now threw its weight in support of the Finance Minister's scheme.

The Chamber Yields under Protest

The Chamber, on the other hand, was far from sharing the same prudent outlook. Indeed, the presentation of the bill was followed by five weeks of stormy debates. It was suggested on many sides that the proposals of the Government could only be interpreted as a capitulation to Germany. Hitherto everyone had been repeating in every key the refrain: "Germany will pay"; but now the Government itself had admitted that the payer would be France, and that France was now trying to show the world she could do without German payments. So the Right argued.

[17] *Doc. Parl.*, 1924, *Chambre, Sess. Ord.*, Doc. No. 6972, p. 137 *et seq.*

[18] *Ibid.*, p. 156.

The Left, on the other hand, protested against the inclusiveness of the *double décime* and proposed increased taxation of the rich as the correct solution.

For all that, the Left must have been greatly pleased at the election prospects which the highly unpopular bill of their opponents was preparing for them. The moderate parties, on the other hand, felt uneasy. How much had been said and suggested during those five weeks early in 1924 to avoid the abhorred *double décime!* The creation of a national lottery for purposes of war reconstruction,[19] an exceptional capitation tax ranging from 10 to 100 francs,[20] another lottery for general financial rehabilitation,[21] the conversion of *Bons de la Défense Nationale* into long-term premium bonds, involving an economy of 3 billions,[22] were a few of the deputies' suggestions. Finally, however, the Government's *projet*, somewhat modified, was voted, 350 to 210, and dispatched to the Senate. The franc in the meantime had touched new low points.

The Senate Agrees

The Senate Commission, which only a few months previously had thought it logical to relieve the general budget of some 3.5 billion francs by transferring them to the debit of the German budget, must have found it somewhat awkward to approve of an operation which was the exact opposite of what it had advocated itself. But the monetary position was growing more alarming every day, and if the Senate rapidly voted, and only slightly modified the Chamber's bill, it was not with conviction that the bill was good, but out of self-defense. The Senate could not, through holding up the bill, risk being blamed for the collapse of the franc. So it voted the economies, the *double décime* and the other tax measures, the new measures against tax evasion, and finally the utilization of these new resources for paying the interest on the "German" debt. "We have refused

[19] *Doc. Parl.*, 1924, *Chambre*, *Sess. Ord.*, Doc. No. 6986, p. 177.
[20] *Doc. Parl.*, 1924, *Chambre*, *Sess. Ord.*, Doc. No. 6987, p. 179.
[21] *Doc. Parl.*, 1924, *Chambre*, *Sess. Ord.*, Doc. No. 7117, p. 328.
[22] *Doc. Parl.*, 1924, *Chambre*, *Sess. Ord.*, Doc. No. 7135, p. 343.

the Government none of the immediate measures it had asked of us." [23]

What else, in all reason, could they have done? M. Poincaré himself had gone to the Senate and had declared that "France, with the fall of the franc, is passing through dangers that may become mortal. We must remedy this by the means we propose to you; it is not a question of weeks, it is a matter of days — even a matter of an hour. . . . Every hour of delay increases the danger and lessens the chances of a rapid restoration of our national currency." [24] But after complimenting itself on its own sense of patriotic duty, the Senate Commission proceeded to explain what it thought of the Government; and it did not think much of it.

Not only did it attack the new Government proposals, but it was also very unkind to M. de Lasteyrie, whose past optimistic policy had contributed so much to preparing the present difficulties. It quoted numerous passages from the Finance Minister's recent speeches in which he had been persuading everybody that pessimism was "totally unjustified." They blamed him for not having effected in time the necessary economies, and of having expressed the view that budget deficits did not matter. And then, suddenly, among all this optimism, there had come the crash, and the panic that overwhelmed the Finance Minister was just as foolish as his early cheerfulness had been. All things considered, he had proved that the right job was not always filled by the right man. "However, it would be cruel to go on recalling what happened only a few months ago." [25]

As for the new measures, and particularly the *double décime* that the Senate had voted, M. Bérenger, the Commission's *Rapporteur,* was far from finding them satisfactory. The *double décime* was the main piece of the new financial armor. He had no illusions regarding the quality of that piece. He thought that the Chamber could have found a better way of raising taxes. Indeed, he feared that the *double décime* would result in a rise in prices, in underconsumption and a constant diminution in

[23] *Doc. Parl.,* 1924, *Sénat, Sess. Ord.,* Doc. No. 160, p. 127.
[24] *Ibid.,* p. 126.
[25] *Ibid.,* p. 127.

budget revenue in place of its remarkable increase during 1923. But as the Senate had neither the time nor the full authority to substitute for the Chamber's bill proposals of their own, and as they did not wish to refuse the Minister of Finance what he had asked from them, and what he was needing so urgently, they granted it, but they also left to him, before the country, the complete and full responsibility for the new measures.[26]

This act, passed on March 22, 1924, prescribed economy cuts during 1924 to the extent of 1 billion francs. It added the *double décime* to most direct and indirect taxes and increased the rates to some extent in nearly all the others, notable exceptions being sugar and wine.

The act also prescribed, subject to certain exemptions, an exceptional revaluation of houses which would be taken for the new assessment basis as from January 1, 1926, and a provisional revaluation of land followed by a regular periodical revaluation to be begun in 1927.

Penalties and surcharges were respectively increased on fraudulent tax declarations and delays in payment. The right to pay the war-profits tax in government *rentes* at their nominal value was abolished. No dividends could be paid or coupons cashed without a register (*bordereau de coupons*) being signed by the holder of the securities, these registers to be communicated by the banks, etc., to the tax authorities.

The *double décime* and the *bordereau de coupons* were described by M. Bokanowski as " the earthen bags of our financial Verdun." If he intended to emphasize the makeshift character of the defenses chosen, the figure of speech was apt. But if he meant that this parliamentary skirmish in the early months of 1924 was the climax in the battle of the franc, it is clear that his rhetoric was better than his foresight.

Budgetary Readjustment

As finally passed, the yield of the new fiscal and financial measures was officially estimated at 3,341,131,000 francs to

[26] *Ibid.*, p. 127.

which, of course, should be added the 1 billion francs in economy cuts.[27] What then was the new relation that had been established between the general budget and the "German" budget of recoverable expenditure? Nine billions of short-term bonds, authorized by the Finance Act of 1924, were now reduced to 3 billions. The receipts of the general budget were increased by 3,341 millions. A sum roughly corresponding to that amount (3,433 millions) was turned over to the "German" budget. But even then the revenues of the "German" budget were insufficient to meet its recurring "permanent" expenditures. This deficit, according to the figures published at the time, was 1.5 billions. A few months later M. Clémentel, the new Finance Minister, in submitting his *projet* for the 1925 budget, estimated that the new arrangement would involve for the year 1924 a budgetary deficit of at least 2,775 billions. To this figure could be added the expenditure of the non-permanent part of the special budget. As for the act of March 22, he described it as a "belated and insufficient remedy in a monetary crisis which had been neglected for only too long." [28]

Though "belated," the act of March 22 was nevertheless the most important step that had been taken since 1920 towards a sounder financial basis. The fact that it did not instantly solve the budgetary problem and do away at once with the "German" budget was perhaps to have been expected — especially if one considers the enormous opposition met by the new measures. But it is important as a symbol. It is the first statutory evidence of the abandonment of a policy of optimistic illusions, a reluctant but clear confession that the "Germany-will-pay" program had been a will-o'-the-wisp.

[27] *Bulletin de Statistique*, April, 1924, pp. 415–418.

[28] *Doc. Parl.*, 1924, *Chambre, Sess. Ord.*, Doc. No. 441, p. 1388.

CHAPTER VII

THE CARTEL DES GAUCHES TAKES THE HELM, 1924

It is difficult to say what contributed most to the defeat of the *Bloc National* in the elections of May 11, 1924. It was partly the constitutional issue that had been raised by the *décrets-lois*,[1] partly the incomplete success of the Ruhr policy, but above all, perhaps, the feeling of dissatisfaction that had been aroused by the fall of the franc, the rise in prices, and the increase in taxes. On the other hand it should be remembered that although the seats of the *Bloc National* in the new Chamber were reduced from 356 to 247, the actual total of votes obtained by all candidates sponsored by the *Bloc* (as compared with the 1919 elections) had only decreased from 31,784,309 to 30,419,847.[2] It may therefore be reasonably suggested that the defeat of the *Bloc National* was not so much due to the fiasco of its policy as to the superior electoral tactics of M. Poincaré's opponents.

That much dissatisfaction had been aroused throughout the country by the *double décime* seems certain, but it may be doubted that any promises of reducing taxation made by the Left in their election campaign could have been taken very seriously by a majority of the electorate. If any did believe such a reduction possible, they were facing disappointment.

As the conservatives passed the control to the Left, their disappointment must have been greatly tempered with relief. The financial situation which they bequeathed to the new Government was a desperate one. The Dawes Plan was to go into effect in the fall of 1924, giving for the first time something which approached a firm basis for estimating receipts from Germany, and all values had to be readjusted to the changed expectations regarding the size of these receipts. The loan market was prac-

[1] *Cf. Doc. Parl.*, 1924, *Sénat, Sess. Ord.*, p. 127.

[2] Huddleston, "France after the Elections," *Contemporary Review*, July, 1924.

tically dead. Late in the fall of 1924 an effort was made to float an issue of 10-year *Bons du Tresor,* but in spite of the fact that the net yield to the investor was made 8.62 per cent [3] less than 5 billions was produced. Altogether only 6.8 billions of paper francs (net) could be borrowed in 1924 and even less (4.4 billions) was to be available in 1925.[4]

A bitter draught was brewing for the people of France. But more than two years were to pass before they could be persuaded to take the nauseating dose. It was to be the task of the *Cartel des Gauches* to convince them of its absolute necessity. And when at last this task was accomplished, the people insisted that the spoon should be in the hand not of Caillaux, or any other leader of the Left, but of Poincaré, whom now they were removing from office largely because they did not like the first faint whiffs of the medicine.

New taxes were to be necessary and a new and lower level was to be established for the franc. During the time the people were being reconciled to this program, conservatives could wait in patience, for they possessed effective methods of blocking any policy which could operate seriously to their disadvantage. They carefully clung to two trump cards. In the first place, if disgruntled they could send much of their wealth abroad. Again, they could precipitate a " confidence crisis " by merely refraining from renewing their subscriptions to the huge quantities of short-term Treasury paper which were outstanding. Taxes might be necessary, but the conservatives were to dictate the particular kinds of taxes. These two years were to be years during which it would be quite as well not to be in titular control of the events.

Clémentel's 1925 Budget Bill

The first financial measure the new Government proposed was to cancel article 1 of the act of March 22, 1924, relating to the economy cut of one billion francs on the ground that such an *a priori* decision was impracticable.[5] Soon afterwards, on August

[3] See p. 266. [4] See p. 185.

[5] *Doc. Parl.*, 1924, *Chambre, Sess. Ord.*, Doc. No. 120, p. 972. This measure has an important political background. The Cartel des Gauches had benefited

1, came the financial manifesto of the *Cartel des Gauches,* M. Clémentel's budget bill for 1925, which made it clear that the new Government not only intended not to diminish taxation, but that it proposed to follow the course of M. Poincaré earlier in the year towards attaining budgetary unity and equilibrium.

M. Clémentel, however, went much further than his predecessors. His budget contained not only the recurring expenditure of the "German" budget, but also the capital expenditure that M. Poincaré had left outside. "The proposals of the Government attain for the first time in eleven years both unity and equilibrium of the budget. They bring back to the country a normal budgetary régime which has disappeared only too long ago. They mark an end of a policy of illusions which hindered the country from measuring the full extent of its fiscal duty."[6] The budget reached the unheard-of figure of 33.5 billions.

Such an immediate solution of the whole budgetary problem, which had given so much trouble to all the earlier finance ministers may seem rather surprising, and one is tempted to suspect a certain element of pretentiousness in this first budget bill presented by the *Cartel des Gauches.* But though the task M. Clémentel had proposed to himself seemed to present insuperable difficulties, the impression produced by his budget declaration was a good one, and many thought that here at last was a Government which would pursue a policy based on well-defined and sound principles. This impression was confirmed by the promise the Government had made at the time it took office to make public a detailed survey of the whole financial situation of France.

The Inventaire, December, 1924

This promise was fulfilled by the publication in December, 1924, of an appendix to the budget bill entitled "*Inventaire de*

---

considerably in the elections by the article in the act of March 22 prescribing the economy cut to be effected by ministerial decrees — the fear of losing their jobs had set a large number of small government employees against the *Bloc National.* (See *Revue de Paris,* Année 31, No. 3, June, 1924, p. 713.)

6 *Doc. Parl,* 1924, *Chambre, Sess. Ord.,* Doc. No. 441, p. 1388.

la Situation financière de la France au Début de la Treizième Législature." This valuable document is an exposé of the various fiscal and financial problems that confronted the Herriot Government upon its coming into office. Although restrained in tone, this "sincere and impartial" *Inventaire* contains much criticism of the financial policy hitherto pursued by the *Bloc National.* The *Inventaire* was published at a particularly suitable moment. The time had come when France had to abandon her loan policy, and it is interesting to contrast the position in 1924, with that M. Klotz had outlined at the end of 1919.[7] While the outstanding problem then had been reconstruction, the outstanding problem now was the consequences of that reconstruction — the enormous growth of the public debt.

Analysis of the Debt. — On July 31, 1924, Clémentel estimated, the public debt was as follows, in billions of paper francs: domestic, 277.8; foreign, 136.7; total, 414.5.

Of the above internal debt nearly 160 millions had been contracted since the war. The following approximate figures (in billions of francs) show how this amount had accumulated: [8]

	1919	1920	1921	1922	1923	1924
Revenue	11.6	20.1	23.1	24.2	27.7	31.1
Expenditures	54.2	58.1	51.1	48.9	45.8	40.2
Deficit	42.6	38.0	28.0	24.7	18.1	9.1

The expenditure Clémentel subdivided as follows:

	Military	Debt	Civil	Recoverable	Special Treasury Accounts	Total
1919	18.2	7.9	9.2	15.5	3.4	54.2
1920	7.6	11.7	11.4	22.3	5.1	58.1
1921	6.0	11.1	9.9	21.4	2.7	51.1
1922	5.0	13.6	7.7	22.1	0.5	48.9
1923	4.8	12.8	6.5	21.7	...	45.8

7 See pp. 56–59.

8 *Inventaire,* p. 21.

"In considering the origin of our debts," said M. Clémentel, "we are led to regret that since the very beginning of the war the strongest effort had not been made to ask for a larger yield from taxation, in order to avoid the issue of loans, which now weigh so heavily on our financial situation. Whatever were the obstacles in the way of such an increase, the principle of a sane policy should have been to reject such issues so long as no permanent resources had been created to cover their interest charge."[9] The incorporation in the "recoverable" budget of recurring expenditure fed out of loans had been particularly disastrous, and the payment of the debt service by such means "increased the debt, one might say, at compound interest." The hope of receiving payment from Germany did not justify that procedure.[10]

Criticisms of Tax System.—Of greater interest was the definition of the new Government's attitude toward taxation. M. Clémentel analyzed the tax revenues of 1913 and of 1923 and concluded that, in spite of the income-tax reform, the "taxes on consumption proper" bore a slightly higher percentage of the aggregate tax burden in 1923 than in 1913. In his budget bill for 1925 he proposed to raise the "direct" taxes and lower the consumption taxes. A considerable increase in direct taxation was, he felt, quite within the capacity of the French taxpayer.

Improvement could, for example, be expected from the *impôt foncier*, which, being based on the valuations made in 1908–1912, was yielding revenue on a pre-war basis. M. Clémentel thought that a revaluation of real estate, account being taken of currency depreciation, would result in a yield at least twice the current amount.[11] Such a revaluation would also automatically improve the yield of the agricultural profits tax. As the coefficients used in calculating the tax were low, M. Clémentel suggested that in addition to the revaluation, the tax-rate itself should be raised from 6 per cent to 8 per cent.

The yield of the liberal-professions schedule left even more to be desired. The care of respecting the professional secrets of

[9] *Ibid.*, p. 10. [10] *Ibid.*, p. 20. [11] *Ibid.*, p. 126.

a doctor, lawyer or notary had hitherto prevented the legislator from allowing the fiscal authorities to investigate documents of a strictly private nature. " No doubt the desire to avoid painful shocks and friction may justify the moderation displayed in such matters. But as a result of the abuses resulting from the lack of fiscal control in this class of incomes, the losses of the Treasury attain at present such figures that equity and the needs of the State cannot permit their toleration any longer. It cannot be allowed that the high degree of honor connected with certain professions should degenerate into a real tax-exemption. Important improvements in this matter must be introduced into our present legislation." [12]

Investment income taxed at the source did not admit of much evasion. The difficulty lay with the declaration of such income under the *impôt général*. It seemed obvious that a large part of such taxable income was not declared. The *bordereau de coupons* would, of course, remedy this evil to a considerable extent, but there was still room for tax evasion so far as foreign securities were concerned. M. Clémentel expressed the pious hope that the committee of government experts assembled at Geneva would solve this international problem.

The turnover tax received a surprisingly good bill of health. Clémentel said that it was a tax of great value to the Treasury, and, on the whole, it would be better not to change it except in some minor details. It might be desirable to offer some exemption in the matter of indispensable foodstuffs. Being an *ad valorem* duty, with high rates on consumption of luxuries, it did not share the imperfections and iniquities of the older forms of indirect taxation.

Revision of Customs.—The customs duties needed general revision. During the latter part of the war, the State had exercised the strictest control over all exports and imports and had completely prohibited the importation of non-essentials. The sale of certain commodities such as petrol, coal, wool and cotton had been handled by the State itself. After the war these regulations were rapidly relaxed, but the economic position was such that it

12 *Inventaire*, pp. 127–128.

was necessary to adopt some new measures soon afterwards, particularly with regard to the exportation of foodstuffs. Complete prohibition of export was subsequently modified by the decree of April 7, 1924, instituting an *ad valorem* export tariff ranging from 5 per cent to 15 per cent on meat, preserved meat, animal fats, condensed milk, cheese, fresh vegetables, fruit, etc.

As to imports, the veto of the State — except for certain monopolistic goods — had ceased on January 1, 1921. The subsequent policy consisted in restoring again, for certain national industries, the protective tariffs which had been reduced during the war owing to war needs; and further to coördinate the customs tariff with the general rise in the price level. Owing to the instability in prices, there had been created soon after the war a special commission, on which were represented industrial and commercial interests. This commission was to determine the increased tariff rates in accordance with the rise of prices. The limit of such increases had been fixed at 300 per cent over the pre-war tariff, but in later years this figure had been increased, for certain types of goods, to 900 per cent. Some specific rates were also replaced by *ad valorem* rates. M. Clémentel thought that this system, being devoid of a clear line of policy, was open to criticism. Moreover, there had been numerous instances where the rates had been raised merely on the request of some special interest. On the whole, M. Clémentel believed that a general revision of tariff rates, and the abolition of the temporary commission, would be a desirable step.

The Tobacco and Match Monopolies. — The fiscal monopolies — tobacco and matches — showed the following increase between 1913 and 1923 (in millions of francs): [18]

	Tobacco		Matches	
	1913	1923	1913	1923
Gross	545.1	1806.7	44.6	127.3
Expenses	108.7	524.2	12.6	55.6
Net	436.3	1282.5	32.0	71.7

[18] The figures have been evened to the nearest 100,000 francs.

Thus the proceeds of the two monopolies had increased by 289 per cent. Judging from these figures, it could not be said, as had often been done, that state monopolies were unproductive. As for delay in introducing more up-to-date methods of production, this was due to the stiff task of obtaining budgetary credits for the purpose. The need to respect the limits set by the budget had compelled the monopoly authorities to go slowly in perfecting the technical equipment of the factories. It also had to be admitted that the commercial side of the question left much to be desired. "While being firmly resolved to maintain our fiscal monopolies, in view of the constantly growing revenue yielded by them, we are nevertheless determined to give its due to the true part of the criticism directed against them."[14] The Finance Minister announced that a special commission had been formed, consisting mainly of eminent manufacturers and qualified representatives of trade and agriculture. This commission had not been, on the whole, unfavorably impressed by the present working of the monopolies. M. Clémentel, however, recognized that there were many disadvantages connected with the bureaucratic handling of an industry and he had sought a method of placing the monopolies on a business footing while maintaining over them at the same time the control of Parliament. He proposed that the monopolies be endowed with financial autonomy and that the additional resources needed by them be supplied by issuing state-guaranteed obligations. Their budget should be independent of the state budget, but subject to the approval of the Minister of Finance and of Parliament. M. Clémentel thought that this more elastic and more businesslike handling of the monopolies would considerably increase their productive capacity.

Sick Treasury.—On the whole, the problem of the budget was considered less troublesome than the problem of the Treasury, with its embarrassing debt maturities. France was in a state of nervous excitement. Clémentel made an interesting effort to construct a national balance sheet, listing the public debt among the liabilities and a figure representing taxes capitalized at 5 per cent among the assets. This balance sheet served principally

[14] *Inventaire*, p. 138.

to emphasize the exposed position of the Treasury traceable to the absence of quick assets with which to meet the large items of floating debt.

"The evils suffered by the Treasury," said the report, "are due to this lack of correspondence between the respective maturities of the claims on the State, which are grouped over a short period, and the resources at its disposal, which are spread over a long period."[15] The only way to overcome this divergence was to "discount our future resources by means of more or less long-term loans,"[16] that is, to consolidate the floating debt.

M. Clémentel pointed out that 1925 would be a difficult year for the Treasury. Besides the foreign debt maturities, it would be confronted with the repayment, at the option of the holders, of nearly 22 billion francs of domestic short-term debt. M. Clémentel blamed his predecessors for a lack of foresight when they let so many maturities accumulate all in one year. The fact was, of course, that the situation for years had been quite out of control.[17] The Treasury needed all the money it could borrow and had to allow the lender to select the type of security he fancied. No solution of the problem of these maturing obligations was proposed in the budget bill. M. Clémentel intended to make the necessary proposals at a later date; he hoped the task would then be easier. In the meantime, the holders of bonds might be blessed with an accession of faith.[18]

CLÉMENTEL'S PROPOSED "NEW FISCAL MEASURES"

It will be recalled[19] that the 1925 budget as introduced by M. Clémentel contemplated a complete consolidation and an aggregate figure of about 33.5 billions. It showed a prospective surplus of only 38 millions[20] and to achieve even this margin it was necessary to ascribe 1,611 millions to "new fiscal measures."

[15] *Ibid.*, p. 233.

[16] *Ibid.*, p. 233.

[17] See p. 192.

[18] *Ibid.*, p. 244.

[19] See p. 101.

[20] Revenue: 33,528 millions; expenditure: 33,490 billions. *Doc. Parl.*, 1924, *Chambre, Sess. Ord.*, Doc. No. 441, p. 1387.

M. Clémentel supported the creation of these new measures by arguments of a moral order:

> If the great fiscal reform of 1914 and 1917 . . . was inspired by a profound democratic sense, the same cannot be said of the new taxes created just after the war by the acts of June 25 and July 31, 1920. Other principles had prevailed at that time, and recourse was largely had to taxes on consumption and other indirect taxes. . . . The all-round addition of the *double décime* increased still further the draw-backs and dangers of those principles. It was our duty to break with their tendency, and we have decided to demand entirely from acquired wealth and from income the supplementary revenue necessary for balancing the budget. Before proposing the creation of new taxes we have, however, made a careful and meticulous study of our fiscal legislation; and have taken note of all its loopholes and imperfections and of the evasions it lends itself to, as well as of the insufficiently justified exemptions it allows.[21]

But it should be particularly noted that M. Clémentel's budget bill fulfilled none of the sensational promises — such as the abolition of the *double décime* and the turnover tax[22] — that had shone in red letters on the election banners of the *Cartel des Gauches*.

The principal modifications contained in it related to a stricter control of incomes from liberal professions,[23] to the taxation of bonuses paid to company directors (*tantièmes*) which had hitherto escaped taxation to a large extent; to an official valuation in the case of real-estate transfers, in order to suppress the payment of taxes on fictitious deeds showing a figure lower than the real amount paid; further, to an increase in the tax rate on *bénéfices agricoles* in the case of some large-scale agricultural concerns which were "practically identical with industrial enterprises" — and to the replacement of the *forfaitaire* methods of assessment in certain classes of business by those of direct declaration. Numerous "democratic" modifications were proposed

[21] Revenue: 33,528 millions; expenditure: 33,490 millions. *Doc. Parl.*, 1924, *Chambre, Sess. Ord.*, Doc. No. 441, p. 1387.

[22] See London *Economist*, May 17, 1924.

[23] Doctors, lawyers, etc. would have to keep a register showing their receipts and expenses, and, moreover, the authorities could take "external signs" into consideration for purposes of control.

in indirect taxation, including the suppression of the salt tax. New exemptions in the turnover tax were counterbalanced by the application of that tax to exporters, who had hitherto been exempt.[24]

The new taxes proposed in "that first budget of a truly democratic parliament" [25] were three in number. The first was a tax on the sale and purchase of foreign currency (*opérations de change*), an activity particularly popular in those days of inflation. The tax was a slight one of 5 centimes per 1,000 francs or fraction thereof and the yield was estimated at nine millions.[26] The next measure related to insurance companies whereby the companies themselves — and not the policy holders — were to pay one-half of one per cent on all premiums paid to them.[27] The third tax [28] was a progressive rate on increment value of houses and businesses — the same tax that Klotz had proposed in 1920.[29]

Leisurely Consideration in Parliament, 1924–1925

Although the proposed budget was simple in its structure in comparison with the double and treble budgets of earlier years, the mass of petty tax modifications in it was great.

The complexity of this budget was one of the reasons for the considerable delay its examination and voting involved at each stage through which it had to pass. M. Bérenger remarked that "nearly every one of the 398 articles of the bill is in itself a bill of civil, criminal or fiscal legislation." [30]

Presented to the Chamber as late as November 4, 1924, it was subjected to a long and careful examination by the Finance Commission, and was voted by the Chamber only after a number of important modifications had been made. It was unfortunate for

[24] *Doc. Parl.*, 1924, *Chambre*, *Sess. Ord.*, pp. 1394–5.

[25] *Ibid.*, p. 1395.

[26] *Ibid.*, pp. 1395, 1408, 1451.

[27] The proposed insurance tax was subsequently replaced by a 20 per cent tax on the net income of such companies.

[28] *Ibid.*, pp. 1395, 1409, 1452.

[29] See p. 61.

[30] *Doc. Parl.*, 1925, *Sénat*, *Sess. Ord.*, Doc. No. 140, p. 441.

the painfully achieved equilibrium of M. Clémentel's budget that the government employees and pensioners, to whom many rash electoral promises had been given by the *Cartel*, suddenly had the bad grace to remember these promises somewhere about Christmas-time. The budget voted by the Chamber was thus considerably larger than that prepared by M. Clémentel. Beside these wage increases, the Chamber also thought it its duty to include in the budget the interest on the Morgan loan of 1924 as well as the interest (amounting to 450 millions) on new bonds issued during the same year. All this added over 1.5 billions to the budget. With measures of a more or less exceptional kind, (the exclusion from the budget of some important post-office expenditure, a supplementary receipt under the Dawes Plan, etc.) and with a revaluation of certain tax receipts the Chamber succeeded in covering the increased expenditure. All this took a long time, and it was not until the end of March, 1925, that the Senate was able to begin the examination of the budget.

"A certain number of expenditure budgets had been voted, and the discussions were proceeding normally when suddenly there came a political crisis. M. Clémentel handed in his resignation on April 2, 1925. He was replaced by M. de Monzie but, a few days later, M. Herriot's Cabinet was placed in the minority by the Senate. M. Painlevé's Cabinet was formed and M. Caillaux became Minister of Finance." [31]

Clémentel Gives Up the Task, April, 1925

This sensational crisis, culminating in the famous telephone call to Caillaux at Mamers, will be discussed in more detail in the next chapter.[32] Naturally, it did little to hasten the voting of the budget. Besides, it was not in the character of M. Caillaux to let matters take their own course. On May 12 he presented himself as Finance Minister before the Chamber Commission to explain (as M. Lamoureux put it) "his financial and budgetary conceptions." [33] These he also communicated on May 20

[31] *Lamoureux Report, Doc. Parl.*, 1925, *Chambre, Sess. Ord.*, Doc. No. 1759, p. 875.

[32] For details of this crisis, see pp. 116–119.

[33] *Doc. Parl.*, *loc. cit.*, p. 1759.

to the Senate Commission. In the interval the Senate had adopted as the basis of its discussion the proposals of its Commission wherein both the revenue and expenditure had, as compared with the budget voted by the Chamber, been reduced by over one billion, mainly by means of economy cuts.

M. Caillaux proposed among other things the non-inclusion in the budget of the Dawes payments, the reintroduction of twelve articles relating to measures against tax-evasion which the Senate had discarded, and, further, to meet the deficit that the withdrawal of the Dawes payments would cause, the insertion of a line reading: " Revenue to be expected from new taxes." He said he would shortly submit to the Chamber his proposals relating to these new taxes. He further proposed an 800-million increase in the tax estimates. On the expenditure side, he asked for an increase in credits amounting to 419 millions.[34]

After much discussion, the Senate Commission suppressed a number of tax reductions. and also refused to exclude from the budget the Dawes payments.[35] On the other hand, it reduced the estimates of the Chamber by a number of important modifications. One of them related to the six-months delay in the voting of the budget, resulting in a loss of over 500 millions.[36] As a net result of these plus and minus modifications the total revenue was fixed by the Senate Commission at 33,712 millions.[37]

THE 1925 BUDGET IN ITS FINAL FORM, JULY, 1925

A few more weeks were to elapse before the budget was beaten into its final shape on July 13, 1925. The modifications that were introduced during that time both by Senate and Chamber are, however, of minor interest, and when the budget was finally voted it presented the following prospective balance: revenue, 33,151 millions; expenditure, 33,137; surplus, 14 millions.

[34] *Doc. Parl.*, 1925, *Sénat, Sess. Ord.*, Doc. No. 275, pp. 875–876.

[35] While refusing to do so, the Senate Commission agreed on principle with M. Caillaux's theoretical views on the subject, and symbolically reduced the budget receipts under that head by 1 million francs! *Ibid.*, p. 876.

[36] *Idem.*

[37] *Ibid.*, p. 866.

It seems that, on the whole, Parliament could have done better; but so much time had already been lost that the budget had to be passed at all costs. It was agreed that the 1925 budget, though showing considerable progress over the earlier budget from the standpoint of budgetary unity, was no more than a *budget d'attente*, and that the real *assainissement financier* would only begin with the budget of 1926. Besides, as the *Économiste Français*[38] remarked, the Chamber at the time of the final budget discussions was more concerned with the local elections (*élections cantonales*) than with the equilibrium to be established between the receipts and the expenditure of the State.

What then were the imperfections that had been allowed to remain in the 1925 budget? The principal fault was this, that while showing a surplus on paper, the 1925 budget was not really balanced. The Dawes payments and other payments "relating to the reparation of war damages," amounting to a total of 1,275 millions, had been included on the revenue side of the budget, while of the "non-recurring" reparations expenditure only a trifling sum of 15 millions was inscribed. Thus the largest part of the reconstruction expenditure had been left outside the budget.

None of the tax measures in the 1925 budget law as finally passed was of outstanding importance. Methods of assessment and control were somewhat altered — the *bordereau de coupons*, having proved impracticable after a year's experience, was abolished; a more thorough revaluation of land was substituted for the rough method of revision which had been adopted in 1924 but which aroused so much protest[39] among the farmers that it had been abandoned; administrative expert valuation of real property for purposes of the (registration) tax on transfer would, it was hoped, check fraud; and members of the liberal professions were required to keep books showing their income liable to the schedule tax under penalty of being taxed on an estimated basis with a 50 per cent surcharge.

Three new taxes were introduced, rates on some of the others raised, and additional favors granted to income-taxpayers bur-

[38] Sept. 12, 1925.

[39] *Cf.* Allix and Lecerclé, *L'Impôt sur le Revenu*, Vol. 1, p. 244.

dened with family expenses. The new taxes were (1) the *taxe d'apprentissage,* levied on the business man at 0.2 per cent on wages and salaries paid during the year, the proceeds to be used mainly to aid vocational training schools; (2) a tax of 0.01 per cent on foreign currency transactions; (3) the so-called "replacement taxes," levied on imports, and sales by mines, of coal, and on the slaughtering of animals for meat, both of these to replace the turnover tax on these commodities. Higher rates were applied to the agricultural-profits tax (by raising the assessed valuation 75 per cent), to the tax on incomes from foreign securities not taxed at the source, to the annual transmission tax on securities, to the automobile tax and to the advertisements tax. Initial exemptions were raised for the agricultural, wages and non-commercial income taxes.

Thus the budget as a whole did not appreciably change the tax policy that had existed before the Left had come to power. The turnover tax had not been abolished; even the salt tax had been maintained; the increment-value taxes once again failed of realization; and the income taxes hardly altered their relative importance in the budget.

CHAPTER VIII

CAPITAL LEVY, FORCED CONSOLIDATION OR INFLATION? 1925–1926

THE resignation of M. Clémentel, in April, 1925, served to clarify the character of the struggle which was to be waged during the next fifteen months, the struggle to determine who should bear the weight of the burden of war and post-war finance. The Treasury had borrowed literally hundreds of billions of francs. Who would pay? The first answer had been: "Germany." But it was now obvious that Germany's payments would be wholly inadequate. Nearly half of the Treasury's promises-to-pay were held by England and America. Certainly, they, remembering France's great contribution in blood, would take into account Germany's failure to restore the devastated regions and would not insist upon payment if it meant that the money was to be wrung from the French taxpayer. But England had also made tremendous sacrifices and was even now straining every economic resource to reëstablish the pound sterling and to avoid the stigma of repudiation. A large part of her problem was her own debt to America, representing to a considerable extent her endorsements of France's indirect borrowings from the United States. England decided that her generosity to France was somewhat dependent upon the extent of America's generosity to her. But the war was now over and America was observing Europe with cold and disillusioned eyes. Anything salvaged from this doubtful paper of England and France lying in the strong-box of the federal Treasury meant that much more off the federal income tax. Let these militaristic European powers honor their notes or, if really bankrupt, let them be assessed according to their "ability-to-pay" as determined by the Debt-Funding Commission! Even the liberals insisted that any concessions made be utilized as a lever to force upon France and England American conceptions as to what their domestic and foreign policies should be. Above all, let no sentimental imponderables be brought into the discussion. Far better to have the reputation of being "hard-boiled" than of being "a good thing." If the payments could not be made by the present generation, let their children's children pay, even unto the sixty-second year. Such in substance was to be America's reply to Caillaux and Bérenger. The problem thus became an internal one for France. Three possible courses of action were seriously considered.

Clémentel resigned rather than sponsor the first method, the capital levy, which was the announced policy of the *Cartel des Gauches*. This plan contemplated that a large part of the Treasury's obligations be paid by making a heavy draft upon all who possessed property. Bondholders would be cared for at the expense of property-holders. To a limited extent, of course, the classes were identical. If government securities were evenly distributed among property owners the net result would be as if every one tore up his government paper. Each would pay himself off. He might feel poorer as the result, but, if the assessment were fairly made, no poorer than he should have felt all the time. With the ownership of the government paper distributed, as it was, in a manner very different from property in general, the proposal in its most simple form really was that the amount of a man's possessions should be accepted as fair measure of the sacrifice he should make toward the financial salvation of France. But such a plan had great administrative difficulties and really held little promise of success unless the enthusiastic coöperation of the propertied interests could be enlisted. Instead of coöperating, they fought it with all the weapons at their disposal. Additional taxes were to be levied, but they were to be taxes of a type thoroughly acceptable to the conservative propertied classes — taxes which, in the phrase of Wells, would "throw the burden on the voiceless mass of the common people."[1]

The second method was forced consolidation of the debt. This amounted fundamentally to a proposal that the holders

[1] *Outline of History*, Vol. II, p. 237.

of securities, bearing high rates of interest and with short maturities, would be denied payment and would be required to accept in exchange long-term securities with low interest rates. This would reduce the burden of the debt service and relieve the Treasury of the threat of insolvency. This course would throw the burden upon such owners of property as had invested in government bonds, obviously a less fair arrangement than the capital levy. Moreover, it involved a frank confession of bankruptcy, a bitter dose indeed.

The third course was to debase the currency and let the chips fall where they might. Where the chips would fall, few people knew certainly, a circumstance highly favorable to the adoption of the plan. All obligations were destined to be met — but with francs four-fifths of whose value had been clipped away. The bondholder would lose if the francs he had loaned were more valuable than the francs he now received in return. But working outward through effects upon prices and interest rates, the debasement would affect property owners in diverse and complicated ways. Proprietorship interests would be favorably affected as compared with creditor interests. Business men with a rapid turnover would be affected differently from those with a slow turnover. The burden would vary with the facility with which operations could be adjusted to price changes.[2] Fortunes would fall into the laps of the shrewdest of the speculators. The professor at the Sorbonne would see the purchasing power of his meager fixed salary dwindle until oil for his study lamp would seem a luxury.

The Crisis of April, 1925. — In the history of French budget deficits and Treasury troubles, the appointment of M. Caillaux to the post of Finance Minister was a dramatic incident, but it was an incident easily susceptible of exaggeration. The Hon. George Peel, in his *Financial Crisis of France*[3] makes the telephone call to Mamers a colossal climax in the drama of French public finance. " M. Painlevé, the new Prime Minister, in April, 1925, conceived an inconceivable plan. He rang up Mamers on the telephone, ur-

[2] See p. 184. [3] London, Macmillan, 1925 (2d edition, 1926).

gently offering the post of Minister of Finance to 'the best hated man in France,' to the outcast who had been solemnly proscribed by the Senate five years before as a public enemy, the 'protégé of Germany,' the despised and detested 'Catiline.' M. Caillaux answered the call with the words, '*Je marche.*' Instead of the Tarpeian rock, the Treasury!"[4] The literary value of the situation may be indisputable, but to regard it as a decisive moment in French financial history is to put the whole position of 1925 out of focus. Time was soon to show that M. Caillaux neither at this juncture nor later possessed the peculiar qualities demanded of the man who was to save the franc. The reason why M. Painlevé offered him the finance portfolio was that the Left, after the unfortunate experience of the Herriot Cabinet, were at a loss to find a financier of recognized ability among their ranks to grapple with a situation that was admittedly a difficult one; the only man with a good financial record among their "own" people was Caillaux, the "father of the income tax."

On the eve of the crash, early in April, even such newspapers as the *Journal des Débats* were not feeling apprehensive about "maturities," that sensitive confidence barometer. If there was some feeling of insecurity, it was due not so much to the real difficulties of the Treasury, as to the utterances of M. Herriot himself "who had sown the seeds of anxiety by ringing the alarm bell over the Treasury maturities, and by repeating on every occasion he borrowed from the Bank that inflation was mortal."

The crisis of 1925 began, a few days later, with the resignation of M. Clémentel from the Herriot Cabinet. The reason for this, according to the *Journal des Débats*, was a fundamental one. In the view of this conservative journal, M. Clémentel had been condemned to the very worst of tasks — "of combining decent finance with the most detestable politics."[5]

M. Herriot has uttered some rather vague words; perhaps they are meaningless, but if they are not, they seem to announce mad plans of a capital levy or of forced loans . . . M. Clémentel, knowing things somewhat better than M. Herriot, who has turned fanatic of socialist

[4] Preface to first edition, pp. 6, 7.

[5] April 4, 1925.

metaphysics, is said to have refused to take part in such dangerous adventures; if this is so, he deserves approval, and his resignation may become a healthy warning to the Cabinet. . . . Having seen more clearly, and wishing to be reasonable, M. Clémentel could not stay on in a cabinet of fiscal visionaries.[6]

All this shows clearly the bitterness with which the conservatives opposed the capital levy.

After M. Clémentel's resignation, M. de Monzie, "a man with a reputation of great competence," entered "the worn-out and discredited cabinet."[7] Immediately a bombshell burst, which had a shattering effect upon confidence. M. Bérenger, *Rapporteur* of the Finance Commission of the Senate, made the sensational disclosure that the Bank of France, under pressure from the Government, had falsified its published accounts and that the figures in the weekly statement were not trustworthy.[8] M. Herriot defended himself by alleging that these irregularities had been in existence before his Cabinet had come into office, but the revelation excited such a nervous feeling in the country that the Government, together with its new Finance Minister, was already doomed. The finishing touch to the Government's discredit was added by M. de Monzie himself, who—probably against his own will[9]—proposed a mildly camouflaged capital levy in the shape of a forced loan issued at par and yielding 3

[6] April 5, 1925. The *Ère Nouvelle* of April 4, 1925 explains M. Clémentel's decision to resign as follows:

"During the course of the Cabinet meeting on Wednesday (April 1) M. Clémentel had proposed as a remedy for the Treasury crisis, a 50 per cent increase in the general income tax, a doubling of all the schedule taxes except that on wages; an increase in the price of tobacco; these taxes would cover the new issue of bank notes that had been proposed. M. Clémentel estimated these resources at 6 billions per annum.

"The Cabinet unanimously rejected the suggestions made by the Minister of Finance, and showed itself more favorable to another proposal relating to a forced loan or a national levy on acquired wealth. This levy amounted to 10 per cent payable at once or in 10 annuities.

"M. Clémentel is reported to have said: 'My idea was to ask the few billions we need from the income tax, spirits and tobacco, instead of undertaking vast levies which, I think, can only succeed in a time of peace and agreement.'"

[7] *Ibid.*, April 3, 1925.

[8] See p. 213.

[9] On coming into office he had made some much more moderate proposals.

per cent interest. It was clear enough that in those days of high interest rates this could hardly be regarded as a loan at all.

> It is brother to a pure and simple levy on private fortunes. It is only for the gallery that the Socialists pretend to prefer to it an open levy. . . . This loan (compulsory on one-tenth of all private fortunes above a certain figure assessed on the basis of the available income tax returns) is to be issued at the rate of 3 per cent and at par. Moreover, the coupons will be subject, like other securities, to taxation. In reality, instead of 3 per cent it will be 2.25 per cent. As a consequence, the new *rentes* will immediately suffer a tremendous depreciation. The old 3 per cent *rente,* free of tax, is quoted at about 46, the new *rente* will inevitably fall to about 33. The mechanism of this robbery transaction is easy to grasp.[10]

The *bilan truqué* of the Bank of France, the radical financial program outlined by M. de Monzie, the general atmosphere of hopelessness that surrounded M. Herriot himself; all this brought about the fall of the Cabinet. In the Senate on April 10 the Herriot Ministry was defeated by 158 against 132 votes on a motion of confidence. M. Herriot resigned.

Caillaux's Garantie-de-Change Loan Fails.—After the first excitement caused by Caillaux's return had subsided and M. Briand had at last reluctantly agreed to collaborate with him, the question began to be asked on all sides what the magician intended to do. At first M. Caillaux's utterances—perhaps also his ideas—regarding his financial program were not very clear. Two weeks after his appointment this is all that he chose to say:

> My financial plan consists of several distinct parts. The first relates to the budget equilibrium, which will be established by incorporating in the budget all the expenditure that at present is not inscribed in it; in this way we shall give the world the assurance of our absolute sincerity. I do not wish to make any declarations regarding the other parts of my financial plan. It is only after establishing the absolute equilibrium of our budget and after covering all the expenditure of France by taxes, that I shall be able to undertake a series of further measures which will enable me to restore our finances.[11]

[10] *Journal des Débats,* April 17, 1925.

[11] *Ère Nouvelle,* May 3, 1925.

"M. Caillaux did not show any anxiety as to the high figure of short-term bonds maturing during the course of the year. He was convinced that the Treasury would meet all its obligations provided the Finance Minister took the necessary precautions." Judging by the favorable attitude of the Bourse, M. Caillaux had every hope that a large proportion of the maturing bonds would be renewed this year, and that their consolidation could consequently enter into a general plan which would be elaborated at a later date.[12]

Apparently M. Caillaux, full of confidence in his own luck, and trying to ignore the dangers of the parliamentary game, intended to go slowly about his task. Much to the disappointment of the Socialists, whose capital levy dreams had collapsed with the Herriot Cabinet, it was clear that M. Caillaux had no intention of using any such drastic measures. He had denounced the capital levy, and his two watchwords were "a balanced budget" and "consolidation."

As to the budget, there was no time to waste on any serious innovations. As has been seen,[13] it was already five months overdue, and would have to be patched up and passed in the shortest possible time. The real restoration could only begin with the 1926 budget.

The Treasury question was more urgent. In a remarkable article published in the July 1927 number of the *Revue de Paris,* M. Georges Suarez [14] remarked that there were three choices open to M. Caillaux: one, known as the *plafond unique* of bonds and banknotes, he firmly rejected on the ground that it constituted inflation. The capital levy was not even listed among the possibilities. As for the other two he seems to have hesitated between them. One was the issue of a long-term loan sufficiently attractive to eliminate the bondholders' desire for reimbursement. The other was a compulsory consolidation of the whole short-term and floating debt. According to M. Suarez, who was apparently well informed on what went on behind the political scenes, M.

[12] *Ibid.*

[13] See pp. 110–111.

[14] "L'Expérience Caillaux," *Revue de Paris,* Année 34, No. 4, July, 1927, pp. 115–142.

Caillaux had expressed himself strongly in favor of that compulsory consolidation, and was actually prepared to sign the decree prescribing it when he was abruptly overcome by personal qualms. With the pen in his hand he suddenly wavered and made this tragic admission: "Oh, it is terrible to emerge from an ocean of unpopularity and then to think that a stroke of the pen will plunge one back again!"[15]

Instead, he decided at last to issue a 4 per cent *garantie-de-change* loan, subscriptions payable in short-term bonds. The interest paid (in francs) would vary with the exchange rates. Thus, issued at 95 francs, it would pay 5.4 per cent interest with the pound sterling at 120, 5.88 per cent with the pound at 140, and so forth. It was suggested at the time that it indicated a future plan of M. Caillaux to stabilize the franc at 100 to the pound, which was approximately its value at this time.

M. Caillaux expected great things from this loan — the conversion of about 20 billions of *Bons de la Défense Nationale.* But months passed and at the closing of the subscriptions in October only 6,011 millions had been converted. Admittedly, in view of the unsettled outlook, it would seem that a *garantie-de-change* loan was a particularly attractive proposition. Perhaps M. Caillaux had overestimated the pessimism of the French investor, who had been offered a yield of 8.64 per cent on the last issue; would he subscribe to a 4 per cent loan in the grim hope of seeing a collapse of the franc? Moreover, as M. Suarez suggested, many small investors did not understand the full significance of the *garantie-de-change;* what they grasped was that they were being offered what appeared to be only a 4 per cent security.

Caillaux Breaks with the Cartel, July, 1925. — At the final stage of the 1925 budget debates an issue of political rather than fiscal importance had been raised. Several Left groups were in favor of exempting from the turnover tax all sales of food products, and most retail sales of other articles. The Senate Commission rejected this "reform," and was supported in its rejection

[15] *Ibid,* p. 124.

by Caillaux. He argued that on the eve of important foreign debt negotiations, he could not assent to any material reduction in the tax burden.[16]

With the turnover-tax exemptions written at the head of the *Cartel's* electoral promises, and with Caillaux's unexpected veto, a dangerous political conflict became imminent. What saved the Government this time, however, was the confidence vote granted it by the Centre and Right groups in the early hours of the morning of July 12–13, 1925. The Socialists, whose help, as M. Léon Blum bitterly put it, the Government was now needing no longer,[17] voted against Caillaux. M. Marcel Cachin pithily remarked on behalf of the Communists: "*De Profundis pour le Cartel.*"[18]

This vote was pregnant with dangerous consequences. M. Caillaux had ruined the *Cartel* and thrown away the support of the Socialists to gain even less reliable support from the Centre and the Right.

Caillaux's Inflation Program Fails, October, 1925.—While the position of France was to show a considerable improvement in other respects during the months to come—the successful end of the Moroccan war, the signing of the Locarno agreement—the financial and political situation remained difficult. M. Caillaux's trips to London and Washington to settle the question of interallied debts were not considered successful; the franc was far from stable; the 4 per cent *garantie-de-change* loan had proved a failure, and large short-term maturities were threatening the Treasury at the end of the year. The legal limit of advances of the Bank had already been raised by 4 billions in April, "to legitimize the bastard,"[19] and by a further sum of 6 billions in June.[20] By doing nothing, the Government was adopting the option of inflation. The December maturities were approaching and nothing effective had been done to meet the situation.

16 *Débats*, 1925, *Chambre, Sess. Ord.*, July 12, p. 3459.

17 *Ibid.*, p. 3467.

18 *Idem.*

19 *Ère Nouvelle*, April 16, 1925. See pp. 213, 214.

20 See p. 209.

During the parliamentary vacation following the vote of July 12[21] which was to prove so damaging to Caillaux, M. Herriot had been busy rallying around himself the shattered forces of the *Cartel des Gauches*. At the Radical Congress in Nice, on October 16–17, which was attended by both Herriot and Caillaux, it became obvious that no compromise was possible between the two men. Herriot was still determined to save the situation with a capital levy; Caillaux was refusing to lend himself to that measure.

The vote of July 12 placed M. Painlevé in a painful dilemma. The alternatives were these: either to dismiss the Radical-Socialists from his Cabinet, or to dismiss Caillaux. "For all my affection for M. Painlevé," M. Herriot had declared at the Congress, "if he needs only a single vote, I shall tell all my friends to vote against him."[22]

Following the Nice Congress there were a number of ineffectual attempts by the various members of the Cabinet to save the position of the Government; M. Caillaux's proposals to create the *plafond unique* and, to please the Left, additional inheritance taxes, met with less than half-hearted approval. M. Briand insisted on the resignation of M. Caillaux alone; Caillaux refused; Painlevé was wondering how he could save the moderate Radicals from becoming hopelessly compromised. In the end it was apparent that, if Caillaux were to stay in the Cabinet, the Government would be defeated by the Left, the Right vote, even at its best, being a very uncertain factor. On the other hand, if Caillaux alone resigned, who could take his place? A partisan of the Herriot program? But that would merely mean a repetition of April 10. All things said and few things done, the Cabinet took in the end the only possible course. On October 27 it called on President Doumergue and handed in its resignation.

The second Painlevé Cabinet, in which the Premier took charge of the finance portfolio, and in which M. Georges Bonnet was appointed to the newly improvised post of "Minister of the Budget," had a short and troubled life. From the very beginning its chances of success were poor. On November 3, a day hailed

[21] See p. 122.

[22] *Revue de Paris*, July, 1927, p. 135.

by the *Ère Nouvelle* as " a great parliamentary day in the annals of the Republic " — because the Cabinet had managed to obtain a small majority in the Chamber — the Socialists had abstained from voting, indicating thereby that the life of the Government lay in the hollow of their hand. With the Socialists on one side and the moderate Radicals on the other, the position of the Painlevé Cabinet was necessarily a precarious one, and whatever financial program it proposed, the chance of escaping both Scylla and Charybdis was small.

Painlevé's Capital Levy and Moratorium Plans Fail, November, 1925. — The financial problems confronting M. Painlevé were far from easy. Apart from the 2.5 billions (provisional) deficit in the 1925 budget, caused largely by the delay in its voting, there were the large December short-term maturities which had to be met one way or another. Should resort be had to either forced consolidation or inflation by borrowing from the Bank of France?

To the minds of most Frenchmen, the terror of forced consolidation was eclipsed by a far more drastic proposal that M. Painlevé made a few days later. Perhaps to insure the coöperation of the extreme Left, perhaps because he really thought it the only possible salvation of French finance, he proposed a capital levy, in a form somewhat different from M. Herriot's capital levy of April, 1925, but a capital levy nevertheless. Its object was to amortize, in 14 years, 45 billions of short-term bonds, 7 billions of the short-term foreign debt, and 15 billions of the internal floating debt.[23]

It consisted of two parts: (1) a yearly poll tax of 20 francs plus a progressive tax on salaries exceeding 50,000 francs, and (2) the *Contribution Extraordinaire,* the heart of the whole scheme.

The *Contribution Extraordinaire* was made up of a number of separate taxes, payable over a period of 14 years. In some cases it was a super-tax on incomes; in others it was more like a true capital levy payable in instalments. On houses, for ex-

[23] *Doc. Parl.*, 1925, *Chambre, Sess. Extraord.*, Doc. No. 2047, p. 75.

ample, it was fixed at 150 per cent of the rental value as determined for the assessment of the schedule tax; in the business schedule the tax amounted to 50 per cent of the average annual profits made during the past three years; on securities 15 per cent of the annual revenue was to be paid to the State, every year for fourteen years, and this levy also applied to state securities (with the exception of bonds of not more than one year's maturity); unproductive capital (furniture, works of art, jewellery, etc.) would be taxed at 8 per cent. Certain allowances were made for wife and children.

A sinking fund for the amortization of the internal debt would be created and the entire proceeds of this capital levy would be devoted to it. In addition, the sinking fund would be endowed with a standing credit from the budget amounting to 2,630 millions per year and also with the proceeds resulting from the sale of state property.

But it was not through the capital-levy proposal that the Government was destined to fall. Under Socialist pressure,[24] M. Painlevé agreed to declare a "moratorium" on a part of the bonds maturing on December 8. He decided, moreover, to have recourse to the Bank of France for an extra 1.5 billions.

At a meeting of the *Ligue Républicaine,* at which MM. Millerand and de Lasteyrie spoke, the latter declared: "Never has one seen the Government in such a state of insolvency, such an abdication from governmental dignity. . . . For the first time since the French Revolution is the Government failing in its obligations by postponing its payments and by taxing the *rente.*" The ex-Finance Minister referred to the "extraordinary levy" as an infringement of the right of property, as an intrusion of the State into private affairs, as "pure collectivism."[25]

Whatever M. Painlevé thought of the capital levy, it is apparent that he felt uneasy regarding the "bankruptcy" arguments that were being put forward with regard to the "moratorium" and there is an obvious feeling of weakness in the declarations he made during the stormy debate of November 22.

[24] *Ère Nouvelle,* November 23, 1925.
[25] *Ibid.,* November 15, 1925.

"The Government will not let the word of the State be compromised. It has chosen between two solutions: either to let the franc slip — and that is not keeping the word of the State — or else to endeavor to pay the creditors of the State in good money." [26]

It was on this issue that the Government fell. A small group of moderate Radicals, including MM. Nogaro, Montigny, Raoul Péret, and Le Trocquer voted against the Government, and the "moratorium" clause was rejected, 278 to 275. The Government resigned; and with it went its capital levy and its "breach of contract." All that remained was a state of confusion and the urgent necessity to borrow from the Bank of France. Two days after the fall of the Cabinet the legal limit of advances was increased 1.5 billions.[27]

The Loucheur Surtaxes, December, 1925. — To form a cabinet after M. Painlevé's fall now became an almost insuperable task. M. Briand tried and failed. M. Doumer tried and failed. M. Herriot tried and failed. Seldom had the parliamentary party system shown itself in a worse light. Finally, after a whole week's impotent efforts, M. Briand was asked to try again and succeeded. The man of Locarno was the only politician on the Left whose authority, both in France and abroad, was unshaken.

M. Louis Loucheur, "*le gros financier,*" was given the post of Minister of Finance. His first task was to solve the problem of the bonds falling due in six days.

Before accepting the post in the Cabinet he had already prepared a bill "instituting exceptional measures to insure the equilibrium of the Treasury," which was immediately presented to Parliament.[28] This bill dealt with two aspects of the problem — one relating to the budget, the other to the Treasury.

Owing to the seven months' delay in the voting of the 1925 budget and to the consequent delay in the dispatch of demand notes to the taxpayers, the tax yield was slow. In December about 3 billions in direct taxes were still outstanding. Although

[26] *Débats,* 1925, *Chambre, Sess. Extraord.,* Nov. 22, p. 3904.

[27] See p. 209.

[28] *Doc. Parl.,* 1925, *Chambre, Sess. Extra.,* Doc. No. 2128, p. 147 *et seq.*

the poor taxpayer was in no way to blame for this delay, M. Loucheur thought it well not to be too considerate at a time when the Treasury was on the verge of collapse. He demanded that all taxes due in 1925 be paid before the end of the year; anyone slow in paying his bill would have his tax increased by 10 per cent after a month's delay. These taxes applied to the regular budget expenditure. M. Loucheur stated that, despite this delay in the collections, the 1925 budget would actually show a "fairly important surplus." [29]

Even more dangerous was the problem of the maturities of December 8. "To meet the payment of these short-term bonds," M. Loucheur wrote, "we propose the increase of certain direct taxes (on the basis of the 1925 assessments involving only very little additional work), which will supply the Treasury with three billions, roughly corresponding to the above maturity." [30]

This was, therefore, a retroactive surtax, payable for the year 1925, after the regular tax for that year had in many cases already been paid. The tax was far from negligible. It represented an addition of 50 per cent to the regular *impôt foncier* paid in 1925, to the business-profits tax, to the *valeurs mobilières* tax and to the *taxe de transmission,* and 20 per cent to the *impôt général.*[31] These "Loucheur surtaxes" were payable before March 1, 1926 (a date changed later to May 1). Never had the French taxpayer been treated so brutally. "We, however, realize," M. Loucheur continued, "that these measures — prompt collections and increases in the taxes — even if immediately voted by Parliament, cannot give their full yield except after some time; though the effect will be felt at once, the final result will not be attained until later. In the meantime, we have to meet the maturities on the fixed dates. We, therefore, ask your permission to make an agreement with the Bank of France which, by raising the advances to the State by 6 billions, will constitute in a way an advance in respect of the tax receipts referred to above." [32]

[29] *Ibid.*, p. 147.

[30] *Idem.*

[31] The estimated yield was 2,990 million francs. *Ibid.*, p. 148.

[32] *Doc. Parl.*, 1925, *Chambre, Sess. Extraord.*, Doc. No. 2128, p. 147 *et seq.*

In addition M. Loucheur remarked that the Bank of France had proposed to increase the note circulation by 1.5 billions for the requirements of trade and industry.

The Loucheur taxes were passed[33] and collected, but they never served their original purpose. They were credited to the Sinking Fund which had been created on April 29, 1925, instead of against the advances of the Bank. The bondholder was correctly considered a more exacting creditor than the Bank of France.

Loucheur's Tax Program Fails, December, 1925.—Attention was now directed to the 1926 budget. The happy time was over when budget deficits could easily be covered by loans, and M. Loucheur realized that the budget would have to be completely self-contained and actually cover certain items—such as capital outlay for post-office improvements which would normally be met by the issue of bonds—until such time as "the loan market would once more be approachable."

Unfortunately, the 1926 budget, which had been submitted by Caillaux in July as "irreproachably balanced,"[34] was in Loucheur's eyes far from such a state. The total deficit, he calculated, was 5.6 billions.[35] This does not reveal Caillaux's position clearly, however, for of this amount, he had planned to cover about 3.5 billions by increased taxes largely on the schedule incomes. The rest of the deficit had arisen since Caillaux had left office.

On December 8, 1925, Loucheur presented to Parliament a formidable bill[36] containing proposals to raise additional revenue to the extent of 6,825 millions for the year 1926, and 8,040 millions for each following year. The object of these sensational measures was, according to Loucheur, to check inflation. Four

[33] The Chamber Commission added to Loucheur's proposals a 25 per cent increase on wages and professional incomes, and raised the rate on income from foreign "non-abonnées" securities from 18 per cent to 25 per cent, for 1926. *Doc. Parl.*, 1925, *Chambre, Sess. Extraord.*, Doc. No. 2147, pp. 280–281.

[34] *Doc. Parl.*, 1925, *Chambre, Sess. Ord.*, Doc. No. 1956, p. 1407.

[35] *Doc. Parl.*, 1925, *Chambre, Sess. Extraord.*, Doc. No. 2180, p. 298.

[36] *Ibid.*, p. 296 *et seq.*

times during 1925 had the Government been compelled to increase the legal limit of advances from the Bank of France,[37] 17.5 millions in the aggregate. During the year 1925, the outstanding Treasury paper had dropped 8.28 billion francs.[38] Owing to the increased habit of hoarding bank notes, said Loucheur, indicative of a loss of confidence in government bonds,[39] and owing also to a certain scarcity of notes for business needs, the tempo of the subscription to government bonds had diminished and the Government had thus been denied the "reëmployment of billions of notes that had been issued." In other words, the expectation that bank notes would be exchanged for government bonds had not fully materialized, and this in itself constituted definite, instead of temporary, inflation. M. Loucheur thought that the only way of avoiding further inflation would be to make the budget and all other state expenditure independent of both the Treasury and the Bank of France. The phrase that "the Treasury would see to these expenses"[40] would have to be forgotten once and for all.

The budget deficit was not the only reason why more resources were needed at once. The Treasury had a number of important maturities to meet during 1926. The foreign commercial debt repayable during the year amounted to 1,600 millions; further, there were over 6 billions of bonds maturing in May, repayable at their holders' option. M. Loucheur estimated that, even if it could rely on the successful conversion of many bonds, the Treasury would require about 3 billions a year for amortization. "Anxious not to burden the country too heavily, we did not wish to reach that total figure which would necessitate the immediate voting of 8.5 billions in new taxes, and have, therefore, reduced our request to 8 billions for 1927 and to 7 billions for 1926. . . . In 1926, the most heavily burdened year, we can, moreover,

[37] See p. 209.

[38] See p. 231.

[39] It is not clear from M. Loucheur's statement in what respect the hoarding of Bank of France's notes is preferable to the investment in government bonds in times of inflation, unless it be the psychological distinction between "Bank," and "Government," and the idea of discredit attached to the latter. Perhaps the fear of forced consolidation had something to do with it. *Cf. Doc. Parl.*, 1925, *Chambre, Sess. Extraord.*, Doc. No. 2180, p. 297.

[40] *Ibid.*, p. 297.

utilize 3 billions of exceptional resources provided by the act of December 4." [41]

Both direct and indirect taxes were suggested to raise the sums needed. A 20-franc capitation tax, higher rates in almost all the schedule income taxes and in the security income tax, were to be supplemented by higher stamp duties, alcohol and petrol taxes, tobacco prices, postal and telegraph rates, and by extending the turnover tax to exports. In addition, a 10 per cent tax on the first sale of houses and businesses, and special inheritance and gift taxes were to yield about 2.2 billions, to go to a special amortization fund.[42]

The Finance Commission of the Chamber, after five days' discussion, sent the whole bill back to the Finance Minister. None of its aspects had satisfied them. M. Lamoureux thought that neither the amortization plan nor the solution of the budget problem "corresponded to the needs of the moment." All that the Commission retained was a supplementary bill submitted by M. Loucheur on December 10, relating to new measures against tax evasion.[43]

The people of France were not yet ready for such heavy taxation as that proposed by M. Loucheur. "Journals of every shade of opinion," wrote the London *Economist* at that time, "have been ruthless in their attacks since the earliest of M. Loucheur's detailed proposals." [44] On December 15, having braved the storm for eighteen days, M. Loucheur resigned his post and the Premier asked M. Doumer, the sober-minded old senator from Corsica, to take his place.

Doumer's Payments Tax Fails, March, 1926. — Several days elapsed before M. Doumer was able to present his financial program to the Chamber. Owing to the hybrid composition of the Cabinet itself, some of its members were unable to accept all the

[41] *Cf. Doc. Parl.*, 1925, *Chambre, Sess. Extraord.*, Doc. No. 2180, p. 298.

[42] *Doc. Parl.*, 1925, *Chambre, Sess. Extraord.*, Doc. No. 2181, p. 306.

[43] One of these "new" measures was the introduction of the "carnet de coupons," which its inventor, M. Bokanowski, had recommended again with particular emphasis a few days earlier in the Chamber. *Débats*, 1925, *Chambre, Sess. Extraord.*, Dec. 2, p. 3938.

[44] Dec. 19, 1925, p. 1047.

proposals he presented to them on taking office. There were particularly strong protests from the *Cartel* ministers against M. Doumer's suggestion to double the turnover tax. This clause had subsequently to be withdrawn, and substituted by another which did not so completely abandon the electoral promises of May, 1924.

M. Doumer's program differed very considerably from M. Loucheur's. He did not intend to throw the whole burden of financial reconstruction on the *poires,* the simple-minded but honest taxpayers, and he hoped to increase the revenue from indirect taxation.

In his *exposé* [45] he spoke once more grave words of warning:

> The seriousness of the financial crisis cannot escape anybody's attention. . . . While the nation prospers, works, saves, and produces, and would become richer if it were not for the depreciation of money which frustrates the result of its labors, the financial position of the State grows worse every day. Dragging painfully from one maturity to another, from one crisis to another, from inflation to inflation, it lives in constant danger of a catastrophe which would be fatal to the whole country.
>
> The credit of the State is seriously shaken. It must be restored by declaring loudly once and for all that there can be no question of that dangerous expedient labelled "consolidation," but the true name of which is bankruptcy. For only too long has our expenditure exceeded our normal resources. The difference has amounted every month to hundreds of millions, sometimes billions. . . . With these constant loans we have increased the debt, the burden of which has now become intolerable.[46]

M. Doumer recalled that in the 1926 budget bill the debt charge (not counting pensions), amounting to nearly 15.4 billions, represented 42.5 per cent of the total expenditure. But

> the debt is not only terrible by its weight. It is also terrifying by its nature. The resources that the *Bons de la Défense Nationale* bring to the Treasury are essentially precarious. Their flow depends indeed on factors both economic and moral, and these variations, which are

[45] *Doc. Parl.*, 1925, *Chambre, Sess. Extraord.*, Doc. No. 2332, p. 492 *et seq.*

[46] *Ibid.*, p. 492.

difficult to anticipate, condemn our Treasury to live in a state of intolerable insecurity. . . .

As for the part of the debt representing the advances of the Bank of France, it is by far the most disastrous; it involves inflation and its whole train of calamities. . . . For the large majority of Frenchmen, it is infinitely worse than the heaviest of taxes. We have not another hour to lose if we wish to save the finances of France from the terrible danger that is threatening them.[47]

His plan, like Loucheur's, was composed of two parts: one aimed at budgetary equilibrium; the other at an alleviation of the Treasury difficulties. The amount he intended to raise with new taxation was 5.8 billions, to which sum he proposed to add the 3 billions of Loucheur taxes.

Of the total sum of 8.8 billions he proposed to repay 2 billions to the Bank of France, to spend 2.5 billions on debt amortization and to credit 4.3 billions to the 1926 budget, this being the deficit shown in the latest parliamentary statements of the budget. M. Loucheur's estimates of expenditure had thus been considerably cut down.

Of the taxes with which M. Doumer had chosen to raise the rather formidable sum of nearly 9 billions, 3 billions (the Loucheur surtaxes) already had been voted by the act of December 4.

"In view of these heavy taxes, it went without saying that it was impossible to add anything to the burden of direct taxation during 1926."[48] M. Doumer said that if it had not been for that act he would have concentrated on the income tax for raising additional revenue, and suggested that he would have done it on a basis different from M. Loucheur's.

But the damage had been done, and the income-tax *poires* would now have to be left in peace for some time. M. Doumer proposed to raise the revenue from tobacco by 1 billion. "Of all taxes none has seemed to us less painful than one on optional consumption, the extent of which can always be determined by the taxpayer's own free will. The proposed increase will not, however, result in raising the monopoly prices to an exorbitant

[47] *Doc. Parl.*, 1925, *Chambre, Sess. Extraord.*, Doc. No. 2332, p. 492 *et seq.*

[48] *Ibid.*, p. 493.

and prohibitive level; our aim is merely to reach the average present price level as compared with pre-war prices." [49]

Both financially and politically the most important measure proposed by M. Doumer was an exceptional 1.2 per cent tax on payments. This tax, practically identical with the turnover tax, "has not only been suggested by the example of foreign countries — Germany, Belgium, Italy — which have found in such taxes (whatever their name, tax on transactions, tax on payments, general stamp duty on commercial transactions) one of the best instruments of financial restoration; but it has also been inspired by practical considerations, as well as by our concern for fiscal justice." [50] "Fiscal justice" was clearly an afterthought.

Immediately afterwards, however, M. Doumer explained that the real reason for deciding on this tax was the ease and promptness with which it would give a large yield. It would be collected together with the turnover tax and would bring in 320 millions a month or 3.8 billions a year.

> On the other hand, being so widely distributed, it will escape the criticism incurred by the consumption taxes on common foodstuffs, of being inversely progressive. . . . It is proportionate to everybody's needs. If one cannot try to measure the degree of a taxpayer's wealth by his use of sugar or wine, it is undeniable that the total of his expenditure is closely connected with his capacity to spend. Lastly, the tax will exempt the essential foodstuffs, because it will affect neither agriculturists' sale of their produce, nor in a general way the trade in cereals, nor the sale of bread and meat. . . . A high cost of living tax? Such criticism can be expected and we are anxious to explain.[51]

The explanation amounted to this, that in times when prices take quick jumps of ten, twenty, and thirty per cent, an extra franc or so per hundred francs will surely not make much difference. Doumer also proposed to extend the turnover tax to exports. Thus he rested almost his entire plan of action upon an increase and extension of the tax which the Left politicians had promised to suppress.

His other proposals included an increase in the tax on stock exchange transactions, and the reinforcement of the financial

49 *Ibid.*, p. 493. 50 *Idem.* 51 *Idem.*

administration which would result in a supplementary revenue of 300 millions.[52]

The Finance Commission once more disagreed with a Finance Minister.[53] It rejected the proposed addition to the turnover tax in the guise of a "tax on payments," though approving the extension of the tax to exports. Other indirect tax rates (e.g., those on spirits, automobiles, coffee, and salt) should be raised, and the yield from the schedule income taxes increased by stricter methods of assessment, involving abandonment of much of the *forfaitaire* practices. For the rest, the deficit should be covered by economies in administration, and improvements in the tax administration. "For some time," it said, "as a result of the mediocre status of the direct-tax employees, and the insufficiency of the remuneration, a large number among them have abandoned their posts to look for better ones in business. On the other hand, the recent competitive examinations organized by the administration have given poor results, and have not even sufficed to recruit a number of employees to replace those who have left. The administration of direct taxes is far from having at its disposal the functionaries it actually needs." [54]

The Chamber had already voted some special credits for the reorganization of that important financial department, and the Commission estimated that "the improvement made in the status of these functionaries will make it possible to attract a larger number of new employees and to stop the resignations. Thus, the control for which these functionaries are responsible will be

[52] M. Doumer's budget (*ibid.*, p. 495) may be summarized as follows:

(In millions of francs)

Expenditure		*Revenue*	
Deficit in 1926 budget *projet*	4,500	Loucheur taxes	3,000
Economies	200	Administrative improvements	300
	4,300	Tax on Bourse transactions	100
Reimbursement to Bank of France	2,000	Increase in tobacco prices	1,000
Sinking Fund annuity	2,500	Turnover tax on exports	600
		Tax on payments	3,800
	8,800		8,800

[53] *Doc. Parl.*, 1926, *Chambre, Sess. Ord.*, Doc. No. 2458, p. 68 *et seq.*

[54] *Ibid.*, p. 72.

exercised with greater strength and severity, and a greater yield can be expected in the future from the general income tax and the schedules." [55]

As the voting of the budget bill, with its new taxes, would considerably ease the situation, the Commission wished the Chamber to vote the *projet* now presented, which, it incidentally remarked, involved for the majority no breach in their electoral promises. This was obviously an allusion to the tax on payments, which resembled too closely the turnover tax.

The Chamber spent some three weeks discussing the financial program of the Commission. M. Doumer was far from satisfied with the Commission's *rapport* and would not abandon his tax on payments. As a concession to those who spoke of the burden it imposed on the consumer, he agreed to exempt retail sales from the tax.[56] The Chamber, however, declined to be satisfied even with that. At the end of its deliberations it had succeeded in voting only some 1.6 billions of new tax measures, and the budget, still showing a deficit of 2.4 billions, and without any special provisions for debt amortization, was sent to the Senate.

The Senate Commission adopted the majority of measures voted by the Chamber and added 3,385 millions, including 800 millions from tobacco and 2,400 millions from a modified payments tax. The total receipts voted by the Senate itself came to 5,185 millions, nearly the figure aimed at by M. Doumer.

But with the return of the bill to the Chamber, the equilibrium was again completely upset. The Finance Commission bluntly rejected the tax on payments; and, though it introduced into the bill a few minor measures, there still remained a deficit of over 2 billions.

After much discussion, the Commission finally agreed to consider a half per cent tax on payments (excluding retail sales) which was accepted by 12 votes against 11. This article read as follows: " Beginning on the first day of the month following the passing of the present act an exceptional tax on payments shall come into force, payable by means of adhesive stamps.

" This tax, the rate of which is 0.50 per cent, is due on pay-

[55] *Ibid.*, p. 72. [56] *Débats*, 1926, *Chambre*, *Sess. Ord.*, Jan. 29, p. 323.

ments received in settlement of professional sales . . . made by persons subject to the tax on business profits and mining profits." [57]

Exceptions were allowed in the case of (1) retail sales, (including sales of food on the seller's premises), (2) export sales, and (3) in general, the exemptions already allowed for the turnover tax.

In the heated debate of March 5, 1926, the tax was torn to pieces. First came M. Bedouce who, on behalf of the Socialists, condemned it as another tax on general consumption. "We are offered a new tax," he said, "the disastrous effects of which will add themselves to those of the turnover tax." [58] M. Doumer tried in vain to appease the Left with the not very convincing argument that the tax on payments he was proposing would be useful as an experiment looking toward the tax on production demanded by the opponents of the tax on turnover. But this "hope of a future dream," as M. Ernest Lafont put it, did not change the fact that the payments tax was "not even a new variety, but merely a new name for the turnover tax." [59] M. Charles Reibel, on the Right, without putting forward any concrete arguments against the tax, condemned the general financial policy of the Government. "The Treasury, whether you like it or not," he said to M. Doumer, "is directly dependent on the renewal of the *Bons de la Défense Nationale* and should some anxiety persist among the holders of these securities, it is certain that you will be unable to ask Parliament for a sufficient number of taxes to assure their repayment. You will, therefore, be inevitably condemned to inflation. . . . Gentlemen, you can well feel that you will never be able, whatever you do, to reassure public opinion so long as it feels the socialist-revolutionary spell hanging over the Government." [60] This speech indicated the general defiant attitude of the *Bloc National* towards the Government.

M. Briand spoke eloquently of the interests of the nation, and of the parliamentary Locarno spirit, but his plea was of no avail.

[57] *Débats*, 1926, *Chambre*, *Sess. Ord.*, Mar. 5, p. 1272.
[58] *Ibid.*, p. 1273.
[59] *Ibid.*, p. 1275.
[60] *Ibid.*, p. 1277.

Parliament would not lend the Government its coöperation. M. Doumer explained how careful he had been to find the best solution. The direct taxes could not be touched, after the Loucheur surtaxes of December 4. The indirect taxes that the Finance Commission had proposed had been badly received. During the first discussions nearly all had been discarded. With the greatest difficulty had the Government obtained an increase in tobacco prices. M. Doumer knew that the name "turnover tax" was unpopular, and he had, therefore, refrained from using it; he saw that the only possibility of saving the situation was to vote a "tax on payments," even though both its rate and its breadth of application had been greatly reduced as compared with the original proposals. He concluded:

If you do not fear the return of inflation, if you are not terrified at the prospect of a new crisis, and of that anxiety which surrounded us during 1925, you may certainly reject our proposals. . . . Gentlemen, when I agreed to go to the Ministry of Finance, the position, I assure you, was not an enviable one.

M. LE RAPPORTEUR GÉNÉRAL — That's quite true.

M. DOUMER — I have made every effort to improve it. [Cheers.] I may repeat here what I already said in January to the Finance Commission: There is still time; if you will give us what we ask, we shall succeed in avoiding a crisis, and you will have nothing to fear of the near future. Otherwise, another must take the responsibility of governing.[61]

Such was the question of confidence put to the Chamber by the Minister of Finance, in the session of March 5. The vote resulted in the defeat of the Government by 274 votes against 221.

The Péret Tax Act, April, 1926. — Before M. Doumer's resignation the Chamber, though refusing to vote the tax on payments, had adopted "on principle" over 3 billions in new taxation. There was still a deficit of more than 2 billions to be made good.

M. Raoul Péret, the Finance Minister in the new Briand Cabinet, was confronted with the unenviable task of finding new fiscal resources for that amount, and his first proposals indicate that his fiscal program did not differ essentially from M. Doumer's

[61] *Ibid.*, p. 1275.

except that he was prepared to ask for an additional contribution from taxation in the form of a progressive *taxe civique* (in effect, an addition to the income tax), estimated to yield 500 million francs. The most important measure he proposed was, however, analogous to M. Doumer's — *viz.*, a raise from 1.3 to 2 per cent of the tax on turnover payable by all except retailers. He further proposed a voluntary contribution.

According to the parliamentary correspondent of the *Ère Nouvelle*, there was a feeling of unrest in the corridors of the Palais Bourbon before the opening of the finance debate. " To be quite candid," he wrote, " the corridors looked bad. Small groups of deputies were discussing M. Péret's financial proposals, but from whatever angle they approached them they inevitably returned to this conclusion — yes, but there is that tax on turnover! That was, evidently, a huge dose. Two ministers had already tried to force it down the Chamber's throat, and both times they had had to give up. . . ." It was true that " M. Raoul Péret would engage in the battle with weapons that M. Doumer completely lacked — amiability and subtlety," but it was doubtful that these would win over some 60 or 70 deputies who had voted against the tax on payments.[62]

Contrary to expectations, however, the increase in the turnover tax was accepted by the Chamber, partly no doubt because M. Péret made the proposal on the understanding that in 1927 the whole turnover tax would be replaced by a general production tax and by higher tax rates on income. This tax increase was incorporated in the " new fiscal measures " act of April 4, 1926.

This act falls into two parts. The second, dealing with " new resources," included: the increase of the turnover tax to 2 per cent except for retailers; the new *taxe civique;* an increase in various registration and stamp duties, including the transfer tax on real estate; an increase in the taxes on spirits, salt, petrol, lubricants, perfumery; an increase in the coal production tax and *taxe d'abatage;* the extension of the turnover tax to exports; an extension of the field of application of the business-profits tax; and an increase in tobacco prices.

[62] See p. 137.

The first part, of perhaps more fundamental importance, introduced radical changes in the methods of assessing the income taxes. It was on the initiative of the Chamber that this was done, for Doumer had written in December, 1925, that it would be impossible to elaborate a well studied and careful reform until the budget for 1927 was prepared.[63] As Allix and Lecerclé remark, "The majority of these new measures testify indeed to the lack of reflection with which the act was elaborated. Inflicting . . . annoying formalities . . . rashly modifying regulations which were better than the new ones, disconcerting both the administration and the taxpayers who beg that they be left in peace so that they may have the time to assimilate the existing laws before others are voted, the act merely undermines the fiscal system instead of strengthening it."[64]

As to the general income tax, article 1 of the new act completely transformed the rules governing the declaration of incomes. Until then only those had to make a declaration whose income was, at least in part, taxable, i.e., bachelors with over 7,000 francs income, married couples without children with incomes over 10,000 francs, those with one child, if their income exceeded 13,000 francs, etc. Now — with certain exceptions — declaration of total income had to be made even though no general income tax was due.

Allix and Lecerclé thought this would be impossible in any case, both for practical and moral reasons. All the humble people liable to the thirty-franc penalty for non-declaration could not be taxed in any case; and to pick out a few at random would be an injustice.[65]

Furthermore, only "householders" had been subject to the general income tax. Henceforth persons residing permanently in hotels, furnished rooms, etc., were to be included.

The most drastic change was introduced in the business schedule. Here no class of business was taxable any longer on the presumptive, turnover basis. Businesses were divided into two

[63] *Doc. Parl.*, 1925, *Chambre, Sess. Extraord.*, Doc. No. 2332, p. 492 *et seq.*

[64] Allix and Lecerclé, *L' Impôt sur le Revenu, Supplément* (1926), p. 19.

[65] *Op. cit.*, p. 72.

classes — those with incomes over 50,000 francs and those with incomes less than that figure. In the first case a full statement showing the net income had to be produced; in the case of the smaller incomes it was sufficient for the taxpayer to declare himself as belonging to a " class " of income (e.g., between 10,000 and 15,000 francs); and he was taxed accordingly, provided the authorities did not dispute such a declaration. Declarations in the professional schedule might be subjected in matters of dispute to examination of a special commission comprising members of the taxpayer's own profession.

Regarding investment incomes, two new attempts were made by the act of April 4 to eliminate tax evasion in the general income tax. One was the creation of " order shares "[66] or " endorsement shares." Any sale transfer had to be communicated by registered letter to the company that issued the share. The attraction of such stock was to be the suppression of transfer duties and the reduction by 50 per cent of the transmission tax.

The other measure, though advocated by M. Bokanowski ever since 1923, was to prove no more effective. The *carnet de coupons,* though prescribed by the act, never came into force, and was suppressed a few months later before the *carnets* themselves had actually been printed. The practical difficulties connected with this system made it unworkable.[67]

[66] A director of one of the largest French banks and member of the Experts Committee of 1926 has testified that he has never yet seen a " titre à ordre," and that he thinks there are very few, if any, in the market, partly because of the trouble connected with the compulsory postal notification of any transfer.

[67] It was simple enough if the taxpayer kept only one account and entrusted his banker with the cashing of all his coupons; the banker could then make the entries in his customer's " carnet." The matter was more difficult if the taxpayer had, say, several accounts. In that case banker B could not credit his customer with a coupon until he received the " carnet " from banker A; in the meantime, banker C was also asked to credit the customer with another coupon; would he have to write for the " carnet " to A or B or to the customer himself? Moreover, if, as such things happen, the " carnet " were lost in the post, on what basis could the taxpayer then be assessed? And seeing that it was to his interest to lose the " carnet," was it likely that he would take special care not to do so? Another reason for the suppression of the " carnet " was that it complicated immensely the position of foreign investors. Mr. Smith, of London, having invested 100 pounds in French railway bonds deposited in Paris, could not draw dividends until he either got a " carnet de coupons " or proved by affidavit that he was a

The taxation of agricultural profits, despite the recommendations of the Finance Commission, was left unchanged by the act of April 4.

The Budget of 1926. — Only about two weeks had elapsed since M. Péret had replaced M. Doumer and he had already succeeded in practically solving the budgetary problem. The budget, voted on April 29, was no more than a formal completion of what had already been achieved by the tax law of April 4. It showed the following balance: expenditure, 37,338,389,202 francs; revenue, 37,498, 739,468 francs.

The revenue was almost entirely composed of normal tax receipts,[68] with "exceptional resources" amounting to only 415 millions. Of this last item 400 million francs were expected under the war-profits tax, an item which was to prove an illusion.[69] One of the most important features of the budget was the inscription in it of the total pensions charge amounting to 5,143 millions. The corresponding item in the 1925 budget had been only 3,776 millions.

The debt charge (excluding pensions) in the budget act of 1926 amounted to 15,144 [70] millions, showing an increase over the 1925 budget of 360 millions.

The budget act instituted an independent amortization fund managed by a council representing the various financial services of the Government, and also the various commercial, business and labor interests of the country. The principal resources of the fund were to be the following: special budgetary credits opened for the purpose, the proceeds of the Loucheur taxes, budget surpluses, gifts and legacies made to the State without mention of any special purpose, and the voluntary contributions created by the act of March 31, 1926. This fund should not be confused with the

non-resident foreigner and not subject to the French income tax. Such formalities naturally tended to turn the already not over-enthusiastic foreign investor away from French securities. *Cf.* Allix and Lecerclé, *op. cit.*, Vol. II, p. 192 *et seq.*

68 Including "ordre" receipts.

69 See pp. 330–336.

70 It should be noted that this does not agree with the figure given in the *projet* of 1928, p. 71.

Caisse d'Amortissement, which was established by Poincaré later in the year.

The struggles of the twelve-month period surveyed in this chapter, negative and futile though they appear on the surface, were far from being without significance. A succession of finance ministers had analyzed the possible courses of action and practically every possible plan had been laid before Parliament for action by one minister or another in perfectly definite form. In disposing of these issues it had been shown that the *Cartel des Gauches* did not possess sufficient strength to impose a capital levy. It had become clear also that forced consolidation would not be countenanced. A little was done to increase taxes, but the event was to show [71] that the 1926 tax collections were no greater than those of 1925, measured in francs of constant value. By shouting " no " to everything, Parliament had, in effect, whispered " yes " to the policy of inflation. But perhaps more important than anything else, the public generally had been awakened to the necessity of firm leadership. By stultifying itself, Parliament had prepared the way for the return of M. Poincaré.

[71] See p. 400.

CHAPTER IX

POINCARÉ "SAVES THE FRANC," 1926–1927

THE acute financial crisis which began in May, 1926, and culminated in the panic of July 21–24, was a phenomenon the fundamental causes of which lay rooted deep in the general policies and practices of the post-war period. Of immediate and obvious causes there was a notable lack. On the surface things seemed to be moving along about as usual — little better or worse. But distrust and pessimism, which had been steadily accumulating for a long time, had now reached significant proportions. The avalanche began to move. This is clearly reflected in exchange rates and in prices.

In April, 1925, the month when Caillaux was summoned to the Ministry of Finance, the average quotation for francs was 19.20 to the dollar. In the following October, when he resigned, the average quotation for the month was 23.92. During the winter, the value of the franc continued to sag to lower and lower levels. In May, 1926, when the storm began to break upon the head of M. Péret, the dollar would buy 30.60 francs. In June, the quotation was to become 34.93, and in July, 41.15. All these figures are monthly averages.[1] In individual transactions at the height of the panic, the franc, normally worth twenty cents, sold for approximately two cents.

The story of prices is similar. In April, 1925, Caillaux found the wholesale price index at 512.8, and in the following October left it at 572.3. Péret faced the crisis of May, 1926, with prices at 687.9. In June they were to rise to 738.4, and in July to 836.2.[2]

PÉRET YIELDS TO CAILLAUX, JUNE, 1926

At the beginning of the crisis M. Péret tried to take things calmly. On May 21, he was able to state at a council of the

[1] See p. 449. [2] See p. 448.

Cabinet that the debt maturity of the preceding day had been met "in the most satisfactory conditions and that the position of the Treasury was a healthy one." "There is nothing," he said, "to justify the fall of the franc. The budget is balanced. The Treasury has regained ease in its transactions."[3] And most important of all, the *Bons de la Défense Nationale* were showing once more an excess of subscriptions over withdrawals. But the franc still went on falling. What was to be done? A committee of experts was appointed on May 31, to analyze the incomprehensible situation and to find the remedies that the Finance Minister knew not where to seek.

Before the Finance Commission on June 3 M. Péret recalled how the Treasury had only had to disburse one billion francs of the 3,100 million maturity of May 20, the rest having been converted. The Loucheur taxes had been steadily coming in — nearly 2.5 billions had already been collected on April 30. He said that, taken as a whole, the position of the Treasury would be normal until December 31, 1926. Nevertheless, he was seriously concerned about the monetary situation which he ascribed to numerous causes, such as the sale of francs by foreigners, speculation, the general economic crisis, the deficit in the trade balance, etc.[4]

Various measures were considered by the Government. They thought of suppressing the regulations regarding the export of capital, and tried to encourage the repatriation of French capital that had emigrated; they suppressed a useless bogey like the *carnet de coupons;* they prescribed new food restrictions. One of the gravest dangers rested in the political instability of the Government. On June 1, M. Briand referred to this in the Chamber. "The most important thing is for the Government not to let its authority be weakened at all. . . . The [present] difficulties would be made worse by feebleness in the Government. There is no doubt that the weakness (*fragilité*) of the Government's authority is one of the most dangerous elements of the present time."[5]

[3] *Ère Nouvelle,* May 22, 1926.

[4] *Ibid.*, June 4, 1926.

[5] *Débats,* 1926, *Chambre, Sess. Ord.*, pp. 2306–2307.

The appointment of the experts' committee brought matters to a head. M. Péret was violently attacked not only on the Left, but also by moderate members of the *Cartel*, for seeking the co-operation and advice of the experts' committee, a committee composed predominantly of bankers and capitalists,[6] for acting contrary to his political principles, and for undermining the authority of Parliament.

M. Nogaro went so far as to insinuate that the Finance Minister seemed to "take more than mere advice from those manipulators" (meaning the bankers on the experts' committee).

M. Raoul Péret: — You have uttered a word that, as an honest man, you have certainly already regretted. I wish to point out that the Government has all liberty of action; that it is not placed in anybody's hands, that it obeys no injunctions [cheers from Centre, Right, and several Left benches], and that, once it has thought necessary to constitute a committee of financial experts —

M. Desoblin: — Who are not disinterested —

M. Raoul Péret: — after the model of what has been done in several other countries, . . . it is because the questions confronting us are essentially of a technical order.[7]

The Minister explained that the experts' report would be used by the Government only as a basis for its own proposals. To the question, what policy the Government intended to follow, M. Péret gave the following reply, which aroused serious indignation among the Socialists:

I shall not enter into any details. I wish only to say that ours shall be a policy that will aim at reassuring the owning classes, by which I mean all that mass of savers who have made it their duty in difficult hours to help the State — [Ironic cheers on extreme Left — cheers on Right — general disturbance.]

M. Pierre Renaudel: — Very fine for the owning classes!

M. Raoul Péret — to give confidence to labor and saving and to contribute in that way to the rehabilitation of the franc. [Cheers from Centre, Right, and various Left benches.][8]

[6] The committee consisted of one representative from the Ministry of Finance, three from industry, one from the Bank of France, six from the largest French banks, and two university professors, MM. Jèze and Rist.

[7] *Débats*, 1926, *Chambre, Sess. Ord.*, June 1, pp. 2308–2309.

[8] *Ibid.*, p. 2309.

The indication of such an "attitude" set fire to the "democratic Chamber." While M. Péret might personally have gained the support of the Centre and Right groups (their applause during his declaration was probably significant), he could hardly expect solid support from any party combination on the Left. On June 15, at the end of a cabinet meeting, he made an official statement in which he announced that "in face of the rising exchange rate, and in the absence of the necessary support upon which the Government could count, he could not accomplish his duty to the full extent." He was resigning because "it seemed necessary to him to make it possible for a new political and parliamentary combination to take shape, which would satisfy public opinion demanding a combined effort in view of the general danger." For the fourth time in succession M. Briand had to select a new Minister of Finance and M. Caillaux was given another chance.

The Report of the Committee of Experts, July, 1926

In the meantime, the experts, disregarding parliamentary squabbles, were working night and day. Their report, an exceedingly able document considering that it was produced in one month's time, appeared July 3. While primarily concerned with the monetary problem, the experts thought it necessary to survey the whole field of public finance.

Importance of Currency Stability.—In their preface they stressed the necessity of rapid action on the part of Parliament. The situation was serious. The stabilization of the currency must be brought about.

> The fall of the franc [they wrote] has caused great ravages in our national economic life. It has continued the destruction of capital which the war had begun. The country believed that it was maintaining its spending capacity, whereas in reality it was consuming its own capital. No doubt, trade and industry have experienced a period of apparent prosperity; even as yet there is no unemployment, sales are easy, and exports active. Many Frenchmen live in a state of illusion; in reality, in spite of nominally increased profits, there is in many cases an absence of real profit. The French are working and producing; but most of them are becoming unconsciously poorer.

A few new fortunes have been created, but only too often they are the unhealthy and temporary fruit of currency depreciation. This depreciation gives debtors, by the automatic reduction of their debts, an easy way of becoming rich; but creditors grow weary, the spirit of saving disappears, credit becomes impossible, and production is threatened.

In France, a country of the middle classes and of small-scale industrialization, where prosperity is based on the capacity to save, the consequences of monetary instability are particularly serious. If thrift were to become the quality of fools, if the attractions of speculation and gambling were to take the place of productive labor, we should see before very long the disappearance of our national virtues. To safeguard the economic life of the country, the franc must be given the fundamental quality of a currency — stability.[9]

Therefore, in the first place, borrowing and inflation must stop; the credit of the Treasury, which, through the issue of *Bons de la Défense Nationale*, had become the largest deposit bank in the country, must be restored. To be able to renew and to consolidate these bonds, the Treasury must be able to pay its creditors in a stable and reliable currency.

As to the rate of stabilization, the experts rejected the idea of complete revalorisation. Such a procedure would involve continuous and systematic deflation which would be ruinous to the taxpayer, as well as to industry, trade and agriculture, on account of the necessity of lowering prices indefinitely, and of keeping to contracts made in times of monetary depreciation. Moreover, "those who would benefit by such a deflation would not be the same people who had suffered during the preceding period. In present-day economic life, agreements are renewed, securities change hands and wealth is transferred too rapidly to enable one to atone for the injustice suffered by many in the past by a lengthy revalorization of the franc."[10]

The experts considered that complete stabilization meant a gold convertibility of the currency notes; not at the pre-war rate, but at some new rate determined by law. Such a stabilization, of course, would not be effected immediately, and would have to be attained by degrees. Besides the technical factors, there was also

[9] *Rapport du Comité des Experts*, p. 8. [10] *Ibid.*, p. 9.

to be considered the morale of the public; and to restore confidence it was necessary that the Government should guarantee the absolute security of capital and the fulfillment of all its undertakings (no forced consolidation of short-term bonds, etc.). Consistency in financial policy was essential.

Return of confidence would have to rest on several technical measures. French capital that had emigrated should be encouraged to return. This continuous emigration of French capital had considerably upset, during the past years, the trade balance of France, and had affected the rate of exchange in a disastrous way.

Budget Suggestions. — Though since 1924 immense improvements had been made in the French budgetary policy, the experts considered that the 1926 budget was still imperfect. A few expenditure items were left to the charge of the Treasury, and others required supplementary credits not provided for by revenue.

In one respect, however, the budget was in a fortunate position. The Dawes payments, which were not included in the budget, sufficed in 1926 for the first time to take care of the remaining expenditures on the devastated regions, so that the Treasury was entirely freed from that burden. Any future obligations issued in respect of the devastated regions would be financed by future Dawes payments.

The difficulty regarding the 1926 budget was the extremely small surplus, and, in addition, (1) the risk of having the budget balances upset by the changes in the exchange rates, (2) the inevitable additional expenditure on increased government salaries, and the military needs in Syria and Morocco, and (3) certain expenses which had still been left outside the budget.

The experts incidentally criticized the lack of publicity in matters of public finance, which in many cases increased the uneasiness of the public who were not always able to see the actual position.

With regard to expenditure, the experts "cherished no illusions that any immediate and important economies could be effected by way of compressing the budget," [11] and that only administrative reforms, involving the suppression of certain government

[11] *Rapport du Comité des Experts*, p. 19.

departments, could tend to diminish administrative expenses. The Ministry of the Liberated Regions, for example, was one for which there was no further need.

As for revenue, the experts thought it necessary to increase it by 2.5 billions for 1926, and by 5 billions for 1927. How could these sums be raised after all the heavy tax increases in 1925 and 1926?

The treatment of the tax problem is certainly not the most impressive portion of the experts' report. One sympathizes with M. Jèze, who felt unable to give it his personal approval.[12] It is significant that the fiscal measures they proposed were in many respects similar to those adopted by M. Poincaré two months later, except that they wished to leave direct taxes even more completely out of their program.

> The direct taxes [they wrote] are collected on the basis of *rôles*, the establishment of which normally precedes the collection. These *rôles* correspond either to incomes estimated on a *forfaitaire* basis a long time ago, or else to actual incomes made one or two years previously. At a time of monetary depreciation, however much care one may take to speed up collections, the gold value of the tax gradually shrinks between the times of assessment and collection. Repressions and increases in rates may well be applied, but they only encourage the export of capital and accentuate, indirectly, the exchange crisis. . . .[13]

Particularly startling and unorthodox was the experts' indictment of the income tax because of its alleged effects upon prices:

> The Committee does not consider that a system of heavy direct taxes, striking production and labor, will spare the large mass of consumers. The fiscal burdens which, in the form of direct taxes, weigh on agriculture and on business activity, will eventually be incorporated in prices, and, in many cases, in a proportion higher than their real amount.[14]

But, above all, the direct taxes did not conform with the depreciation of money, which meant in every case a loss to the Treasury.

A number of interesting comments on the various taxes were

[12] *Ibid.*, p. 21. [13] *Idem.* [14] *Idem.*

made by the Committee. They pointed out that the nominal rate of 60 per cent in the general income tax, while giving little additional benefit to the Treasury, merely tended to demoralize the taxpayer. They condemned both the *bordereau* and the *carnet de coupons* as ineffective and as likely to cause the export of capital. What was necessary was the reorganization of the government services, and particularly the amalgamation of the direct tax and registration administrations. This would enable the direct-tax official to have full access to all the information available for the registration authorities. "Such a tightening in the control would be much more effective than all those vexing methods which make capital seek to escape." [15]

Further, the experts thought an increase in the number of tax officials very desirable. The direct-tax services were understaffed by 13 per cent; several hundred posts were vacant. There was a particularly important lack of higher-grade officials.

Regarding the assessments themselves, they considered that the initial exemption should be raised from 7,000 to 10,000 francs. "The administration would find itself freed of a multitude of troublesome and unproductive declarations, and could concentrate better on the more significant taxpayers." [16]

The tax on land and on agricultural profits, being based on the cadastral valuation of 1910, did not, naturally, correspond to the real incomes of the taxpayers. The experts suggested that the basis of the tax be increased by one hundred per cent. They also drew attention to the fact that, in the case of agricultural profits, the taxpayer was able to diminish his tax by producing evidence of having an income smaller than that administratively determined, but that, on the other hand, the tax controller could not increase the tax even if he had the means of proving that it was larger. The *forfait*, therefore, always operated to the detriment of the Treasury.

The experts further considered the taxes on securities, and stressed the exorbitant charges striking incomes from that source. In an appendix they showed the cumulative effect on such incomes of the schedule tax, the transmission tax and the stamp

[15] *Rapport du Comité des Experts*, p. 23. [16] *Ibid.*, p. 24.

duty. These taxes alone, (i.e., not counting the *impôt général*) amounted in several cases to 50, 60, 70 and, in one case, to 256 per cent of the actual dividends! [17]

The Committee also suggested that the distinction between *abonnées* and *non-abonnées* foreign securities be abolished for the sake of simplicity, and that both classes pay a stamp duty at their time of issue and a special tax of 8 or 10 per cent over and above the regular 12 per cent tax on *valeurs mobilières* incomes.

The theoretical maximum tax of 80 per cent on inheritances should, in the opinion of the experts, also be reduced; it was never applied in practice and "merely acts upon the taxpayer as an unnecessary bogey." [18]

While the experts were anxious to reduce to a certain extent the rates in the direct taxes, they considered that it was quite possible to increase a large number of indirect taxes. The tax on sugar was only 100 per cent higher than before the war; by doubling it an additional revenue of 400 millions could be expected. An 0.05 franc surtax per litre of wine would yield 300 millions more.

They also recommended an increase in the customs tariff and an all-round raise to 2 per cent of the turnover tax. The various exceptions and modifications introduced in the tax during the past two years had made it very complicated, and the experts thought that above all it should be an essentially simple and productive tax.

Finally they considered an increase in railway fares quite practicable and estimated that a 15 per cent increase would yield 1,800 millions.

It is not to be wondered that the Left was not favorably disposed towards the "Committee of Experts."

The Treasury Problem. — In considering the Treasury problem, the experts first dealt with the floating and short-time debt. The private current accounts, amounting at the end of June, 1926, to 1,600 millions, were an uncomfortable liability of the Treasury,

[17] The figures quoted include the Loucheur supertaxes. Without them, the taxes represent usually between 30 and 40 per cent of the income. *Ibid.*, pp. 136–137.

[18] *Ibid.*, p. 25.

and apt to necessitate repayments at most inopportune moments. They were, however, of minor importance compared with the *Bons de la Défense Nationale* where every excess of repayments over subscriptions placed the Treasury in a very awkward position. While for several years after the war, the subscriptions constantly showed a surplus over the withdrawals, since 1924 the reverse movement had set in, which had become particularly strong since the question of forced consolidation had been raised. The Committee vigorously rejected any scheme of forced consolidation and forced reduction of interest and declared itself in favor of progressive voluntary consolidation to begin at the first opportunity.

In the meantime, it was necessary to take a number of measures "which would surround the repayment of the *Bons de la Défense Nationale* by every possible guarantee."[19] The securities, a legacy of the past, must be separated from the Treasury. A special *Caisse de Gestion* endowed with special powers and funds should be established to care for them. To make the working of the fund elastic, it should be allowed a temporary 6 per cent margin of issue over the actual amount of bonds outstanding (*viz.*: 49 billions).

The *Caisse* should be endowed with several resources. There should be an annuity from the budget equal to the interest due on the bonds outstanding at the beginning of the year. Of this sum, any unused balances would be used for amortization. Further, there should be an amortization annuity from the budget of at least 500 millions. It should further be given an initial endowment of 4 billion francs out of the foreign "stabilization" loan.[20] In later years a part of the Dawes payments should also be credited to the *Caisse*. And, most important of all, it should also receive all the net revenue of the tobacco monopoly. "Being surrounded by all these guarantees, the bonds will keep the favor of the public."[21]

The *Bons Ordinaires du Trésor* amounting to 2.6 billions, should also be handled by the *Caisse*.

19 *Rapport du Comité des Experts*, p. 33.

20 See p. 154.

21 *Ibid.*, p. 35.

The 3-to-10-year *Bons du Trésor* and *Crédit National* Bonds, 7 billions of which were to be repayable at the option of their holders in 1927 (3 in February and 4 in September), should to a large extent be easily converted with the return of confidence. Even in the most unfavorable conditions similar maturities had resulted in the conversion of 50 per cent of the bonds.

Regarding the Bank of France, the experts recommended the gradual reduction of the advances to the State and fixed the budgetary annuity for that purpose at 1 billion.

Extra-Budgetary Expenditures.—The extra-budgetary expenses, such as capital outlay on Alsace-Lorraine railways, should have the indispensable funds inscribed in the budget until it again became possible to issue bonds.

The interest on Bank of France advances should also be fully inscribed in the budget. Repayments of foreign debts should be made from the receipts from the Dawes Plan. To cover the temporary divergences between the Treasury receipts and payments, it should be allowable to issue *Bons Ordinaires du Trésor* to the extent of 5 billions [22] per year. These bonds would be independent of those handled by the *Caisse.*

The experts recalled in this connection the evils resulting from the late voting of the budget.

The Process of Stabilization.—All that has been said was only the indispensable preliminary to the real aim of the experts' report. This aim was the stabilization of the franc. The principal agent in the attainment of this was not to be the Treasury, but the Bank of France, because, they said, the State was not in position to undertake the essential market operations. "The intervention on the money market," the experts wrote, "does not imply large-scale strategic operations, but merely a constant supervision of exchange rates, the Bank buying one day the excess of foreign currency, and selling the next day when francs are scarce.

"In England, the Bank, being freed by law from internal payments in gold, merely keeps up the international value of its notes by using directly or indirectly its metal reserve, which it is able

[22] Before the war, on a 5-billion budget the Treasury was permitted to issue 600 millions of such bonds. *Ibid.*, p. 39.

to protect by its discount policy. An analogous system should be aimed at in France." [23]

The desirable time for stabilization was not clearly indicated — it should be as soon as possible — nor was the rate specified at which the franc should be stabilized. It should be fixed, they said, between the two extreme limits of the value of the franc as determined by the index number of prices, and its international value at the same period. To induce French capital to return to France, it would be desirable to fix the rate at a figure lower than the prevailing one (about 170 to the pound).[24] The stabilization would have to be effected with the assistance of the following credits: (1) long-term loans already obtained, or later to be obtained, by the Government from abroad (Morgan loan, etc.); (2) credits obtained by the Bank of France; and (3) private and commercial credits.

But to obtain credits from abroad, it would be necessary to ratify as early as possible the Washington Agreement and also to begin negotiations with England regarding the inter-Allied debts. As for the private credits, the Bank of France should be able to attract a considerable number of foreign currency deposits from abroad.

The restrictions on the export of capital, which, in any case, were ineffective, should be suppressed and full liberty should be given to the movement of funds both into and out of France.

The process of stabilization would then fall into three periods: (1) a period of pre-stabilization with the rates oscillating around a rate fixed in advance; (2) a period of *de facto* stabilization dur-which it would be known that the Bank bought and sold gold and foreign currency at a fixed rate; and (3) the period of *de jure* stabilization, at which time only could the question of the gold standard and of convertibility be definitely settled. This, in brief, was the chart and compass which was to guide France to the final solution of its financial problem. As will be seen, save for minor exceptions, such as the suggestions regarding foreign credits and certain taxes, the plan here developed was to be adopted as the program of the restoration.

[23] *Rapport du Comité des Experts*, p. 42.

[24] See p. 173.

Caillaux Denied Special Powers, July, 1926

In July the financial sky looked black. In many quarters, however, the publication of the experts' report brought the conviction that the worst was over. For here was at last a program, no political improvisation or mere expedient, one which did not neglect a single aspect of the whole financial situation and which, if adopted, would likely prove a solution. The burning question of the time was whether there would be a sufficiently strong government in France to apply the experts' plan in practice. On July 4 the Paris correspondent of the London *Times* wrote:

> Everything depends on how far M. Caillaux and the Government are prepared to maintain the indivisibility of the whole scheme. If they show that they are ready to resign rather than let any of its essential points be modified, they will give it double weight. The failing of all the governments in the past years has been that they have lent themselves to compromises. The compromises did not save them from defeat, but people had been led to believe that there are many ways of conducting sound finance, whereas, as the Report indicates, there are very few.[25]

M. Caillaux, in his long speech to the Chamber on July 6,[26] was disconcertingly vague as to what he intended to do, and his main point was the announcement that a bill would be presented to Parliament giving special powers to the Government to do by decree what was necessary to increase taxation within certain limits and to initiate a policy of stabilization. While accepting in a general way the experts' plan and recalling that its main conclusions coincided with the bills he had prepared for the Chamber a year before and which "events had prevented him from bringing into effect," M. Caillaux nevertheless differed from the experts in some respects. He proposed to increase taxation by not more than 3 billion francs, the additional revenue being devoted to an increase in government salaries, to repayments to the Bank of France, to the cancellation of *Bons de la Défense Nationale* and to expenses connected with stabilization. In the fiscal and finan-

[25] London *Times*, July 5, 1926, p. 14.

[26] *Débats*, 1926, *Chambre, Sess. Ord.*, p. 2730 *et seq.*

cial measures which he proposed to take, he followed, as will be seen, the experts' plan fairly closely. There was particularly one point on which his views coincided with theirs, and on which M. Poincaré was later to differ, *viz.*, the urgent necessity of obtaining foreign credits. With this object in view he impressed upon the Chamber the need of ratifying the Washington Agreement and of reaching a settlement in respect of the French debt to Great Britain.

A few days later he flew to London, where he signed an agreement with Mr. Churchill.[27] From the English point of view the terms were considered very generous, and were "frankly intended as an encouragement to the French people in the task of serious financial reform that lay before them."[28] Though the French did not view it in exactly the same light,[29] the agreement had at least this merit, that the repayments were spread over a large number of years and were smallest at the beginning.

On his return from London, M. Caillaux promptly prepared his "special powers" bill.[30] Under the terms of this plan the Government would be authorized until November 30, 1926, to effect by decree, and within certain limits, a whole "*programme d'ensemble.*"

Modification of the taxes was to result in redistribution of the burden, without greatly modifying the total tax yield, as follows: maximum rate of the general income tax to be reduced to 30 per cent; readjustments in death duties, etc., by simplification of assessments and suppression of excessive rates; reduction not exceeding 50 per cent in the transmission tax; increase of not

[27] France was to pay as follows: 1926–27, 4 million pounds; 1927–28, 6 million pounds; 1928–29, 8 million pounds; 1929–30, 10 million pounds; 1930–31 to 1956–57, 12½ million pounds per annum; 1957–58 to 1987–88, 14 million pounds per annum. Including accrued interest the total of the debt of France to Great Britain on March 31, 1926, stood at 647,106,000 pounds, or, deducting the French gold deposited in England, at about 600 million pounds. If payment were to be made in full on the terms on which the money had been originally lent, the annual interest charge alone would have amounted to about 30 million pounds. —*French War Debt*, (London, H. M. Stationery Office, 1926), 7 pp.

[28] *Ibid.*, p. 15.

[29] London *Times*, July 15, 1926, p. 16.

[30] *Doc. Parl.*, 1926, *Chambre*, *Sess. Ord.*, Doc. No. 3192, p. 1076 *et seq.*

more than 25 per cent in the schedule taxes; pending a new valuation, the cadastral value, for purposes of assessment under the *impôt foncier,* to be increased by 75 per cent; agricultural-profits tax also to be increased and *carnet de coupons* to be abolished.

Supplementary revenue was to be created as follows: a readjustment of specific taxes to the depreciated value of the currency, the new rates not to exceed five times the rates in force on July 1, 1914 (this clause applying primarily to stamp and registration duties, sugar, customs, colonial foodstuffs, monopoly products and post-office rates), the application of a turnover tax at a 1.3 per cent rate to export trade, and unification of its rates (save of course the *de luxe* rates) at 2 per cent on all domestic transactions; the extension of the *de luxe* rate to the export trade with certain exceptions; the transport taxes to be increased.

A sinking fund was to be created, managed by the *Caisse des Dépôts* and entrusted with the handling of interest, repayment and renewal of the *Bons de la Défense Nationale* and *Bons Ordinaires du Trésor.* The total amount of such bonds was to be fixed at 49 billion francs though temporarily the issue might exceed this maximum by 6 per cent.

The limit of issue of *Bons Ordinaires du Trésor* for working capital of the Treasury was to be reduced to 5 billions.

The Government might effect conversions and consolidations of the internal debt and also conclude conventions with the Bank of France for the reduction of the note issue.

The Government was to be authorized to undertake the following measures for the purpose of stabilizing the currency: securities and exchange credits held by the Government to be handed back to the Bank of France, which was to be authorized to purchase gold at a price to be fixed by it in agreement with the Minister of Finance, the notes issued by the Bank in exchange for gold and foreign exchange not being included within the circulation limit.

Finally, the Government was to be authorized to increase government salaries and wages by a total sum of not more than 1 billion francs, the pay in each category of officials to be raised by at least 200 per cent over the rates prevailing before 1919. Economies were also to be effected by the Government where possible.

The rest of the story is primarily political. On July 6 the Socialist Left attacked M. Caillaux at his mention of "special powers." The attack, moreover, was not confined to the Left, for when M. Blum declared that what M. Caillaux proposed amounted to no less than a violation of the Constitution, the Marin group on the Right also applauded.[31] As the *Times* correspondent remarked two days later, "the Government's political credit goes up when M. Caillaux holds forth, and down when M. Louis Marin or M. Léon Blum asks awkward questions."[32] The "special powers," were, however, to M. Caillaux's mind, the only possible instrument of successful reform. On July 16 he bluntly declared to the rather unfavorably disposed Finance Commission that "he could do nothing and attempt nothing unless he had special powers, and if he did not get them, he would resign."[33] The Commission particularly objected to M. Caillaux's wording of the "special powers" bill and substituted for it another text according to which the Finance Minister could not pass any decrees unless "deliberated upon and approved by the Council of the Ministers," and emphasized the limits within which the Government could legislate by decree.[34]

But the debate in the Chamber on July 17 soon showed that the "special powers" bill had raised not only a political, but also a personal issue. Not only was the Chamber unwilling to grant "dictatorial" powers, but it was particularly averse to giving them to M. Caillaux.

The first sensation of the day was created when M. Herriot, the president of the Chamber, appeared dressed in informal clothes and took his seat in the body of the house, as the leader of his party, and not in the presidential chair.[35] When he rose to speak it was felt that the Government was doomed. He said that the bill which the Government had proposed, with its "little

[31] London *Times*, July 8, 1926, p. 16.

[32] *Ibid.*, July 9, 1926, p. 14.

[33] *Ibid.*, July 17, 1926, p. 12.

[34] *Doc. Parl.*, 1926, *Chambre*, *Sess. Ord.*, Doc. No. 3215, p. 1044 *et seq.*

[35] London *Times*, July 19, 1926, p. 12.

cutting, sharp and peremptory clauses," [36] had wounded many republican consciences. As one who had opposed legislation by decree when proposed by M. Poincaré (in 1924) he declared that the present proposals were far more dangerous.

On the other side of the Chamber M. Louis Marin made a personal attack on M. Caillaux. "To some men," he said, "we would perhaps vote full powers. I do not wish to go back into your past, but it has indeed the inconvenience of dividing Frenchmen and that is a serious consideration when one is trying to restore confidence." [37] M. Tardieu, seconding M. Marin, read the famous "Rubicon" document which had been found among M. Caillaux's papers in Florence, and figured prominently in his trial before the Senate. This was to show that M. Caillaux was making use of the difficult situation France was in, in order to obtain those dictatorial powers for which he had striven for many years past.

In this way the Government had against it, and particularly against its Finance Minister, a hybrid majority composed of Radical-Socialists, Socialists and Communists on the one side and the conservative group of Louis Marin on the other. They defeated the Government by 288 votes against 243. The main responsibility for this defeat rested on M. Herriot.

Herriot Found Wanting, July, 1926

"The fall of the Government," wrote the *Times* on July 18, "occurring at a moment when an ordered plan recommended by non-political experts was beginning to be put into operation, has disconcerted public opinion, and in some quarters has caused dismay. The old fear of an Herriot Cabinet supported by Socialists has revived." On July 20, the day on which the Herriot Cabinet was formed, the franc fell to 235 to the pound, practically to two cents.

As the Socialists had formally refused to take part in M. Herriot's Cabinet, and had given the usual answer that they were prepared to support the Government "within the limits fixed by

[36] *Idem.*, also, *Débats*, 1926, *Chambre*, *Sess. Ord.*, p. 2964.

[37] *Ibid.*, p. 2972; also, London *Times*, July 19, 1926, p. 12.

the congresses of Grenoble and Clermont-Ferrand" — which implied a capital levy — and as a considerable section of M. Herriot's own friends disapproved of his rash decision to overthrow the Briand-Caillaux Cabinet, it was unlikely that the new ministry would survive the first vote of the Chamber.

Already on July 20 statements were appearing in the press to the effect that 250 deputies belonging to all parties, except the Socialists and the Communists (i.e., including members of M. Herriot's own party) had signed a manifesto in favor of the formation of a "Government of public safety." [38] It was clearly felt in the political world of France that if the situation was to be saved and if the parliamentary form of government was not to be finally compromised, a stable Government with national instead of party interests would have to be formed.

On July 21, the memorable day on which the franc reached the depths of 240 to the pound, Herriot and his Finance Minister appeared before the Chamber. De Monzie had the gift of prophecy; he addressed himself to the present, he said, rather than the future, "for a Minister of Finance often has only the length of a week, perhaps even less." [39] The future of this Finance Minister was to be not more than one day.

His Government fell, not upon any technical question, but because of a general lack of confidence in its ability to take quickly whatever measures were necessary. If one reads de Monzie's speech [40] outlining his fiscal plans, one finds it difficult to discover just what he had in mind. He spoke of applying the experts' plan, he mentioned foreign credits to be obtained through farming out monopolies, he hinted at a forced consolidation of the floating debt; but as Franklin-Bouillon, at that time a Radical-Socialist, put it:

I have gathered from the debate but one definite thing — that is the presentation of a *projet,* the same, apparently, which had been drawn up by the preceding Cabinet. Was it worth the trouble to make a crisis for this? [Applause from various benches; lively interruptions

[38] London *Times,* July 21, 1926, p. 14.

[39] *Débats,* 1926, *Chambre, Sess. Ord.,* p. 3020.

[40] *Ibid.,* pp. 3020–3022.

on the Extreme Left.]. . . . The country cannot be saved by a party Government; no energetic financial policy, no plan of profound reforms can succeed if you have not first transformed the atmosphere of this Chamber so that there may exist, as in Belgium, a Government composed of representatives of all the parties.[41]

A hostile demonstration took place in the streets outside the Palais-Bourbon, a demonstration, according to the London *Times* correspondent, "not only against M. Herriot himself, but against the fatuousness of the Chamber."[42] Inside the Palais-Bourbon the Government was overthrown when it asked for a general vote of confidence, by 290 to 237. From the *Journal Officiel:*[43]

[The President of the Council, followed by the members of his Cabinet, except the Minister of Finance, leaves the chamber. At the Extreme Left and on various benches at the Left, deputies arise and applaud the President of the Council.]

From the Left: *Vive Herriot!* [Applause from the Left and the Extreme Left.]

From the extreme Communist Left: *Vivent les Soviets!* [Noise from Centre and Right.]

From the Centre and Right: *Vive la France!* [Applause from the Centre and Right.]

As the sitting drew to a close in the early morning hours of July 22, the Chamber shouldered the responsibility for further inflation, and ratified a convention with the Bank of France, ceding the balance of the Morgan loan to the Bank, and authorizing it to raise its note circulation by the amount of the proceeds from this cession.[44]

Poincaré Takes Charge, July, 1926

Poincaré was called on to form a National Union Cabinet. This he did, distributing the posts among the various party leaders, Herriot himself being given the Ministry of Education.

For a time, at least, the party game was up. The nation had tired of it and was sufficiently frightened to take its medicine, if

41 *Ibid.*, p. 3025.
42 London *Times*, July 23, 1926, p. 14.
43 *Débats*, 1926, *Chambre, Sess. Ord.*, p. 3027.
44 *Ibid.*, pp. 3029–3030.

administered by a man it thoroughly trusted. The acute crisis was over.

Poincaré has described the situation he had to face when he took office: [45]

> The day the present ministry was formed, July 24, 1926, the margin over the advances [of the Bank to the State] was found to be reduced to one million, and on the morning of July 27, it was only up to 10 million francs.
>
> On July 27, in conformity with the convention of July 24, the current account of the Treasury [with the Bank] was credited with 771 million francs, the proceeds of the transfer of the balance of the Morgan loan; the margin above the advances on the morning of July 28 was 688 million francs. This margin was insufficient to provide for the end-of-the-month maturities, which absorb in general from 1,200 to 1,500 millions. The Government, however, had at no time planned a new rise of the limit of the advances of the Bank of France. Convinced that the restored confidence of the public in the credit of the State would lead to a rapid amelioration of the Treasury situation, and resolved on the other hand to obtain from Parliament without delay the vote of all the taxes necessary to reëstablish at once the balance between public revenue and expenditures, it decided that an exceptional and temporary advance should suffice the Treasury.

On July 30–31, temporary arrangements were made with private banks to loan nearly a billion francs. Thus the Treasury was tided over its embarrassing end-of-the-month shortage of current assets.[46]

The Tax Law of August 3.—Meanwhile Poincaré had drawn up his tax bill and submitted it to the Chamber Commission, which made a hurried report. Discussion in the Chamber began—and ended—on July 31.

[45] Letter to the President of the parliamentary Finance Commission, quoted in *Revue de Science et de Législation Financières*, Vol. 24, 1926, p. 674.

[46] The manner in which such advances were made was thus explained by Poincaré: " C'est dans ces conditions qu'à la date du 28 juillet le trésor a été crédité d'une somme de 88 millions correspondant, aux bordereaux d'effets remis à la Banque de France par la Caisse centrale du trésor, et que, d'autre part, le 30 et le 31 juillet, divers établissements ont présenté à l'escompte à la Banque de France, pour 930 millions d'effets. Ces avances sont, à ce jour, entièrement remboursées." *Ibid.*, p. 647.

Poincaré's *projet* shows that he was obviously concerned with the fright the French taxpayers had exhibited in their flight from the franc to foreign securities, which, commonly attributed to their panic over the uncertain future of the monetary unit, was probably due in large part to a desire to escape heavy taxation, already existent or impending.[47] So although additional taxation was needed, the taxpayer was to be wooed, not threatened — taxed where he could not escape rather than where theories of social justice might dictate. Indeed, to a large extent one may say the financial fate of France lay in the degree of willingness with which the large taxpayers faced their duty. If they wished fraudulently to avoid heavy taxes, such as the 60 per cent section of the general income tax, and the still more severe parts of inheritance and estate taxes, they could do so, to an extent that no additional raising of the rates could compensate.

Therefore the new tax law[48] took long strides in a direction which to many of the Socialists must have seemed to lead straight away from the goal they had fought for ever since the 1924 electoral campaign with its slogan of lifting the burden from indirect taxes.

The highest rate of the general income tax was cut from 60 per cent to 30 per cent. The rates of the inheritance and estate taxes were cut, and at the same time made less steeply progressive. The annual transmission tax on securities was lowered by about 40 per cent; the *carnet de coupons,* devised to check evasion of the general income tax as concerned revenue from securities, was abolished.

Then the burden of indirect taxes was raised almost everywhere. A sweeping provision gave the Government power to raise all specific taxes up to six times the pre-war rates, and decrees were soon issued, increasing almost all the indirect specific taxes (e.g., on sugar, coffee, etc.) and many of the stamp taxes. The turnover tax was set at 2 per cent for practically everyone, whole-

[47] See his remarks in the 1927 budget *projet* — *Doc. Parl.*, 1926, *Chambre, Sess. Ord.*, Doc. No. 3248, p. 26 of the *projet;* and also Chappedelaine, Finance Commission reporter, in *Débats*, 1926, *Chambre, Sess. Ord.*, p. 3082.

[48] *Cf.* article by Émile Giraud in *Revue d'Économie Politique*, Vol. 41, March–April, 1927, pp. 329–344.

saler or retailer, and its extension to exports was now made particularly noticeable by raising rates to a scale of 1.30 per cent to 12 per cent. Customs duties were raised; the wine tax was heavily increased (though to December 31, 1926 only); postal rates were increased; the automobile tax rates were marked up; and the tax on passenger and freight revenue was made heavier by applying its rates to the present transportation charges instead of to those used before the war. This is not a complete list of the additional indirect tax burdens, but it gives an idea of the widespread "*majoration*" which applied to the system.

Those fighting for more direct taxation did not come out of the debates empty-handed, however. All the schedule income-tax rates were raised — those of the land-income and securities income taxes from 12 to 18 per cent; the business-profits tax from 10 to 15 per cent; and the taxes on labor alone — i.e., on wages, non-commercial income, and agricultural profits — from 7.20 to 12 per cent (this lower rate was raised in a greater proportion than the 10 and 12 per cent rates, but the increase was not made to apply in full force to wages and non-commercial incomes of less than 40,000 francs). Finally, perhaps as a slight concession to the Socialist longing for a capital levy, a once-for-all tax of 7 per cent was laid on the first sale of real estate or of businesses. In addition, several other minor alterations were made in the tax laws.

It is clear that when the crisis came, the remedy was sought in lightening the burden on rich taxpayers, which the latter, and perhaps others too, thought unfair, and by increasing the levy on those of more moderate means, both through raising the schedule income rates and through increasing and extending indirect taxes.

Under the law as finally passed it was estimated that during the full calendar year 1927 the added indirect tax burden would bring in 6,104.3 millions, and the revised schedule (including securities income) and inheritance tax rates, 3,088.5 millions, making the annual burden newly imposed, 9,192.8 millions. For the rest of 1926, the new taxes would bring in 2,458.3 millions.[49]

The above provisions are taken from the law as finally passed,

[49] *Revue d'Économie Politique*, Vol. 41, p. 322.

but the *projet* as submitted by Poincaré had been almost the same, except, indeed, that it had not been quite so severe. Before the *projet* had gone through the Chamber Commission, several additional taxes had been grafted on to it. The resulting bill was virtually whisked through Parliament.[50]

The speedy vote was due largely to a series of drastic changes the Chamber had introduced, during July, in its rules of procedure. These culminated in the exceptional suppression of the right of amendment, passed on July 30, to apply only to the *projet* then under consideration. No individual deputy was allowed to suggest amendments to Poincaré's bill; only the Chamber Commission could do so.[51]

" Parliament effaced itself before the Government. It gave to the ministers large powers to deal successfully with the task of financial restoration. . . . Public opinion was decidedly hostile; it reproached Parliament with losing its time and energy in interminable discussion, in interpellations, in pitiless criticism which overthrew cabinets and increased the mess, without advancing the desired solution." [52] This was a long step from that December day in 1925 when the Chamber Commission had considered Loucheur's tax proposals, had kept the articles relating to fraud, and had sent the rest back to the Minister, causing his resignation.[53] Nevertheless the bill did not escape some critical comment on its rush through the Chamber. Vincent Auriol said:

This ministerial combination is nothing but a political combination where the parties of reaction have had the skill to divide the former majority; with the powerful personality of the President of the Council, aided by the tenacious skill of M. Maurice Bokanowski, one has succeeded in making triumphant a policy which the country wishes no more. [Applause on the Extreme Left and from several benches at the Left]. . . . How many times have we not had to fight these indirect taxes, not only for the social injustices they bring but also for their economic consequences, for their repercussions on the cost of living, and likewise, on inflation? [Applause on the Extreme Left.] [54]

[50] *Cf. Débats*, 1926, *Sénat*, *Sess. Ord.*, p. 1443.

[51] *Revue de Science et de Législation Financières*, Vol. 24, 1926, pp. 679–688.

[52] *Ibid.*, pp. 674–5.

[53] *Ibid.*, p. 678.

[54] *Débats*, 1926, *Chambre*, *Sess. Ord.*, p. 3083.

Auriol admitted that the general income-tax rate of 60 per cent was too high, but if it were to be reduced he wanted more, not less, means of control of tax evasion.[55]

However, Poincaré had the winning argument: "If the resources which we ask of you were not voted without delay, the State would be delayed in receiving 16 millions per day, 660,000 francs per hour, 11,000 francs per minute."[56] And he added: "I have never declared to the Commission that after these taxes I would demand others. Quite to the contrary, I indicated that I was holding firmly to the idea that this fiscal effort should be the last one."[57]

Gagged by its own amendment rule, and perhaps placated by an increase in salaries, the Chamber voted the *projet* in quick time, by 295 to 188.[58]

When the Senate met on August 3 it made even quicker work of the bill. "Gentlemen," said Henry Chéron, reporter of the Finance Commission, "Your Commission of Finances has decided to ask from you the ratification pure and simple of the financial *projet* voted by the Chamber (*Tres bien!*)"[59]

Poincaré reaffirmed his intention to check the franc's fall by a balanced budget:

> There have been . . . several theorists who say to us ". . . at the point where the franc is, it is better to let it collapse completely. We shall imitate Germany, and, on the débris of the franc, we will raise the edifice of a new money." This language has never, be it understood, been that of the Government, of any French Government whatsoever. . . . As to the indirect taxes, several of my Senate friends would, I think, have liked less diversity; they would have preferred the concentration of the main burden on the turnover tax, but here I have to take account of the well known, incontestable dislike of the other Chamber to raise this tax, and also of the positions already taken either by the experts or by preceding Governments.[60]

The Senate voted the complete *projet* the same day, 250 to 13.[61]

[55] *Débats*, 1926, *Chambre*, *Sess. Ord.*, p. 3084.
[56] *Ibid.*, p. 3087.
[57] *Ibid.*, p. 3090.
[58] *Ibid.*, p. 3115.
[59] *Débats*, 1926, *Sénat*, *Sess. Ord.*, p. 1449.
[60] *Ibid.*, p. 1459.
[61] *Ibid.*, p. 1472.

The Caisse d'Amortissement Established. — By the law of August 7, and the constitutional law of August 10, voted with much ceremony at Versailles, that part of the floating debt represented by the *Bons de la Défense Nationale* and the *Bons Ordinaires du Trésor* was removed from the Treasury's charge and taken over by an autonomous *Caisse d'Amortissement*.[62] To cover the interest payment on these bonds, and any that it might issue itself, the *Caisse* was to have the net revenues from the tobacco monopoly (which it was to manage itself) and such subventions from the general budget as might be needed; and for amortization purposes it was to have the total receipts from the inheritance and estate taxes, and the new 7 per cent tax on first sale of real estate and businesses. These revenues no longer appeared in the general budget.

The 1927 Budget. — One more major parliamentary task remained to be accomplished before the year ended. The 1927 budget had to be voted. Even more striking than the swift passage of the tax bill of August 3, was the speed with which the new budget was rushed through the Chamber and Senate. Poincaré's *projet* was dated July 27, 1926, and within five months the budget was passed.

In his *exposé des motifs*,[63] Poincaré declared his primary aims to be "achievement of budgetary equilibrium, amortization of the public debt, adoption of indispensable measures to attract or retain capital in our country."[64] He took it for granted that no one would contest the necessity of a truly balanced budget, and summed up the post-war financial history of France in one sentence: "It escapes no one that the origin of our financial difficulties resides, for a large part, in the present burden of the loans which have been imposed on us by the . . . expenses resulting from the prolonged insolvency of Germany."[65]

But what is a balanced budget? Poincaré was resolved to take the most prudent course possible; in the expenses of the

[62] See p. 242.

[63] *Projet de loi, budget général de l'exercice 1927. Chambre*, 1926, *Sess. Ord.*, Doc. No. 3248.

[64] *Ibid.*, p. 7 of the (separately printed) *projet*.

[65] *Ibid.*, p. 8.

1927 budget were included even such items as capital outlays for the postal, telephone and telegraph system, which might ordinarily be met by refunding operations or new loans, but which could not be so met now, because " the exigencies of public credit, in fact, no longer permit any appeal, even temporary, to resources from loans."[66] There were also included expenses which had formerly been considered Treasury items — e.g., the entire interest on the advances to the Bank of France.

However, he did not pretend that such debt maturities as those of the *Crédit National* bonds and the *Bons du Trésor* should be included in the budget. During 1927, over 7.5 billions of these were to fall due, but one had no way of knowing how many of these would be presented for repayment, or how many could be refunded. Provisions for amortization of various other loans were nevertheless scattered throughout the budget chapters so that Poincaré was able to calculate that of the total budget expenses of 39,382 millions, almost 3,133 millions were for repayment of the public debt. This, of course, was entirely apart from the amortization the *Caisse d'Amortissement* was supposed to accomplish. As to advances for reconstruction, they would be considered later when the payments in kind made by Germany could be calculated more accurately.

On the receipts side the total was 39,960 millions. The Finance Minister stressed the conservative evaluation of the revenue, based on the yield in 1925, when the price level was lower. Time was to justify this method for the 1927 budget. Nor did Poincaré omit to comment on the economies that were hoped for from many administrative changes made by the Government under the power of decree granted by the law of August 3, 1926, e.g., the fusion of administrations of direct and registration taxes.[67]

As intimated above, the 3 billions put in the budget for amor-

[66] *Projet de loi, budget général de l'exercice 1927. Chambre*, 1926, *Sess. Ord.*, Doc. No. 3248, p. 9.

[67] Seventy-six " economy decrees " were issued under this law between Aug. 3 and Nov. 10, 1926. *Doc. Parl.*, 1926, *Chambre, Sess. Ord.*, Doc. No. 3386, p. 1218. For a description of the more important of these, see Cahill, *Report on the Economic and Industrial Conditions in France, 1925–1926*, pp. 31–35.

tization did not complete the Government's plans for debt repayment. There were two other sources: from the payments to be made by Germany, 1,542 millions were to be taken to meet that part of the foreign commercial debt maturities not covered by the budget; and most important of all, the *Caisse d'Amortissement* was to apply the revenue from the inheritance and estate taxes and the tax on the first transfer of real estate and businesses to amortization of the *Bons de la Défense Nationale,* all of which were now in its charge. Altogether, Poincaré totalled the amortization allowances from all sources at 8,174 millions for the 1927 fiscal year.

No important tax changes were contemplated in the budget bill itself. Capital had already been frightened too much, declared the Finance Minister, by repeated elevation of tax rates, especially on income from securities, and stability of taxes was felt to be the one thing above all others necessary to attract and keep capital.[68]

Thus the 1927 budget would, if Poincaré had his way, provide for all expenses except those to be met by the *Caisse* and the Treasury out of funds which — unlike those of the past years — were practically certain to accrue to them, and a substantial reduction of the public debt would be accomplished. No more would the governors of the Bank of France have to worry about the incessant demand of the State for advances; "we have the firm intention henceforth to do away with any appeal to the Bank of France for the satisfaction of the needs of the State." [69]

The Finance Commission of the Chamber showed no disposition to tinker extensively with the 1927 budget. It made some minor changes, so that the final balance came out: receipts, 39,959 millions; expenditures, 39,260 millions. It contented itself for the most part with a hope that stabilization would take place as soon as possible. and with the remark that "We think that this [budget] will now destroy the legend, too long spread among foreigners, that the French do not pay taxes proportionate to their capacity to pay and to the financial necessities." [70] True,

[68] *Projet de budget,* 1927, pp. 26–27. [69] *Ibid.,* p. 12.

[70] *Doc. Parl.,* 1926, *Chambre, Sess. Ord.,* Doc. No. 3386, p. 1213.

the Commission made a supplementary report on November 17,[71] in which it made several minor tax alterations. But the budgetary equilibrium was not imperiled.

The Chamber, contrary to custom, deferred general discussion on the budget until it had voted the separate expense items. This took from November 13 to December 7. Representatives of the various parliamentary groups were then given their chance to comment on Poincaré's policy as a whole.

As no tax revision of importance was under discussion, the speakers concerned themselves almost entirely with the question of stabilization, and on the whole refrained from bitter attacks. Auriol, speaking for the Socialists, demanded a capital levy, with reduction of interest;[72] and Garchery expressed the Communist opinion that the business depression resulting from Poincaré's policy was ruining the working classes.[73] But the others contented themselves with wondering what the final rate of stabilization would be, and the tax structure of August 3 was not seriously attacked.

The Chamber had raised the expenditure total to 39,634 millions, but it now succeeded in raising the revenues to 40,099 millions, largely through imposing a heavier tax on foreigners' identity cards, an increase soon abandoned because of protests.[74] When the budget came back from the Senate, it was still balanced, though rather more delicately. Twice more it was sent to the upper house and returned and on December 18, 1926, the budget as a whole was voted, in its definitive form, by the Chamber, 405 to 140. Once more a French budget was voted before its fiscal year opened. Poincaré had had his way, both in method and content, for this prompt budget law did not differ in important respects from his original *projet*. There were a few tax changes, but they were of little importance compared to the budget as a whole, and its precious equilibrium. The final figures were: receipts, 39,728,310,592; expenditures, 39,541,443,921.

71 *Ibid., Sess. Extraord.*, Doc. No. 3534, p. 74.

72 *Débats*, 1926, *Chambre, Sess. Extraord.*, pp. 4129–4133.

73 *Ibid.*, pp. 4118–4122.

74 As explained in Senate report, *Doc. Parl.*, 1926, *Sénat, Sess. Extraord.*, Doc. No. 655, p. 65 *et seq.*

Local Tax Reforms. — In the exciting atmosphere of state finances, one is apt to slight a significant change in post-war French finance, a change which took place in the fall of 1926 while the franc was rising and *confiance* was being restored. The local bodies — the départements and communes — were now given a measure of freedom over their sources of revenue far greater than they had previously had. The law of August 13, 1926, authorized the transformation, and the administrative decree of December 11, 1926, gave the details.

Briefly, the reform allowed the départements to levy taxes of their own, and gave the communes greater liberty in shaping existing taxes, and in adding new ones. The départements had hitherto been unable to collect any money (with minor exceptions) from taxes other than the *centimes* added to the old state direct taxes on real estate, business and rentals. Now they were given practically the same opportunity as communes to levy taxes of their own. As to the communes, they were released from the condition of abolishing their *octrois* before establishing other taxes, and from the necessity of approval by a special law of Parliament for each tax. The kinds of taxes they might impose were still limited, however, the list being drawn up in the law of August 13, 1926. The general effect of the reform was to decentralize the local tax levy and collection, putting more responsibility on the local bodies and less on Parliament.[75]

The Situation under Control, 1927

Dramatic parliamentary scenes such as those of July, 1926, were absent in the year 1927. There was still tension between Poincaré and his opponents, but it remained tension, never breaking with the loud crash that had been heard so often in the preceding years. The " Savior of the Franc " has remained in power up to the date of writing (February, 1928),[76] and to all appearances has had his way when he has attached sufficient importance

[75] For a detailed discussion of this, see Roger Bonnard, " La Réforme des Taxes locales," in *Revue de Science et de Législation Financières*, Vol. 25, No. 2, 1927, pp. 361–384.

[76] For later developments as to stabilization, see pp. 438–446.

to having it. But on more than one occasion some parts of his financial policy have met with determined check. Each time, he did not choose to make the issue one of confidence, and it is impossible to determine whether he acted thus because he knew the opposition was too strong, or whether the opposition was strong because he acted thus.

The most important of these occasions arose from the match monopoly and customs revision. In March, 1927, the Government tried to persuade Parliament to turn the match monopoly over to a French private corporation, on the understanding that the state would receive at least the same profit it was realizing under the existing régime.[77] The plan never got beyond the Chamber Commission, which rejected it on April 6 after a brief discussion.

The Chamber discussed a proposal to " farm out " the match monopoly on May 24, May 31 and June 2. Poincaré gave his views on May 31. The Chamber rejected, 281 to 243, the Government's proposal on June 10. As Poincaré had not made the issue one of confidence in the Government, no serious political consequences followed. In October he announced that he had a new plan under consideration, which he would reveal later.[78]

Another step in Poincaré's fiscal reform which up to the present has not received the sanction of Parliament is the readjustment of the customs duties to conform to the existing price level and beyond that to meet the demands of agriculture and many new industries for protection. The history of the customs since 1914 is one of intricate and almost constant change. The import prohibitions and export restrictions of war times were followed by a system of ever rising coefficients applied to the normal tariff duties, in an effort to keep the rates up to the advancing price level.[79] For a while the Government varied the coefficients as it pleased, by decrees, but in December, 1922, Parliament again

[77] See the " projet " of the last week in March. *Doc. Parl.*, 1927, *Chambre, Sess. Ord.*, Doc. No. 4233, p. 508.

[78] *Économiste Européen*, Vol. 72, No. 1857, October 7, 1927, p. 232. For the subsequent loan by the Swedish Match Company, see p. 356.

[79] *Cf.* Chatin-Ollier, *La Politique douanière et la Stabilité dans les Relations commerciales;* and *Économiste Européen*, Vol. 71, No. 1827, March 11, 1927, p. 147.

took control, and the changes became less frequent. General increases of 30 per cent were made on April 6, 1926, and August 14, 1926, but such a blanket change did not, of course, remedy the existing maladjustments.

The Chamber began discussion of customs reform May 13, 1927, but delayed the decision on the rates. The rest of the law it passed on May 17. Parliament gave the Government power to alter certain tariff rates by decree (subject to later ratification by Parliament), in order to facilitate conclusion of the pending commercial discussions with Germany.[80]

The commercial treaty with Germany was concluded on August 17, and on August 30 about half the customs schedule was upset by new import rates — some higher, some lower. Protest from the United States led to the agreement of November 15, whereby France modified the harshness of the tariff. But the general revision of the customs schedule is still unaccomplished.

Meanwhile, the franc had been in effect stabilized at around 124 to the pound, or approximately 4 cents; the Bank of France, in December, 1926, entered the exchange market, buying when the franc went down and selling when it rose. At times, rumors circulated that Poincaré favored a further upward move for the franc, but he kept to his policy of secrecy on plans for the future. "Whatever be the results achieved," he declared, "the task is far from accomplished. Never was it truer than at present to say that nothing has been done as long as something remains to do."[81] Whenever he raised the issue of confidence in his Government, as when a certain part of the 1,591 million surplus from the 1926 budget was turned over to state employees in retroactive salary and pension increase, he was supported by the Chamber, even though the Chamber's Finance Commission might disagree.[82] He even succeeded in initiating provisional payments on the political war debt to the United States without much protest from the Chamber.

[80] *Économiste Européen*, Vol. 72, No. 1845, July 15, 1927, p. 40; *ibid.*, No. 1846, July 22, 1927, p. 56.

[81] *Ibid.*, No. 1847, July 22, 1927, p. 67. *Cf.* also, Vol. 71, May 6, 1927, pp. 275, 279.

[82] *Ibid.*, Vol. 72, Nos. 1844–45 (July 8, 15, 1927) pp. 23, 39–40.

It was a waiting game. Poincaré appeared to be waiting for the elections of 1928 before effecting legal stabilization, to have an excellent campaign issue in the threat of what might happen if the Left once again assumed control, and the Left parties appeared to be waiting too, not caring to take responsibility before that time. They were hoping that Poincaré would definitely stabilize the franc before elections.[83] He had escaped criticism by adding nothing to the tax burden after August, 1926; indeed, taxes had to some extent been reduced, if one excepts changes in the customs rates — the *taxe civique* and the higher rates on wines had not been carried over into 1927, the turnover tax was removed from exports at the beginning of the year, and the *carte d'identité* charge on foreigners was reduced.[84] If the total debt had not actually decreased (the *Caisse d'Amortissement* had floated additional bonds to secure working capital), at least the terms on which the State could borrow had become much more favorable, and the danger of constantly recurring maturities had been disposed of.[85] There was not much the opposition could clamor for, except the reduction of already existing taxes — if they dared — and immediate stabilization.

The 1928 Budget

Poincaré submitted his 1928 budget on April 7, 1927. It contained few important changes from the 1927 budget but the aggregates were higher than the previous year: receipts, 42,161 millions; expenditures, 41,528 millions. As Poincaré informed Parliament:

> Amelioration of the situation of the [State's] personnel with a fixed income, hard hit by the rise in prices; reorganization of our army and navy which harmonizes the needs of our national defense and the lightening of the obligations imposed on each citizen; maintenance and development of expenses necessary to our capital equipment, to the intensification of our agricultural production and to our commercial expansion; firm equilibrium assured without increase in taxes, through the yield

[83] *Cf.* Caillaux's speech as reported in the *New York Times*, Oct. 30, 1927.

[84] *Projet de loi, budget général de* 1928, *Doc. Parl., Chambre*, 1927, *Sess. Ord.*, Doc. No. 4310, p. ix of the *Projet*.

[85] See Poincaré's list of measures taken to meet these ends. *Ibid.*, p. xii.

of existing taxes and savings on the interest payments of the public debt — thus are summarized the general characteristics of the *projet de budget* which we submit in full confidence for your deliberation.[86]

The Finance Commission of the Chamber worked through September and October on the 1928 budget, and was apparently in complete accord with Poincaré when suddenly it decided that something had to be done about reducing transfer taxes on real estate, taxes on securities, the agricultural-profits tax, and the land tax. Poincaré, seeing a vision of his cherished budgetary equilibrium destroyed, flatly refused to agree.[87] He declared that he would make a question of confidence of any issue tending to diminish the receipts or increase the expenses of the budget, and after reconsideration, the Commission decided to let him have his way, with minor exceptions.[88]

" Never has it been more indispensable," stated Poincaré, " to complete in order and in mutual confidence a monetary and financial reform which is not finished, which can be forever compromised by imprudent action, by budgetary frivolity or prodigality, and which controls . . . the whole future of France." [89]

Poincaré reaffirmed his intention, September 26, to keep the National Union Cabinet together to complete the work of financial restoration, or to resign at once if his policy was defeated in any essential point. At the same time, Caillaux was calling attention to the extremely heavy taxes, and what seemed to him the exaggerated rate of amortization. Thus the shadow of a forthcoming struggle over the tax burden was cast on the political arena — a struggle which " may, whether one wishes it or not, become one of the most important factors in the next political battle." [90]

The Chamber Finance Commission returned from its vacation September 20, eager to know if the Government would consent to a lightening of the tax burden. It would not. If but one favor were granted, floods of others would necessarily follow.

86 *Ibid.*, p. xxvi of the *Projet*.

87 *Économiste Européen*, Vol. 72, No. 1858, Oct. 14, 1927, pp. 243–248.

88 *Ibid.*, Vol. 72, No. 1859, Oct. 21, 1927, p. 264.

89 Quoted, *ibid.*, p. 264.

90 *Revue Politique et Parlementaire*, Vol. CXXXIII, Oct. 10, 1927, p. 128.

It would not even admit a lowering of the 7 per cent tax on first sales of real estate and business, or a lightening of the burden on securities, which men of the caliber of Caillaux and de Chappedelaine publicly demanded.[91] The Commission was persuaded by Poincaré and by circumstances in general not to change any vital part of the tax system.

After all, elections were approaching. No one dared take the responsibility for what might happen if the budgetary equilibrium were disturbed and Poincaré resigned; and the Socialists apparently thought it to their advantage to keep Poincaré in power until the 1928 elections — the better to overthrow him then.[92]

The Chamber reconvened on November 3, 1927. Poincaré's waiting policy was further strengthened when Daladier, leader of the Radical-Socialist party, gave assurance that he would let the Government's experiment run its course until the May elections.[93] On November 8 the budget discussion was opened in the Chamber.

More than once Poincaré had to raise the question of confidence in the Government, when some proposal that he thought would endanger the budgetary equilibrium came to a vote.[94] "For not a single instant," remarked *Le Temps*,[95] "from the beginning to the end of the discussion . . . has the President of the Council ceased to . . . direct the course [of the budget]. . . . More than ever, perhaps, have the demands for increased expenditures and reduced revenues been multiplied. For any one to abandon these ideas from time to time, it sufficed that the question of confidence be raised." On December 11, 1927, the *projet* as a whole was voted, 392 to 125 (the Socialists and Communists voting *en bloc* in the negative) and sent to the Senate.[96] The Senate hurried through its discussion on the understanding that the general financial policy would come up for special debate in January, 1928.[97]

91 *Ibid.*, p. 130.
92 *Ibid.*, Nov. 10, 1927, p. 310.
93 *Économiste Européen,* Vol. 72, No. 1860, Oct. 28, 1927, p. 275.
94 *Ibid.*, No. 1863, Nov. 18, 1927, p. 327.
95 Dec. 13, 1927.
96 *Idem.*
97 *Ibid.*, Dec. 21, 1927.

As finally voted, on the morning of December 25 after an all-night session, the budget expenditures were set at 42,445 millions, and the receipts at 42,497 millions. A few tax changes were made, but they were unimportant — excepting a lightening of the tax on agricultural profits, the extension of the production tax system to sugar, which was now relieved of the turnover tax, and the placing of foreign registered securities on the same basis as similar French securities in relation to the transmission and conversion taxes. The first two had been inserted by the Chamber in the course of the debates; the last was sponsored by Poincaré.[98]

The Outlook

As the months have passed since the advent of the Poincaré Ministry, the precise character of France's *assainissement financière* has gradually become clear. Poincaré has "saved the franc" — or rather he has saved about one-fifth of it. He has done this by persuading the people of France that the other four-fifths were beyond salvation.

To raise the franc from the panic quotation of two cents to the present four-cent level was on its face no mean achievement. That achievement may be placed to the personal credit of M. Poincaré. His qualities and reputation marked him as preëminently the man for the task. What was required at this juncture was confidence — confidence that the policy of drift would cease, and confidence, on the other hand, that nothing "radical" would be done. Assurance on these two points probably sufficed in itself to double the value of the franc. There is truth in the aphorism, ascribed to a witty German, that "Poincaré did everything that was necessary by doing nothing at all." His value lay largely in the things he could be trusted not to do. The author of the Ruhr policy could be trusted not to allow Germany to escape the payment of all that it was possible to extract. He could be trusted not to "sell out" France to her foreign creditors. He could be trusted not to impose a capital levy or to resort to a "forced consolidation." He could be trusted not to abuse his

[98] *Économiste Européen*, Vol. 72, No. 1867, Dec. 16, 1927, p. 391.

"special powers" by doing anything "unconstitutional." Finally, he could be trusted not to waver and compromise. He did not possess Caillaux's reputation for technical competence in finance or Briand's genius for inspiring friendship and loyalty. But on technical matters he was intelligent enough to seek advice, and affection he could dispense with. For the particular task he had to do, what mattered it if no one loved him if everyone trusted him?

His positive task, of course, was to reconcile the country to the economic consequences of the policy of inflation. When all is said and done, the increase in taxation by the act of August 3, 1926, merely made it possible to cease drifting down the stream. To tax for the purpose of pushing back up stream against the current was not attempted. Taking into account the changed value of the franc, the tax collections in 1927 were only about 70 per cent greater than the tax collections in 1913.[99] Practically this entire increase[100] was required for payments of interest (in depreciated francs) to the holders of the enormous domestic debt.[101]

From the point of view of taxation and the budget, the stabilization of the franc at about one-fifth its old value offers a problem the seriousness of which depends primarily upon the future with respect to France's receipts from Germany and France's payments to England and America. These are the two great unsettled items. However averse America may be to the linking of the reparations problem with the war-debt problem, the plain fact is that France's ability to pay England and America will be vitally affected by her success in securing reparations from Germany. France has made her financial sacrifice by writing off four-fifths of the value of the franc. She sincerely believes she is now taxing herself to the limit. He would be an ingenious person indeed who could devise methods of taxing her much more heavily. There is no room in the budget for payments to England

[99] See p. 400. Even if one deflates the 1927 tax collections according to the new stabilization rate for the franc, the amount has only doubled.

[100] 15.3 billion francs.

[101] 17.1 billion francs.

and America. France hopes that reparations will provide the means to meet these obligations and besides to amortize the securities which were issued to rebuild the devastated region. "What if the reparations fail?" the French ask. Convinced that the tax system cannot be made to produce more, the only solution France can see is further inflation. Thus it may be for America to decide whether the financial history of post-war France is ended or is only beginning. Let America trust and hope that the reparations will not fail.

PART TWO

THE PUBLIC DEBT OF FRANCE

CHAPTER X

GENERAL SUMMARY OF THE PUBLIC DEBT

In view of the fact that it was by loans almost exclusively that France financed herself during both the war and the post-war period, it has been considered appropriate to describe and to analyze in considerable detail the growth, character and extent of the French debt.

Treasury Profits from Franc Depreciation. — At the end of 1926 the total public debt of France was approximately 500 billion paper francs.[1] This is equivalent to about 80 billion pre-war francs.[2] At the end of 1913 the total public debt of France was, in francs of the same value, 33.1 billions.[3] Consequently, eliminating the element of the fluctuations in the value of the franc, the debt is now only about two and one-half times what it was before the war.[4]

These statements give some conception of the comparative size of the public debt in France at the outbreak of the war and at the present time but they throw almost no light on the question as to the use France made of the borrowing method in financing the war. The benefit which France derived from loans is

[1] 497.1 billion francs.

[2] This figure, 79,346 million francs, results from the use of the *Statistique Générale* index of wholesale prices, transferred to 1913 as a base. See p. 448. If the wholesale price index of the Federal Reserve Board is used, the figure becomes 83.97 billions. According to Professor Ogburn's Cost-of-Living Index (see Volume III of this series) the figure of 95.2 billions is obtained. Deflated by means of the exchange rate, the figure is 102 billion francs.

[3] This figure, 32,594 million francs, is as of December 31. At this time the wholesale price index was 98.5 as compared with an average of 100 for 1913. To be strictly accurate the 1913 debt figure should be adjusted. The result is 33,080 million francs.

[4] Deflating with exchange rates rather than with wholesale prices, the real increase in the debt becomes approximately three times instead of two and one-half times. With the Cost-of-Living Index a result lying between these two is obtained.

by no means measured by the size of her debt to-day in deflated francs as compared with its size in 1913. She has collected from her investors vast sums, the repayment of which she is now in a position partially to escape as a result of the process of inflation.

Table 1 presents in summarized form data (the derivation of which is explained in greater detail later in this chapter) indicating that during this period France borrowed over and above reimbursements[5] some 285 billion paper francs. When these borrowings are translated into francs of pre-war value, the figures show that, as the money came to the French Treasury year by year, the Government actually received during the years 1914–1926 the equivalent of 100.4 billions of pre-war francs. If to-day France owes only 46.3 billions more in pre-war francs than she did in 1913, the difference between this amount and the 100.4 billions (the worth of her annual borrowings) is a rough measure of the extent to which the Government through inflation has in effect levied a tax primarily upon the domestic investors and indirectly upon all whose economic interests are unfavorably affected by the variations in value of the French bank notes. This figure is 54.1 billion pre-war francs.

A very substantial part of the total French debt consists of foreign borrowings, 205 billions out of a total of 497 billions of paper francs, or 32.8 billions out of a total of 79.3 billions of pre-war francs.[6] If the interest and amortization on the foreign debt can be financed from some outside source such as the Dawes Plan, the public debt which will continue as a charge on the future French budgets will amount to only 46.5 billions pre-war francs as compared with 33.1 billions in 1913. Finally, if the proposed formal legal stabilization is accomplished by a reduction in the item of advances to the State[7] by the Bank of France, amounting to 17 billion paper francs or 2.7 billion[8]

[5] It should be noted that these statements do not take into account budgetary appropriations for amortization. [6] As of December 31, 1926.

[7] *Palmade Report, Budget général, 1928, Ministère des Finances, Chambre*, p. 36.

[8] This was done, the advances to the State, as of June 21, 1928, of 17,900 million francs being completely wiped out through the surplus coming from the revaluation of the Bank's gold stock. See p. 443. However, this does not in-

TABLE 1

ANNUAL NET BORROWINGS,[a] 1914–1926

(In millions of francs. Source: Table 4)

	In Paper Francs[b]	In Pre-War Francs[c]
1914	6,257	6,154
1915	20,306	14,526
1916	29,236	15,529
1917	35,121	13,425
1918	37,226	10,976
1919	48,655	13,657
1920	37,686	7,398
1921	24,863 [d e]	7,208
1922	17,351 [d e]	5,311
1923	15,843 [d e]	3,781
1924	6,780 [d e]	1,388
1925	4,393 [d e]	799
1926	1,549 [d e f]	220
Total: 1914–1926	285,266	100,372

[a] All reimbursements are believed to have been taken into account except the budget appropriations for amortization.

[b] When deflated with exchange rates, the following figures are obtained. Attention is, however, called to the fact that until March, 1919, the rates of the French franc were artificially sustained by Great Britain and the United States. Immediately after the "unpegging" of the franc in March, 1919, there began a precipitous fall. (*Gold and Silver Inquiry* [1925], p. 327.)

	Gold Francs		Gold Francs
1914	6,275	1921	10,396
1915	17,999	1922	6,548
1916	25,958	1923	4,193
1917	31,949	1924	1,894
1918	35,416	1925	847
1919	23,981	1926	318
1920	11,468	Total	177,242

A real index of retail prices does not exist in France. The one prepared by the *Statistique Générale* and published under the name of "Indices des prix de détail" cannot be used for the present purposes, it being little more than one of foodstuffs. (See in this regard J. H. Rogers, *op. cit.*, p. 130.)

[c] According to index of wholesale prices, 1913 = 100.

[d] Includes "contrevaleur" of the emissions of "jetons métalliques."

[e] After subtraction of payments from the amortization account of the Bank of France, as follows (figures from the annual reports of the Bank of France):

1921	1,279 million francs
1922	809 " "
1923	795 " "
1924	838 " "
1925	955 " "
1926	1,322 " "

[f] Includes 2,350,000,000 francs, estimated net increase due to operations of the *Caisse d'Amortissement.*

pre-war francs, the figure of 46.5 billions is reduced to 43.8 billions. In other words, the debt charge on the French budgets of the future need be only an amount sufficiently great to cover the service on an amount of indebtedness approximately one-third (32.3 per cent) greater than that which was outstanding in 1913.

The statements made in the preceding paragraph undoubtedly give an impression of a higher degree of precision than is justifiable. The dependability of the indices used for deflation is of course open to question. Moreover, the statements made with regard to the future assume a continuance of prices and exchange rates on approximately the same level which obtained at the end of 1926. Furthermore the statements which are made regarding the necessary budgetary appropriations in the future French budgets must not be interpreted to mean that these charges may be expected to be only one-third greater than they were in 1913. The interest rate for government borrowings is now nearly double what it was before the war. As will appear from an examination of Table 2, the interest and amortization charges in the 1927 budget are more than three times those in the 1915 budget, in terms of pre-war francs. Nevertheless, it is believed that the figures quoted give an approximately correct impression both of the prospective burden of the French debt and of the extent to which France financed the war by borrowing francs of high value and repaying francs of low value.

General Statistics of the Debt. — Table 3 is a consolidated statement of the public debt showing the amounts outstanding at the end of each year. In the chapters which follow will be found a detailed discussion of the composition of each of the elements included in this table. It is helpful to study in conjunction with

---

clude the 5,930 million francs (as of June 25, 1928) of the Russian debt (see p. 220) which the *Caisse d'Amortissement* is now amortizing. Under the Young Plan, which was announced while this book was in the hands of the printer, the payments to be received by France are more than sufficient to meet the payments to England and America under the debt settlements.

Attention should also be called to the deposits of the *Caisse d'Amortissement* with the Bank of France which at the end of 1926 amounted to 1,824 million paper francs.

TABLE 2

PUBLIC DEBT BURDEN (INTEREST AND AMORTIZATION) 1913 AND 1927

(In thousands of francs)

	In Paper Francs		In Pre-War Francs	
	1913 [b]	1927 [c]	1913	1927 [a]
Total debt charges, excluding *dette viagère* ...	958,097	18,067,849	958,097	2,910,414
Dette viagère............	325,982	6,193,000	325,982	997,584
Total	1,284,079	24,260,849	1,284,079	3,907,998

[a] Deflated by index of wholesale prices, average (620.8) for 8 months only of 1927.
[b] *Compte Général* for 1914, pp. 146–148.
[c] Table 8 and footnote to p. 197.

this table the data presented in Table 4. These highly interesting figures were published in the *Report of the Committee of Experts* [9] and have been brought up to date with information furnished by the Ministry of Finance.[10] Table 4 summarizes the net results of the borrowing operations of the Treasury for the entire period under consideration. It provides a basis for drawing some general conclusions regarding the manner in which the deficits accumulated from year to year and the indebtedness increased. In fact it is the best guide available for gauging the French financial situation from year to year during the period. It does not give a complete picture of the situation because, although it does include, except for 1926, a complete statement of receipts from loans, it does not take into account the reimbursement of loans made through appropriations included in the budget [11] or as the result of drafts made upon certain minor

[9] Pp. 148–149. The same table appears also in somewhat different form in the budget *projet* of 1923, p. 91.

[10] It is only fair to the reader to state that the writer has ventured to analyze the 1926 situation with the aid of the data in this table in spite of a written warning from the Ministry of Finance that "on ne saurait, en effet, sans s'exposer à aboutir à des conclusions erronées, ajouter les chiffres de 1926 à ceux des années 1913 à 1925."

[11] Until the *Compte Général* for the years included in this period become available it will apparently be impossible to present definitive statements as to

TABLE 3

THE PUBLIC DEBT OF FRANCE[a] AT END OF EACH YEAR, 1913-1927

(In millions of paper francs. Source: See footnotes)

	Domestic Debt			Foreign[d] Debt	Total Domestic and Foreign
	Floating[b]	Funded[c]	Total		
1913	1,432	31,162	32,594	0	32,594
1914	7,462	31,966	39,428	102	39,530
1915	12,442	46,999	59,441	2,949	62,390
1916	22,014	58,183	80,197	8,783	88,980
1917	36,696	70,420	107,116	21,572	128,688
1918	46,541	97,779	144,320	28,973	173,293
1919	82,991	102,636	185,627	67,076	252,703
1920	85,573	133,599	219,172	105,149	324,321
1921	92,725	148,701	241,426	83,962	325,388
1922	93,562	160,877	254,439	97,984	352,423
1923	91,541	183,750	275,291	140,903	416,194
1924	92,362	193,147	285,509	142,858	428,367
1925	98,900	192,693	291,593	213,855	505,448
1926	96,121	195,653	291,774	205,326	497,100
1927 (Sept. 30)[e]	88,915	208,426[f]	297,341[f]	210,805[f]	508,146

[a] These figures do not include the local debt. See p. 274.

[b] From Table 9 where these totals are broken down so as to show the various elements in the floating debt. (These figures include advances by the Bank of Algeria and advances to Russia.)

[c] From Table 25.

[d] From Table 31.

[e] From *Chéron Report, Budget général, 1928, Sénat* (manuscript), the foreign political debt excepted, for which figures from Table 32 have been used and translated into francs at 124 francs to the pound sterling.

[f] These figures include the railway loans, as follows:

Domestic funded debt .... 2,602 million francs (internal loans)
Foreign debt .... 2,146 " " (foreign loans)

The "service" on these loans (interest and amortization) is entirely at the charge of the railways, which have an autonomous budget (for details see Table 7).

---

expenditures which have been made from the various budgets for amortization. The debt service provided for the "exercice 1927" ("crédits accordés") amounted to 1,513 million francs. However, this included a non-recurring item of 833 millions for the repayment of certain miscellaneous external commercial loans. Moreover, the practice of issuing securities which carry amortization requirements is one which was not followed to any great extent until the last two years. In view of these facts it seems probable that the distortion due to the absence of these figures is not important and, in any case, it is one which with our present knowledge it is impossible to correct.

accounts, such as the amortization account of the advances from the Bank of France. The figures given in Table 4 for increases and decreases in the bank advances do not check with the figures shown in Table 18 [12] for the year 1918 and the years 1920 to 1926. Inquiries made at the Ministry of Finance elicited the information that the discrepancies were due to several causes: first, the explanation lies in part in the fact that the figures of the Treasury table are as of the last day of the year, whereas the figures of Table 18 are as of the day of the last bank statement of the year. Again the Treasury table does not take into account the reductions made in the advances through drafts upon the amortization account of the Bank of France.

It must be borne in mind that Table 4 is essentially a Treasury table. A point of special significance is that the operations of the *Caisse d'Amortissement* during the last three months of 1926 are not taken into account. It is important consequently to bring the operations of the *Caisse* into the picture for the last three months of 1926. The facts with regard to its operations during this period are set forth in Table 5. The increase in the amount of the securities outstanding is shown to be 4,174 million francs. However, it should be noted that, by the end of December 1926, the *Caisse* had accumulated a cash balance at the Bank of France amounting to 1,824 million francs.[13] Presumably any deposits which the *Caisse* had to its credit with the Treasury had been taken into account in the Treasury table. It appears then that in the net the operations of the *Caisse d'Amortissement* during the period October 1 to December 1, 1926, resulted in a net increase of indebtedness amounting to about 2,350 million francs.

The data which have been presented on page 185 (Table 1) contain the writer's best estimates of the annual net borrowings taking into account the facts with regard to the *Caisse d'Amortissement* set forth above.

[12] After eliminating increases due to the Russian debt, which are not taken account of in Table 4.

[13] Amount estimated by J. H. Rogers, *op. cit.*, p. 168. See p. 255.

TABLE

TREASURY STATEMENT OF ANNUAL RECEIPTS FROM EXCEPTIONAL

(In millions of francs. Sources: 1913–1925, *Report of the*

	1913	War Period					
		1914	1915	1916	1917	1918	Total
I. Exceptional resources, 1913–1926:							
A. Internal loans:							
Perpetual loans [a]	..	.....	6,265	5,425	5,174	7,246	24,110
Bonds maturing later than one year (*emprunts à terme*)	..	465	......	......	......	......	465
Treasury paper of various maturity lengths (*bons et obligations*) (Net)	..	1,858	10,487	12,955	13,054	16,611	54,965
Deposits with the Treasury	91	.....	......	53	360	436	849
Total	91	2,323	16,752	18,433	18,588	24,293	80,389
B. External loans: [b]							
America	..	51	1,845	1,624	7,532	5,388	16,440
Great Britain	..	.....	814	6,968	3,997	1,594	13,373
Spain	..	.....	......	131	67	570	768
Switzerland	..	.....	......	......	46	164	210
Scandinavian countries	..	.....	147	47	11	......	205
Other countries	..	.....	......	30	232	979	1,241
Loans for railways of the State and of Alsace and Lorraine	..	.....	......	......	......	......	....
Total	..	51	2,806	8,800	11,885	8,695	32,237
C. Advances by the Banks of France and Algeria	..	3,925	1,150	2,350	5,160	4,680	17,265
D. Loans issued to provide funds for payment of war damages:							
Crédit National loans	..	.....	......	......	......	......	....
Annuities and bonds given to war sufferers	..	.....	......	......	......	......	....
Total	..	.....	......	......	......	......	....
Grand Total	91	6,299	20,708	29,583	35,633	37,668	129,891
II. Repayments (net) made by the Treasury, 1913–1926, not included among the budgetary expense items:							
Pre-war Treasury Paper (*bons et obligations*)	..	.....	149	......	......	......	149
Deposits with the Treasury	..	42	68	......	......	......	110
External loans [e]	..	.....	185	347	512	442	1,486
Bank advances	..	.....	......	......	......	......	....
Repayment of January 1922 *Bons du Crédit National*	..	.....	......	......	......	......	....
Repayment of July 1922 *Bons du Crédit National*	..	.....	......	......	......	......	....
Repayment of *Bons du Trésor* 3 and 5 years, 1922	..	.....	......	......	......	......	....
Repayment of *Bons du Trésor* 3, 6, and 10 years, 1923	..	.....	......	......	......	......	....
Bons de la Défense Nationale, Bons du Trésor, and *obligations*	..	.....	......	......	......	......	....
Total	..	42	402	347	512	442	1,745
III. Surplus of receipts over repayments (I minus II)	91	6,257	20,306	29,236	35,121	37,226	128,146
Subsidiary metal coinage issued [h]	..	.....	......	......	......	......	....
Estimated receipts of Treasury from reparation payments [g]	..	.....	......	......	......	......	....

[a] Net receipts, i.e., not including results of consolidation and conversion operations.
[b] Translated into francs at the average exchange rate for the year.
[c] Not including 1,070 millions of Bons de la Défense Nationale given in exchange for Crédit National bonds in November, 1921.
[d] Not taking account of the November, 1924 loan floated in the United States, the proceeds of which went to repay part of the Bank of France advances.
[e] Translated into francs at the average exchange rate for the year.
[f] Not including the repayment made by the proceeds from the loan floated in the United States in November, 1924.
[g] These figures do not represent *total* reparation payments to France; a large part does not come under

FOUR

LOANS, REIMBURSEMENT OF LOANS AND CERTAIN RESOURCES, 1913-1926

Committee of Experts, pp. 148–149; 1926, Ministry of Finance)

Post-War Period									Total 1914-1926
1919	1920	1921	1922	1923	1924	1925	1926	Total	
......	11,278	......	......	......	......	......	......	11,278	35,388
653	7,035	......	......	......	......	......	......	7,688	8,153
25,454	15,569	22,724	8,911	7,431	3,294	......	240	83,623	138,588
1,546	617	379	670	1,031	532	1,218	495	6,488	7,337
27,653	34,499	23,103	9,581	8,462	3,826	1,218	735	109,077	189,466
9,267	3,295	1,449	......	......	......[d]	......	......	14,011	30,451
1,759	205	......	......	......	412	252	......	2,628	16,001
......	78	......	......	......	......	......	......	78	846
73	......	......	......	......	......	......	......	73	283
......	......	......	......	......	......	......	......	....	205
249	......	3	......	......	......	......	......	252	1,493
......	......	......	......	......	......	......	1,103	1,103	1,103
11,348	3,578	1,452	......	......	412	252	1,103	18,145	50,382
8,370	865	......	......	......	......	14,150	1,050	24,435	41,700
3,960	3,880	1,871[e]	7,822	4,951	1,567	......	......	24,051	24,051
......	......	4,694	2,632	4,388	5,293	3,020	3,663	23,690	23,690
3,960	3,880	6,565	10,454	9,339	6,860	3,020	3,663	47,741	47,741
51,331	42,822	31,120	20,035	17,801	11,098	18,640	6,551	199,398	329,289
......	......	......	......	......	......	......	......	....	149
......	......	......	......	......	......	......	......	....	110
2,676	4,901	2,966	1,238	847	1,397	911	2,253	17,189	18,675
......	235	2,100[h]	850	604	592[f]	634	668	5,683	5,683
......	......	......	......	......	1,691	......	......	1,691	1,691
......	......	......	......	......	......	1,729	......	1,729	1,729
......	......	......	......	......	......	3,669	......	3,669	3,669
......	......	......	......	......	......	2,666[i]	3,160[j]	5,826	5,826
......	......	......	......	......	......	3,798	......	3,798	3,798
2,676	5,136	5,066	2,088	1,451	3,680	13,407	6,081	39,585	41,330
48,655	37,686	26,054	17,947	16,350	7,418	5,233	470	159,813	287,959
......	......	88	213	288	200	115	51	955	955
......	......	......	......	309	1,553	550	2,845	5,257	5,257

"Treasury receipts," and there were receipts prior to 1923, not shown here. (*Cf.* Chapter XVI). The figures above do not include 1,100 millions which belongs to the budgetary receipts of 1925. The costs attributable to the armies of occupation are not deducted from these figures.

[h] In the *Projet de loi, budget général de l'exercice 1923*, Doc. No. 4220, p. 91, this figure is given as 850 millions with the following footnote: "Déduction faite du solde créditeur du compte d'amortissement (1,250 millions)."

[i] First series.

[j] Second series.

[k] These figures represent the net benefit accruing to the Treasury as the result of the issuance of this subsidiary coinage.

TABLE 5

CAISSE D'AMORTISSEMENT. AMOUNTS OF SECURITIES OUTSTANDING AT BEGINNING AND AT END OF 1926 OPERATIONS.

(In millions of francs. Source: Tables 20 and 27)

	September 30, 1926	December 31, 1926	+ −
Bons de la Défense Nationale	46,850	49,079	+ 2,229
40-year bonds — Tobacco loan of October 1, 1926	Nil	3,013	+ 3,013
Bons Ordinaires du Trésor	1,314	246	− 1,068
	48,164	52,338	+ 4,174

Diagram II is based on the data set forth in Tables 3 and 9.

As will be shown in the detailed chapters which follow, the debt situation was in reality out of control for a considerable portion of the period under discussion. By this is meant that the Treasury was not in a position to fix or to dictate the terms under which it would receive subscriptions to loans. The need for funds was so great that practically the only possible policy was to keep on sale more or less continuously government paper of every possible type. For example, as will be clear from Diagram II, the bank advances played a far more permanent rôle than would have been desirable. Through inability to draw sufficient funds from other sources, these bank advances really became permanent loans. Again, in the case of the Treasury paper, it proved impossible to carry through refunding operations on a scale which would have kept the average level down to a reasonable figure. As a consequence, during almost the entire period, the Government had to operate in the presence of demand liabilities of tremendous volume. Thus, the Treasury paper became in a sense a permanent resource. The graph also makes clear the relative importance of foreign borrowing as compared with domestic funded debt as well as with Treasury paper and bank advances. In considering the graph, care should be taken to note

Diagram II

Component Parts of French Public Debt, and Totals, 1913–1927
(In billions of francs)

TABLE 6

THE PUBLIC DEBT OF FRANCE AS OF SEPTEMBER 30, 1927

(In millions of francs. Source: *Chéron Report, budget général*, 1928, *Sénat*. Taken from manuscript)

I. INTERNAL DEBT [a] (*Dette Intérieure*)	
1. *Dette perpétuelle*	
Rentes 3%	19,740
Rentes 5% 1915 *et* 1916	18,866
Rentes 4% 1917	8,996
Rentes 4% 1918	20,608
Rentes 6% 1920	27,604
Rentes 4% 1925	5,927
	101,741
2. *Dette amortissable*	
Rentes 3% *amortissables*	2,591
Rentes 3½% *amortissables en* 30 *ans*	11
Rentes 5% 1920 *amortissables en* 60 *ans*, not including those *rentes* which the State has since bought up (*déduction faite des rentes dont l'État est devenu propriétaire*)	11,134
Rentes 6% 1927 *amortissables en* 50 *ans*	18,220
Rentes d'Alsace et de Lorraine	73
Obligations 6% 1927 *amortissables en* 50 *ans*	4,642
Bons du Trésor 1927 *amortissables en* 15 *ans*	3,629
Bons du Trésor 1926 *amortissables en* 10 *ans*	1,285
Émissions du Crédit National:	
Obligations 1919 *amortissables en* 75 *ans*	3,932
" 1920 " " 75 "	3,960
" 1924 " " 50 "	1,604
Obligations de la Caisse Autonome d'Amortissement 1926 *amortissables en* 40 *ans*	3,013
Capital value of various annuities at the charge of the State (*Capital des annuités diverses à la charge de l'État*)	9,582
Capital value of thirty-year annuities given to war sufferers (*Capital des annuités trentenaires remises aux sinistrés*)	12,608
Capital value of ten-year annuities given to war-sufferers (*Capital des annuités décennales remises aux sinistrés*)	1,840
	78,124
3. Debt of moderate and short term for which no formal provision for amortization has been made (*Dette à moyen et court terme à échéance massive*).	
Émissions du Crédit National:	
Bons 1921 *de* 10 *à* 15 *ans*	2,978

[a] These were securities issued in France. A considerable share of these is doubtless held abroad but it was impossible to secure from the Ministry of Finance any estimate as to how large a share.

TABLE 6 (Continued)

Bons février 1922 *à* 2, 5 *et* 10 *ans*	1,644
Bons juillet 1922 *à* 3, 6, 12 *et* 18 *ans*	939
Bons janvier 1923 *à* 25 *ans*	2,984
Bons juin 1923 *à* 25 *ans*	1,990
Obligations de la Défense Nationale:	
Sexennales type 1919	150
Décennales 1919–1929	2,181
Décennales 1922–1932	254
Sexennales type 1925	3,240
Bons du Trésor à court terme:	
à 3 *et* 5 *ans* 1922	450
à 3, 6 *et* 10 *ans* 1923 (*1ère série*)	2,706
à 3, 6 *et* 10 *ans* 1923 (*2ème série*)	1,810
à 10 *ans* 1924	4,633
Permanent advances by the Bank of France (*Avances permanentes de la Banque de France*)	200 [b]
	26,159
4. Floating Debt (*Dette flottante*)	
Bons ordinaires du Trésor under the control of the Treasury (*gérés par le Trésor*)	248
Bons ordinaires du Trésor et Bons de la Défense Nationale under control of the *Caisse d'Amortissement* (*gérés par la Caisse Autonome*)	44,131
Temporary advances by the Bank of France (*Avances temporaires de la Banque de France*)	24,400 [c]
Deposits held by the Treasury (*Dépôts de fonds à la Caisse Centrale et dans les Trésoreries Générales*)	13,042
Balance due to individuals in postal check accounts (*Solde des comptes de chèques postaux* [*particuliers*])	1,288
	83,109
II. FOREIGN DEBT — COMMERCIAL (*Dette Extérieure Commerciale*)	
1. In francs at par:	
United States:	
Loan 1920	374
Loan 1921	315
Loan 1924	458
Loan of the cities of Lyons, Bordeaux, Marseilles	233
Bons remis en prix des stocks	2,110
Balance of the English-French loan	mémoire
Balance of the $5\frac{1}{2}$% loan	11

[b] This item is eliminated from the total in arriving at the figures used in the tables of aggregates. See p. 202.

[c] It should be noted that the amounts of the Russian advances have been added for the purpose of arriving at the aggregate figures in the general tables. See p. 220.

TABLE 6 (Continued)

England:	
Bonds floated in England (*Bons émis en Angleterre*)	38
Bons du Trésor deposited with the Bank of England (*remis à la Banque d'Angleterre*)	Nil
Purchase of war-stock from England (*Cession des stocks anglais*)	57
Loans granted in Holland	Nil
Loans granted in Argentine	92
Loans granted in Uruguay	16
Total in francs at par (*Total en francs au pair*)	3,704
2. External commercial debt translated into francs at 124 francs to the pound sterling. (*Contrevaleur du total de la dette extérieure commerciale en francs sur la base de la livre à 124 francs*)	18,150
III. Foreign Debt — Political (*Dette Extérieure Politique*)	
1. In francs at par (*en francs au pair*):	
Advances by the American Treasury [this item does not include interest accrued and unpaid] (*Avances de la Trésorerie américaine*)	15,194
Bons du Trésor deposited with the British Treasury; this item includes interest overdue, capitalized (*Bons du Trésor remis à la Trésorerie britannique [y compris les intérêts capitalisés]*)	17,328
Total in francs, at par	32,522
2. External political debt, translated into francs at 124 francs to the pound sterling (*Contrevaleur du total de la dette extérieure politique en francs sur la base de la livre à 124 francs*)	159,358
SUMMARY	
I. Internal Debt (*Dette Intérieure*) (in paper francs)	
1. *Dette perpétuelle*	101,741
2. *Dette amortissable*	78,124
3. Debt of moderate and short term for which no formal provision for amortization has been made (*Dette à terme à échéance massive*)	26,159
4. Floating Debt (*Dette flottante*)	83,109
	289,133
II. External Commercial Debt (*Dette Extérieure Commerciale*)	
In francs, at 124 francs to the pound sterling (*En francs sur la base de la livre à 124 francs*)	18,150
General total of the internal debt and the external commercial debt (*Total général de la dette intérieure et de la dette extérieure commerciale*)	307,283
III. External Political Debt (*Dette Extérieure Politique*)	
In francs, at 124 francs to the pound sterling (*En francs sur la base de la livre à 124 francs*)	159,358

the different scale used for the total debt and to disregard the width of the bars representing the foreign debt.

Present Status of the Debt. — The last available statement of the public debt was published in the *Chéron Report* on the 1928 budget (Senate) which gives the facts as they stood on September 30, 1927. Because of the aid it gives in the understanding of the manner in which the French classify their debt, the figures are here shown in detail (Tables 6 and 7).

TABLE 7

DEBT OF STATE RAILROADS AND ALSACE AND LORRAINE AS OF SEPTEMBER 30, 1927

(In millions of francs.)

INTERNAL DEBT (*Dette Intérieure*) (in paper francs)		
State Railroads	*Obligations* 4%	524
	Obligations 5%	924
	Obligations 6%	595
	Obligations 6%	474
	Obligations 7%	25
	Obligations 7%	60
		2,602
EXTERNAL DEBT (*Dette Extérieure*)		
1. In francs, at par (*En francs au pair*)		
State Railroads	*Obligations* 7% floated in Switzerland, 1926	60
	Obligations 7% floated in Switzerland, 1927	149
	Obligations 7% floated in Holland, 1926	62
	Obligations 7% floated in Holland, 1927	52
Railroads of Alsace and Lorraine	*Obligations* 7% floated in Switzerland, 1926	75
	Obligations 6% floated in Switzerland, 1927	40
		438
2. Translated into francs at 124 francs to the pound sterling (*Contrevaleur en francs sur la base de la livre à 124 francs*)		2,146
General Total (in paper francs)		4,748

Debt Service and Classification of Interest with Reference to Tax Exemptions — The appropriations made for 1927 to care for interest and amortization are set forth in detail in Table 8. As will be seen, the aggregate appropriations for those purposes amounted to the staggering sum of 18 billion paper francs.[14] The

[14] Including the interest charge on securities under control of the *Caisse*, but not including the "service" of the "dette viagère" (pensions, etc.) which amounted, in 1927, to 6,193 million francs.

TABLE 8

DEBT SERVICE (*CRÉDITS ACCORDÉS*) FOR THE *EXERCICE* 1927, WITH CLASSIFICATION OF THE INTEREST ACCORDING TO STATUS REGARDING EXEMPTION FROM INCOME TAX[a]

(In thousands of francs. Source: *Projet de Budget*, 1928, Vol. II, p. 32 *et seq.* Classified according to data supplied by the Ministry of Finance.)

	Amortization	Interest: Exempt from both normal and surtax	Interest: Exempt from normal tax only	Interest: Exempt from neither normal nor surtax	Interest: Total	Total amortization and interest
BUDGET:						
Rentes, 3 per cent	....	....	589,372	.....	589,372	589,372
" 5 per cent	....	....	942,822	.....	942,822	942,822
" 4 per cent, 1917	....	....	359,687	.....	359,687	359,687
" 4 per cent, 1918	....	....	823,732	.....	823,732	823,732
" 6 per cent, 1920	....	....	1,658,225	.....	1,658,225	1,658,225
" 4 per cent, 1925	....	374,500	....	.....	374,500	374,500
" 5 per cent *amortissables*, 1920	147,763	....	762,213	.....	762,213	909,976
" 3 per cent "	74,744	....	78,854	.....	78,854	153,598
Amortization of the funded debt	3,203	....	....	.....	....	3,203
Rentes 3½ per cent, *amortissables*, 1914	732	....	....	386	386	1,118
Rentes d'Alsace et de Lorraine	380	270	....	2,310	2,580	2,960
U.S. Loan, 1920 (31 francs to the dollar)	136,400	181,900	....	.....	181,900	318,300
U.S. Loan, 1921 (31 francs to the dollar)	....	141,600	....	.....	141,600	141,600
U.S. Loan, 1924 (31 francs to the dollar)	130,200	190,800	....	.....	190,800	321,000
Short-term loans made abroad (translated into francs at the current rate of exchange)	....	142,250	....	.....	142,250	142,250
Bonds given to the American Government in payment for war stocks	....	631,400	....	.....	631,400	631,400
External commercial debt[b]	833,000	....	....	.....	....	833,000
Annual payment to the *Caisse d'Amortissement*	....	490,000	....	.....	490,000	490,000
Annual payment to the *Caisse des Dépôts et Consignations* to amortize *rentes*	10,243	4,057	....	.....	4,057	14,300
Loans floated by railroads for the account of the State in 1871, 1872	502	1,996	....	.....	1,996	2,498
Payment to the Eastern Railroad for that part of its lines given to Germany by the Treaty of Frankfort	3,701	16,799	....	.....	16,799	20,500
Payment to the P.L.M. Railroad resulting from reorganization of system in 1897	915	1,632	....	.....	1,632	2,547
Payment to the Orleans Railroad resulting from reorganization of system in 1883	75	1,598	....	.....	1,598	1,673
Repayment to the *Caisse des Dépôts et Consignations* of advances made by it to the State, to be given to the *Office National du Crédit Agricole* for distribution of electricity in rural districts	....	4,000	....	.....	4,000	4,000
Repayment to the *Caisse des Dépôts et Consignations* of advances made by it to the State, to be given by the latter to certain building and loan societies	....	93,117	....	.....	93,117	93,117
Payment to the *Crédit Foncier* for part of the loans advanced by it to earthquake victims of 1909 in certain *départements*	....	295	....	.....	295	295
Obligations de la Défense Nationale	....	....	534,300	.....	534,300	534,300
Ten-year annuities given to war sufferers in payment for war damages	....	294,556	....	.....	294,556	294,556
Three- or five-year *Bons du Trésor*	....	....	259,309	.....	259,309	259,309
Three-, six-, and ten-year *Bons du Trésor*	....	....	580,929	.....	580,929	580,929
Ten-year *Bons du Trésor* of 1924	....	....	399,990	.....	399,990	399,990

[a] Does not include interest on the new loans issued during the year 1927.

[b] Does not include the provision for 1,542 million francs for amortization coming from German payments.

TABLE 8 (Continued)

	AMORTIZATION	INTEREST: EXEMPT FROM BOTH NORMAL AND SURTAX	INTEREST: EXEMPT FROM NORMAL TAX ONLY	INTEREST: EXEMPT FROM NEITHER NORMAL NOR SURTAX	INTEREST: TOTAL	TOTAL AMORTIZATION AND INTEREST
Payment to the *Crédit Foncier* for part of the loans advanced by it to flood victims of 1910	....	33	....	.....	33	33
Annual payment to Spain for certain frontier rights	....	17	....	.....	17	17
Subventions to railroads and repayment of money advanced by them to the State for capital outlays	....	39,730	....	.....	39,730	39,730
Repayment of other loans advanced to State by Railroads	....	129	....	.....	129	129
Loans floated by the *Crédit National* [c]	100,841	....	1,657,319	.....	1,657,319	1,758,160
Thirty-year annuities given to war sufferers	....	933,696	....	.....	933,696	933,696
Repurchase of canal concessions	....	198	....	.....	198	198
Floating debt of the Treasury	....	1,770,611	....	.....	1,770,611	1,770,611
Subventions granted to Alsace and Lorraine credit institutions in 1922 at time of monetary reform	....	28,358	....	.....	28,358	28,358
Reimbursements to communes of Alsace and Lorraine	....	25,388	....	.....	25,388	25,388
Interest on guarantee money deposited with the Government	....	....	....	1,772	1,772	1,772
Amortization of *rentes* received in payment of war-profits tax and included in the tax receipts thereof	70,000	....	....	.....	....	70,000
	1,512,699	5,368,930	8,646,752	4,468	14,020,150	15,532,849
Caisse d'Amortissement excess over budget credit [d]	....	2,313,000	222,000	.....	2,535,000	2,535,000
	1,512,699	7,681,930	8,868,752	4,468	16,555,150	18,067,849

[c] See footnote on p. 271.

[d] A budget credit of 490,000,000 francs is shown above. The total interest charge on the securities under the control of the *Caisse* was estimated to be 3,025,000,000 francs. (*Bons de la Défense Nationale*, 2,803,000,000 francs and the 40-year Tobacco bonds of 1926, 222,000,000 francs.) No interest was included on the small amount of *Bons Ordinaires du Trésor* (those under control of the Treasury, not those under control of the *Caisse d'Amortissement*) outstanding in 1927 (246,000,000 francs capital amount on January 1, 1927, and 150,000,000 francs on May 1, 1927), the interest on these securities being paid in advance. No amortization figure is given for the *Caisse*.

interest has been classified so as to show the degree to which it is exempt from income taxes. Approximately one-half of the total interest is entirely exempt from all income taxes, both normal (*cédulaire*) and surtaxes. Almost all of the remainder is exempt from the normal (*cédulaire*) tax.[15] The fact that these huge sums pass into the hands of the holders of the securities free of taxes to the extent indicated is of great significance when one is drawing conclusions regarding the burden of the French tax system.

Estimates for 1928 show a somewhat similar situation, the addition of the *dette viagère* charges and the amortization charges

[15] As regards details of the fiscal régime applied to the *Crédit National* issues, see footnote *d* to Table 59 and footnote *d* to Table 42.

borne by the Dawes Plan payments bringing the total up from 18.9 billions to 30 billions. In detail the estimates follow: [16]

Budget		
Interest	10,700 millions	
Amortization	3,000 "	
Total		13,700 millions
Caisse		
Interest	2,700 millions	
Amortization	2,500 "	
Total		5,200 "
Total (budget and *Caisse*)		18,900 millions
Dette viagère (budget)		7,500 "
Total		26,400 millions [17]
Amortization from the Dawes Plan		3,600 millions.
Total interest and amortization charges of the French State in 1928—26,400 millions plus 3,600 millions		30,000 millions.

The respective charges of the *dette viagère*, interest and amortization [18] are as follows:

Dette viagère	7.5 millions	
Interest	13.4 "	(10.7 are provided from the budget and 2.7 outside the budget)
Amortization	9.1 "	(3 are provided from the budget and 6.1 outside the budget)
Total	30.0 millions	

[16] *Palmade Report, loc. cit.*, pp. 17–18.

[17] This amount represents the interest and amortization charges borne by the French taxpayers.

[18] The total "crédits accordés" on the 1928 budget are 42,444,948,760 francs. (*Loi du 27 Décembre 1927 portant fixation du budget général de l'exercice 1928.*)

CHAPTER XI

THE FLOATING DEBT: I. BANK BORROWINGS

THIS chapter and the two chapters which follow are devoted to a discussion of the floating debt. The aggregate figures which emerge as the result of the analysis are shown in Table 9.

The strategy of the French credit operations, though it has become complicated in its details, was quite simple in its general outlines.

TABLE 9

FLOATING DEBT AT THE END OF EACH YEAR, 1913–1927

(In millions of francs. Sources: Tables 18, 19, and 23)

	Bank Borrowings [a]	Treasury Paper	Deposits with the Treasury and Miscellaneous Items	Total	
				In Paper Francs	In Pre-War Francs [b]
1913	0	410	1,022	1,432	1,453
1914	3,925	1,735	1,802	7,462	6,753
1915	5,705	7,006	*−169*	12,542	7,685
1916	9,225	12,618	171	22,014	10,818
1917	15,805	19,552	1,339	36,696	12,059
1918	20,891	22,915	2,735	46,541	13,192
1919	29,490	48,052	5,449	82,991	19,634
1920	30,580	50,899	4,094	85,573	19,681
1921	28,742	60,362	3,621	92,725	28,469
1922	27,955	59,070	6,537	93,562	25,853
1923	27,883	57,720	5,938	91,541	19,961
1924	27,472	56,408	8,482	92,362	18,210
1925	41,163	48,128	9,609	98,900	15,639
1926	41,576	44,449	10,096	96,121	15,343
1927	30,206 [c]	44,379 [d]	14,330 [d]	88,915	14,812

[a] Including the advances of the Bank of Algeria and the Russian advances. See pp. 220, 224.

[b] Deflated according to the index of wholesale prices, 1913 = 100. See p. 448.

[c] As of September 29, 1927.

[d] As of September 30, 1927, *Chéron Report*, *Budget général*, 1928, *Sénat*.

Advances from the Bank of France were to be counted on to supply a working fund for immediate purposes at the time of the first onslaught, and in addition to provide an ultimate refuge in an extremity. A continuous appeal was to be made to the people to invest every possible franc in short-time Treasury paper, offered for sale at thousands of convenient points like the post offices. At considerable intervals and at propitious times, long-time loans were to be issued to refund the accumulated short-time paper and to attract cash which had not been caught in the net of the short-time offerings.

In what manner, then, did the Bank of France play its double rôle as first and last line of national defense?

"Permanent" Advances of the Bank of France

First it will be well to explain and to eliminate an item of 200 million francs carried among the assets of the Bank of France under the title, "Permanent Advances to the State." This item covers sums aggregating this amount paid by the Bank to the State from time to time upon the occasion of the extension or renewal of certain of the Bank's privileges.[1] In character they resemble more closely franchise taxes than loans. They bear no interest and are to be repaid only if the charter of the Bank is cancelled.[2] The proceeds have been used to aliment the resources of certain public credit organizations, such as the *caisses de crédit agricole*. It seems improper to include them in a tabulation of the public debt of France.[3]

War Advances of the Bank of France

Legal Limitations on Advances. — Three years before the outbreak of the war, the Treasury made its plans for a financial mobilization. When the crisis came, a secret convention which had been arranged with the Bank of France on November 11,

[1] Laws of June 9, 1857; convention of March 29, 1878; law of June 13, 1878, *prorogée;* laws of November 17, 1897, December 29, 1911, and December 20, 1918.

[2] Convention of October 26, 1917, article 5.

[3] *Inventaire*, p. 55.

1911, was immediately submitted to Parliament and ratified by a law of August 5, 1914.[4] This law enabled the Treasury to borrow 2.9 billion francs from the Bank and permitted the Bank, in turn, to increase its note issue to the extent of 5.2 billion francs. Within a few months, the Treasury had borrowed the full amount permitted.[5] The limit was obligingly raised.

This process was repeated at intervals of a few months throughout the war. During the five years ended June, 1919, the legal limit of advances was increased no less than eight times, carrying it from 2.9 billion to 27 billion francs. Then, for nearly six years, there were no increases, but rather several small reductions, which, by April, 1925, had diminished the limit 4 billion francs. In the next eight months, however, covering Caillaux's term as Minister of Finance and the weeks immediately following, this reduction of 4 billions was swamped in a series of four increases aggregating 17.5 billion francs, which carried the limit to its peak of 39.5 billions. During 1926 and 1927, there have been reductions which have brought the limit down to 32 billion francs. Finally, a convention of December 28, 1927, reduced the limit to 31 billion francs.[6]

Legal Limitations on Circulation. — Closely articulated with these changes in the limit of advances to the State have been changes in the legal limit of bank-note circulation, but the changes in this limit have been ever upward, never downward. From a pre-war level of 6.8 billion francs, a height of 41 billions was reached in the six years by a series of eleven steps. Then there was a pause[7] of five years until 1925, when, by three large steps, the limit rose to 58.5 billions. Finally, in 1926, the limit was extended above this figure by flexible provisions permitting the

[4] For the arrangement with the Bank of Algeria, see p. 224.

[5] According to the Bank statement for December 10, 1914, as published in *L'Économiste Français*, the allowances on that date stood at 3.6 billion francs, although the law raising the legal limit above 2.9 billions was not passed until December 26, 1914.

[6] *Annual Report* of the Bank of France for the year 1927.

[7] Thus Fisk was able to write in 1922: "France has accomplished one important step toward stabilization in bringing the volume of her currency under control." — *French Public Finance*, p. 67.

issuance of bank notes, not to count against the legal limit, to pay for the balance of the Morgan loan taken over by the Bank and to pay for bullion and foreign exchange purchased by the Bank.

Significance of the Legal Limitations. — It is quite possible to attach too much importance to these legal limits on advances and on circulation. Diagram III pictures clearly the lively game of "touch and go" which they played. Contemplation of this chart gives the impression that certainly until the middle of 1919 the limits sprang lightly out of reach whenever the figures of actual circulation or advances approached uncomfortably close. In the case of circulation, indeed, the adjustment of the legal limit between August, 1914, and July, 1919, was made simply by decree. But during the remainder of the period, so far as circulation is concerned, and during the entire war and post-war period, so far as advances are concerned, the necessity did exist of seeking the formal consent of Parliament whenever the Treasury wished to increase its credit at the Bank or the Bank wished to increase its power to issue notes. This made it possible for opponents of the policies of a Government in power to make their opposition embarrassing. Whereas, during the war, the increases seem to have been granted automatically upon request, it is clear that the increase of July, 1919, was obtained "with great difficulty"[8] and that five years later, in 1925, the situation was even more troublesome. At that time the reluctance to ask Parliament for increases was so extreme that it led to serious irregularity and to the falsification of the published statements of the Bank.[9]

Variations in Advances. — The first of the great war loans[10] was not floated until late in 1915. But it produced only 6.3 billion francs in cash and by that time the Treasury had borrowed 7.4 billions from the Bank. Clearly the Treasury could not from this source repay the Bank for the funds advanced as a first line of defense. Indeed its needs were so pressing that it could repay

[8] Allix, *Science des Finances*, p. 320.
[9] See pp. 118, 213.
[10] See p. 264.

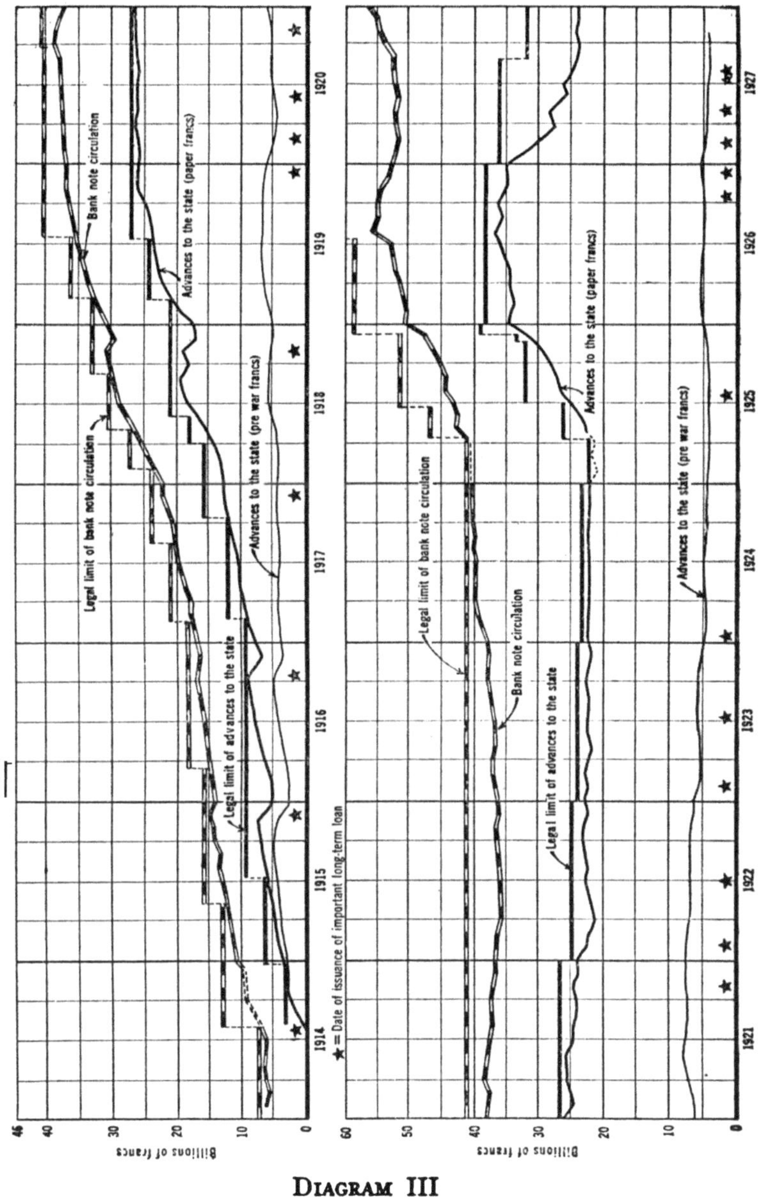

DIAGRAM III

Relationship between Legal Limit of Bank-Note Circulation and Actual Circulation, and between Legal Limit of Advances to the State and Actual Advances, 1921–1927

TABLE 10

ADVANCES TO THE TREASURY BY THE BANK OF FRANCE ON DAY OF LAST PUBLISHED BANK STATEMENT IN EACH MONTH, 1914–1927

(In millions of paper francs. Sources: *Journal Officiel* and *L'Économiste Français*)

	1914	1915	1916	1917	1918	1919	1920
January	.....	3,900	5,400	8,100	12,800	19,550	25,300
February	.....	4,400	5,700	8,800	12,950	20,500	25,800
March	.....	4,700	6,700	9,500	14,000	21,600	26,300
April	.....	5,200	7,200	9,900	15,650	22,400	25,300
May	.....	5,500	7,500	10,500	16,800	22,900	26,050
June	.....	6,000	7,900	10,600	18,450	23,250	26,000
July	.....	6,300	8,300	10,700	18,900	23,300	25,550
August	? [a]	6,300	8,400	11,200	19,150	23,600	25,800
September	2,100[b]	6,700	8,500	11,650	18,000	24,150	26,600
October	? [a]	6,900	8,600	12,150	18,800	25,450	26,600
November	3,600[c]	7,400	6,500	12,550	17,000	25,850	26,600
December	3,900	5,000	7,400	12,500	17,150	25,500	26,600

	1921	1922	1923	1924	1925	1926	1927
January	25,600	23,000	23,100	22,800	21,200[d]	34,200	32,550
February	25,600	22,500	23,200	23,100	21,900[d]	34,500	29,600
March	26,200	21,500	23,100	22,700	21,800[d]	35,000	28,150
April	26,000	22,100	22,500	22,700	23,250[d]	35,150	29,300
May	26,200	22,450	23,000	22,700	23,850	35,900	26,600
June	25,000	23,300	23,100	23,000	25,650	36,600	26,850
July	25,100	23,000	23,000	23,000	27,250	37,450	25,650
August	24,900	23,900	23,400	22,800	27,750	36,450	25,050
September	24,900	24,000	23,700	23,000	28,900	36,650	24,400
October	25,100	23,600	23,400	22,700	29,950	35,750	24,850
November	24,500	22,900	22,800	22,600	31,950	35,700	24,450
December	24,600	23,600	23,300	22,600	35,950	36,000	24,550

[a] No figures, except those shown above, have been made public for these late months of 1914. The investigator has seen the unpublished figures for this period but permission to print them could not be obtained.

[b] The figure is for October 1.

[c] The figure is for December 10.

[d] The figures during these months are not reliable. See p. 204.

TABLE 11

NOTE CIRCULATION OF THE BANK OF FRANCE ON DAY OF LAST PUBLISHED BANK STATEMENT IN EACH MONTH, 1914–1927

(In millions of paper francs. Sources: *Journal Officiel* and *L'Économiste Français*)

	1914	1915	1916	1917	1918	1919	1920
January	5,894	10,474	13,858	17,328	23,534	31,983	37,583
February	5,764	10,962	14,295	17,889	24,308	32,716	37,889
March	5,743	11,177	14,952	17,460	25,179	33,372	37,569
April	6,038	11,584	15,278	19,010	26,395	33,978	37,688
May	5,812	11,828	15,435	19,479	27,303	34,061	37,915
June	5,852	12,105	15,806	19,823	28,550	34,442	37,544
July	6,683	12,593	16,091	20,202	29,148	35,025	37,696
August	? [a]	12,050	16,425	20,569	29,434	35,090	37,905
September	9,299[b]	13,458	16,714	20,995	29,922	35,787	39,208
October	? [a]	13,868	16,589	21,705	30,782	36,974	39,084
November	9,986[c]	14,287	16,119	22,691	29,072	37,424	38,807
December	10,043	13,310	16,677	22,337	30,250	37,275	37,902

	1921	1922	1923	1924	1925	1926	1927
January	37,913	36,433	36,780	38,834	40,516[d]	50,618	52,172
February	37,808	36,151	37,055	39,345	40,792[d]	50,991	51,697
March	38,435	35,528	37.188	39,950	40,892[d]	51,492	52,385
April	38,211	35,787	36,548	39,824	43,050[d]	52,208	52,210
May	38,233	35,674	36,741	39,556	42,703	52,735	51,801
June	37,422	36,039	36,689	39,665	43,000	53,073	52,107
July	36,941	36,050	36,929	40,324	44,496	56,022	52,756
August	36,783	36,385	37,364	40,034	44,702	55,147	52,672
September	37,129	36,603	37,626	40,339	45,557	55,010	54,156
October	37,154	36,694	37,670	40,529	46,679	54,578	54,700
November	36,336	36,114	37,329	40,447	48,085	53,263	54,962
December	36,487	36,359	37,905	40,604	51,085	52,907	56,551

[a] No figures, except those shown above, have been made public for these late months of 1914.

[b] The date is October 1.

[c] The date is December 10.

[d] The figures during these months are not reliable. See p. 204.

TABLE 12

DEFLATED STATISTICS OF ADVANCES TO THE TREASURY BY THE BANK OF FRANCE ON DAY OF LAST PUBLISHED BANK STATEMENT IN EACH MONTH, 1914-1927

(In millions of pre-war francs. Figures from Table 10, deflated by use of the index of wholesale prices, 1913=100)

	1914	1915	1916	1917	1918	1919	1920
January	.....	3,264	3,127	3,757	4,092	5,624	5,197
February	.....	3,534	3,204	3,901	4,054	6,022	4,943
March	.....	3,629	3,604	4,150	4,280	6,434	4,743
April	.....	3,910	3,772	3,992	4,694	6,743	4,306
May	.....	4,068	3,939	4,102	5,007	7,044	4,736
June	.....	4,367	4,193	3,982	5,613	7,073	5,277
July	.....	4,506	4,499	3,993	5,603	6,684	5,155
August	.....	4,478	4,516	4,148	5,471	6,791	5,147
September	2,041	4,637	4,505	4,162	5,069	6,708	5,060
October	.....	4,560	4,458	4,284	5,224	6,666	5,302
November	3,374	4,657	3,293	4,280	4,750	6,383	5,774
December	3,529	3,064	3,636	4,108	4,861	6,033	6,118

	1921	1922	1923	1924	1925	1926	1927
January	6,296	7,330	5,971	4,615	4,121	5,399	5,235
February	6,783	7,343	5,500	4,249	4,252	5,428	4,687
March	7,280	6,994	5,448	4,546	4,245	5,540	4,389
April	7,491	7,045	5,426	5,044	4,534	5,407	4,605
May	7,954	7,086	5,658	4,951	4,588	5,219	4,234
June	7,692	7,169	5,653	4,943	4,727	4,957	4,313
July	7,604	7,075	5,655	4,789	4,894	4,479	4,138
August	7,516	7,216	5,664	4,784	4,980	4,737	4,054
September	7,238	7,288	5,595	4,736	5,201	4,658	4,065
October	7,576	6,995	5,565	4,566	5,233	4,757	4,230
November	7,384	6,504	5,148	4,489	5,277	5,221	.....
December	7,553	6,521	5,081	4,456	5,685	5,746	.....

TABLE 13

LEGAL LIMITS OF ADVANCES TO THE STATE BY THE BANK OF FRANCE, 1914–1927

(In millions of francs. Sources: *Inventaire*, page 48; *Journal Officiel*, *passim*)

Effective Date[a]	Legal Limit of Advances to State
August 5, 1914. (Law of that date. Convention dated November 11, 1911)	2,900
December 26, 1914[b]. (Law of that date. Convention dated September 21, 1914)[c]	6,000
July 10, 1915. (Law of that date. Convention dated May 4, 1915)	9,000
February 16, 1917. (Law of that date. Convention dated February 13, 1917)	12,000
October 4, 1917. (Law of that date. Convention dated October 2, 1917)[d]	15,000
April 5, 1918. (Law of that date. Convention dated April 4, 1918)	18,000
June 7, 1918. (Law of that date. Convention dated June 5, 1918)	21,000
March 5, 1919. (Law of that date. Convention dated February 13, 1919)	24,000
July 17, 1919. (Law of that date. Convention dated April 24, 1919)	27,000
January 1, 1922. (Law of December 31, 1920. Convention dated December 29, 1920)	25,000
January 1, 1923. (Law of December 31, 1922. Convention dated December 21, 1922)	24,000
January 1, 1924. (Law of December 27, 1923. Convention dated December 14, 1923)	23,200
January 1, 1925. (Law of December 31, 1924. Convention dated December 22, 1924)	22,000
April 15, 1925. (Law of that date. Convention dated April 7, 1925)	26,000
June 30, 1925. (Law of June 27, 1925. Convention dated June 30, 1925)	32,000
November 24, 1925. (Law of November 23, 1925. Convention dated November 24, 1925)	33,500
December 7, 1925. (Law of December 4, 1925. Convention dated December 7, 1925)	39,500
January 1, 1926. (Law of April 15, 1925 and law of December 31, 1920. Convention dated December 29, 1920)	38,500
January 1, 1927. (Law of December 31, 1920. Convention dated December 29, 1920)	36,500[e]
August 31, 1927. (Law of August 7, 1926. Convention dated June 13, 1927)	32,000
January 1, 1928. (Law of December 31, 1920. Convention of December 28, 1927)	31,000

[a] The date of the law is accepted as the effective date, except when the date of the convention is later.

[b] Germain-Martin, *Les Finances publiques de la France et la Fortune privée*, p. 131, gives this date as December 29.

[c] In Allix, *Science des Finances*, p. 322 this date is given as September 20, apparently a typographical error.

[d] Allix, *op. cit.*, p. 321, gives this date as October 20.

[e] This diminution of two billion francs has escaped notice in some quarters. Thus the *New York Times*, in its weekly article on the report of the Bank of France, for several months, gave the legal limit as 38,500,000,000 francs instead of 36,500,000,000 francs.

TABLE 14

LEGAL LIMITS OF BANK-NOTE CIRCULATION, 1914-1927

(In millions of francs. Sources: *Inventaire*, page 53; *Journal Officiel*, *passim*)

Effective Date	Legal Limit of Bank Note Circulation
December 29, 1911. (Law of that date)	6,800[a]
August 5, 1914. (Law of that date)	12,000
May 11, 1915. (Law of August 5, 1914. Decree of May 11, 1915)	15,000
March 15, 1916. (Law of August 5, 1914. Decree of March 15, 1916)	18,000
February 15, 1917. (Law of August 5, 1914. Decree of February 15, 1917)	21,000
September 10, 1917. (Law of August 5, 1914. Decree of September 10, 1917)	24,000
February 7, 1918. (Law of August 5, 1914. Decree of February 7, 1918)	27,000
May 3, 1918. (Law of August 5, 1914. Decree of May 3, 1918)	30,000
September 5, 1918[b]. (Law of August 5, 1914. Decree of September 5, 1918)	33,000
February 25, 1919. (Law of August 5, 1914. Decree of February 25, 1919)	36,000
July 17, 1919. (Law of that date)	40,000
September 28, 1920[c]. (Decree of that date)	41,000
April 15, 1925. (Law of that date)	45,000
June 27, 1925. (Law of that date)	51,000
December 4, 1925. (Law of that date)	58,500
July 22, 1926. (Law of that date)	58,500 +[d]
August 7, 1926. (Law of that date)	58,500 ++[e]

[a] In the *Projet, Budget général*, 1923, p. 54, this limit is incorrectly stated as 6,900,000,000 francs.

[b] This date is incorrectly given as September 3, 1919 by the *Gold and Silver Inquiry*, Serial 9, Vol. 1, p. 310.

[c] The law of July 31, 1920, authorized an increase of the legal limit to 43 billions by decree of the Conseil d'État, upon proposal by the Ministry of Finance. This authority, however, was not exercised in full, only 1 billion being added to the limit under its provisions. In the *Gold and Silver Inquiry* table (*loc. cit.*), 43 billions is given at this date as the legal limit.

[d] This law permitted the issuance of bank notes above the limit of 58,500 million francs to the extent of the balance of the Morgan loan taken over by the Bank from the Treasury.

[e] This law permitted additional bank notes to the extent of the bullion and foreign exchange purchased.

only about 2.4 billions.[11] Moreover, by the time five months had passed, it had become necessary to reborrow the entire payment and more besides.

When the second of the great war loans was issued, in October, 1916, the same story was repeated in a more rapid tempo. The yield in cash was 5.4 billions. The Treasury repaid the Bank only 2.1 billions.[12] Within three months all of this and more had been loaned back to the Treasury.

The third loan, launched in November, 1917, did not cause a ripple in the rising line of advances, as shown in Diagram III. Some of the later loans were accompanied by temporary reductions in advances but the Treasury fairly steadily increased its borrowings of the Bank until, when the Treaty of Versailles was signed, the figure stood at 23.25 billion francs. The Bank then had supplied a first line of defense to the extent of advancing 7.4 billions before the machinery for issuing permanent loans could be brought into operation. By the end of the war it had also supplied nearly 16 billion francs in addition which the Treasury had been unable to get from other sources. Finally, coming to the rescue again in 1925 and 1926, when the long-term bond market failed, the Bank increased this 16 billion of "extremity loans" to 30 billions. At the end of 1927, as the result of a series of operations described elsewhere,[13] the total advances by the Bank had been reduced to about 24.5 billion francs.[14]

Thus far the discussion of advances had been entirely in terms of paper francs. When deflated and stated in terms of 1913

[11] These statements are not precise, of course, being based on the monthly figures. Truchy (*Les Finances de Guerre de la France*, pp. 45–46) gives the following figures of the reimbursements of bank advances from the proceeds of loans (in billions of francs):

5% *Rentes*, 1915	2.4
5% *Rentes*, 1916	2.2
4% *Rentes*, 1917	.3
4% *Rentes*, 1918	2.5

[12] See p. 206.

[13] See p. 251.

[14] The first Bank statement issued in 1928 gives the advances as 23.9 billion francs.

francs, the advances of the Bank of France to the State (plotted at the bottom of Diagram III) show a tendency to remain remarkably constant. At the time of the first great issue of *rentes* near the end of 1914, the advances amounted to approximately 5 billion pre-war francs. In spite of the enormous increases in these advances expressed in paper francs, the total amount, expressed in pre-war francs, never reached as much as eight billions. Even during the hectic days of 1926 when the advances of paper francs rose above 37 billions, the figures in pre-war francs rode along evenly at about five billion francs. Indeed the line has remained practically level at about this figure since January, 1923. In other words that portion of the loans of the Bank to the Treasury, described above as "extremity loans," as contrasted with "first line of defense loans," actually performed the function of restating the account from time to time in such a manner as to offset in a high degree the effect of the changing value of the franc.

It is not the purpose here to suggest causal relations but merely to point out that the enormous variations in the amounts borrowed was accompanied by relatively slight variations in the real purchasing power of the Bank advances.[15] Whatever its significance may be from the point of view of the real limitations which circumscribe the utilization of bank borrowings as a source of public revenue, it is certainly an interesting fact that, during the last five years, in spite of the great variations in advances in paper francs, the Treasury continued to owe the Bank practically a constant amount of 1913 francs.

Indirect Advances. — The figures of advances of the Bank of France shown in Table 10 were taken from the bank statements published from week to week. In presenting them it is necessary to mention that it is freely acknowledged that for extended periods the Treasury availed itself of additional bank credits with the indirect and more or less irregular assistance of the Bank of France.

[15] It may be noted that the addition of the item of advances to Russia (see p. 220), would make the line even more level than it is. For a discussion of the close correlation between advances and circulation, see J. H. Rogers, *op. cit.*, p. 60 *et seq.*

The manner in which these indirect advances were made is described by Professor Rogers, as follows: [16]

> Finding the Treasury in desperate need of funds and at the same time, because of the maximum legal limit to advances from the Bank to the State, unable to secure further direct credit from the Bank of France, the Minister of Finance appealed to other banks to relieve the emergency. A number of them agreed to provide the necessary funds in return for the issue to them of short-term Treasury paper. But this important understanding was included in the agreement: that the Bank of France would at once rediscount for the banks paper in sufficient quantity to pay for the Treasury paper thus purchased — as in the cases made public it actually did on the day following the loan negotiation. Thus the Bank, although in reality lending to the Treasury, was enabled to enter the additional advances under "Portfolio" instead of under "Advances to the State" and, consequently, to fulfill the letter but not the spirit of the law.

The successive Governments had had recourse to this practice ever since 1920 and, although it called for additional issues of bank notes, the Bank of France had been able to keep the circulation within the legal limit, which was never exceeded until the early months of 1925. Seeing no other way out of the situation and unwilling to alarm public opinion by an open transgression of the legal limit (fixed at 41 billion francs by decree of September 28, 1920), the Government of M. Herriot induced the Bank of France deliberately to understate the volume of money in circulation. M. Herriot was in hopes that the volume of the currency might be brought back within the limits permitted by the law before the public became aware of the situation. But the disclosure was made in the discussions in Parliament early in April, 1925. On April 7, in the Senate, M. Bérenger plainly stated that the Bank of France had become involved in irregularities and, on the same day, M. de Monzie filed a request with the Finance Commission to increase the limits of both advances and circulation by 4 billion francs, justifying his request by stating that "these increases had for their single object the regularization of an actual situation which the Bank and the new Minister of Finance agreed should not be permitted to con-

[16] J. H. Rogers, *op. cit.*, p. 198.

tinue."[17] This announcement precipitated a violent debate in Parliament. Replying to veiled charges by M. Herriot, M. François-Marsal frankly admitted that under his own administration the private banks had been accustomed to discount a part of their commercial portfolio[18] at the Bank of France in order to make advances to the State, but he insisted that the limit of circulation had never been exceeded by the Bank of France in the course of such financing under the previous Governments. M. Poincaré also contended that when earlier Governments asked for advances outside the legal limit, they succeeded in accomplishing it by absolutely legal means.[19]

Even before the public disclosure of this situation, M. Herriot had been greeted in the Senate by shouts of "resign," and the storm which now arose precipitated the downfall of his Government. There seems to be no doubt that the admission that the Bank had published figures which it knew to be incorrect had a profound effect in undermining general confidence in the French financial situation both at home and abroad. The general feeling seems to have been well expressed by M. Bokanowski when he plaintively protested that *"de temps immémorial on avait l'habitude de croire les bilans de la Banque de France."*[20] According to the best information obtainable, the actual misstatements in the bank statements were restricted to the period of a few months between January 1 and April 16, 1925.

The advances which the Bank of France made to the Government indirectly through various private banks date back to 1920, but the existence of such borrowings appears not to have been generally recognized until the time of the debate in the Senate.[21] In the statement issued by the Bank of France on April 16, 1925,

[17] *L'Éclair,* April 8, 1925.

[18] Jèze, *Revue de Science et de Législation Financières,* 1927, p. 348, states that Treasury paper rather than commercial paper was discounted by the private banks.

[19] Jèze, *op. cit.,* 1925, p. 560.

[20] *L'Éclair,* April 10, 1925.

[21] Jèze calls attention to a mention of the "hidden" advances in a report to the Minister of Finance by M. de Mouy, Directeur du Mouvement Général des Fonds, on December 13, 1923. (*Revue de Science et de Législation Financières,* 1927, p. 348.)

after the passage of the new law establishing a new legal limit for advances, the Bank explained that the figure of 22,350 million francs, given as the amount of advances, was "without prejudice to the sum of 1,350 million francs which the Treasury still owes to various credit establishments. This amount will be indicated little by little in future statements of the Bank of France."

In his speech of February 3–4, 1928, made in the Chamber, M. Poincaré, speaking of the relations of the State and the big banks, gave an apparently complete list of figures of the indirect advances since 1920:

October, 1920	893 millions
September, 1922	300 "
December, 1922	525 "
October, 1923	525 "
March, 1924	900 "
June, 1924	1,140 "
September, 1924	1,050 "
December, 1924	1,175 "
February, 1925	1,025 "
April, 1925	700 "
November, 1925	200 "
July, 1926	905 "

Such advances, he said, had been always repaid in a very short time and bore no interest. He also added that measures had been taken in order to avoid the necessity of having recourse to such advances from private banks in the future.[22]

Variations in Circulation. — The assistance of the Treasury by the Bank of France was accompanied by a great expansion in bank notes. In the middle of 1919, when the Treaty of Versailles was signed, the loan of about 23 billion francs to the Treasury had involved an increase in the bank-note circulation of about 28 billion francs. At the end of 1927, when advances stood at about 24.5 billion francs, the increase in bank notes amounted to approximately 50 billion francs.[23]

[22] *Le Temps*, February 4–5, 1928.

[23] It is interesting to note the close correspondence between this figure and the amount which it is estimated was gained by the Government at the expense of investors in government securities.

The Cost of the Advances.—The temptation to depend upon advances from the Bank of France was doubtless accentuated by the relatively slight interest burden which such advances placed upon the Treasury. The original arrangement called for an interest payment of 1 per cent.[24] In 1917 the Bank agreed to relinquish for amortization purposes one-half of the interest accruing to its benefit.[25] Two years later,[26] when the limit was raised from 21 to 24 billions, instead of continuing the 1 per cent rate (net ½ of 1 per cent to the Bank), it was agreed that on the new increment of 3 billions, the rate should be ¾ of 1 per cent, of which one-half was to go to amortization, making the net interest rate accruing to the credit of the Bank on the increment only .375 of 1 per cent. Later in 1919,[27] when the limit was raised 3 billion more, it was stipulated that no interest at all should accrue to the benefit of the Bank, but that ¾ of 1 per cent should be credited to the amortization account. In April, 1925, by which time the limit had dropped to 22 billion, an increase in the limit of 4 billions was agreed to on condition no interest should accrue to the credit of the Bank, the entire ¾ of 1 per cent going to amortization.[28] In June, 1925,[29] when the limit was once more extended beyond 26 billions, the terms (which remained in force until December 31, 1927) entitled the Bank to benefit only to the extent of ⅕ of 1 per cent on advances beyond that figure.[30]

[24] *Projet, Budget général, 1923,* p. 54. Convention of November 11, 1911, ratified by law of August 5, 1914.

[25] Convention of October 26, 1917, ratified by law of December 20, 1918. This arrangement, whereby a part of the interest was foregone by the Bank, was accepted in lieu of payment of war-profits taxes by the Bank for the period beginning January 1, 1918. A lump sum of 200,000,000 francs was credited to the amortization account in lieu of war-profits taxes for the period before that date.

[26] Convention of February 13, 1919, ratified by law of March 5, 1919.

[27] Convention of April 24, 1919, ratified by law of July 17, 1919.

[28] Convention of April 7, 1925, ratified by law of April 15, 1925.

[29] Convention of June 30, 1925; law of June 27, 1925.

[30] It should be noted further that, under a provision of the convention of November 11, 1911, the interest accruing to the credit of the Bank was really reduced by a requirement that the Bank pay a "redevance" to the Treasury on the amount of the advances equal to ⅛ of the interest of 1 per cent specified in this convention. This reduced the interest to ⅞ of 1 per cent. In addition the Bank of France pays other taxes.

Amortization of the Advances.—It must be noted that, in addition to the interest mentioned in the preceding paragraph,[31] part of which went to amortize the debt to the Bank, the Treasury agreed to make certain additional payments to be credited to the amortization funds. Thus as early as September, 1914, the Treasury promised that from one year after the cessation of hostilities, it would begin to credit the amortization account with 2 per cent of the amount of the advances,[32] making the total of interest and amortization, 3 per cent. Even after the interest rate was cut, it was still required that this total of interest and amortization payments should not drop below 3 per cent,[33] the excess over the specified interest going to the amortization account. The situation as it now stands is summarized in Table 15.

The difficulty experienced in 1919 in securing the increase in the limit of advances from 24 to 27 billion francs has already been pointed out.[34] At this time it was understood that the increase was to be a temporary concession to be repaid from the proceeds of the next succeeding loan.[35] Circumstances, however, did not permit the Government to carry out this agreement and, in 1920, a new convention was arranged under the terms of which the State agreed to reduce the advances on January 1 of each year, beginning in 1921, by a sum of not less than 2 billion francs.[36] Toward the end of 1920, however, it became apparent that the scheduled payment of 2 billion francs could not be made and, by the convention of December 29, 1920,[37] the arrangement was postponed another year. On January 1, 1922, the limit was

[31] Note also the income of the amortization account from the accrued discounts on the Russian loans. See p. 221.

[32] Convention of September 21, 1914, ratified by law of December 26, 1914. Allix, *Science des Finances,* p. 322, is apparently incorrect when he states that these 2 per cent payments were to begin from the date of the cessation of hostilities. The date when the 3 per cent rate became effective was October 24, 1920. (*Inventaire,* p. 51; *Report of the Bank of France,* 1920.)

[33] *Inventaire,* p. 51; Allix, *op. cit.,* p. 322; *Report of Bank of France,* 1920.

[34] See p. 204.

[35] Convention of April 24, 1919, ratified by law of July 17, 1919.

[36] Convention of April 14, 1920, ratified by law of April 22, 1920.

[37] Ratified by law of December 31, 1920.

dropped 2 billion francs. In 1923 this figure was decreased by one billion francs.[38] A year later, instead of a decrease of 2 billion francs, 800 million was agreed to.[39] On January 1, 1925, the limit was reduced 1.2 billion francs,[40] bringing it to the level of 22 billions. After this date it was impossible to reduce the limit further until January 1, 1926, and, even then, the reduction amounted only to 1 billion [41] from the level of 39.5 billion which had now been reached. Finally, on January 1, 1927, the limit was reduced by the full 2 billion francs, fixing the level at 36.5 billion francs.

The arrangement regarding allotment to the amortization account was further modified by the convention of June 13, 1927,[42] to take effect on January 1, 1928. This convention provided that the Treasury should reduce the Bank advances by a sum equal to the face value (*capital nominal*) of the *obligations,* 6 per cent, *amortissables,*[43] issued in June and July, 1927, drawing on the amortization account for the difference between the face value

TABLE 15

INTEREST AND AMORTIZATION RATES APPLYING TO ADVANCES OF THE BANK OF FRANCE, VALID UNTIL DECEMBER 31, 1927[a]

Increments of Advances	Interest Accruing to the Benefit of the Bank	Amortization				Total Interest and Amortization
		In lieu of war-profits taxes	Excess interest	General rate	Total	
	Per cent	*Per cent*	*Per cent*	*Per cent*	*Per cent*	*Per cent*
First 21 billions	0.5	0.5	0.0	2.0	2.5	3.0
22d billion	0.375	0.375	0.25	2.0	2.625	3.0
23d to 25th billion	0.0	0.75	0.25	2.0	3.0	3.0
Excess over 26 billions	0.2	0.55	0.25	2.0	2.8	3.0

[a] For rates subsequent to this date, see p. 219, footnote 44.

[38] Convention of December 21, 1922, ratified by law of December 31, 1922.

[39] Convention of December 14, 1923, ratified by law of December 27, 1923.

[40] Convention of December 22, 1924, ratified by law of December 31, 1924.

[41] Convention of April 7, 1925, ratified by law of April 15, 1925.

[42] Authorized by the law of August 7, 1927.

[43] Strictly speaking, not the face value of "obligations" issued, but the face value of the "obligations" issued for cash and those issued for *Bons de la Défense Nationale,* to the extent that the "bons" were accepted for discount by the *Caisse d'Amortissement.* Not quite all of the "bons" were so accepted.

and the proceeds of the loan (*valeur d'émission*). The legal limit was to be reduced by the same amount. The Government, desiring to be able to say that this refunding of a portion of the advances into long-term obligations involved no addition to the debt service and being uncertain regarding the extent of the response to the loan, had a difficult task in fixing the future rate of interest and amortization on advances. The formula adopted results in a reduction of the total interest and amortization rate on advances from 3 per cent to about 2.5 per cent.[44] The Bank continues to receive exactly the same rates of interest as before, the reduction in the rate being at the expense of the amortization fund. From the point of view of the Bank this is, of course, satisfactory, for, from the proceeds of the loan of June and July, 1927, four and one-half billions of the advances were paid off. Since, however, the interest on the long-term *obligations* is far in excess of interest which would have accrued to the Bank on the advances which these *obligations* replaced, it is obvious that the Treasury succeeded in preventing an increase in the amount of the debt service only by reducing the amount to be credited to amortization.

The Committee of Experts, in its report submitted in 1926,[45]

[44] Article 5 of the convention of June 13, 1927, reads as follows: "Beginning with January 1, 1928, the rate of interest on the *Bons du Trésor* delivered to the Bank of France in support of its advances should be fixed in such a manner that the interest on the new maximum of advances to the State, augmented by the fixed annuity to be inserted in the general budget for the service of the 'obligations' described in article 1, shall be equal to the interest, at the rate prescribed by article 4 of the convention of September 21, 1914, on the maximum of advances at present authorized." The maximum was reduced from 36.5 to 32 billion francs and the item of 293,807,685 francs has been inserted in the 1928 budget for service on the new "obligations." On the basis of these figures the formula stipulated in the convention yields a rate of 2.5037. In his *Report* on the budget of the Finance Ministry for 1928, pp. 112–113, M. Palmade gives the following formula:

$\frac{X}{100} \times 32{,}000$ millions $+ 293{,}807{,}685 = \frac{3}{100} \times 36{,}500$ millions; $X = 2.55$ per cent.

It should be noted that X really equals 2.5037, as given above. There may be a provision, however, for evening to the next higher half of one-tenth of one per cent.

[45] Pp. 37–38. An examination of the budget *projets* indicates that a part of the interest on advances which accrued to the credit of the Bank was made a budgetary charge in the years prior to 1926.

asserted that interest on the advances of the Bank of France was still being considered a Treasury rather than a budgetary charge and recommended that this interest be entirely assumed by the budget. By a supplementary credit [46] granted in August, 1926, the charge was inserted in the 1926 budget. Since that date the budget allowances have covered the full three per cent on the advances.

The Advances to Russia

In addition to the advances to the State already described, there is a closely analogous and highly significant item listed among the assets in the Bank's balance sheet as "*Bons du Trésor Français* discounted for advances of the State to foreign governments." [47] This item is the result of a series of loans made to Russia during the course of hostilities, amounting in the aggregate to the capital sum of 3,241 million francs.[48]

Bank and Treasury Relations in the Russian Advances. — The procedure followed in making these loans to Russia is interesting. The Bank advanced the funds to the Russian Government, the understanding being that it should receive interest from Russia for the loan at its current discount rate. The French Treasury acted as guarantor by depositing with the Bank its *Bons du Trésor,* renewable at three-month intervals. Russia got the money, the Bank secured possession of the French *Bons du Trésor,* and the French Treasury, when Russia collapsed, was left with a real instead of a contingent liability, *a liability which steadily accumulated interest* from month to month. Even yet, however, the French Treasury has not written the item off as a bad debt and formally assumed the liability.[49]

Peculiar Treatment of Amortization Allowances. — At the time of the Russian collapse, in 1917,[50] the Bank agreed that 85 per cent of the interest which was accumulating on the Russian

[46] Law of August 3, 1926.

[47] Laws of April 1 and December 29, 1915; February 15 and August 4, 1917; March 22 and December 20, 1918.

[48] 3,240,504,737.68 francs. *Le Temps,* February 27, 1927.

[49] For recent developments, see below, p. 444, footnote *e*.

[50] Convention of October 26, 1917, ratified by the law of December 20, 1918.

loan should go to the amortization fund, retaining only 15 per cent for itself. However, the transaction was handled in a very peculiar manner in the accounts. Each week the published balance sheet of the Bank shows this item of the Russian loan among its assets entered at a higher figure than the previous week, the weekly increase corresponding to the accumulated interest. At the same time, on the liability side, each week the amortization account grows, until some date, usually the end of the year, when the account is drawn upon to reduce, not the amount of the Russian loan item on the asset side, but interestingly enough, another and a distinct asset, the advances to the French Treasury. Thus the Russian debt item has steadily grown until the original capital sum of 3,241 million francs now (on December 29, 1927) stands as a Bank asset of 5,881 million francs. The Treasury has paid nothing to the Bank as interest on this loan but nevertheless the Bank appears to have credited the amortization account with 85 per cent of the increase from 3,241 to 5,881 millions (or 2,244,000,000 francs) and then reduced advances to the State by that amount.[51] In other words, the accruing book-interest on a bad Russian debt, which does not fall within the legal limitation upon Bank accommodations to the State, has been used to reduce the item of advances to the State, which has a legal limit. Moreover, this legal limit has been so closely approached that, many times during the period, the addition of an item of this size would have caused serious embarrassment. Thus by a bit of financial legerdemain, the Bank has in form increased its loans to Russia (which the French Treasury almost without doubt will ultimately have to pay) and has devoted the proceeds to reducing the French Treasury's debt to the Bank. The Russian debt, in effect, has been assumed to be good and the accruing interest on this debt, in spite of the fact that in all probability it will never be collected,

[51] Except for a portion used to meet the losses of the Bank on account of the guarantees made by the Bank in connection with the moratorium declared at the outbreak of the war. *Inventaire,* p. 52. Convention of September 21, 1914, ratified by the law of December 26, 1914; convention of October 26, 1917, ratified by the law of December 20, 1918.

has been used to reduce the debt of the French Treasury to the Bank. Or, assuming Russia to have dropped out entirely as a factor in the situation, the French Treasury has been steadily borrowing from the Bank, under cover of this Russian item, to pay its debt to the Bank.

All in all, this history of the advances to Russia is a rather astonishing episode. The temptation was doubtless strong to adopt the particular procedure which was followed. But the practical effect has certainly been to obscure the true state of affairs and to make it appear much more favorable than it actually is. When the French themselves describe the situation as "purely fictitious," [52] all will agree they do not use extravagant language. While the device of borrowing from Peter to pay Paul has long been recognized in public and private finance, it has remained for the French Treasury to evolve the device of borrowing from Peter to pay Peter!

The Convention of February 3, 1927.—The anomalous character of this transaction seems to have been fully appreciated by the Treasury and the Bank.[53] Early in 1927, the first time since the end of the war that a comfortable margin below the legal limit of advances was available, steps were taken to adjust the situation. On February 3, 1927, a convention was arranged with the Bank (ratified by law of March, 1928) proposing to abandon the process of pyramiding the interest, to stabilize the item on the books of the Bank at the level reached on the date of ratification, to fix the interest rate at 1 per cent, one-half of the interest going to the amortization account, and to recover from the Bank for the benefit of that account any excess of interest which has accrued to the Bank since January 27, 1918, above the proposed new level.[54] It was estimated in February,

[52] Report of M. de Chappedelaine. *Le Temps*, October 30, 1927.

[53] The Committee of Experts (*Rapport*, p. 37) remarked that "it would be well to make uniform the conditions applying to the account of the new advances to the State and to the account of the 'Bons du Trésor Français escomptés pour avances de l'État aux gouvernements étrangers.'"

[54] M. Palmade (Report on the 1928 budget of the Ministry of Finance p. 36) states that one should add this Russian loan item to the advances to the State. See also Jèze, *Revue de Science et de Législation Financières*, 1927, p. 347.

1927, that this excess interest would amount to approximately 111 million francs.[55]

The Advances to Russia Considered as Additional Advances to the State.—The securities deposited with the Bank in connection with this transaction apparently are not included under the heading of *Bons du Trésor* in the general debt statement. So far as the French Treasury accounts are concerned, the Russian debt is still a sound asset. The prospect of collection is certainly extremely remote and a French debt statement which ignores it is open to severe criticism.

In view of the fact that the convention of February 3, 1927, has the practical effect of placing the Russian advances on substantially the same basis as the war advances to the State, it seems proper so to consider them in compiling a general statement of the French debt. This is the course which has been followed. The amounts of the Russian advances as they stood in the Bank accounts at the end of each year are shown in Table 16.

TABLE 16

ADVANCES OF THE BANK OF FRANCE TO RUSSIA (FRENCH *BONS DU TRÉSOR* DISCOUNTED FOR ADVANCES OF THE STATE TO FOREIGN GOVERNMENTS) ON DAY OF LAST PUBLISHED STATEMENT IN EACH YEAR, 1915–1927

(In millions of paper francs. Source: *Journal Officiel*)

1915	630
1916	1,800
1917	3,220
1918	3,526
1919	3,755
1920	3,980
1921	4,142
1922	4,355
1923	4,583
1924	4,872
1925	5,213
1926	5,576
1927	5,881

[55] *Le Temps*, February 27, 1927.

ADVANCES OF THE BANK OF ALGERIA

In addition to the advances by the Bank of France, the Treasury received advances, relatively insignificant in amount, from the Bank of Algeria during the period 1915 to 1920. As the Treasury officials explain the situation, the Bank of Algeria acts as fiscal agent for the Treasury in Algeria and honors drafts for accounts payable in that country, the Treasury transferring funds as soon as possible through the Bank of France to correct the situation when overdrafts occur. It is known, however, that the arrangement of November, 1911,[56] in addition to providing for accommodations at the Bank of France in case of mobilization, included a promise from the Bank of Algeria to make advances to the Treasury to the extent of 100 million francs. The amounts of these advances at the end of each year are shown in Table 17. They must be included in any comprehensive statement of the public debt.

TABLE 17

ADVANCES TO THE TREASURY BY THE BANK OF ALGERIA ON DECEMBER 31 OF EACH YEAR, 1915–1920

(In millions of paper francs. Source: *Rapport du Comité des Experts*, page 150)

1914	25
1915	75
1916	25
1917	85
1918	215
1919	235
1920	0

AGGREGATE BANK BORROWINGS OF THE FRENCH TREASURY

It is now possible to consolidate the figures developed in this chapter. In Table 18 totals are presented, which include (1) figures ordinarily given as the war advances of the Bank of France, (2) the Russian advances, and (3) the advances of the Bank of Algeria.

[56] See pp. 202–203.

TABLE 18

AGGREGATE BANK BORROWINGS OF THE FRENCH TREASURY ON DAY OF THE LAST PUBLISHED STATEMENT OF THE BANK OF FRANCE IN EACH YEAR, 1915–1927

(In millions of paper francs. Source: Tables 10, 16, and 17)

1914	3,925
1915	5,705
1916	9,225
1917	15,805
1918	20,891
1919	29,490
1920	30,580
1921	28,742
1922	27,955
1923	27,883
1924	27,472
1925	41,163
1926	41,576
1927	30,431

CHAPTER XII

THE FLOATING DEBT: II. TREASURY PAPER

THE history of the use of short-term Treasury paper constitutes one of the most interesting chapters of the recent French financial history. The magnitude of the resources which the Treasury succeeded in mobilizing by the use of such paper is truly remarkable.

The Pre-War Situation. — The use of the short-term Treasury paper is a device of long standing in France as in other modern countries. Operating under an *ordonnance* passed on August 4, 1824 [1] the French Treasury had been accustomed to supply its temporary needs by the issuance of such paper,[2] termed in the early days *bons royaux* and in the later days *Bons du Trésor.*[3] The term of such paper was restricted to one year and the interest rate was varied from time to time in accordance with the conditions of the market in such a manner as to supply the Treasury with the precise sums needed to meet budgetary expenditures pending the collection of taxes. It was customary for Parliament to specify a limit for the Treasury to observe in contracting liabilities of this kind. At the outbreak of the war this limit stood at 600 million [4] and the amount of the *Bons du Trésor* actually outstanding had reached the rather unusually high figure of 434.5 million francs.[5]

[1] Allix, *Science des Finances,* p. 309.

[2] Truchy, *Les Finances de Guerre de la France,* p. 57.

[3] In this chapter the term *Bons du Trésor* is to be understood as referring to securities of this name, with a maximum term of one year. Such paper came to be described in the French documents as *Bons Ordinaires du Trésor.* Very recently the term *Bons du Trésor* has also been applied to securities issued for longer terms. This later portion of the French debt is discussed in Chapter XIV.

[4] *Loi de Finances* of July 15, 1914, art. 75.

[5] Jèze, *Revue de Science et de Législation Financières,* 1927, p. 521.

The clientèle upon which the Treasury depended to absorb this paper consisted of a rather small and specialized group of large business and financial institutions, which had become accustomed to utilize this method of employing their surplus working capital. The outbreak of the war, bringing with it a moratorium, practically destroyed for the time being the demand for the *Bons du Trésor* from this old clientèle.

The Creation of the Bons de la Défense Nationale.— It was in the face of this situation that M. Ribot evolved the brilliant plan which was to transform a broken sword into a new weapon of tremendous power. If the few old customers of the *Bons du Trésor* were unable to buy, he suggested that an entirely new market be sought by changing the terms and conditions attached to the bonds, so as to make them appeal to the great masses of the French population.[6] Perhaps most important of all was the change in the very name of the bonds, the new securities being christened *Bons de la Défense Nationale,* a title which in itself had a tremendous appeal. In the next place their interest rate was fixed at 5 per cent,[7] a rate which at the time seemed very high for French government securities. The terms of the paper were made 3 months, 6 months and 1 year. The securities were issued in denominations as low as 100 francs. The greatest pains were taken to render subscriptions easy. In addition to the ordinary outlets through the banks, stocks of the paper were kept at all of the post offices and all of the numerous local offices of the Finance Ministry, where they could be purchased and redeemed with as little formality as buying a loaf of bread. No tracks were left to cause embarrassment with some future tax collector, not even a signature being required in connection with the transaction. The interest was paid in advance in the form of a discount, in the same manner as the War Savings Certificates in the United States. Whereas the old *Bons du Trésor* had carried with them no privileges with respect to discounts or advances of the Bank of France, the new *Bons de la Défense Nationale* received special treatment

[6] *Report to the President of the Republic by the Prime Minister, the Minister of Finance and the Minister of Commerce,* dated September 13, 1914.

[7] *Décret* and *arrêté* of September 13, 1914.

at the Bank. The bearer of paper due within three months could call upon the Bank of France at any time for the face value minus the discount at the prevailing bank rate. The bearer of paper with a longer maturity could secure a loan from the Bank to the extent of 80 per cent of its face value.[8] Furthermore the paper was given special preferences in connection with any future loans. A campaign of publicity was inaugurated appealing to the people to subscribe and, as a final touch, the government employees and others who issued the bonds were given a commission on their sales to stimulate their avidity. These various terms and conditions were subjected to subsequent modifications,[9] but the general characteristics of the *Bons de la Défense Nationale,* as established under the decree of September 13, 1914, were retained throughout the entire period.

It was expected that the new *Bons de la Défense Nationale* would entirely replace the old *Bons du Trésor.*[10] However, it was discovered that, even with their apparently less attractive characteristics, including lower interest rates and lack of privileges with respect to rediscount and advances, there still persisted a demand for paper of the old type. The French Treasury promptly arranged to continue the issuance of the old *Bons du Trésor* to those who desired them. Thus it happens that throughout the period the French short-time Treasury paper consisted of these two types of securites, differing considerably in their precise terms and conditions, but being essentially alike in character. However, the *Bons du Trésor* played a relatively minor rôle. During the war, the amount outstanding never exceeded 750 million francs. Beginning in 1918 when the interest rate on the shorter-term *bons* was raised and the habitual clients were once more in a position to subscribe, the demand for them became much more substantial, the amount rising above 5 billion francs on several occasions. This post-war demand, it is suspected, came to a

[8] For a more complete description of the characteristics of the *Bons de la Défense Nationale,* see Jèze, *Revue de Science et de Législation Financières,* 1927, pp. 502–503.

[9] See p. 238.

[10] By a literal reading of the decree of September 13, 1914, the *Bons du Trésor* should have disappeared.

considerable extent from the private banks which coöperated in the arrangement to enable the Bank of France to make indirect advances to the State.

Statistics of Treasury Paper. — The response from the country to the new *Bons de la Défense Nationale* was very large. "It seems that not even the Minister of Finance who created them was able to picture clearly the brilliant success to which they were destined."[11] The francs literally poured into the Treasury from thousands of wickets opened throughout the country. By the end of 1914 more than 1.5 billion francs were outstanding and, by the end of 1915, the figure had reached nearly 7 billion. The issuance of these huge amounts largely in small denominations created a problem of accounting and control which the Treasury, with its forces diluted by the military mobilization, was unable immediately to solve.[12] The records fell into a condition of confusion, with the result that even to-day there is doubt as to the trustworthiness of the statistics which are currently published by the Treasury regarding the amounts of these securities outstanding at various times during and after the war. Truchy, for example, presents his statistics with the arresting remark, "*Il est nécessaire de faire observer que les chiffres ne peuvent être considérés comme exacts qu'à quelques milliards près.*"[13]

Early in March, 1922, the country was astounded to learn from a statement included in the budget *projet*[14] that the amount of the *Bons de la Défense Nationale*, in circulation on December 31 preceding, which had been stated to be 65,420 millions, was in reality only about 58,500 million francs. The Minister of Finance stated that the "discrepancy which existed in the total amount of the bonds in circulation is explained by the haste with which it was necessary to organize in 1914, without adequate personnel and supplies, an emission of quantities of securities without precedent, involving entirely new practical problems."

11 Truchy, *Les Finances de Guerre de la France*, p. 59.

12 See p. 24.

13 *Ibid.*, p. 60.

14 *Projet de loi portant fixation du budget général de l'exercice 1923*, Doc. No. 4220, p. 86.

At the Ministry of Finance it was explained that it was customary to make up the statistics by tabulating the coupons which were returned to Paris by the issuing offices and that in the confusion of taking off the figures from the bales of stubs, there was a great deal of double counting which became apparent only later when the paper was renewed or reimbursed.

The effect of the discovery of this huge discrepancy, even though it was in favor of and not against the Government, created an unfortunate impression. It gave rise to wild rumors of huge losses to the Treasury because of the looseness with which the accounts had been kept, but M. Clémentel effectively disposed of these rumors in 1924 by an official statement that a verification by the *Cour des Comptes* of the records for the period 1914–1920 had revealed only a single case of fraudulent payment amounting to 172,000 francs in a total of 230 billions.[15]

Under the circumstances it is not surprising that almost every published statement differs from every other. Probably the most dependable data are those which were presented in the *Experts' Report* in 1926. These are given in Table 19, together with data recently made public relating to the years 1926 and 1927.

For the purposes of studying the interaction of the various elements in the floating debt, it is helpful to have available the figures of Treasury paper outstanding at more frequent intervals than one year. In the Chappedelaine report on the budget of 1928, monthly figures are given for the period from July, 1926, to August, 1927.[16] Moreover, in two documents by Georges Lachapelle, published under the imprint of the *Société d'Études et d'Informations Économiques*,[17] monthly figures are given for the period 1914 to 1926. The Lachapelle data do not agree with the official Chappedelaine data for the few months during which they overlap and they do not entirely agree with the data given in the *Experts' Report* for December, 1918, 1920, and 1921. Lachapelle gives no specific reference to the source of his data,

[15] *Inventaire*, p. 43.

[16] Except that no figures are given for August, 1926.

[17] *L'Évolution de la Circulation, des Changes, des Prix et de l'Émission des Valeurs à court terme du Trésor de 1914 à 1926* (1926).

TABLE 19

AMOUNTS OF OUTSTANDING TREASURY PAPER (*BONS DE LA DÉFENSE NATIONALE* AND *BONS ORDINAIRES DU TRÉSOR*) AT END OF EACH YEAR, 1913–1927

In millions of francs. Sources: 1913–1925, *Experts' Report*, page 150; 1926, *Chappedelaine Report*, *Budget 1928*, *Chambre*, page xxxiii; 1927, *Chéron Report*, *Budget 1928*, *Sénat* (manuscript)

	Bons de la Défense Nationale	*Bons Ordinaires du Trésor*	TOTAL
1913	0	410	410
1914	1,619	116	1,735
1915	6,963	43	7,006
1916	12,574	44	12,618
1917	19,522	30	19,552
1918	22,335	580	22,915
1919	46,140	1,912	48,052
1920	48,938	1,961	50,899
1921	58,420	1,942	60,362
1922	56,431	2,639	59,070
1923	54,723	2,997	57,720
1924	54,538	1,870	56,408
1925	45,735	2,393	48,128
1926	([a])	([a])	49,449
1927 (Sept. 30)	([b])	([b])	44,379[b]

[a] The Ministry of Finance furnished the writer with these figures as of December 31, 1926 (in millions of francs):

Bons de la Défense Nationale	49,075
Bons du Trésor under control of the *Caisse*	246
Bons du Trésor under control of the Treasury	123
Total	49,444

It will be noted that the total is 5 million francs less than that given in the *Chappedelaine Report*. All these securities except 123 millions of *Bons du Trésor* were in the hands of the *Caisse d'Amortissement*.

[b] The *Bons du Trésor* under control of the Treasury outstanding at this date amounted to 248 millions. The old *Bons du Trésor* and the *Bons de la Défense Nationale* outstanding (all in the hands of the *Caisse d'Amortissement*) amounted to 44,131 million francs.

contenting himself with the statement that they "*ont été relevés avec le plus grand soin sur les documents officiels.*" The writer, not being able to locate any published "*documents officiels*" containing the monthly figures for the period, appealed to the Treasury for information and was assured that the Lachapelle data had "been copied by the author from the official documents of

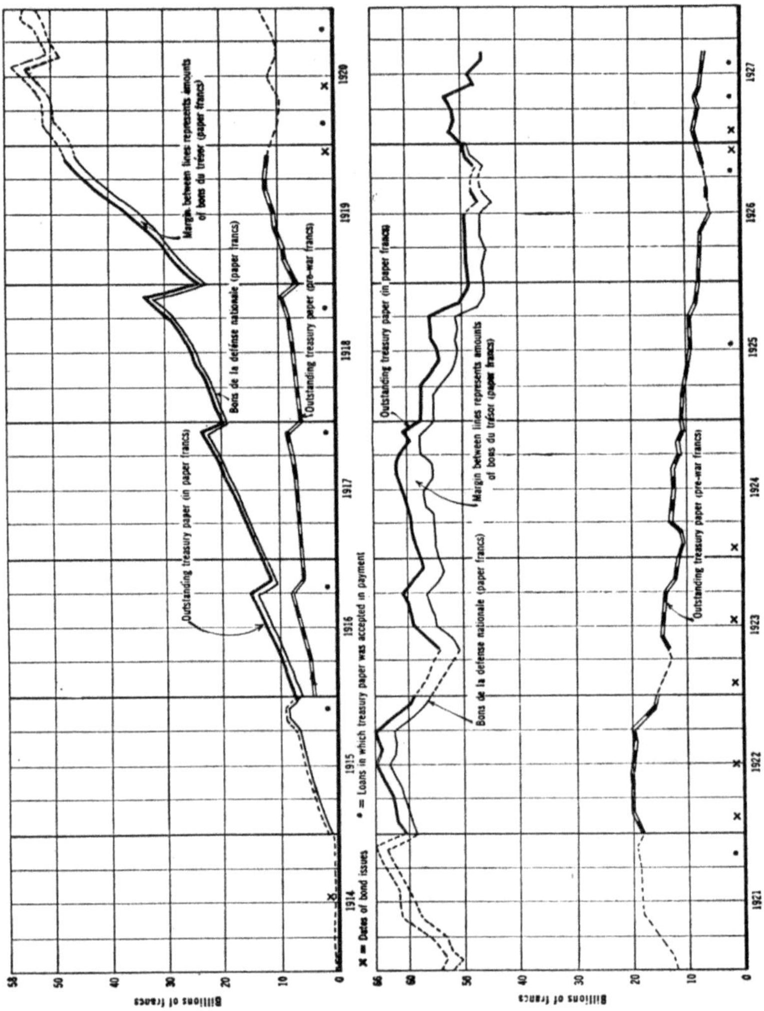

DIAGRAM IV

Outstanding Treasury Paper, in Both Paper and Pre-War Francs, 1914–1927

la Direction du Mouvement Général des Fonds with the special authorization of the Minister of Finance." [18]

Table 20 (see pages 234–235) presents the available data, the figures which are particularly open to suspicion being italicized. The same data are shown in Diagram IV.

Variations in the Amount of Treasury Paper Outstanding. — The rôle which was played by Treasury paper is made clear in Diagram IV. During the war period the amounts outstanding increased rapidly and constantly, the only interruptions in the upward curve being those which were occasioned by the four large issues of *rentes,* in payment for which this Treasury paper was accepted. It should be noted, however, that not one of these four issues of *rentes* absorbed enough of the Treasury paper to reverse more than momentarily the general upward trend of the curve. Each great war loan served only to fund a fraction of the new Treasury paper which had been issued since the last. Thus the original notion that the paper would serve primarily as a temporary resource in anticipation of large permanent loans was not borne out by the events.

When the figures of outstanding Treasury paper are deflated, this interesting story emerges. After the first *rentes* issue, toward the end of 1915, the outstanding Treasury paper amounted to 4.3 billions of 1913 francs; after the second *rentes* issue, late in 1917, the corresponding figure was 6 billions; after the third issue of *rentes,* late in 1917, the figure was 6.4 billions; and, after the fourth of the war issues of *rentes,* the figure was 6.5 billions. In other words between 1915 and 1919, the amount of the Government's real debt in this form remained remarkably constant in the neighborhood of 6 to 6.5 billions of pre-war francs.

It is worthy of comment that the French investors should have preferred to keep their investments in government securities of this short-time liquid form. It is clear that this Treasury paper, in spite of the fact that its term was very short, developed into a permanent and continuing resource. As a result of a large number of influences,[19] a very substantial portion of the French investors,

[18] Communication from M. Bizot, under date of December 31, 1927.

[19] Truchy, *op. cit.*, pp. 58–59.

TABLE 20

AMOUNTS OF OUTSTANDING TREASURY PAPER (*BONS DE LA DÉFENSE NATIONALE* AND *BONS ORDINAIRES DU TRÉSOR*) AT THE END OF EACH MONTH, 1914–1927

(In millions of francs. Sources: 1914, *Experts' Report*, page 150; 1915–1926, G. Lachapelle, *L'Évolution de la Circulation, des Changes, des Prix et de l'Émission des Valeurs à court terme du Trésor de 1914 à 1920*; 1926–1927, *Chappedelaine Report, Budget 1928*, *Chambre*, page xxxiii)

BONS DE LA DÉFENSE NATIONALE

	1914	1915	1916	1917	1918	1919	1920	1921	1922	1923	1924	1925	1926	1927[e]
January	....	2,478	7,809	13,421	20,256	24,740	47,879	51,101	59,787	.....	54,889	54,886	46,089	.....
February	....	3,018	8,570	14,353	21,231	26,494	49,343	53,009	60,092	.....	54,682	54,992	46,068	.....
March	....	3,970	9,283	15,353	22,010	28,400	49,445	53,858	61,087	.....	54,522	53,945	45,783	.....
April	....	4,338	10,020	16,388	22,553	29,758	49,907	56,482	61,529	51,577	56,194	52,246	46,212	.....
May	....	5,114	11,251	17,503	24,086	31,465	51,078	58,812	62,891	52,947	56,780	51,244	46,384	.....
June	....	5,593	12,089	18,515	24,492	33,578	52,703	59,380	63,811	54,841	56,343	50,569	46,157	.....
July	....	6,418	13,159	19,619	25,374	36,314	54,060	60,282	62,527	55,655	56,288	50,690	44,230	.....
August	....	6,977	14,175	20,761	26,452	38,844	48,720[a]	61,584	62,663	56,352	56,598	50,330	46,003	.....
September	....	7,694	15,074	21,631	28,011	41,083	49,758	62,798	63,131	56,679	57,180	51,202	46,850	.....
October	....	8,533	11,590[a]	22,538	30,741	43,513	50,429	63,688	60,781	54,991	57,181	46,623[c]	45,886	.....
November	....	8,817	12,181	23,674	32,930	45,445	51,239	64,199	57,675	53,939	57,047	45,569	48,542	.....
December	1,619	6,963[a]	12,574	19,521[a]	22,334[a]	40,140	52,352	58,420[b]	56,431[c]	54,723	54,538	45,735	49,079	.....

BONS ORDINAIRES DU TRÉSOR

	1914	1915	1916	1917	1918	1919	1920	1921	1922	1923	1924	1925	1926	1927[e]
January	...	....	41.4	29.9	29.9	630.1	1,841.5	2,680.9	1,967.4	3,231	3,535	2,275	2,172	.....
February	...	....	44.2	29.9	29.9	799.9	1,837.7	2,049.6	1,863.2	3,469	3,878	1,824	2,722	.....
March	...	....	56.4	29.9	29.9	803.4	1,724.4	3,482.3	1,261.6	3,072	3,783	2,929	2,756	.....
April	...	....	40.6	29.9	87.5	1,014.4	1,312.5	3,364.7	1,304.8	2,947	3,302	2,667	2,666	.....
May	...	....	40.6	29.9	99.3	1,379.9	1,517.6	2,837.6	1,693.5	3,283	3,109	2,740	2,577	.....
June	...	....	40.6	29.9	240.7	1,868.9	1,652.8	2,883.5	1,903.4	4,066	3,875	3,211	2,643	.....
July	...	....	44.1	29.9	239.6	1,752.2	1,615.6	1,751.1	2,023.9	3,910	5,212	4,125	2,460	.....
August	...	....	44.1	29.9	672.5	1,809.7	1,630.1	1,672.2	2,299.5	3,634	5,123	4,487	2,027	.....
September	...	....	44.1	29.9	733.6	2,176.9	1,837.2	1,835.4	2,842.1	3,754	4,169	4,348	1,530	.....
October	...	....	44.1	29.9	681.5	2,054.8	2,024.6	1,818.5	2,273.1	3,815	1,169	3,623	897[d]	.....
November	...	....	44.1	29.9	749.7	2,115.7	3,838.6	1,999.2	2,170.3	3,426	2,855	2,813	517[d]	.....
December	116	43.3	44.1	29.9	534.9	1,912.0	1,961.3	1,941.3	2,639.0	2,097	1,870	2,394	369[d]	.....

TOTAL TREASURY PAPER

	1914	1915	1916	1917	1918	1919	1920	1921	1922	1923	1924	1925	1926	1927[e]
January	....	......	7,850.4	13,450.9	20,285.9	25,370.1	*49,720.5*	*53,781.9*	61,754.4	.....	58,424	57,161	48,261	51,401
February	....	......	8,614.2	14,382.9	21,260.9	27,293.9	*51,180.7*	*55,058.6*	61,955.2	.....	58,560	56,816	48,790	50,843
March	....	......	9,339.4	15,382.9	22,030.9	29,203.4	*51,169.4*	*57,340.3*	62,348.6	.....	58,305	56,874	48,539	50,664
April	....	......	10,060.6	16,417.9	22,640.5	30,772.4	*51,279.5*	*59,846.7*	62,833.8	54,524	59,496	54,913	48,878	52,393
May	....	......	11,291.6	17,532.9	24,185.3	32,844.9	*52,595.6*	*61,649.6*	64,584.5	56,230	59,889	53,984	48,961	47,168
June	....	......	12,129.6	18,544.9	24,732.7	35,446.9	*54,355.8*	*62,263.5*	65,714.4	58,907	60,218	53,780	48,800	47,851
July	....	......	13,203.1	19,648.9	25,615.6	38,066.2	*56,575.6*	*62,033.1*	64,550.9	59,565	61,500	54,815	*46,690*	45,571
August	....	......	14,219.1	20,790.9	27,124.5	40,653.7	*50,350.1*[a]	*63,256.2*	64,962.5	59,986	61,721	54,817	48,030	44,894
September	....	......	15,118.1	21,660.9	28,742.6	43,259.9	*51,595.2*	*64,633.4*	65,973.1	60,433	61,349	55,550	48,380	44,379
October	....	......	11,634.1[a]	22,567.9	31,422.5	45,567.8	*52,453.6*	*65,506.5*	63,054.1	58,806	58,350	50,246[c]	*46,783*[d]	.....
November	....	......	12,225.1	23,703.9	33,688.7	47,560.7	*55,077.6*	*66,198.2*	59,845.3	57,365	59,902	48,382	49,059[d]	.....
December	1,735	7,006.3[a]	12,678.1	19,550.9[a]	*22,868.9*[a]	48,052.0	*54,313.3*	60,361.3[b]	59,070.0	57,720	56,408	48,129	49,448[d]	.....

[a] At this time there was an issue of rentes.

[b] At this point deduction was made of 7 billion francs representing the amount by which the accounts had been found to be in error, see p. 229.

[c] This figure was definitely fixed by the Comptabilité Publique after various corrections had been made.

[d] The figures given for October, November and December, 1926 (*Bons Ordinaires du Trésor*) were arrived at by combining data given by the Lachapelle document of February 15, 1927, p. 4, which represent the amounts of the *Bons du Trésor* under control of the *Caisse d'Amortissement*, with data given in the *Chappedelaine Report*, p. xxxiii, which represent the amounts of the *Bons du Trésor* under control of the Treasury. The actual figures are as follows:

	Bons in Caisse	*Bons du Trésor under control of the Treasury*	*Total*
October	720	177	897
November	379	138	517
December	246	123	369

The figures for October, 1926 are in italics as being open to suspicion because of a discrepancy between the Chappedelaine and the Lachapelle figures. Chappedelaine gives the new *Bons du Trésor* as 177 millions and the old *Bons du Trésor* and *Bons de la Défense Nationale* under control of the *Caisse* as 46,588, or a total of 46,765 million francs. On the other hand, Lachapelle gives the amount of the *Bons de la Défense Nationale* as 45,886 and the amount of the *Bons du Trésor* under control of the *Caisse* as 720 million francs. If one adds to the Lachapelle figures the Chappedelaine item of new *Bons du Trésor*, he reaches the total of 46,783 million francs, the figure given in the table as the total for October, 1926. Just where the discrepancy lies is impossible to say.

[e] The *Chappedelaine Report*, p. xxxiii, and the *Chéron Report* (*Budget général*, 1928, *Sénat*, for the September figures) gives the following figures for 1927:

	Bons du Trésor not including old Bons under control of the Caisse	*Bons du Trésor and Bons de la Défense Nationale under control of the Caisse*
January	3,968	47,433
February	4,422	46,421
March	3,214	47,450
April	1,807	50,586
May	990	46,178
June	714	47,137
July	583	44,988
August	511	44,383
September	248	44,131

The total figures above, for 1927, are the sum of these two items.

TABLE 21

DEFLATED STATISTICS OF OUTSTANDING TREASURY PAPER (*BONS DE LA DÉFENSE NATIONALE* AND *BONS ORDINAIRES DU TRÉSOR*) AT THE END OF EACH MONTH, 1914–1927

(In millions of pre-war francs. Figures from Table 20, deflated by use of the index of wholesale prices, 1913 = 100)

	1914	1915	1916	1917	1918	1919	1920
January	....	....	4,546	6,239	6,485	7,299	10,214
February	....	....	4,842	6,375	6,657	8,018	9,807
March	....	....	5,024	6,720	6,738	8,699	9,228
April	....	....	5,270	6,620	6,791	9,263	8,728
May	....	....	5,930	6,849	7,209	10,103	9,561
June	....	....	6,438	6,967	7,524	10,784	11,032
July	....	....	7,156	7,332	7,594	10,920	11,416
August	....	....	7,645	7,700	7,750	11,699	10,044
September	....	....	8,012	7,739	8,095	12,017	9,815
October	....	....	6,031	7,958	8,731	11,935	10,455
November	....	....	6,193	8,085	9,413	11,743	11,955
December	1,570	4,293	6,201	6,425	6,482	11,368	12,491

	1921	1922	1923	1924	1925	1926	1927
January	13,227	19,680	.....	11,827	11,112	7,618	8,266
February	14,589	20,220	.....	10,771	11,032	7,676	8,050
March	15,932	20,283	.....	11,677	11,076	7,683	7,899
April	17,242	20,030	13,148	13,221	10,708	7,519	8,234
May	18,716	20,387	13,833	13,062	10,386	7,117	7,507
June	19,158	20,220	14,417	12,942	9,912	6,609	7,686
July	18,792	19,856	14,646	12,786	9,845	5,584	7,351
August	19,093	19,614	14,521	12,950	9,838	6,242	7,266
September	18,789	20,034	14,267	12,634	9,996	6,121	7,393
October	19,773	18,688	13,985	11,738	8,780	6,225	....
November	19,951	16,997	12,952	11,897	7,990	7,174	....
December	18,533	16,322	12,586	11,121	7,611	7,893	....

while willing to give the Government the use of their money, preferred to make their arrangements on a purely temporary basis.

Turning to the post-war period, a study of the diagram shows that during the four years, 1919–1922, there was a tremendous increase in the amounts of the Treasury paper outstanding, measured both in terms of paper and in terms of pre-war francs. The peak was apparently[20] reached toward the middle of 1922, when the amount outstanding reached 66 billions of paper francs and 20.4 billions of francs of pre-war value. During this period refunding operations were insignificant in their influence.

Beginning late in 1922 the curves show a distinct downward trend. The fluctuations for nearly three years were due entirely to influences other than refunding operations. Between October, 1921, and July, 1925, when Caillaux issued his *rentes* with a guarantee based on exchange, there were no issues at all in subscription for which the Treasury paper was accepted.[21] At the time of the issue of *rentes* by Caillaux, the outstanding Treasury paper amounted to 54.8 billions of paper francs, or 9.8 billions of 1913 francs. The Caillaux conversion brought the amount of Treasury paper down to the neighborhood of 48 billions of paper francs, where it remained fairly constant until the political crisis in the middle of 1926. Since that time the amounts outstanding have varied considerably, the bulk of the paper being under the control of the *Caisse d'Amortissement* which pursued a vigorous policy of consolidation described more fully hereafter. Attention is called particularly, however, to the relatively slight fluctuations during 1926 and 1927 in the line representing the amount of outstanding Treasury paper in terms of pre-war francs. According to the last available figures, those for September, 1927, the Treasury owed 7.4 billion pre-war francs to the holders of this type of paper. In spite of the violent fluctuations in the amounts outstanding measured in paper francs, the debt expressed in pre-war francs did not vary more than one billion francs during the period of approximately two years, dating from October, 1925, shortly after the issue of the Caillaux *rentes*.

Variations in the Terms of Issues. — The conditions originally attached to the issue of the *Bons de la Défense Nationale* have already been described. Both the *Bons de la Défense Nationale* and the *Bons du Trésor* have been continuously on sale through

[20] It is impossible to make the statement more definite because of the discrepancies revealed in the 1922 figures.

[21] The only refunding operation during this period was made in 1923, when 2,073 million francs of 2-year *Bons du Trésor*, 6 per cent, 1921, were accepted in payment for the *Bons du Trésor*, 6 per cent, 1923 (first series). See Table 27.

the entire period. The conditions under which they were sold have, however, been modified from time to time.

The changes made in the rate of interest on both types of paper are set forth in detail in Table 22. It should be borne in mind that from the beginning, with certain minor exceptions,[22] the interest on the *Bons de la Défense Nationale* was paid in advance. In the case of the *Bons du Trésor* the rates are not strictly comparable because until July 13, 1918, the interest was not paid in advance, while later it was.[23] It will be observed that the rates of interest on the *Bons du Trésor* were in almost every case slightly lower than those on the *Bons de la Défense Nationale.*

It is also possible, from Table 22, to trace the variations of the length of terms of the two types of Treasury paper.

The denominations in which the loans were issued also varied from time to time. In the case of the *Bons de la Défense Nationale,* as has already been noted, the paper was available from the beginning in denominations as low as 100 francs. In 1915[24] this limit was made even lower and bonds of 5 and 20 francs were made available. The amounts of these denominations in circulation, however, were never large[25] and the 5- and 20-franc *bons* were abandoned in 1922.[26]

The absence of any record of the holders of the Treasury paper made it impossible to exercise any control over the returns of interest for purposes of income tax. From the beginning the interest on this paper had been exempt from the normal income tax (*valeurs mobilières*). The law of March 13, 1924, granted complete exemption on these securities, even from the *impôt général sur le revenu,* but this was simply a recognition of an existing state of fact.

22 The denominations of one-month bonds, the holders of which exercised the privilege of carrying them 60 or 90 days before cancellation and the bonds of very small denominations, 5 and 20 francs, which were issued at 5 per cent between 1915 and 1922.

23 Decision of the Minister of Finance of July 12, 1918.

24 Decree of August 10, 1915. This date is frequently given incorrectly as August 15. Germain-Martin, *Les Finances publiques de la France et la Fortune privée,* p. 150; Jèze, *Revue de Science et de Législation Financières,* 1927, p. 502.

25 Germain-Martin, *op. cit.*, p. 150.

26 *Arrêté* of March 11, 1922.

During the war period the issues of Treasury paper were practically without control by Parliament as to their amount. From time to time decrees were issued specifying the maximum limit, but these decrees were not submitted to Parliament for ratification. This became a subject of sharp criticism after the war and, beginning December 31, 1921,[27] it became a custom to consult Parliament with regard to changes in the limits.

Treasury Paper as a Source of Danger and Embarrassment. — The existence of outstanding Treasury paper of short maturity in such huge amounts proved to be a source of great embarrassment and danger to the French Treasury during the periods of stress after the war. It is obvious that the holders of this paper could within a very short time, merely by refraining from renewing it, raise problems of the first magnitude. There are no data available to show what portion of the Treasury paper was held by the financial institutions and what portion by the public in general,[28] but charges have been freely made in France that the holdings of the large financial institutions in the post-war period were so great that it was necessary for the Governments at every moment to consult them and conform to their wishes with regard to policy. For example, M. Herriot himself, speaking in the Chamber on April 9, 1925, remarked, "This situation is difficult and I can say even somewhat humiliating; for it is already apparent — and our country, which is above all that has been said of it, especially when it is being calumniated, is well aware of this fact — that *domestic politics are no longer free when they are to be controlled and restricted by money interests.*"[29] (Italics in the original text.) Jèze, in commenting on the situation, flatly says: "The

[27] Finance law of that date.

[28] In a speech on June 25, 1915, Ribot announced that the subscribers were predominantly small rather than large capitalists. According to Germain-Martin, (*op. cit.*, pp. 155–156), not until 1918 did the large financial institutions begin to invest heavily in this paper.

[29] Jèze, *Revue de Science et de Législation Financières*, 1927, p. 506. "Oui, messieurs, situation difficile, et je dis même un peu humiliante; car il est déjà démontré — et le pays, supérieur à tout ce que l'on dit de lui, surtout quand on le calomnie, le sent bien déjà — que la politique intérieure n'est plus libre si elle est dominée et restreinte par les ménaces de l'argent." *Débats, Chambre, Sess. Ord.*, April 9, 1925, p. 2152.

TABLE 22

RATES OF INTEREST ON TREASURY PAPER

BONS DE LA DÉFENSE NATIONALE

DATE OF DECREE, ARRÊTÉ OR DECISION	EFFECTIVE DATE	1 MONTH PER CENT[a]	3 MONTHS PER CENT	6 MONTHS PER CENT	1 YEAR PER CENT	2 YEARS PER CENT
September 13, 1914	Same	....	5.	5.	5.	...
December 10, 1914	December 21, 1914	....	4.	5.	5.	...
April 16, 1918	Same	3.6	4.	5.	5.	...
December 28, 1918	January 1, 1919	3.6	4.	4.5	5.	...
February 25, 1922	March 12, 1922	3.	3.5	4.	4.5	...
February 14, 1923	February 19, 1923	3.	4.	4.5	5.	...
July 31, 1926	August 1, 1926	3.6	5.	5.5	6.	...
December 1, 1926	December 2, 1926	3.	5.	5.5	6.	...
December 16, 1926	December 17, 1926	....	4.	4.5	5.5	6.[b]
February 3, 1927	February 4, 1927	....	...	...	5.	6.
April 11, 1927	April 12, 1927	....	...	...	4.	5.
May 6, 1927	May 7, 1927	....	...	...	3.	5.
June 22, 1927	June 23, 1927	....	...	...	...	4.5

[a] The one-month *Bons de la Défense Nationale*, if not presented for payment at the end of one month, bore interest during two succeeding months at slightly increased rates. Various French writers have erroneously stated that these "bons" of one month carrying interest at an increased rate if held beyond one month were first authorized by the *arrêté* of February 26, 1922. They were really authorized in 1918. Moreover, the date, February 26, 1922, is itself an error. The true date of the second *arrêté* dealing with such issues is February 25, 1922. Germain-Martin, *Les Finances publiques de la France et la Fortune privée*, p. 150; Jèze, *Revue de Science et de Législation Financières*, 1927, p. 502.

[b] Effective date January 1, 1927.

BONS DU TRÉSOR

Date of decree, arrêté or decision	Effective date	Of 1 month to 2 months per cent	More than 2 months to 3 months per cent	More than 3 months to 6 months per cent	More than 6 months* to less than 1 year per cent	For one year per cent
August 19, 1914	August 20, 1914	1.	1.	1.	4.	5.
April 23, 1918	April 24, 1918	3.	3.5	3.5	4.	5.
June 25, 1918	June 26, 1918	3.	3.5	4.5	4.5	5.
December 28, 1918	January 1, 1919	3.	3.5	4.25	4.75	5.
February 25, 1922	March 12, 1922	3.	3.25	3.75	4.25	4.5
February 14, 1923	February 19, 1923	3.	3.75	4.25	4.75	5.

* Under the 1914 arrangement, this class apparently included securities of six months. Under the later arrangements, the "bons" of this precise term were included in the preceding group.

large holdings by the banks of *bons* and the menace of their eventual presentation for reimbursement, permitted the banks to exercise a powerful pressure on the governments in order to induce them to follow a certain fiscal policy or to abstain from certain fiscal measures." [30]

In the *Experts' Report* the following classification is given of the outstanding *Bons de la Défense Nationale* according to the length of term: [31]

	One-year bonds Per cent	*Six-months bonds Per cent*	*Three-months bonds Per cent*	*One-month bonds Per cent*
First half of January, 1924.	52.2	23.1	10.6	14.1
First half of January, 1925.	48.8	21.2	15.4	14.6
First half of January, 1926.	40.6	9.7	11.5	38.2
First half of May, 1926...	42.3	7.1	15.2	35.4

It will be noted that in May, 1926, when about 46 billions were outstanding, more than one-third of the *bons* were for a term of only one month. In other words, in case of any shock to *la confiance,* the Treasury might be called upon to repay practically upon demand not less than 16 billions of francs. It seems unnecessary to stress the possibilities of trouble unavoidably connected with such a situation. Clearly any tax proposal such, for example, as a forced consolidation, or a capital levy, which would be unpalatable to the security holders, could be effectively and promptly vetoed by extra-political means.

The Caisse d'Amortissement.—The threat which constantly hung over the Treasury because of this floating debt is recognized by everyone who has commented on the situation. It was discussed in considerable detail in the report of the committee of experts, who recommended the organization of a separate *Caisse* to assist in bringing the situation under control.[32] One of the first steps taken by Premier Poincaré, after the organization of his Ministry in July, 1926, was to transfer the management of the outstanding Treasury paper to the *Caisse Autonome de Gestion*

[30] Jèze, *loc. cit.*

[31] P. 147.

[32] *Rapport du Comité des Experts,* pp. 33 and 53.

des Bons de la Défense Nationale et d'Amortissement de la Dette Publique,[33] which was created by law of August 7, 1926, and set up with pomp and dignity at the session of the *Assemblée Nationale* in Versailles on August 10, 1926.[34] Having taken over from the Treasury at the date of October 1, 1926, a total amount of 46,164 [35] million francs of Treasury paper (*Bons de la Défense Nationale* and *Bons Ordinaires du Trésor*) the *Caisse* proceeded to act with vigor. The issuance of the *Bons Ordinaires du Trésor* was discontinued. The renewals of such bonds were made by the *Caisse* only in the form of the *Bons de la Défense Nationale.* The amounts of the *Bons du Trésor* to be issued by the Treasury itself was fixed at 5 billion francs a year by the law of August 7, 1926. The *arrêté* authorizing the first issue of such *Bons du Trésor* was dated December 30, 1926 (effective January 1, 1927). It also set forth the conditions governing such issues, which were as follows:

Interest rate:	*Per cent*
Bons of one month to two months	3
" " two months to three months	3.5
" " three months to four months	4
" " four months to six months	4.25
" " six months to eight months	4.75
" " eight months to one year	5

The interest was paid in advance. The smallest denominations of such *bons* had to be of 100,000 francs. This is indicative of the fact that the new *bons* were destined to the pre-war clients of the Treasury. The issue of the new *bons* was suspended beginning February 4, 1927.[36]

The law of August 7, 1926, creating the *Caisse d'Amortissement,* also put an end to the item of the budget which provided for the payment of interest on the old *Bons de la Défense Na-*

33 A complete description of the organization of the *Caisse* will be found in Professor Rogers' volume, *op. cit.*, pp. 46–47.

34 See p. 167.

35 *Palmade Report, Budget 1928, Chambre,* p. 21.

36 *Arrêté* of February 2, 1927.

tionale and *Bons Ordinaires du Trésor* now placed under the control of the *Caisse*. Under the new arrangement this "service" was at the charge of the *Caisse* itself, but a certain relation between the *Caisse* and the budget still subsisted in the budget of 1927 in the form of an allowance of 490 millions placed at the disposal of the *Caisse* to be used in case of insufficiency of its own resources. But already, in the budget of 1928, the *Caisse* thought proper to give up even this last protection and will henceforth assume the whole responsibility for the payment of the interest on the *bons* under its control.

The maximum limit of the circulation of *Bons de la Défense Nationale* and *Bons Ordinaires du Trésor* (those under control of the *Caisse*) was fixed at 49 billion francs by article 5 of the law of August 7, 1926. This maximum, according to the law, must be reduced every year by the amount of the *bons* redeemed by the *Caisse*. In case of emergency the circulation limit may, however, be exceeded by no more than 6 per cent (*marge de tolérance*) and for very short periods only. By decision of January 13, 1927, the Financial Committee of the *Caisse* fixed at 46 billions the limit for the year 1927.

The first refunding operation of the *Caisse* was to issue in January, 1927, a 40-year loan (the so-called tobacco loan) [37] by which it succeeded in withdrawing more than 3 billions of the Treasury paper. An issue of 6 per cent 50-year *rentes amortissables* in April and May, 1927, resulted in a conversion of approximately 7.4 billions additional.[38] Finally, the issue of 6 per cent 50-year *obligations amortissables* in June and July, 1927, brought in another $1\frac{1}{4}$ billion.[39] Beginning in December, 1926, a

[37] The interest and amortization "service" on this loan is entirely at the charge of the *Caisse*.

[38] The *Caisse* has obligated itself to remit to the Treasury the necessary amounts to cover interest and amortization charges on the rentes paid for by a surrender of *Bons du Trésor* and *de la Défense Nationale* (*Avenant* of June 10, 1927, convention of April 1, 1927, passed by the State with the *Caisse d'Amortissement*).

[39] The *Caisse* will bear the charge pertaining to the obligations issued in exchange for *Bons du Trésor* and *Bons de la Défense Nationale* which have not been rediscounted by the *Caisse* to the Treasury at the close of the operation. (*Chappedelaine Report, Budget général, 1928, Chambre*, p. xvii.)

series of decisions [40] of the *Caisse* resulted in a suspension of the issue and renewal of all *Bons de la Défense Nationale* of terms of less than 2 years. By the end of July, 1927, all the six-month *bons* had been withdrawn. Under the plan put into operation all of the one-year *bons* outstanding will have disappeared by June 3, 1928. Even at the present time, although the total amount of the *Bons de la Défense Nationale* is still very large (44,131 billion francs, as of September 30, 1927, see Table 20), the operations of the *Caisse* have practically removed from the situation the danger of a serious embarrassment through a demand for immediate reimbursement by the holders. It is interesting to compare the figures appearing on p. 242 with the data furnished in the recent speech [41] by M. Lebrun, *Président du Conseil d'Administration de la Caisse d'Amortissement,* which refer to the situation as of September 1, 1927. A striking redistribution within the groups of the various maturities will be observed. At this date the only *bons* in circulation were of one- and two-year maturity, one-third of them being of longer term.

[40] Decree of December 10, 1926, stopped "prolongation" of 1-month bons; decision of December 10, 1926, suspended issue of 1-month bons from December 11; decision of December 16, 1926, suspended renewal of 1-month bons from December 17; decision of December 22, 1926, suspended issue of 3-month bons from December 23; decision of January 13, 1927, suspended renewal of 3-month bons from January 14; same date, suspended issue of 100-franc denominations for bons of all categories; decision of January 29, 1927, suspended issue of 6-month bons from January 30; decision of June 2, 1927, suspended issue and renewal of 1-year bons from June 3.

[41] *Le Temps,* September 28, 1927.

CHAPTER XIII

THE FLOATING DEBT: III. DEPOSITS WITH THE TREASURY AND MISCELLANEOUS ITEMS

THE treatment of the floating debt is divided into three parts. Having discussed first the bank borrowings (Chapter XI) and next the Treasury paper (Chapter XII), we are now to consider certain miscellaneous items, the most important of which are the deposits with the Treasury. Following a practice which seems to find no exact counterpart in Anglo-Saxon countries, the French Treasury is constantly in possession of substantial sums which have been left on deposit. These "*Comptes de Dépôts de Fonds*" played an especially important part in the financial history of 1926 and 1927. In addition to these deposits, certain other items must be brought into the tables, such as the balance of the postal money orders account and the resource which the Treasury has created through the issuance of the small metal coins (*jetons métalliques*).

Statistics of Deposits with the Treasury and of Miscellaneous Items. — In the Report of the Committee of Experts, the table of the floating debt includes a column headed "*Divers. (Dépôts et c/c, solde des comptes de chèques postaux, jetons métalliques, etc.)*". The figures there given are reproduced in the last column of Table 23. These figures are understood to be comprehensive in the sense that they include all items which may properly be termed floating debt and which are not included under Treasury paper and bank borrowings. Such figures as are available regarding cash deposits of the Treasury are presented in the first and second columns of Table 23. It will be noted that the data are not complete. It would be very interesting to have information regarding the variations of the amount of these deposits with the Treasury from week to week. However, as Allix remarks, it is the policy of the Treasury to give these figures "as little publicity as possible."[1]

[1] Allix, *Science des Finances*, p. 318.

TABLE 23

DEPOSITS WITH THE TREASURY AND MISCELLANEOUS ITEMS OF FLOATING DEBT AT END OF MONTH OR YEAR STATED, 1913–1927

(In millions of francs. Source: see footnotes)

Date	Deposits with Treasury		Total Deposits with Treasury and Miscellaneous Items [f]
	At Paris [a]	Total [b]	
1913	.....	.....	1,022 [c]
1914	.....	.....	1,802 [c]
1915	.....	.....	−169 [c, g]
1916	.....	.....	171 [g, h]
1917	.....	.....	1,339 [c]
1918	218 [c]	.....	2,735 [c]
1919	646 [c]	.....	5,449 [c]
1920	928 [c]	.....	4,094 [c]
1921	618 [c]	.....	3,621 [c]
1922	676 [c]	.....	6,537 [c]
1923	556 [c]	.....	5,938 [c]
1924	1,055 [c]	.....	8,482 [c]
1925			
January	.....	7,156	.....
February	.....	7,430	.....
March	.....	7,295	.....
April	.....	7,706	.....
May	.....	8,240	.....
June	.....	7,734	.....
July	.....	7,463	.....
August	.....	7,385	.....
September	.....	7,914	.....
October	.....	7,715	.....
November	.....	8,756	.....
December	2,496 [c]	8,776	9,609 [c]
1926			
January	.....	8,376	.....
February	.....	7,545	.....
March	.....	7,845	.....
April	917 [c]	7,397	8,297 [c]

[a] "Deposits with the Treasury at Paris" represent deposits at the *Caisse Centrale* and are made up, after 1921, largely of the accounts of the banks. Before 1921 only the accounts of firms and of individuals who furnished supplies to the Government are represented. Many large accounts not those of individuals, of banks, or of business firms, such as accounts of the City of Paris, of the *Caisse des Dépôts et Consignations*, and of certain other public institutions, are not included.

[b] "Total deposits with the Treasury" include all deposits at the *Caisse Centrale* and, in addition, those at the *Trésoreries Générales* in the provinces. These figures were furnished to J. H. Rogers by the Ministry of Finance.

[c] *Rapport du Comité des Experts*, p. 150.

TABLE 23 (Continued)

DEPOSITS WITH THE TREASURY AND MISCELLANEOUS ITEMS OF FLOATING DEBT AT END OF MONTH OR YEAR STATED, 1913–1927

(In millions of francs. Source: see footnotes)

Date	Deposits with Treasury		Total Deposits with Treasury and Miscellaneous Items [f]
	at Paris [a]	total [b]	
May	.....	7,681	.....
June	.....	8,338	.....
July	2,167 [e]	8,378	9,566 [e]
August	.....	7,904	.....
September	1,717 [e]	7,833	.....
October	2,606 [e]	8,925	.....
November	2,255 [e]	8,571	.....
December	2,629 [e]	8,975	10,096 [d]
1927			
January	2,111 [e]	8,090	.....
February	3,330 [e]	9,630	.....
March	6,179 [e]	12,258	.....
April	6,894 [e]	13,254	.....
May	9,214 [e]	16,010	.....
June	10,882 [e]	17,776	.....
July	9,862 [e]	16,911	.....
August	6,349 [e]	13,457	14,478 [e]
September	.....	13,042 [i]	14,330 [i]

[d] Furnished by Ministry of Finance.

[e] *Chappedelaine Report, Budget général, 1928*, pp. xxxiii–xxxiv.

[f] "Divers. (Dépôts et c/c, solde des comptes de chèques postaux, jetons métalliques, etc.)"

[g] 1,669 minus 1,838 (amount due the Treasury from subscribers to rentes, 5 per cent, perpétuelles, 1915).

[h] 1,979 minus 1,808 (amount due the Treasury from subscribers to rentes, 5 per cent, perpétuelles, 1916).

[i] *Chéron Report, Budget général, 1928, Sénat*, from manuscript.

Rôle Played by Deposits with the Treasury. — The figures in Table 23 make it clear that a very high percentage of the total sums here under consideration consisted of deposits with the Treasury. For example, in December, 1926, this fraction was nine-tenths, approximately one-third of which was on deposit at the *Caisse Centrale* in Paris. During the early years of the war an important part of these deposits consisted of advances made to the Treasury by the treasurers-general.

It must be explained that it is an old custom in France, dating back to pre-revolutionary times, to permit the treasurers-general, the local representatives of the Ministry of Finance, to accept deposits which, in turn, they were required to place at the disposal of the Treasury.[2] They are allowed an interest return upon such funds and are in position to make a profit upon the difference between the amount of this interest and the sums which they are required to pay to depositors. In the next place, in its business dealings, the Treasury is constantly in possession of a varying sum which represents balances belonging to individuals or firms which have been allowed to remain for some reason or other in the Treasury.

Shortly after the outbreak of the war, the Government made an effort to develop these banking functions of the treasurers-general by assuming added liability for the safety of deposits and by increasing the remuneration (*émoluments*) allowed to the treasurers-general.[3] The above-mentioned guarantee given by the State remained in force, by a series of successive renewals until 1926,[4] but the importance of the rôle played by the treasurers-general was considerably reduced in 1916, when the decree of June 29 authorized the *Caisse Centrale* of the Treasury to accept deposits from its creditors (*créanciers de l'État*) and from départements. It will be noted that at the end of 1918 the advances to the Treasury by the treasurers-general amounted to only 286,502,700 francs[5] and that even the total miscellaneous floating debt did not exceed 3 billion francs. Towards the end of 1920 the banking functions of the Treasury were considerably broadened and the Treasury opened what amounted to a new central bank, through the device of developing its system of deposits at the *Caisse Centrale* in Paris.

By the *arrêté* of December 17, 1920, it was announced that the *Caisse Centrale* would receive deposits from the public generally and pay interest thereon at the rate of 3 per cent for sight deposits. It was required that the first deposit be of at least

[2] Fisk, *French Public Finances*, p. 227.

[3] Decree of December 11, 1914, ratified by law of December 26, 1914.

[4] Allix, *Science des Finances*, p. 318.

[5] *Projet de budget*, 1920, p. 168.

500,000 francs and that additional deposits be made in substantial round amounts. This arrangement at first attracted no considerable amounts of money; not until the end of 1924 did the *Caisse Centrale* have to its credit as much as one billion francs. No particular effort seems to have been made to increase the attractiveness of these deposits. In fact, in 1922, the interest rate was cut down to 2.5 per cent.[6] Nevertheless, by the end of 1925, the total amount of deposits had reached the level of approximately 2.5 billions. At the end of 1926, the amount of deposits was practically the same. On December 10, 1926,[7] the Treasury established a system of time deposits, offering 4 per cent in case the depositor would agree to give one month's notice of contemplated withdrawal. The interest rate on such deposits was dropped to 3.5 per cent on February 3, 1927,[8] and the time-deposit arrangement was entirely withdrawn by an *arrêté* of February 22, 1927, effective as of March 23, 1927. During the early months of 1927 the effect of the Poincaré policy was becoming apparent in the form of a rapid influx of capital from abroad. This movement brought about a state of remarkable ease in the money market and a marked decline in the interest rate of short-term paper. Since it was very important that these funds should not bring about a business expansion and an increase of prices, the Treasury was urged to take responsibility for providing an outlet for the excess short-term money. The amount of deposits at the *Caisse Centrale* increased from 2.1 billion francs in January, 1927, to 3.3 billions at the end of February. During March this amount nearly doubled and during April, in spite of a reduction in rate from 2.5 to 2 per cent,[9] the deposits still continued to grow rapidly. This movement was doubtless accentuated by the withdrawal from the market of the *Bons de la Défense Nationale* for the shorter terms. By the end of May, the deposits were in excess of 9 billions; by the end of June they reached the remarkable total of 10.9 billion francs. By this time the Treasury was alarmed and embarrassed. On June 27,[10] it had already put on

[6] *Arrêté* of February 25, 1922.

[7] *Arrêté* of same date.

[8] *Arrêté* of same date.

[9] *Arrêté* of April 11, 1927.

[10] Decree of June 13, 1927.

sale the issue of a 50-year loan (*obligations 6 pour cent amortissables*), one of the announced purposes of which was to change a part of the Treasury deposits into a more manageable form. Moreover, by the *arrêté* of July 27, the interest rate on these deposits was reduced to 1.5 per cent. Still a third measure of steadying the situation consisted in a slight relaxation of the regulations governing the exportation of capital. By action taken on August 16, 1927,[11] the Government provided means whereby French funds could be invested temporarily on foreign markets through the purchase of foreign bills of exchange, it still being required, however, that the funds be definitely earmarked for return to France within a 90-day period. It is not possible to trace accurately the effect of these various steps, but the figures show that during July the deposits at the *Caisse Centrale* dropped approximately one billion and in August over 3 billions more. The last published figure, however, that for the end of August, 1927, shows the deposits at the *Caisse Centrale* to have been even then 6.3 billion francs.

The Treasury utilized these deposits to reduce its advances from the Bank of France.[12] During the time when the deposits were increasing by such phenomenal amounts, the Treasury issued no information as to what was happening, but persistently called attention to the reductions which were being made in the advances from the Bank. It is true that there occasionally appeared in the Paris newspapers surmises as to the important part the Treasury deposits were playing, but there was in general no adequate appreciation of the extent to which the Treasury, while apparently improving its position by reducing Bank advances, was to a very large extent merely substituting another liability, much more expensive and much more pregnant with possible embarrassment than the bank advances themselves. Indeed, these huge deposits constituted a menace even more threatening than that of the *Bons de la Défense Nationale*,[13] which during these

[11] *Arrêté* of same date.

[12] Premier Poincaré's speech of February 3-4, 1928, before the Chamber, *Le Temps*, February 5, 1928.

[13] See p. 239.

months the *Caisse d'Amortissement* was making valiant efforts to bring under control. Professor Allix [14] calls attention to the fact that the only real difference between the deposits and the *Bons de la Défense Nationale* was that the investors in one case received a formal security and in the other case a mere receipt. Moreover, these deposits could be used as a basis for a demand of immediate payment, whereas, after the end of June, 1927, it was impossible to purchase *Bons de la Défense Nationale* for a period of less than two years.

However, it must be pointed out that the Government seemed to be well aware of this danger. In a speech of M. Poincaré, from which a quotation has already been made in a different connection, the Premier assured the Parliament that this demand liability of the Treasury was always covered, for at least a like amount, by demand assets of the State, namely by the available margin between the legal limit of advances to the State by the Bank of France and the actual sums outstanding.[15]

Although there are no data available after the end of August, 1927, it seems clear that the most acute danger is now passed. It is obvious, however, that if the Treasury still has funds on deposit with it to the extent of 5 or 6 billions, any sudden demand for reimbursement will probably involve an increase in the advances from the Bank of France to a corresponding extent.

The development of this banking function by the Treasury

[14] Allix, *Science des Finances*, p. 331.

[15] This available margin in 1927 (at the end of each month) was approximately as follows:

January	4	billion francs
February	6.9	" "
March	8.4	" "
April	7.2	" "
May	9.9	" "
June	9.7	" "
July	11.1	" "
August	11.5	" "
September	7.6	" "
October	7.2	" "
November	7.6	" "
December	7.5	" "

(See Tables 10 and 13); M. Poincaré's statement appears, consequently, to be perfectly correct.

seems to have rested upon no direct parliamentary authority.[16] The whole question was frankly discussed by M. Chappedelaine in his report. He pointed out that it was difficult to see how the Treasury was able to avoid the restrictions imposed by the law of December 31, 1920, which required that no further State loan should, under any circumstances, be made without specific authority from Parliament. He recognized, however, the importance of providing an occupation for the superabundant supply of liquid capital, which, if not guided, might produce very harmful results. It seems probable that the amount of deposits can be successfully controlled by the further use of the same methods which were applied during the middle of 1927; indeed, the entire removal of the restrictions upon the export of capital which was accomplished by the decree of January 10, 1928[17] is doubtless to be interpreted as a further effort on the part of the Treasury to rid itself of this function of providing a form of investment for surplus short-term money.

Jetons Métalliques.[18] — A word should be said regarding the extent to which the Government was able to utilize as a resource the subsidiary coinage. The withdrawal of silver early in the war brought about a scarcity of small currency which was at first cared for through the issuance of notes of small denominations by the Chambers of Commerce. These notes were secured by an equivalent amount of bank notes deposited with the Bank of France and, later, by funds deposited with the Treasury. Consequently, they made no changes in the computation of the total public debt. However, beginning in 1921, these notes, which had become very dirty and worn, were withdrawn and in their place were issued token coins of 50-centime, 1-franc and 2-franc denominations. Unlike the paper notes of small denominations, these *jetons métalliques* are not unofficial issues by the Chambers of Commerce, but are true government money in spite of the fact that they bear the imprint of the Chamber of Commerce. Behind them is nothing more than the fiat of the Government, the cover-

[16] *Chappedelaine Report, Budget général, 1928, Chambre*, p. liii.

[17] Reported in the *New York Times* of January 11, 1928.

[18] Commission on Gold and Silver Inquiry, U. S. Senate, *Foreign Currency and Exchange Investigation*, Serial 9, Vol. I, 1925, p. 313. Fisk, *French Public Finances*, p. 72.

ing by special deposits in the Bank or in the Treasury having been removed. In the Report of the Committee of Experts,[19] the following data are given of the annual increase of "*contrevaleur des jetons métalliques*":

Year	Annual Increase	Total Outstanding
1921	88	88
1922	213	301
1923	288	589
1924	200	789
1925	115	904
1926	51 [a]	955

[a] Figure furnished by the Ministry of Finance.

It was explained at the Ministry of Finance that the phrase used in describing these figures indicates the net benefit to the Treasury which accrued through the issuance of the *jetons*, the actual cost of minting the coins having been deducted.

The remaining miscellaneous items in the floating debt are too insignificant to demand discussion.

Adjustments for Deposits of Treasury and Caisse d'Amortissement.—It would add to the completeness of the picture of the financial situation, if certain assets could be taken into account. Certainly mention should be made of the cash standing to the credit of the Treasury and *Caisse d'Amortissement* at the Bank of France.

In the case of the Treasury, the cash balances at the Bank of France are found to be insignificant.[20] On the other hand the

19 P. 148.

20 The following figures, furnished by J. H. Rogers, (*op. cit.*, p. 163) show the deposits of the Treasury at the Bank of France for December (averages of weekly data) of each year stated, in millions of francs.

1914	...	1921	35
1915	606	1922	20
1916	35	1923	22
1917	122	1924	18
1918	160	1925	25
1919	76	1926	27
1920	102	1927	30

Caisse d'Amortissement, in addition to its cash deposit with the Treasury, which cannot legally fall below 1200 million francs,[21] has built up a large cash balance at the Bank of France during 1927. The precise figures have not been made public. They have been estimated by Professor J. H. Rogers at the amounts shown in Table 24. No adjustment has been made in the public debt tables to take account of these large sums which are destined for amortization. It is obvious, however, that they should be borne in mind in drawing conclusions regarding the financial situation since the fall of 1926.

TABLE 24

DEPOSITS OF THE *CAISSE D'AMORTISSEMENT* IN THE BANK OF FRANCE

(In millions of francs, estimated amounts for selected end-of-month dates.)

1926		1927	
October	444	May	6924
November	825	June	9177
December	1824	July	9129
1927		August	8945
January	2424	September	7075
February	1252	October	7253
March	957	November	7198
April	3374	December	6981

[21] *Chéron Report, Sénat, Projet de loi portant* (1) *régularisation de crédits ouverts par décrets au titre de l'exercice 1926;* (2) *ouverture et annulation de crédits sur l'exercice 1926*, p. 18–19. Presumably the Treasury in turn transfers these sums to the Bank of France, increasing the amount of the Treasury balance on deposit or reducing the amount of the advances of the Bank to the State.

CHAPTER XIV

THE FUNDED DEBT: INTERNAL

THE war has brought confusion into the terminology of the French debt. As is pointed out in some detail later in this chapter, the sharp lines of division which formerly existed between the various classes of the public debt have lost their distinctness. It is no longer easy to separate even the floating debt from the funded debt and it is very difficult, indeed, to segregate the short-term funded debt from the long-term funded debt. The Ministry of Finance kindly furnished the writer with a tabular statement which classifies the public debt into these three categories, giving figures for each as of the end of each year during the period under review. However, when one attempts to reconcile the figures as given in this table with detailed figures in the various budgets and financial reports published from time to time, he finds it a hopeless task. It has proved impossible to break down the aggregate figures into a complete and reconcilable set of subsidiary statements. Because of this situation and because the short-term funded debt passes by such imperceptible gradations into the field of the long-term funded debt, it was decided to treat both types under the general heading of " Funded Debt."

Table 25 presents the data furnished by the Ministry of Finance relating to the internal[1] funded debt.

Short-Term Bonds — General. — In normal times the French Treasury had found it convenient to use a type of security the duration of which was considerably longer than that of the *Bons Ordinaires du Trésor,* the maximum term of which is one year, but shorter than the very long term or perpetual *rentes* which are formally inscribed on the *Grand Livre de la Dette Publique*. Such securities were called *Obligations du Trésor*. The treatises on

[1] The term " internal " is used when the bonds were floated in France. What part is held abroad is unknown.

TABLE 25

FUNDED DEBT—INTERNAL
OUTSTANDING AT THE END OF EACH YEAR, 1913–1927

(In millions of francs. Sources: 1913–1926, Ministry of Finance; 1927, *Chéron Report, Budget général, 1928, Sénat*, manuscript.)

	Short-term bonds	Perpetual and long-term bonds	Total
1913	0 [a]	31,162	31,162
1914	0 [a]	31,966	31,966
1915	632	46,367	46,999
1916	427	57,756	58,183
1917	516	69,904	70,420
1918	531	97,248 [b]	97,779 [b]
1919	914	101,722	102,636
1920	423	133,176	133,599
1921	10,309	138,392	148,701
1922	26,835	134,042	160,877
1923	39,975	143,775	183,750
1924	46,636	146,511	193,147
1925	39,461	153,232	192,693
1926	38,796	156,857	195,653
1927 (Sept. 30)	27,739	180,687	208,426

[a] In spite of the fact that in the table furnished by the Ministry of Finance no figures are given for short-term bonds outstanding at the end of the years 1913–1914, an examination of the *Compte Général* indicates that at the end of 1913 there were *Obligations du Trésor* of short term outstanding to the amount of 246 millions and, at the end of 1914, of 336 millions. Comparison of the totals indicates that in all probability these sums have been included under the head "Perpetual and long-term bonds." Because of the relatively small size of the amounts, no attempt has been made to recast the figures furnished by the Ministry of Finance.

[b] In both the *Projet de budget, 1920*, p. 62, and in the *Annuaire Statistique, 1926*, p. 157, this figure is given as 67,779 billion francs. When these facts were called to the attention of the officials in the Ministry of Finance, they insisted that the published figures were wrong and that the figures as given above are the correct ones. See p. xviii.

French finance give as term limits for such securities "more than one year up to 30 years."[2] However, if the securities were not to be reimbursed within 15 years after the date of their issue, they would be classed as long-term rather than short-term debt. As a matter of fact, these *Obligations du Trésor* had a narrow and specialized clientèle, consisting in large part of certain financial

[2] *E.g.*, Allix, *Science des Finances*, p. 871.

institutions which did not require for their investments the degree of liquidity furnished by the *Bons du Trésor*, but which nevertheless found attractive the insurance against substantial depreciation in the value, which was given by a definite covenant to redeem the securities within a few years. In 1914 the only type of short-term security in existence was the *obligations sexennaires* or *sexennales* (with a term of six years), the name of which had become synonymous with short-term *obligations* and included all issues of 6 years or less.[3] There were no long-term *Obligations du Trésor* in existence at the outbreak of the war, the last issue outstanding having been repaid by anticipation in 1891 through the consolidation loan of *rentes* 3 per cent *amortissables*.[4]

From the material already presented regarding the floating debt one gains a favorable impression of the resourcefulness of the French in adapting the form of their securities to meet the varied demands of their investment market. The same tendency to elaborate the varieties of public securities is evident in the field of the short-term funded debt. One result is that the line of division between the floating debt and the short-term debt has become hazy and obscure. For example, as has been pointed out, the *Caisse d'Amortissement* since January 1, 1927, has been issuing *Bons de la Défense Nationale* with a term of two years. The amounts of two-year paper of this type are included in the table of the floating debt, in spite of the fact that it falls outside of that classification if one applies the old rule that the floating debt consists only of securities to be reimbursed within one year after their issue.

The same considerations which led the Treasury to rechristen the *Bons du Trésor* as *Bons de la Défense Nationale* led them to rechristen also the *Obligations du Trésor* as *Obligations de la Défense Nationale*. Likewise, after the war, short-term securities being easier to place, the new issues were christened *Bons du Trésor* instead of *Obligations du Trésor*, since the name conveyed the idea of greater liquidity, and the Treasury developed a series of offerings for such *Bons du Trésor* with terms running from

[3] Allix, *op. cit.*, p. 872.

[4] *Idem.*

2 to 15 years. The confusion which might be expected to arise as a result of using the same name of *Bons du Trésor* for floating debt and short-term funded debt was avoided to some extent by inserting the word " *ordinaires* " in the description of the *Bons du Trésor* of the floating debt type, making the title read " *Bons Ordinaires du Trésor.*"

In the next place, when the Treasury's policy developed of liquidating its liability to the war sufferers (*sinistrés*) with securities rather than with cash, it became a custom to utilize a special form of annuities for the purpose.[5]

Finally at the close of the war the Government decided to set up a separate corporation to finance its expenditures in the devastated areas, an organization it called the *Crédit National pour faciliter les réparations des dommages causés par la guerre.*[6] This organization, which must be considered essentially a piece of government machinery, found it convenient to utilize a form of security virtually the same as the traditional *Obligations du Trésor*.

As a result of all these developments one finds the field of the short-term debt to be crowded with a complicated array of securities which, however troublesome to the financial historian, certainly accomplished very well the Government's object of having a full stock of paper for sale, with varieties of terms, titles and conditions calculated to meet the taste of every possible buyer. The difficulty here is one of classification, for not only have the traditional lines of division been obscured as to the lower limit where the short-term debt must be separated from the floating debt, but also as to the upper limit where the short-term debt must be separated from the long-term and perpetual debt (*dette perpétuelle et à long terme*). For example, the third loan of the *Crédit National, Bons 6 pour cent 1921 à lots,* was issued with a term of 15 years. In the table prepared for this study by the Ministry of Finance this issue is classified with short-term debt. Again, in 1927, the issue of *Bons du Trésor* 7 per cent, also with a term of 15 years, is, according to Allix, to be considered a long-

[5] See p. 273.

[6] Law of October 10, 1919.

term issue.[7] In the table as presented on page 257, however, this issue has been classed as short-term debt, the writer having followed the Treasury practice in this respect.

Bearing in mind what has been said concerning the difficulties of classification, attention is once more called to Table 25 which presents the data furnished by the Ministry of Finance as to the amounts of short-term bonds outstanding on the dates specified. It will be observed that not until 1921 had the short-term debt assumed considerable proportions. In only one year, 1924, had the short-term bonds amounted to as much as one-half of the floating debt. This peak figure of 46.6 billions was attained after the issuance of the *Bons du Trésor* 5 per cent, 1924.

Obligations de la Défense Nationale. — An examination of the *Compte Général* for 1914 shows that in December, 1913, there were outstanding 246 million francs of the *Obligations du Trésor* of the old type.[8] During 1914 this amount rose to 336 millions.[9] It was during 1915 [10] that these old *Obligations du Trésor* were rechristened *Obligations de la Défense Nationale.* During that year 581 millions [11] of the new securities were issued. The old *Obligations du Trésor* soon disappeared entirely from the public debt statement, being listed for the last time in the statement issued as of September 30, 1916.

These *Obligations de la Défense Nationale* had this point of difference, as compared with the other issues of the funded debt, and of similarity as compared with the issues of the short-time Treasury paper described under the floating debt, namely, that they were on sale continuously for long periods rather than offered in the form of specific issues to be subscribed for within the space of a few weeks. Consequently it is not possible to construct a table of issues showing terms and amounts realized. Moreover, because of the irregularity of the financial reports during the period, it is impossible to construct a table showing in detail varia-

[7] Allix, *op. cit.*, p. 872.

[8] *Compte Général*, 1914, Vol. II, p. 5.

[9] *Ibid.*, 1915, Vol. II, p. 5.

[10] Decree of February 13, 1915.

[11] *Compte Général*, 1916, Vol. II, p. 5.

tions in the emissions and redemptions by regular periods.[12] A clear picture of the character of these credit transactions can, however, be given by describing in detail the terms surrounding the first of these issues.

By authority of the law of February 10, 1915, of the decree and *arrêté* of February 13, 1915, and of an *arrêté* of February 18, 1915, there were placed on sale on February 25, 1915, 5 per cent *Obligations de la Défense Nationale.* These bonds, no matter when purchased, were to be repaid on February 16, 1925. They were offered in denominations from one hundred to one million francs. The emission price was 96.50 per cent; the interest was payable at six-month intervals in advance. Beginning with the sixth year the Treasury was permitted to call the bonds at par, with an adjustment for any interest which had been paid in advance. This issue remained on sale from February 25 to November 20, 1915. Four months later they were again placed on sale for a period of 7 months (March 20 to October 1, 1916). In 1917 they were again offered to purchasers for 8½ months (February 16 to November 1). Finally, in 1918, they were offered for another period of 8 months (January 21 to September 21). It should be noted that by the time that the issue was finally withdrawn from the market, the term of the securities offered had been reduced to less than 6½ years.

In 1917 while the first issue of 5 per cent 10-year *obligations* of 1915 was still on sale, a second and entirely different issue of 5 per cent 5-year *obligations* was offered. The conditions of this issue were slightly different from those of the previous one. They were issued at par and carried a premium upon reimbursement of 2.5 per cent. The holders of these *obligations* were given the privilege of demanding payment at the end of the first year or at any interest date thereafter.[13] This issue was on sale for 8 months, from March 1 to November 1, 1917. They were again offered in 1918 for 8 months, from January 21 to September 21.

12 These " obligations " were refunded in very large amounts in the course of the issuance of the rentes.

13 See decree of February 9, 1917, and *arrêté* of February 10, 1917.

In the year 1919, the first two issues having been withdrawn, two fresh issues were made available to the public, both bearing 5 per cent interest, one issue having a term of 10 years and the other of 6 years.[14] These 1919 issues were apparently on sale continuously until February 16, 1922.[15]

Again in 1922 there was a special issue of the *Obligations de la Défense Nationale* which was turned over to the banks of Alsace and Lorraine to facilitate substitution of French francs for German marks as the circulating medium in those provinces.[16]

Finally this form of security was utilized to a certain extent in connection with settlement of claims for war damages.[17]

In spite of the various advantages which are enjoyed by the *Obligations de la Défense Nationale* as, for instance, freedom from the tax on income from securities, acceptability in payment for bonds of future loans, certain advantages originally granted exclusively to the *rentes* and subsequently conceded to the *Obligations de la Défense Nationale,* these securities had only a limited success during the first years following their appearance. The favor of the public later turned decidedly towards the *Bons de la Défense Nationale.*[18]

Such data as are available regarding the outstanding amounts of *Obligations de la Défense Nationale* are shown in Table 26. These figures are not presented with confidence. In the first place, they are for scattered dates; secondly, they represent the *capital nominal* rather than the *produit de l'émission.* Finally, in the case of certain years, they are plainly at variance with the figures of the general table furnished by the Ministry of Finance.

Other Funded Debt. — All the other emissions of the funded debt whether of long or short term differ from the *Obligations de la Défense Nationale* in that, instead of being almost continu-

14 See decree and *arrêté* of May 14, 1919.

15 The sale of "Obligations de la Défense Nationale" was definitely suspended by the *arrêté* of February 14, 1922. However, certain amounts of the "obligations" continued to be issued in payment of war damages. See p. 299.

16 See decree of September 5, 1922.

17 See p. 300.

18 Truchy, *Les Finances de Guerre de la France,* p. 67.

TABLE 26

OBLIGATIONS DE LA DÉFENSE NATIONALE
OUTSTANDING AT THE DATES SPECIFIED, 1915–1927.

(*Capital nominal*, not *produit de l'émission*)

(In millions of francs)

1915 — December 31	581 [a]
1916 — "	1,295 [b]
1917 — "	521 [c]
1918 — "	531 [d]
1919 — "	914 [e]
1920 — September 30	933 [f]
1921 — May 31	580 [g]
1922 — March 31	1,730 [h]
1924 — June 30	5,794 [i]
1925 — April 30	8,536 [j]
1926 — March 31	10,395 [k]
1926 — December 31	10,797 [l]
1927 — September 30	5,825 [m]

[a] *Compte Général*, 1915, Vol. 2, p. 5.
[b] *Compte Général*, 1916, Vol. 2, p. 5. Note the discrepancy with table supplied by the Ministry of Finance.
[c] *Projet de Budget général de l'Exercice 1919*, p. 118.
[d] " " " " " " *1920*, p. 164.
[e] " " " " " " *1921*, p. 186.
[f] " " " " " " *1922*, p. 164.
[g] " " " " " " *1923*, p. 304.
[h] *Inventaire*, p. 260.
[i] " p. 260.
[j] *Projet de Budget général de l'Exercice 1926*, p. 216.
[k] " " " " " " *1927*, p. 178.
[l] " " " " " " *1928*, p. 136.
[m] *Chéron Report, Budget général, 1928, Sénat*, manuscript.

ously on sale, they were offered in the form of specific issues opened to subscription for short and definite periods. The variety of these issues is so great that to describe them in detail would consume too much space. The most important facts with regard to them have been assembled in Table 27 which, together with its footnotes, describes briefly each loan in chronological order, according to the dates when they were offered to the public. The variations in the amounts outstanding from time to time are shown with sufficient clarity by Table 25.

TABLE 27

DETAILS OF ISSUES OF INTERNAL FUNDED DEBT, LONG AND SHORT TERM (EXCEPT *OBLIGATIONS DE LA DÉFENSE NATIONALE*), 1914–1927

(Figures, where not otherwise specified, in millions of francs. Sources: 1915–1920, *Projet*, *Budget général*, 1923, p. 58 *et seq.*; 1920–1927, Ministry of Finance; also see footnotes.)

ISSUES	TERM (MAXIMUM) IN YEARS	AUTHORIZATION	PERIOD OF PUBLIC OFFERING	RATE OF YIELD [e'] (PER CENT)	FACE VALUE OF THE SECURITIES ISSUED (CAPITAL *Nominal*) [a]	PROCEEDS OF THE LOANS (*valeur d'émission*) [b']			
						CASH	SECURITIES WITH A TERM OF MORE THAN ONE YEAR (FUNDED DEBT) [b]	SECURITIES WITH A MAXIMUM TERM OF ONE YEAR (FLOATING DEBT) [c]	TOTAL — CASH AND SECURITIES
1914 *Rentes*, 3½ per cent, *amortissables*, 1914	25	Law of June 20, 1914 Decree of June 24, 1914 *Arrêté* of June 25, 1914	July 7, 1914[d]	3.85	885[a]	803[d]	.....	.....	803
1915 *Rentes*, 5 per cent, perpetual, 1915	Indefinite	Law of Nov. 16, 1915	Nov. 25 to Dec. 15, 1915	5.73[e]	15,205	6,285[c]	4,779	2,244	13,308
1916 *Rentes*, 5 per cent, perpetual, 1916	Indefinite	Law of Sept. 15, 1916	Oct. 5 to Oct. 29, 1916	5.71[e]	11,514	5,425[p]	964	3,693	10,082
1917 *Rentes*, 4 per cent, perpetual, 1917	Indefinite	Law of Oct. 20, 1917	Nov. 26 to Dec. 16, 1917	5.83[e]	14,482	5,174[p]	452	4,583	10,209
1918 *Rentes*, 4 per cent, perpetual, 1918	Indefinite	Law of Sept. 19, 1918	Oct. 20 to Nov. 25, 1918	5.68[e]	31,304	7,246[p]	1,415	13,502	22,163
1919 *Crédit National* (First loan), *obligations* 5 per cent, 1919 *à lots*	75	Convention of July 7, 1919 Law of Oct. 10, 1919 Decree of Nov. 20, 1919 *Arrêté* of Nov. 21, 1919	Dec. 12 to Dec. 23, 1919	5.34[f, f']	4,000	3,960[p]	.....	.....	3,960[c]

1920									
Rentes, 5 per cent, *amortissables* 1920........	60	Law of Dec. 30, 1919	Feb. 19 to Mar. 20, 1920	5.75 [g, e]	15,940	7,035 [p]	617	8,289	15,941
Crédit National (Second loan), *obligations* 5 per cent, 1920, *à lots*....	75	Decree of Nov. 20, 1919 *Arrêté* of May 20, 1920	May 31 to June 26, 1920	5.17 [h, i, f]	4,000	3,880 [p]	.....	.....	3,880 [e]
Rentes, 6 per cent, perpetual, 1920........	Indefinite	Law of Aug. 2, 1920	Oct. 20 to Nov. 30, 1920	6.0 [e]	28,089	11,278 [p]	12,654	4,156	28,089
Total, 1920.......					48,029	22,193	13,271	12,445	47,910
1921									
Bons du Trésor, 6 per cent, 1921......	2	Laws of Feb. 10, 1915 and Feb. 16, 1917 Decree and *arrêté* of May 14, 1921	May 23 to June 21, 1921	6.0 [j]	5,665 [e']	5,495 [e']	.....	.....	5,495 [e']
Crédit National (Third loan), *Bons*, 6 per cent, 1921, *à lots*........	15	Decree of Nov. 20, 1919 *Arrêté* of Sept. 24, 1921	Oct. 24 to Nov. 10, 1921	6.03 [h, i, f]	3,000	1,871 [q]	.....	1,099 [r']	2,970 [e]
Total, 1921.......					8,665	7,366	.....	1,099	8,465
1922									
Crédit National (Fourth loan), *Bons*, 6 per cent, February, 1922......	10	Decree of Nov. 20, 1919 *Arrêté* of Jan. 12, 1922	Feb. 1, 1922 and following	6.88 [i, f]	4,710	4,540 [r]	.....	.....	4,540 [r]
Crédit National (Fifth loan), *Bons*, 6 per cent, July, 1922..........	(3 to) 18	Decree of Nov. 20, 1919 *Arrêté* of June 10, 1922	June 26, 1922 and following	6.20 [i, f]	3,290	3,280 [r]	.....	.....	3,280 [r]
Bons du Trésor, 6 per cent, 1922..........	(3 or) 5	Laws of Dec. 31, 1921 and Mar. 31, 1922 Decree of Sept. 20, 1922 *Arrêté* of Sept. 28, 1922	Oct. 9 to Nov. 10, 1922	3-year *bons* 6.38 [d'] 5- " " 6.54 [d']	8,237 [d']	8,196 [d']	.....	.....	8,196 [d']
Total, 1922.......					16,237	16,016	.....	.....	16,016
1923									
Crédit National (Sixth loan), *Bons*, 6 per cent, Jan., 1923, *à lots*....	25	Law of Dec. 31, 1922 Decree of Nov. 20, 1919 *Arrêté* of Jan. 6, 1923	Closing date, Feb. 10, 1923	6.03 [h, i, f]	3,000	2,991 [e]	.....	.....	2,991
Bons du Trésor, 6 per cent, 1923 1st series } 2d series }	(3, 6 and) 10	Law of Feb. 20, 1923 { Decree and *arrêté* of Feb. 24, 1923 { Decree and *arrêté* of Sept. 22, 1923	Mar. 5 to Apr. 7, 1923 Oct. 1 to Nov. 3, 1923	1st series 3-year *bons* 7.23 [d'] 6- " " 7.14 [d'] 10- " " 7.10 [d'] 2nd series 3-year *bons* 7.61 [d'] 6- " " 7.32 [d'] 10- " " 7.21 [d']	10,000 [d'] } 6,189 [d'] }	14,012 [d']	2,073 [d']	.....	16,085 [d']
Crédit National (Seventh loan), *Bons*, 6 per cent, June, 1923 *à lots*.....	26	Decree of Nov. 20, 1919 *Arrêté* of June 9, 1923	Closing date July 13, 1923	6.17 [h, i, f]	2,000	1,960 [e]	.....	.....	1,960 [e]
Total, 1923.......					21,279	18,963	2,073	.....	21,036

TABLE 27 (Continued)

ISSUES	Term (Maximum) in Years	Authorization	Period of Public Offering	Rate of Yield [a'] (Per Cent)	Face Value of the Securities Issued (Capital Nominal) [a]	Proceeds of the Loans (*valeur d'émission*) [b']			
						Cash	Securities with a Term of More than One Year (Funded Debt) [b]	Securities with a Maximum Term of One Year (Floating Debt) [c]	Total — Cash and Securities
1924									
Crédit National (Eighth loan), *obligations* 6 per cent, 1924, *à lots*....	50	Decree of Nov. 20, 1919 *Arrêté* of Dec. 31, 1923	Jan. 2, 1924 and following	6.29 [h, i, j]	1,633	1,567 [e]	.....	.....	1,567 [e]
Bons du Trésor, 5 per cent, 1924..............	10	Law of Dec. 28, 1923 Decree and *arrêté* of Oct. 31, 1924	Nov. 12 to Dec. 10, 1924	8.62 [k]	4,912 [e']	4,912 [e']	.....	.....	4,912 [e']
Total, 1924.......					6,545	6,479	.....	.....	6,479
1925									
Rentes, 4 per cent, perpetual, 1925........	Indefinite	Law of June 27, 1925 Decree and *arrêté* of July 4, 1925	July 20 to Oct. 20, 1925	4.0 [l]	6,011	.....	.....	6,011	6,011
1926									
Caisse d'Amortissement, obligations, 6 per cent, 1926 (Tobacco loan).	40	Law of Aug. 7, 1926 Decree of Sept. 15, 1926	Oct. 7–15, 1926	7.40 [m]	3,013	.....	.....	3,042 [m]	3,042 [m]
Bons du Trésor, 7 per cent, 1926..........	10	Law of June 27, 1925 Decree and *arrêté* of Nov. 13, 1926	Dec. 1–9, 1926	8.67 [m]	1,379	835 [t]	434 [w]	.....	1,269
Total, 1926.......					4,392	835	434	3,042	4,311
1927									
Bons du Trésor, 7 per cent, 1927..........	15	Law of Aug. 7, 1926 Decree and *arrêté* of Jan. 21, 1927	Feb. 15, 1927	8.51 [m]	3,749	2,349 [u]	1,119 [x]	.....	3,467
Rentes, 6 per cent, *amortissables*, 1927.......	50	Law of Aug. 7, 1926 Decree of Apr. 2, 1927, *Arrêté* of Apr. 5, 1927	Apr. 25 to May 25, 1927	6.98 [m]	18,224	.....	10,826	7,398	18,224
Obligations, 6 per cent, *amortissables*, 1927...	50	Law of Aug. 7, 1926 Decree of June 13, 1927	June 27 to July 23, 1927	6.67 [m]	4,642	2,990 [v]	.....	1,281 [y]	4,271
Total, 1927.......					26,615	5,339	11,945	8,679	25,962
Grand Total..					215,163	106,084	35,333	55,298	196,715

NOTES TO TABLE 27.

[a] The "capital nominal" means the par or face value of the securities issued. Certain premiums and lottery prizes are not included and the figures, consequently, cannot be taken as comprehending the total obligations of the State. In the case of the 6 per cent *Obligations de la Caisse d'Amortissement*, (Tobacco loan), 1926, the figure does not include the premiums (minimum 100 francs per 500 francs obligation).

[a'] These rates should be accepted with caution. They have been gathered from scattered sources. Some of them have been computed for the purposes of this table. See footnote *f*. The conditions attaching to the various issues (such as discounts, premiums, lottery prizes, redemption privileges, tax exemptions, etc., etc.) are so complicated that the calculation of an altogether satisfactory series of rates of true yield is an impossible task.

[b] The funded debt (more than one year) received in payment for issues of new funded debt may be subdivided as follows (valeur d'émission; in millions of francs):

Issues of new funded debt	*Obligations de la Défense Nationale*	*Rentes* 3 per cent	*Rentes* 3½ per cent *amortissables*	*Rentes* 5 per cent, 1915, 1916, and 1920; 4 per cent, 1917 and 1918	*Bons du Crédit National*	*Bons du Trésor* 1922	Total
Rentes 5 per cent, 1915	3,317	1,439	22	.....	....	....	4,778
Rentes 5 per cent, 1916	956	....	8	.....	....	....	964
Rentes 4 per cent, 1917	449	....	3	.....	....	....	452
Rentes 4 per cent, 1918	1,412	....	3	.....	....	....	1,415
Rentes 5 per cent, 1920	612	....	4	.....	....	....	616
Rentes 6 per cent, 1920	355	....	3	12,297	....	....	12,655
Bons du Trésor, 1926	.....	....	..	.....	434 Fourth loan	....	434
Bons du Trésor, 1927	.....	....	..	.....	....	1,119 of 1922	1,119
Rentes 6 per cent, 1927	5,077	....	..	.....	622 Fifth loan	5,127 of 1913	10,826
Total	12,178	1,439	43	12,297	1,056	6,246	33,259

The 4 and 5 per cent rentes received in payment for the 6 per cent rentes of 1920 may be further divided as follows: 3,607 millions, rentes 5 per cent, 1915 and 1916; 1,786 millions, rentes 4 per cent, 1917; 4,166 millions, rentes 4 per cent, 1918; 2,739 millions rentes 5 per cent, 1920, amortissables.

[b'] "Valeur d'émission" means the actual money received and par or face value of the securities received in exchange for the obligations of the new issue, the new obligations being taken at the emission price.

[c] The floating debt (of one year maximum) received in payment for issues of funded debt may be subdivided as follows (valeur d'émission; in millions of francs):

NOTES TO TABLE 27 (*Continued*)

Issues of new funded debt	*Bons de la Défense Nationale*	*Bons du Trésor*	*Coupons russes*	*Coupons de rentes de guerre*	*Valeurs diverses non encore reconnues*	Total
Rentes 5 per cent, 1915	2,224	..	...	..	.	2,224
Rentes 5 per cent, 1916	3,693	..	...	..	.	3,693
Rentes 4 per cent, 1917	4,583	..	...	..	.	4,583
Rentes 4 per cent, 1918	13,255	8	239	..	.	13,502
Rentes 5 per cent, 1920	8,226	1	...	62	.	8,289
Rentes 6 per cent, 1920	4,136	15	...	..	5	4,156
Crédit National (Third loan)	1,099	..	...	..	.	1,099
Rentes 4 per cent, 1925	6,011	..	...	..	.	6,011
Caisse d'Amortissement Tobacco loan, 1926........	3,013	..	...	..	.	3,013
Rentes 6 per cent, 1927	7,398	..	...	..	.	7,398
Obligations 6 per cent, 1927	1,281	..	..	..	.	1,281
Total	54,919	24	239	62	5	55,249

[c'] *Projet de Budget*, 1923, pp. 58 and 300.

[d] This loan was offered just before the outbreak of the war. It was over-subscribed many times. Subscriptions were accepted to the amount of 884,614,000 francs (805,000,000 francs, capital effectif). The rentes were offered at 91 francs. But the privilege was given of paying for the rentes by instalments and, when war was declared, practically all the subscribers preferred to abandon the transaction, forfeiting the amounts already paid in, rather than to pay the balance of the subscription. It was not until it was announced (decree dated December 11, 1914) that the rentes could be applied, at 91 francs, to subsequent loans, that subscriptions began to be liberated, through the coöperation of the Bank of France. According to the 1923 *Projet* only 430,000,000 francs had been paid in at the time the rentes were issued and by the end of 1914 the total amount of cash received from the issue amounted to only 490,000,000 francs. (*Projet de Budget général*, 1923, p. 59 *et seq.*) On the other hand, Ribot (*Exposé des Motifs*, law of December 26, 1914, *portant ouverture sur l'exercice 1915 des crédits provisoires* etc.) states that the "montant total des versements" up to September 1, 1914, amounted to 387,000,000 francs and up to November 30 was 515,722,373 francs. The discrepancy in the figures is unexplained. Furthermore, the *Experts' Report* (p. 148) gives 465,000,000 francs as the amount received by the Treasury from "emprunts à terme" in 1914 and nothing from this source during the next four years. By consolidating the figures given in the *Compte Général* for 1914 (p. 261), for 1915 (p. 267) and for 1916 (p. 271), the receipts (under "produit de l'émission") during these three calendar years are found to total 798,055,341 francs. The *Compte Général* for 1917 has not yet been published. In the *Projet de Budget général*, 1920 (p. 176), the slightly larger figure of 798,639,389 francs is given in a statement covering the period ended December 31, 1918. If one adds the amounts shown as "recettes," under the heading of "produit d'émission" (*Services Spéciaux du Trésor*), in the *projets* for each budget since that of 1920, one arrives at the figure of 803,207,595 francs, given above, for the period ended December 31, 1926. These rentes were made acceptable in payment for subscriptions to the series of great war loans and also to the *Obligations de la Défense Nationale*. A total of 43,201,180 francs was accepted in payment for bonds listed in the above table during the period 1914–1927 (*Projet, Budget général*, 1923, p. 58 *et seq.*) The great bulk of rentes, how-

NOTES TO TABLE 27 (*Continued*)

ever, were taken up in exchange for *Obligations de la Défense Nationale*: 22,356,690 francs in 1915 and 674,540,902 francs in 1916 (*Compte Général*, 1916, p. 690). It has not been possible to trace the details of the refunding and redemption of this issue after the end of 1916. On December 31, 1926, only 11,473,200 francs of these rentes remained outstanding (*Projet, Budget général*, 1928, p. 142).

[d'] Ministry of Finance.

[e] *Projet, Budget général*, 1923, pp. 59–60.

[e'] *Projet, Budget général*, 1926, p. 216.

[f] These rates were arrived at by the use of Kent's "formula 64" (*Mathematical Principles of Finance*, 2nd edition, p. 7 of "Compound Interest and Annuity Tables") which reads:

$$P = Cv^{2n} \div \frac{rC}{2} A^{2n}$$

In the computation of these yields the conservative or pessimistic estimates have been utilized, the assumption being that the bonds will run to maturity, that is, not be "called" or reimbursed through the lottery. Tax exemptions were not taken into account.

In the *Inventaire* (p. 36) appears a different table of rates, headed "Taux Réels." No explanation is given of the bases upon which they are calculated. The rates are:

First	loan	5.50
Second	"	5.81
Third	"	6.52
Fourth	"	6.67, 6.72, 6.76
Fifth	"	6.21, 6.30, 6.31
Sixth	"	6.48
Seventh	"	6.71
Eighth	"	6.99

[f'] The calculation of the true yield is complicated. A 500-franc bond was issued at 495 francs. It might be redeemed as early as 20 years or as late as 75 years after the date of issuance, at 600 francs. Finally there were 68 prizes distributed annually by lot.

[g] Jèze (*Cours de Science des Finances*, 1925, p. 24) gives this figure as 5.60.

[h] Plus lottery prizes.

[i] Plus premium or payment of discount on reimbursement.

[j] Approximate rate only.

[k] Germain-Martin, *Les Finances publiques de la France et la Fortune privée*, p. 177. Jèze, *Revue de Science et de Législation Financières*, 1927, p. 623, points out that the yield of this loan was really 6 per cent for the period 1924–1930, and 15 per cent for the period 1930–1934.

[l] This loan carried a guarantee to pay as interest, even if the franc depreciated below 95 to the pound sterling, a sufficient number of francs to be equivalent to four francs on each 100 francs of the "prix d'émission," with the franc exchanging at that rate.

[m] *Chappedelaine, Report, Budget général, 1928, Chambre*, p. xxiv *et seq*. The figure for the yield of the Tobacco Loan is based on the revenue of the first semester of 1927.

[n] *Compte Général*, 1916, p. 690.

[o] In the *Experts' Report* (p. 148) 6,265,000,000 francs is given as the amount the Treasury received from "emprunts perpétuels" in 1915.

It will be observed that during the war it was the custom to offer each year an issue of *rentes*[19] of indefinite term with yields

[19] The so-called "rente" is an annuity certain, in the form of a perpetuity, i.e., a series of payments which are to continue for an unlimited number of periods or forever, at the choice of the borrower. This method of financing owes its origin to the ban placed by the common law in medieval times on ordinary interest-bearing loans. The "constitution de rente," i.e., the creation of the "rente" was, and still is, the name applied to a covenant by virtue of which one party agrees to supply an annuity to the other in consideration of a principal sum of money the repayment of which is left open to the borrower's option, the lender giving up in advance all claim to the reimbursement of the principal so long as the service of the "rente" is continued. In the course of time, although still existing as a legal concept, the "constitution de rente" was gradually replaced in actual practice by the interest-bearing loan, which finally became and now is a legitimate contract protected by the law. The true "rentes" remain as a means of borrowing used by the State, but redeemable "rentes" (rentes amortissables) which have all the characteristics of a simple funded debt are also issued at times.

The issue of the "rentes" whether in the form of a perpetuity or in the form of a redeemable funded debt must be expressly authorized by the legislative bodies, which also make provision for its inscription in the *Grand Livre de la Dette Publique* and direct the Minister of Finance to submit a report to the Parliament as to the results of the issue. The questions of detail are arranged by administrative regulations.

The "rentes" are exempted from practically all the taxes on securities including: (1) the tax on income from securities (with the exception of the 3½ per

---

NOTES TO TABLE 27 (*Concluded*)

[p] These figures agree with those given in the *Experts' Report* (p. 149) representing the cash receipts by the Treasury.

[q] *Experts' Report*, p. 148.

[q'] This figure was arrived at by subtracting 1,871 from 2,970. The exact figure for subscriptions received in securities of one year maximum is 1,070 (*Experts' Report*, p. 148). The discrepancy can be explained by the fact that the figure of 2,970 — total, cash and securities, is only an approximate one. See footnote z.

[r] 7,822,000,000 francs is the amount given in the *Experts' Report* (p. 148) as the proceeds of the "Emprunts du Crédit National" in the year 1922. The *Projet, Budget général*, 1923 (p. 62) states that 4,500,000,000 francs, in round figures, was realized from the February loan.

[s] *Experts' Report* (p. 148.) This document gives 4,951,000,000 francs as the total received by the Treasury from "Emprunts du Crédit National" in 1923.

[t] "Capital nominal," 907,486,000 francs.

[u] "Capital nominal," 2,539,146,000 francs.

[v] "Capital nominal," 3,250,000,000 francs.

[w] "Capital nominal," 471,411,500 francs.

[x] "Capital nominal," 1,209,406,500 francs.

[y] "Capital nominal," 1,392,000,000 francs.

[z] These figures are termed "approximate" in the documents. *Projet, Budget général*, 1923, p. 58 *et seq.*

of approximately 6 per cent. In the case of the first three of these issues approximately one-half of the *rentes* were purchased for cash. In the case of the 1918 issue, although the cash received was greater than for the preceding ones, it amounted only to one-third of the total issue. During the year 1920 there were two large and successful issues of *rentes,* after which none was offered until the ill-fated Caillaux issue of 1925. Finally, 1927 witnessed a return to this type of borrowing in the form of a large refunding issue which involved no cash subscriptions.

In 1919 began a series of loans for the *Crédit National,*[20] which was the corporation set up by the Government to administer the reconstruction of the devastated areas. Between 1919 and 1924 the *Crédit National* appealed to the French investors no less than eight times. The eighth loan offered in January, 1924, was very disappointing in its yield and was the last issued.

In 1921 appears the first of the six issues of the *Bons du Trésor.* In 1926 the *Caisse d'Amortissement* entered the field as an independent borrower with an issue of *obligations* with a term of 40 years, the so-called tobacco loan. Finally there should be mentioned the 50-year *obligations* issued in the summer of 1927 to aid in the process of bringing the floating debt under control.

---

cent amortissables, 1914); (2) the stamp tax; (3) the transfer tax; (4) the tax on exchange transactions (with an insignificant exception). With the exception of the death duties (droits de succession) and the gift taxes (droits sur les donations entre vifs), they are exempted from all the other taxes. *Cf.* Allix, *op. cit.*, p. 596.

[20] The " Crédit National pour faciliter la réparation des dommages de guerre " was created by the law of October 10, 1919. All of its obligations are guaranteed by the State as to both interest and principal. The operating expenses of the corporation as well as the debt service are met by budgetary appropriations. Claims for indemnities in cases of loss are verified by Commissions of Evaluations, but even before this formality is completed the claimant may receive advances from the corporation in order to facilitate the work of rehabilitation. When the indemnity claims have been verified, the Treasury issues certificates of indebtedness. These certificates are in turn discharged in various ways as, for example, by payment in cash, annuities, securities, etc. Interest is paid at the rate of 5 per cent from November 11, 1918, until the day of final settlement. In addition to the assessment and liquidation of damages, the Crédit National also makes loans within carefully prescribed limits for the purposes of encouraging the rehabilitation of industrial and commercial establishments in the devastated regions. (For details as to amount of payments made see p. 299.)

An analysis of the figures of the annual proceeds of these various issues reveals significant fluctuations. In the year 1918 the issues listed in the table were subscribed to the extent of 7¼ billions in cash and 15 billions in securities, the high-water mark up to this time. During 1919 there was only one issue and that a relatively small one. It will be recalled that during this year there was an increase of nearly 23 billions in the Treasury paper issues and an increase of over 8 billions in the Bank advances. This was a year of uncertainty and hesitation. It was succeeded in 1920 by a veritable orgy of long-term issues. In this single year the face value of the three loans issued amounted to more than 48 billions. It is a remarkable fact that these operations resulted in no diminution of the amounts of either the Bank borrowings or the Treasury paper outstanding. The year 1921 was a quiet period, there being only two issues of relatively short term for which subscribers paid a little over 7 billions in cash and one billion in securities. Then for two years no progress whatsoever was made in the refunding operations, all of the issues being paid for in cash. In 1923, only 2,073 million francs of 2-year 6 per cent, 1921, *Bons du Trésor* were refunded by the Treasury by accepting them in payment for the 6 per cent, 1923, *Bons du Trésor,* first series. During these years, it will be recalled, both the Treasury paper and the Bank advances remained almost stationary, but the cash received for issues of funded debt amounted, in 1922, to 16 billions, and, in 1923, to nearly 19 billions. In 1924, the market appears to have been exhausted, both issues of that year being frankly termed " failures " by the French commentators,[21] the yield having been only 6½ billions, in spite of the fact that one issue (that of *Bons du Trésor* 5 per cent, 1924) was offered with a reimbursement premium of 50 per cent, thus making the yield as high as 8.62 per cent. This was immediately followed by the disastrous Caillaux issue of *rentes* early in 1925. From this point onward the long-term market was practically unavailable as a resource for nearly two years, the issue of the *Caisse d'Amortissement* late in 1926 opening a new

[21] Allix, *Science des Finances,* p. 328. Jèze, *Revue de Science et de Législation Financières,* 1927, pp. 624 and 647.

series of long-term credit operations which form a part of the Poincaré program.

Public Debt Incurred for the State Railways and Railways of Alsace and Lorraine. — The State has pledged its credit in various issues of railway securities some of which are classed as internal debt and some as foreign debt (commercial). The portion which is classed as internal debt is included in the aggregate figures in Table 25. The details of such railway *obligations* as of September 30, 1927, divided between the domestic and foreign debt, are shown in Table 7. The amounts involved aggregated at that date less than 5 billion francs, slightly over one-half of which are classed as internal debt. The foreign borrowings for railway purposes are included in the figures for the foreign debt (commercial) given in Table 29.

Various Annuities and Dette Viagère. — Included within the figures of the funded debt of France, as shown in Table 25, are various items which consist of the capital amount corresponding to certain annuities which the State has pledged itself to pay. In the debt statement as of September 30, 1927,[22] this item amounts in the aggregate to approximately 24,030 billions. More than one-half of this sum, (14½ billions), falls under the heading of "*Capital correspondant aux titres d'annuités remises aux sinistrés.*" [23] This represents *obligations* issued by the Government to those who have suffered property damages in the devastated regions.[24]

Quite aside from this item for which a capital sum appears in the accounts, is the so-called "*Dette Viagère,*" literally translated "life debt." While theoretically it should be possible to capitalize the life expectancy of the beneficiaries of these payments, this is, as a matter of fact, not done, the only figures available being the annual charges on the budget. These amounted, on December 31, 1926,[25] to 6,264,734,515 francs. From the point of view of one who wishes to make a comparison with the

22 *Chéron Report, Budget général, 1928, Sénat* (from manuscript).

23 For a short description of the most important among the other annuities see Table 8.

24 See pp. 298–300.

25 *Projet de Budget,* 1928, p. 144.

American situation, it is of course fortunate that this item is not capitalized and included in the formal debt statement. It really represents the annual pension bill, civil and military, of the French Government. It is certainly not to be considered as an item representing a resource to which the Treasury has resorted. It is in no sense a result of borrowings.

Local Debt. — Although the amounts involved are not great, some attention should nevertheless be devoted to the changes which have taken place in the local debt situation. Turning first to the départements, the available data with regard to their indebtedness are shown in Table 28. It will be seen that in the aggregate this debt amounts to slightly less than 4 billion francs.

Only very scanty data are available for the debt of the communes.[26] The figures for 1913, 1921, and 1923 were as follows: [27]

December 31, 1913	4,892 million francs [28]
March 31, 1921	7,449 " " [29]
March 31, 1923	9,230 " " [29]

If one adds the communal and départemental debt for 1923, the last year for which data are available for both, he finds the total figure to be 11.6 billion paper francs. This amounts to 2.5 billion pre-war francs. The corresponding figure for 1913 was 6 billion francs. Thus it is apparent that measured in this fashion the local French debt in 1923 was less than half as great as before the war.

[26] Allix, *Science des Finances,* p. 938, gives the following figures, without citation of source, representing the amounts of loans contracted by the communes in the years specified:

1920	903,174,434 francs
1921	1,303,070,953 "
1922	330,033,158 "
1923	440,098,659 "
1924	772,700,498 "

[27] None of the figures includes Alsace and Lorraine.

[28] *Situation Financière des Communes en 1920,* p. xii.

[29] *Ibid., 1923,* p. x.

TABLE 28

THE OUTSTANDING INDEBTEDNESS OF THE DÉPARTEMENTS [a]

1913–1925

(In millions of francs. Source: *Situation Financière des Départements en 1923*, page 57.)

1913	1,142
1914	1,153
1915	1,158
1916	1,164
1917	1,213
1918	1,224
1919	1,311
1920	1,508
1921	2,160
1922 [b]	2,265
1923 [b]	2,379
1924	2,742 [c]
1925	2,754 [c]

[a] None of these figures includes Alsace and Lorraine.

[b] This figure does not include the debt of 25 million dollars and 3 million pounds which, calculated at the rate of 124 francs to the pound and 25.40 francs to the dollar, the approximate value of the franc, amounts to 1,007 million francs.

[c] Furnished by the Ministry of Interior.

CHAPTER XV

THE FOREIGN DEBT

THE discussion of the foreign debt of France presents peculiar difficulties. The basic figures are themselves in a state of confusion.[1] In the next place, there are the complications due to the fact that the data are in the form of foreign monetary units. Again, in the case of certain items, the accumulated interest has been capitalized and in others it has not. Finally, the figures carried in the accounts are based upon the full amounts of the credits originally extended, although the discussions which have taken place with the American and British treasuries indicate clearly that when a final settlement is arrived at, the amounts will actually be far less.

Statistics of the Foreign Debt.— The confusion which still exists with regard to the fiscal statistics is well illustrated by the situation which developed when an effort was made to secure from the French Treasury a dependable statement of the public debt. In response to a request for a statement as of the end of each year from 1913 to 1927, the data shown in Table 29 bearing upon the foreign debt were supplied.

Since it was desired to show the figures in terms of paper francs, the Ministry of Finance was again requested to supply a detailed table showing the foreign debt in terms of the monetary units in which it was payable. In response to this request the data shown in Table 30 were received. The figures shown in Table 30 were then translated into paper francs; the results are shown in Table 31. Attention is called to the fact that in Table 29 the foreign debt at the end of 1914 is given as 510 millions of francs at par value. Table 32 shows that at this date the debt amounted to 102 million francs. This indicates a serious discrepancy between the two sets of figures, both of which were furnished by the

[1] For examples of similar confusion elsewhere, see pp. 229, 257.

TABLE 29

FOREIGN DEBT, EXPRESSED IN TERMS OF FRANCS AT PAR VALUE, AT THE END OF EACH YEAR, 1913–1927

(In millions of francs. Source: 1913–1926, Ministry of Finance; 1927, *Chéron Report, Budget général, 1928, Sénat* [from manuscript])

	POLITICAL[a]	COMMERCIAL	TOTAL[a]
1913	.....	....	.....
1914	.....	510	510
1915	726	1,245	1,971
1916	3,355	4,098	7,453
1917	14,479	5,559	20,038
1918	23,074	6,208	29,282
1919	25,892	7,674	33,566
1920	29,192	6,767	35,959
1921	29,564	6,091	35,655
1922	29,996	5,448	35,444
1923	30,470	5,255	35,725
1924	31,048	5,431	36,479
1925	31,210	5,229	36,439
1926	31,764	4,980[b]	36,744
1927 (Sept. 30)	32,522	4,142[b]	36,664

[a] In these figures there is included no interest on the American debt. On the other hand, in the case of the British debt, the figures are increased by the amount of the accumulated interest.

[b] Including railway loans floated abroad.

French Ministry of Finance. For the purposes of the consolidated table, (Table 3) the total figures as shown in Table 31 have been utilized.

Distinction between the Political and the Commercial Foreign Debt.—In their accounts the French attach great importance to a distinction between the so-called "*dette politique*" and "*dette commerciale.*" In this country this distinction has not been well understood and the basis for it has commanded no great sympathy. To classify the character of the distinction the following paragraph is quoted from a standard French manual:[2]

The *dette politique* is that which has been contracted by France with the British and American Governments with the object of meeting common military needs. It relates directly to the conduct of the

[2] Allix, *Science des Finances*, p. 876.

TABLE 30

FOREIGN DEBT, EXPRESSED IN TERMS OF THE FOREIGN MONETARY UNITS, AT THE END OF EACH YEAR, 1914–1926

(Three last digits omitted. Source: Ministry of Finance.)

	1914	1915	1916	1917	1918	1919	1920	1921	1922	1923	1924	1925	1926
Great Britain (in pounds sterling)													
Loans by the British Treasury [a]	.....	30,800	131,017	326,143	418,005	475,730	535,730	566,186	586,876	605,681	628,628	635,067	657,038
Loans by the Bank of England (1916–1917)	.....	......	60,000	72,000	72,000	65,000	65,000	65,000	55,000	55,000	50,000	44,000	37,000
Bonds subscribed by the British public (1915)	.....	10,000	8,000	8,000	8,000	8,000	1,240	....	....	....	....	....	....
Loans by Rothschild (1914)	2,000	2,000	2,000	2,000	2,000	2,000	....	....	....	....	....	....	....
War stocks purchased from Great Britain	.....	......	.....	....	....	8,226	8,226	8,226	8,226	8,226	7,476	4,500	3,250
Miscellaneous advances	.....	......	.....	....	....	12,150	11,550	3,550	....	....	3,550	5,055	2,675
Total in pounds sterling	2,000	42,800	201,017	408,143	500,005	571,106	621,746	642,962	650,102	668,907	689,654	689,522	699,963
United States (in dollars)													
Advances by the United States Treasury [b]	.....	......	.....	1,130,000	2,096,427	2,947,500	3,158,800	3,290,000	3,430,791	3,583,307	3,729,885	3,876,544	4,022,804
War stocks — purchased from the United States	.....	......	.....	....	....	400,000	407,341	407,341	407,341	407,341	407,341	407,341	407,341
Commercial debt	10,000	301,200	524,893	612,940	477,043	372,198	238,792	233,648	223,069	209,091	298,043	286,562	277,895
Total in dollars	10,000	301,200	524,893	1,742,940	2,573,470	3,719,698	3,804,933	3,930,989	4,067,201	4,199,739	4,435,269	4,570,447	4,708,040
Spain (in pesetas)	.....	......	36,820	102,513	476,237	592,725	547,950	411,278	204,603	4,827	....	....	....
Switzerland (in Swiss francs)	.....	......	.....	37,500	160,250	146,100	121,800	15,700	....	....	....	....	....
Norway (in Norwegian kröner)	.....	......	25,000	50,000	50,000	60,000	32,400	....	....	....	....	....	....
Sweden (in Swedish kröner)	.....	......	40,000	40,000	46,250	56,250	56,250	....	....	....	....	....	....
Holland (in florins)	.....	......	.....	13,000	18,500	30,000	42,700	48,400	53,300	54,200	55,000	55,000	25,000
Argentina (in Argentine gold pesos)	.....	......	.....	....	100,000	23,252	20,863	18,474	18,474	18,474	18,474	18,464	18,464
Argentina (in Argentine paper pesos)	.....	......	.....	....	12,000	14,000	14,000	2,000	....	....	....	....	....
Uruguay (in Uruguayan gold pesos)	.....	......	.....	....	15,000	15,000	15,000	15,000	15,000	15,000	12,000	9,000	6,000
Egypt (in Egyptian pounds)	.....	......	.....	....	....	4,000	4,000	4,000	4,000	4,000	2,000	1,000	....
Canada (in Canadian dollars)	.....	......	.....	....	....	5,500	5,500	5,730	5,730	5,730	230	230	....
Japan (in yen)	.....	......	.....	76,242	128,218	130,342	133,161	133,161	120,000	70,000	....	....	....

[a] These figures include the accumulated and capitalized interest on the British debt.

[b] These figures include the amount of the unpaid interest on the American debt.

TABLE 31

FOREIGN DEBT, EXPRESSED IN TERMS OF PAPER FRANCS,[a] AT THE END OF EACH YEAR, 1914–1926

(In millions of francs. Source: Table 30)

	1914	1915	1916	1917	1918	1919	1920	1921	1922	1923	1924	1925	1926
Great Britain													
Loans by the British Treasury[b]	...	855	3,641	8,856	10,858	19,736	32,026	29,385	36,801	51,504	54,772	83,086	80,540
Loans by the Bank of England (1916–1917)	...	...	1,667	1,955	1,870	2,697	3,886	3,374	3,457	4,677	4,357	5,757	4,335
Bonds subscribed by the British public (1915)	...	278	222	217	208	332	74	...	...	...	...	...	...
Loan by Rothschild (1914)	50	55	56	54	52	83	...	...	...	...	...	...	...
War stocks purchased from Great Britain	...	...	...	...	...	341	492	427	517	699	651	580	308
Miscellaneous advances	...	...	...	...	...	504	690	184	...	...	309	779	328
Total[c]	50	1,188	5,586	11,083	12,988	23,692	37,168	33,370	40,865	56,881	60,090	90,210	85,601
United States													
Advances by the United States Treasury[d]	...	...	...	6,441	11,426	31,877	53,336	40,500	46,569	70,287	68,807	103,736	101,576
War stocks — purchased from the United States	...	...	...	...	...	4,326	6,878	5,014	5,519	7,990	7,514	10,900	10,285
Commercial debt	52	1,762	3,063	3,494	2,600	4,025	4,032	2,876	3,023	4,101	5,498	7,668	7,017
Total	52	1,762	3,063	9,935	14,025	40,229	64,246	48,390	55,111	82,378	81,820	122,305	118,878
Spain	...	...	23	71	521	1,234	1,233	758	435	12	...	...	...
Switzerland	...	...	...	40	183	283	314	38	...	...	...	...	...
Norway	...	...	42	98	77	131	84	...	...	...	...	...	...
Sweden	...	...	68	78	74	122	190	...	...	...	...	...	...
Holland	...	...	...	32	43	122	227	219	285	403	411	592	253
Argentina (*gold pesos*)	...	...	...	...	565	248	266	175	219	260	310	493	439
Argentina (*paper pesos*)	...	...	...	...	31	68	81	9	...	...	...	...	...
Uruguay	...	...	...	...	98	169	189	138	178	227	222	247	155
Egypt	...	...	...	...	...	2	2	2	3	3	2	1	...
Canada	...	...	...	...	...	55	80	67	78	108	4	6	...
Japan	...	...	...	226	368	722	1,069	796	811	632	...		...
Grand Total	102	2,949	8,783	21,572	28,973	67,076	105,149	83,962	97,984	140,903	142,858	213,855	205,326

[a] The figures as shown in Table 30 were converted into paper francs on the basis of the exchange rates prevailing at the end of each year. The exchange rates utilized were those published in the *Journal Officiel* for December 31 of each year or the nearest day to that date for which quotations were published. The rates appearing in the *Journal Officiel* are the daily rates obtaining at the Paris Bourse. In cases when more than one quotation was given, the average for the day was used. In some instances there were no transactions on the Paris Bourse and, in such cases, the quotations on the London Exchange were taken and transformed into francs at the rate on which francs were quoted at that day on the London market. The source of the London quotations is the London *Economist*.

[b] These figures include the accumulated and capitalized interest on the British debt.

[c] Note that no attempt has been made, in this or other tables, to force the totals to agree with the sum of the several items, when the discrepancy arises from rounding off the true figures to the nearest million.

[d] These figures include the amount of the unpaid interest on the American debt.

TABLE 32

FOREIGN DEBT, EXPRESSED IN TERMS OF FRANCS AT PAR VALUE, AT THE END OF EACH YEAR, 1914–1927

(In millions of francs. Sources: 1914–1926, Table 30; 1927, *Chéron Report, Budget général, 1928, Sénat* [from manuscript])

	1914	1915	1916	1917	1918	1919	1920	1921	1922	1923	1924	1925	1926	1927[a]
Great Britain:														
Political Debt:														
Loans by the British Treasury[b]	...	777	3,305	8,227	10,544	12,000	13,514	14,282	14,804	15,278	15,857	16,020	16,574	17,328
Commercial Debt:														
Loans by the Bank of England (1916–1917)	...	....	1,514	1,816	1,816	1,640	1,640	1,640	1,387	1,387	1,261	1,110	933	.....
Bonds subscribed by the British public (1915)	...	252	202	202	202	202	31	.....	.....	.....	.....	.....	.....	.....
Loan by Rothschild (1914)	50	50	50	50	50	50	.....	.....	.....	.....	.....	.....	.....	.....
War stocks purchased from Great Britain	...	....	....	.....	.....	208	208	208	208	208	189	114	82	57
Miscellaneous advances	...	....	....	.....	.....	306	291	90	.....	.....	90	150	67	38
Total Commercial Debt	50	302	1,766	2,068	2,068	2,406	2,170	1,938	1,595	1,595	1,540	1,374	1,082	95
Total — Commercial and Political Debt	50	1,079	5,071	10,295	12,612	14,406	15,684	16,220	16,399	16,873	17,397	17,394	17,656	17,423
United States:														
Political Debt:														
Advances by the United States Treasury[c]	...	....	....	5,859	10,870	15,283	16,378	17,058	17,820	18,579	19,339	20,100	20,858	21,427[d]
Commercial Debt:														
War stocks purchased from the United States	...	....	....	.....	.....	2,074	2,112	2,112	2,112	2,112	2,112	2,112	2,112	2,112
Other Commercial Debt	52	1,562	2,722	3,178	2,473	1,930	1,238	1,211	1,157	1,084	1,545	1,486	1,441	1,391
Total Commercial Debt	52	1,562	2,722	3,178	2,473	4,004	3,350	3,323	3,269	3,196	3,657	3,598	3,553	3,503
Total — Commercial and Political Debt	52	1,562	2,722	9,037	13,343	19,287	19,728	20,382	21,089	21,775	22,996	23,698	24,411	24,928

TABLE 32 (Continued)

	1914	1915	1916	1917	1918	1919	1920	1921	1922	1923	1924	1925	1926	1927
Spain	...	....	37	103	476	593	548	411	205	5	.....	.....	.....	.....
Holland	...	....	....	27	39	62	89	101	111	113	115	115	52	.....
Switzerland	...	....	....	38	160	146	122	16	.....	.....	.....	.....	.....	.....
Uruguay	...	....	....	.....	80	80	80	80	80	80	64	48	32	16
Norway	...	....	35	69	69	83	45	.....	.....	.....	.....	.....	.....	.....
Egypt	...	....	....	.....	.....	103	103	103	103	103	51	26	.....	.....
Sweden	...	....	56	56	64	78	78	.....	.....	.....	.....	.....	.....	.....
Canada	...	....	....	.....	.....	29	29	30	30	30	1	1	.....	.....
Japan	...	....	....	197	331	337	344	344	310	181	.....	.....	.....	.....
Argentina (*gold pesos*)	...	....	....	.....	500	116	104	92	92	92	92	92	92	92
Argentina (*paper pesos*)	...	....	....	.....	26	31	31	44	.....	.....	.....	.....	.....	.....
Total Commercial Debt	102	1,864	4,616	5,736	6,286	8,068	7,093	6,482	5,795	5,395	5,520	5,254	4,811	3,706
Total Political Debt	...	777	3,305	14,086	21,414	27,283	29,892	31,341	32,624	33,857	35,196	36,120	37,432	38,755
Grand Total — Political and Commercial Debt	102	2,641	7,921	19,822	27,700	35,351	36,985	37,823	38,419	39,252	40,716	41,374	42,243	42,461

[a] As of September 30.
[b] These figures include the accumulated and capitalized interest on the British debt.
[c] These figures include the amount of the unpaid interest on the American debt.
[d] The amount of the American political debt as of September 30, 1927 has been estimated by the writer by adding to the amount of the American debt, as it appears on Table 30 as of December 31, 1926, five per cent interest for the period of nine months on the capital amount of $2,933,173,899 (*Projet de Budget*, 1928, p. 140). The amount in dollars obtained was then translated into francs at par value.

war. It involves only two countries: Great Britain and the United States.

The *dette commerciale* has been contracted not only with Great Britain and the United States but with various other countries: Holland, Argentina, Uruguay, Canada, Egypt, etc. The purpose is also connected with the war, but the proceeds were not employed directly in the conduct of war operations; they were employed, namely, to meet the need of furnishing supplies for national subsistence [*ravitaillement national*] as well as for the acquisition of stocks of materials left in France by the allied armies.

Political Debt. — By reference to Table 29 it will become apparent that this item began to assume large proportions in 1917. It consisted of credits opened for the benefit of France by the American Treasury and of French *Bons du Trésor* deposited with the British Treasury as evidence of similar accommodations. According to the latest statement of the French public debt, as of September 30, 1927,[3] the advances of the American Treasury are shown as amounting to 15,194 millions of francs. This sum includes no accumulated interest. The amount of the *Bons du Trésor* deposited with the British Treasury is shown to be 17,328 millions of francs. Both figures are in terms of francs at par. In the British figures, however, the actual advances have been increased by accumulated interest.

The accommodations given to the French Treasury by the American and British Governments continued for some time after the Armistice, but the changes in the amounts since 1921 represent merely the accumulation of interest.

Commercial Debt. — The commercial debt is relatively small as compared with the political debt. The largest single item consists of the debt due to the United States, based upon the purchase by France of the materials left in that country after the Armistice. There is a similar item due to Great Britain, but it is insignificant in amount. Included also are various bank credits and loans which were made in the foreign currencies. Of these the two largest single items at the time of the last debt statement were the Morgan loans of 1920[4] and 1924 amounting respectively

[3] *Chéron Report, Budget général, 1928, Sénat,* (manuscript).

[4] It is the balance remaining outstanding of this loan which is to be retired

to 374 and 458 million francs at par,[5] the other commercial foreign loans being briefly as follows: [6]

UNITED STATES

Loan of 1921.

Placed in June, 1921. The bonds still outstanding are redeemable at par in 1941. The interest is at 7½ per cent.

Loan of the cities of Lyons, Bordeaux, Marseilles.

Contracted jointly by the three cities in November, 1916, and later placed at the disposal of the French Treasury. The original amount was of 36 million dollars to mature in 3 years. The second issue was made in November, 1919. The proceeds from this loan were $40,586,000. This loan is due in 1934. The interest is at 6 per cent.

Balance of the English-French loan.

This balance represents a partial conversion of the loan of 500 million dollars contracted jointly by Great Britain and France in 1915 and repaid in 1920. On the demand of the holders a part of this loan was refunded in 4½ per cent *obligations* repayable in 1930 and 1940 at the choice of the French Government. Bonds up to the aggregate amount of $13,850 only were thus refunded.

Balance of the Loan 5½ per cent.

This loan was issued in 1917. The existence of this balance is due to the same causes as in the case of the preceding loan. The original capital was of 100 million dollars and was repaid in 1919 with the exception of a small amount refunded, on the demand of the holders, in 5½ per cent *obligations* repayable in 20 years. This balance amounts to $2,110,000.

GREAT BRITAIN

War Stocks.

The amount to be paid to Great Britain for these stocks was fixed at £2,226,069 /1/1. The interest is at 6 per cent.

---

on March 15, 1928, under an arrangement with the Swedish Match Company. New York *Evening Post*, November 5, 1927.

[5] *Chéron Report, Budget général, 1928, Sénat,* (manuscript). A very interesting table is given in the *Rapport du Comité des Experts,* p. 156, which shows a complete schedule by years of the maturities of all of the items of the commercial foreign debt.

[6] *Palmade Report, Budget général, 1928,* p. 82 *et seq.*

Short-term bonds floated in England.

These bonds were floated in England after 1924 to meet the reimbursement of the external debt. Interest at 6 per cent.

ARGENTINA

This loan was contracted in 1918 in connection with purchases of grain and was due in 1927.

URUGUAY

This loan was contracted in 1918 at 5 per cent, to mature in 1927 and 1928.

The purchase of the surplus war stocks left in France by the American expeditionary force constitutes a very interesting episode in the financial history of this period and one which has been the occasion of bitter feeling among the French. According to the French version of the transaction, the price finally agreed upon, which was in the aggregate $407,341,144 [7] was a blind bargain based upon very inadequate information as to the quantities of material involved.[8] The story of the French efforts to dispose of this material is a very dismal one. There were huge losses from deterioration due to failure to protect the goods from the elements. Large sales appear to have been made to speculators at prices so low as to give basis for charges of scandal. Again the dumping of the stocks upon the market resulted in a demoralization of prices. An elaborate study of the details of the transactions is set forth in the *Inventaire*.[9] In this document the figures are translated into dollars according to the average rates of exchange by three-month intervals from 1919 to 1924. The results indicate that these materials, for which France pledged herself to pay over 400 million dollars, were sold for

[7]

Stocks	$400,000,000
Railway material	6,566,762
Machine-tools	774,382
Total	$407,341,144

(*Inventaire*, p. 57).

[8] With respect to the item of stocks of which the price agreed upon was 400 million dollars, it is said that the American asking price was 6 billion francs, whereas the first French offer was 1½ billion francs.

[9] *Inventaire*, pp. 57 and 58.

approximately 270 million dollars, of which at that date only about 220 million dollars had been actually collected. With the data available it is impossible to say to what extent the tremendous loss on this operation was due to sharp bargaining by the American authorities in arriving at the price and to what extent it was due to mismanagement by the French themselves. In any case, it is certainly true that the French public has placed much of the blame upon America. Even Professor Allix, who is not given to exaggeration, speaks of the acquisition of these stocks as "disastrous" and says that "this operation will stand as one of the worst scandals of our modern financial history."[10] It will be recalled that in the pending proposals for the funding of the French debt to the United States the amounts owing to the American Treasury because of the sale of this war material are lumped with the political debt, with the scale of annual payments arranged in such a manner as to cover the liabilities arising from both. In case of failure to ratify the Mellon-Bérenger agreement, the entire sum becomes payable in August, 1929.[11]

[10] Allix, *Science des Finances*, p. 877.

[11] The ratification of the debt agreement in the summer of 1929, while this book was in the hands of the printer, had the effect, of course, of eliminating this maturity.

CHAPTER XVI

REPARATIONS

THE payments made by Germany bear a very vital relationship to the French debt problem. France is depending upon them not only to finance whatever may be required of her by England and America but also to support as large as possible a share of the debt incurred to restore the devastated regions.

Reparations Receipts by France to September 1, 1927. — The reparations problem will be discussed here briefly, from the viewpoint of what France has received, and how these receipts link with the problem of reconstruction of the invaded provinces. The reconstruction problem itself will be considered toward the end of the chapter.

Three blocks of reparations receipts may be distinguished. First, payments, not resulting directly from the Ruhr occupation of 1923–1924, were made by Germany before the Dawes Plan was instituted. Second, the French received a certain net balance of receipts from the occupation of the Ruhr above expenses connected with that occupation. Third, France has been receiving her share of the reparations payments under the Dawes Plan since September 1, 1924. These three classes of receipts are set forth in some detail in Tables 33, 34 and 35. The figures of two of the tables are in gold marks. By transforming the yearly totals into paper francs at the average rate of exchange for each year, the grand totals in francs become: for the first class, 5,430,827,567 francs; for the second class, 1,550,201,987 francs; [1] for the Dawes Plan payments, 10,796,203,559 francs. These total 17,777,233,113 paper francs received from 1919 to September 1, 1927, by France from Germany on account of reparations, after deduction of Ruhr expenses. There seems little doubt that

[1] This perhaps should be somewhat larger. See "undetermined share" item in Table 34.

TABLE 33

REPARATIONS PAYMENTS TO FRANCE BY GERMANY BEFORE DAWES PLAN,[a] WITH STATEMENT OF OFFSETTING EXPENDITURES

(In gold marks, save where otherwise noted. Source: ***Lamoureux Report on 1925 Budget:*** Expenses concerning war damages.[b] Neither receipts nor expenditures from the occupation of the Ruhr are included in this table.)

	To April 30, 1921	May 1, 1921 to April 30, 1922	May 1, 1922 to April 30, 1923	May 1, 1923 to April 30, 1924	May 1, 1924 to June 30, 1924	Total to June 30, 1924
Cash payments	....	....	144,191,200	*−164,700* [c]	....	144,026,500
Deliveries in kind: Coal, cattle, ships, etc.	458,402,800	218,259,400	154,308,100	1,296,100	648,600	832,915,000 [f]
Deliveries in kind: Delivered in execution of the protocols of the Armistice (railroad rolling stock, etc.)	443,301,700	1,667,400	482,500	183,700	*−17,700* [d]	445,617,600 [g]
Saar mines (300,000,000 marks) and German school at Shanghai, ceded to France	302,042,000	....	....	....	....	302,042,000
Total receipts	1,203,746,500	219,926,800	298,981,800	1,315,100	630,900	1,724,601,100
Expenses connected with reparations receipts	....	....	....	....	....	1,620,580,000 [e]
Balance	....	....	....	....	....	104,021,100
Total receipts in paper francs	3,851,988,800	703,765,760	867,047,220	5,155,192	2,870,595	5,430,827,567
Average annual exchange rate used in arriving at paper franc total — francs per gold mark	3.2	3.2	2.9	3.92	4.55	

[a] To be exact, there is a gap of two months between this and Table 34 showing the receipts under the Dawes Plan. But it seems that little if any deliveries were made by Germany during these two months of July and August, 1924.

[b] *Doc. Parl., Chambre*, 1924, Doc. No. 537, Vol. II, pp. 61–64, 89.

[c, d] The amounts represent revisions of figures of previous years, reducing the true amounts of those items. The figures for deliveries in kind for the last three periods would be larger than they are had they, too, not been reduced by revisions for the account of former years.

[e] Costs of army of occupation, 1,381,809,000; temporary reduction granted to Germany in coal receipts, 238,771,000. Of the receipts, 2,147,000 represents profit on exchange of gold marks held temporarily on deposit for Belgium.

[f, g] The total for deliveries in kind thus amounts to 1,278,532,600 gold marks. Yet the Minister of Finance (Loucheur) in a letter to the Chamber Finance Commission of Dec. 5, 1924 (*cf. Violette Report on 1925 Budget, Doc. Parl., Chambre*, Doc. No. 537, 1924, Vol. III of the *Report*, p. 149 *et seq.*) gives figures for deliveries in kind from [Jan. 1 ?] 1920 to May 31, 1924, that total 1,027,000,000 gold marks. The discrepancy may arise from the slight difference in the period covered by the figures, but it is more likely indicative of the approximate character of all such figures.

France is faring better under the Dawes Plan than she did under the old arrangement. Leaving out of account for the moment the Ruhr receipts, France got 1,725 thousand gold marks during the (approximately) five years up to June 30, 1924, while during the three years, September 1, 1924, to September 1, 1927, she received 1,729 thousand under the Dawes Plan.

TABLE 34

RECEIPTS AND EXPENDITURES RESULTING FROM OCCUPATION OF THE RUHR, JANUARY, 1923 TO AUGUST 31, 1924

(In paper francs. Source: *Lamoureux Report*, *op. cit.*, pp. 136–159)

Receipts: Coal tax	619,961,422	
Import and export license taxes on goods entering or leaving the Ruhr	459,272,401	
Ordinary customs duties	762,421,980	
Net receipts from railroad operation	285,000,000	
Receipts from forests	135,186,470	
Deliveries in kind	1,990,852,430	
Marks seized, fines, and contributions	245,614,200	
Miscellaneous receipts	19,055,638	
Total receipts		4,517,364,541
Expenditures: Administration expenses	314,765,314	
Military expenses	695,242,691	
Miscellaneous expenses	2,551,323	
Total expenditures		1,012,559,328
Net balance		3,504,805,213
Add: Bookkeeping profit due to variations in exchange rates		13,703,108
Probable net receipts after Aug. 31, 1924		100,000,000
Balance available for France, Belgium and Italy		3,618,508,321
French share: Delivered in kind	1,237,701,987	
From marks seized and fines (including reserve set aside for possible loss through exchange rates)	312,500,000	
	1,550,201,987	
Add: Undetermined share in approximately 245,750,000 francs	?	

The figure for the French share, as given in Table 34, is calculated in the manner indicated, in order that it may be added to the totals of Tables 33 and 35 to determine the total French receipts from Germany up to September 1, 1927, after deduction only of expenses directly connected with the Ruhr occupation. But there were other expenditures made during this occupation which, though not resulting directly from the Ruhr occupation, were nevertheless chargeable against reparations collections as a whole. If one takes as receipts the amounts directly resulting from the Ruhr occupation, and as expenses all items connected with reparations collections as a whole, the net balance left to France after twenty months of occupation is calculated by Palmade[2] at only 352 million paper francs. Contrasting this with the net balance to be expected from the Dawes payments, Palmade concludes there can be no doubt France was benefited by the change from the Ruhr policy to the Dawes Plan. He asks, however, if Germany would have consented to the Dawes Plan without the forcible suasion of the Ruhr occupation.

Table 35 shows the final forms in which the French share of the gold marks collected under the Dawes Plan have been received. The final total of 1,729 thousand gold marks must not be taken as the amount actually placed at the disposal of the French Treasury during the three years. As will be discussed in more detail further on, the French Government sold its rights to these marks to its citizens at a discount, and, furthermore, on some of the sales it has been able to collect (from its citizen-buyers) only a small amount in cash.

It must be noted that the total from reparations after September 1, 1924, given in Table 35, is, in a manner of speaking, a table of gross receipts. In the tables for the preceding periods, such accompanying costs as those of the army of occupation were deducted to arrive at tentative net receipts. No reliable expenditure figures for this item after September 1, 1924, seem to be available, but using the estimates made in the authorization clauses of various laws, one may present the approximations given in Table 36 (page 292).

As a rough approximation of the net amount France has received from reparations, after deduction of the expenses of the army of occupation, Table 37 (page 292) is presented.

[2] *Op. cit.*, p. 167.

TABLE 35

DAWES PLAN PAYMENTS TO FRANCE, SEPTEMBER 1, 1924–AUGUST 31, 1927

(In gold marks unless otherwise specified. Source: Annual Reports of Agent-General of Reparations Commission)

Final Forms in Which the Marks Were Put at Disposal of France	Sept. 1, 1924–Aug. 31, 1925	Per Cent of Total Payments	Sept. 1, 1925–Aug. 31, 1926	Per Cent of Total Payments	Sept. 1, 1926–Aug. 31, 1927	Per Cent of Total Payments	Grand Total Column for Three Years Sept. 1, 1924–Aug. 31, 1927	Per Cent of Total Payments
Mark payments to armies of occupation	34,012,474.24	8.58	26,216,208.27	4.63	24,491,324.90	3.84	84,720,007.41	5.29
Requisitions and damages under art. 6 of Rhineland agreement	11,130,000.00	2.81	....	....	....	....	11,130,000.00	0.70
Furnishings in kind (to occupation armies) under arts. 8–12 of Rhineland agreement	64,994,640.00	16.39	30,736,225.11	5.43	24,681,026.61	3.87	120,411,891.72	7.50
Furnishings in the Ruhr	26,454,138.65	6.67	....	....	....	....	26,454,138.65	1.65
Reparations Recovery Act (26 per cent import tax on German goods)	25,090,220.95	6.33	41,495,166.17	7.34	59,509,942.99	9.32	126,095,330.11	7.88
Deliveries of coal, coke, and lignite	136,212,112.85	34.35	182,148,096.30	32.20	194,072,856.99	30.40	512,433,066.14	32.02
Transport of combustibles	53,161,379.70	13.40	58,682,689.58	10.37	18,332,181.55	2.87	130,176,250.83	8.13
Deliveries of dyestuffs and pharmaceutical products	5,163,079.35	1.30	2,351,047.85	0.42	3,287,623.30	0.52	10,801,750.50	0.67
Deliveries of chemical fertilizers	19,655,862.09	4.96	47,891,578.25	8.47	47,251,424.36	7.40	114,798,864.70	7.17
Deliveries of coal by-products	....	....	3,023,915.30	0.53	5,799,904.36	0.91	8,823,819.66	0.55
Deliveries of refractory earths	....	....	102,541.61	0.02	154,761.25	0.02	257,302.86	0.02
Deliveries of agricultural products	....	....	17,212,749.77	3.04	18,740,599.12	2.94	35,953,348.89	2.25
Deliveries of timber	....	....	18,110,854.44	3.20	22,379,021.11	3.51	40,489,875.55	2.53
Deliveries of sugar	....	....	12,895,734.49	2.28	17,970,458.96	2.82	30,866,193.45	1.93
Miscellaneous deliveries	20,705,135.50	5.22	83,726,242.92	14.80	84,407.900.68	13.22	188,839,279.10	11.80
Miscellaneous payments	....	....	1,893,145.09	0.33	957,678.55	0.15	2,850,823.64	0.18

TABLE 35 (Continued)

Cash transfers:								
(a) Liquidation of Franco-Belgian Railway *Régie* accounts.	....	....	5,007,229.01	0.89	....	...	5,007,229.01	0.31
(b) Payment of amount owed to Germany for services or deliveries before Sept. 1, 1924..	....	....	350,000.00	0.06	286,584.56	0.04	636,584.56	0.04
(c) In foreign currencies........	....	....	33,820,634.16	5.98	115,980,832.37	18.17	149,801,466.53	9.36
Total payments utilized by France (gold marks)...............	396,579,043.33	100.00	565,664,058.32	100.00	638,304,121.66	100.00	1,600,547,223.31	100.00
Add: France's balance on hand with Agent General [a].........	....		....		....		128,693,821.23	
Total received by France from reparations for first three years of Dawes Plan (gold marks) [b]..	....		....		....		1,729,241,044.54	
Total payments utilized by France (paper francs)...............	1,982,895,216.65		4,157,630,828.65		3,874,506,018.48		10,015,032,063.78	
Average annual exchange rate used in arriving at paper franc totals — francs per gold mark.	5.00		7.35		6.07		....	
Add: France's balance on hand with Agent-General (6.07 francs per gold mark)...............	....		....		....		781,171,494.87	
Total received by France from reparations for first three years of Dawes Plan (paper francs)..	....		....		....		10,796,203,558.65	
French share in each annuity (gold marks)....................	454,512,000.00		584,432,000.00[c]		745,689,000.00		1,784,633,000.00[d]	

[a] Of this amount, 58,406,556.69 marks had to be applied against bills payable for deliveries already made to France. Of the balance, 64,752,410.98 marks was to be spent under contracts already approved. The rest — 5,534,853.56 marks — was not yet disposed of.

[b] On March 19, 1928, the Ministry of Finance issued a statement showing receipts by calendar years, under the Dawes Plan, as follows (in gold marks): Sept. 1 to Dec. 31, 1924, 113,561,000; year 1925, 459,000,000; year 1926, 539,250,000; year 1927, 763,584,000; total, 1,875,395,000. *New York Times*, March 20, 1928.

[c] This figure is taken from the June 10, 1927 *Report of the Agent-General* (Vol. XVI of the Reparations Commission's publications, p. 116).

[d] There is a discrepancy of 55,392,000 marks between this and the figure for "total received." This may be because the figure of the French share in the third annuity may have been made up later than the other figures and may include some changes not noted in the others.

TABLE 36

ORIGINAL CREDITS GRANTED FOR EXPENSES OF ARMY OF OCCUPATION [a]

(In paper francs)

	Fiscal Year			Grand Total
	1925	1926	1927	
Special Treasury Accounts:				
Maintenance of troops of occupation in foreign countries.	613,537,000	479,256,580	541,811,540	1,634,605,120
Payments in kind under Rhineland agreement (to be spent on army of occupation).	. . . . [b]	364,560,000	219,594,390	584,154 390
Total.	613,537,000	843,816,580	761,405,930	2,218,759,510

[a] From budget laws of July 13, 1925 (art. 182), April 29, 1926 (arts. 99, 101, 102), Dec. 19, 1926 (arts. 55, 56). The "payments in kind" item is stated in gold marks (1926: 49,600,000; 1927: 36,177,000), and has been translated into francs at the rate of 7.35 francs to the mark for 1926 and 6.07 for 1927 (from Table 35). It might be thought that these occupation army expenses would be shown by the first and third lines of Table 35, but the amounts shown there are considerably less than those in the above Table 36, indicating they do not come near representing the total expenses under these headings.

[b] This item was treated separately for the first time in 1926.

TABLE 37

NET RECEIPTS FROM REPARATIONS PAYMENTS TO SEPTEMBER 1, 1927

(In paper francs)

Before Dawes Plan, and not including Ruhr receipts (Table 33).	244,971,567 [a]
Net Ruhr receipts (Table 34).	1,550,201,987
Net Dawes Plan receipts (Tables 35 and 36).	7,796,272,554 [b]
Total net receipts.	9,591,446,108

[a] This figure is arrived at by deducting from the receipts, as translated into paper francs (Table 33), the total of expenditures for the period, i.e. 1,620,580,000 gold marks, translated into francs at the rate of 3.2 francs to the mark — the average rate between May 1, 1921 and April 30, 1922 (See Table 33). The resulting figure of net receipts is, of course, only very roughly approximate. Whether it is too high or too low depends, of course, on whether the exchange rate of 3.2 is too low or too high, and that in turn depends upon how the expenses were distributed over the years when the exchange rate

Those figures must be taken with great reserve. The main sources of possible error seem to be: (1) the use of estimates for expenditures in Table 36, and the fact that these estimates cover the period January 1, 1925, to the end of the fiscal year 1927 instead of the period September 1, 1925 — August 31, 1927; (2) the rough-and-ready method used in translating gold marks into paper francs; (3) the unsettled state of the Ruhr accounts existing when the figures reproduced in Table 34 were drawn up; (4) the possibility of double-counting in adding the figures in Tables 33, 34 and 35, although such danger appears to have been avoided in the sources.

How France Uses the Dawes Plan Payments. — France has assigned a definite use to her share of the Dawes Plan receipts during 1928. It may clarify the situation first to see how the reparations payments are to be used during 1928, and then to consider the current expenditures being made for reconstruction.

The Dawes Plan annuities run from September 1 of one year to August 31 of the next. For the calendar year 1928, therefore, France will get the last three-quarters of the fourth (1927–1928) annuity. The fifth annuity is the first one in which Germany is supposed to pay the Allies the full amount of 2,500,000,000 gold marks. It is estimated that France will get 640,470,000 gold marks as her share of the last three-quarters of the fourth annuity, and 374,300,000 gold marks from the first quarter of the fifth annuity — a total of 1,014,770,000 gold marks for the calendar year 1928.[3] In what forms will she receive this amount?

---

was varying. Of the 1,620,580,000 (gold marks) expenses (Table 33) so deducted, about three-fourths arose before May 1, 1921 (*Lamoureux Report*, p. 64), so the exchange rate of 3.2 applied to the expenses is probably too high rather than too low. Unfortunately the report does not give annual figures of expenses; that is why the crude method of applying one exchange rate to the sum total of expenditures cannot be avoided. The figures work out: Receipts, 5,430,827,567 francs; expenditures, 5,185,856,000 francs; net, 244,971,567 francs.

[b] Receipts, 10,015,032,064 francs (Table 35);
Expenditures, 2,218,759,510 francs (Table 36);

Net: 7,796,272,554 francs.

[3] These figures are from the *Palmade Report* (see following footnote). The Agent-General, in his third annual report (p. 175) estimates France's share in the

There are three ways in which the French Treasury will receive this sum. They are (a) deliveries in kind direct to the French Treasury or to the devastated regions; (b) cash payments; (c) rights to goods and services which the Treasury can sell to French citizens.

The amounts to be thus received and the disposal of them are outlined in the *Palmade Report* of 1927.[4] Briefly, they appear as follows (in gold marks):

Deliveries in kind to the army of occupation under the Rhineland agreement........	36,895,000	
Deliveries in kind to war-sufferers in devastated regions	100,000,000	
	136,895,000	
Cash payments (including receipts from 26 per cent import tax on German goods, for which the German seller is reimbursed by his government)		226,000,000
Rights to German goods, to be sold by French Treasury to its citizens		380,000,000
Rights to German labor and construction work (*prestations de travaux*) to be sold by French Treasury to its citizens		271,875,000
Total due from Germany, 1928		1,014,770,000

This total due from Germany does not correspond with the amount to be received by the French Government, however, because the Treasury will not realize the full cash value of the last two items in the above table. The Treasury sells its rights to German goods at a discount of 10 per cent — that is, the French citizen-purchaser gets his rights at 10 per cent below the value set on them for reparations accounting purposes.[5]

fourth annuity at 882,498,000 gold marks. Three-quarters of this is 661,873,500 gold marks, agreeing fairly closely with Palmade's figure.

[4] *Palmade Report, Budget général de l'exercice 1928* (*Ministère des Finances*) *Doc. Parl., Chambre,* 1927, *Sess. Ord.,* Doc. No. 4872, July 13, 1927, pp. 45–60 of the *Report.*

[5] Ultimately the French Government may have lost more than this, through collusion on the part of the German seller and the French buyer. German sellers, it appears, have at times sold live stock and crops to the Agent-General at excessive prices and split the profit with the Frenchmen who bought the right to the goods from their Government. See *New York Times,* January 29, 1928.

As to the rights to German labor and construction work, the Government finds it impossible to collect the entire purchase price from its citizen-purchasers at once; Palmade estimates that the Treasury will be fortunate if during 1928 it realizes, in cash, one-tenth of the sales price. Drawing up a table of receipts available for the French Treasury (rather than of amounts due by Germany) and translating the amounts into francs at 6 francs to the mark, the following results are obtained:

Deliveries in kind, Rhineland agreement	221,370,000	francs
Deliveries in kind, to war-sufferers	600,000,000	
Cash payments	1,356,000,000	
Rights to German goods (allowing 10 per cent discount)	2,052,000,000	
Rights to German labor and construction work (assuming one-tenth realized in cash from French purchasers)	163,125,000	
Amount in fact received by French Government:	4,392,495,000	francs

The deliveries in kind under the Rhineland agreement and to the war sufferers are already dedicated to special uses. There remains a balance of 3,571,125,000 francs which will be disposed of as follows:

Costs of the army of occupation	512,707,160 [6]
Cash payments to war-sufferers	1,250,000,000
Provisional payments on political debts:	
to the United States: $12,132,943 at 25.5 francs	309,000,000
to England £7,000,000 at 124 francs	868,000,000
Payment on English war stocks debt: £1,250,000 at 124 francs	155,000,000
Repayment of Argentine, Uruguayan, and Swiss debts	419,683,951
Total	3,514,391,111
Balance	56,733,889
Total received by French Government after direct deliveries in kind	3,571,125,000

In summary: The receipts from the Dawes payments do not appear in the general budget, nor do the expenditures which they serve to meet (save as authorization clauses). This ensemble of

[6] This amount was 578,630,000 francs in the *projet* as discussed by Palmade, but was cut down in the law as finally passed.

receipts and expenditures forms a separate budget, so to speak, fed wholly by reparations payments and drained chiefly by payments for reconstruction (both in cash and in kind), by provisional payments on the political debts to the United States and England, and by the occupation army's costs. Whether or not the American Treasury believes debt payments should be linked to reparations payments, the French Treasury apparently has no doubts on the matter.

The amount taken from the Dawes payments to be applied to reconstruction does not cover the total payments which the French Treasury must make under the reconstruction program. The schedule of payments under this head for the fiscal year 1928 is planned as follows (in millions of francs): [7]

I. To be met by Dawes Plan payments:	
Deliveries in kind	600
Cash payments	1,250
II. To be met by increase of public debt: [8]	
Capitalized value of debt:	
Ten-year annuities	2,500
Fifteen- to thirty-year annuities	2,500
Six-year bonds (interest payments only, on damages not yet paid for)	250
Six-year bonds (interest and capital payments for damages in Alsace and Lorraine)	150
Rentes 6 per cent [9]	50
III. Cancellation of taxes due by war-sufferers [10]	300
Total reconstruction payments to be made during 1928	7,600

[7] The first six items are reproduced from the budget law of December 27, 1928, arts. 171–176.

[8] It is the custom in French financial circles not to regard these payments as "increases" in the public debt. The Government already owed these sums to the war-sufferers, and surely the payment of a debt is not an increase in it! But for present purposes — to get some idea of the new burden the budget is being called on to bear — the amounts must be considered as adding to the public debt. *Cf. Chéron Report on 1928 budget* (*Doc. Parl., Sénat,* Doc. No. 652, 1928), p. 28 *et seq.;* Poincaré's speech before the Chamber, *Le Temps,* February 4, 1928, p. 5.

[9] This sum is arrived at by capitalizing one-half of the interest charge due on the rentes given or to be given for this purpose in *both* 1927 and 1928. This charge is 6 million francs. The rentes are of the 1920 series, apparently taken in by the Treasury and then given back ("remises") in payment of war damages claims. *Palmade Report,* p. 76.

[10] This sum, like that for the rentes, is an approximation, derived from the

None of the first section above appears in the budget, though the finance law accompanying the budget fixes these amounts. Of the second section, not the capitalized value (as given above) but only the interest and amortization charges (except for the six-year bonds and *rentes*) are borne by the budget.

Reconstruction.[11] — When the war had ended, France saw on one hand a dark shadow, and on the other a cheering light. The shadow was cast by the ruins of the invaded provinces, where property had been destroyed and French citizens ruined both physically and financially. The light came from beyond the eastern border, for France was counting on Germany to make good the war damages. The confidence of France that Germany would pay is in a measure indicated by the generous laws passed in 1919, which enlarged the pension system for the military and civil war-wounded and their families[12] and promised repayment for real and personal property damaged by the invasion.[13] This repayment was based on a cost-of-reconstruction basis if the war sufferer used the money to rebuild practically the same house, factory, etc., on the same place.

The State's adoption of the policy that it should make good to its citizens the losses suffered through invasion was something new for France.[14] It seems certain that the general expectation that Germany would pay had something to do with the decision,

---

sum (300 to 500 millions) that will probably be "paid" in this way during *both* 1928 and 1929. *Palmade Report,* p. 44. It should not, of course, be considered in any balance of state receipts against expenditures, but is useful when calculating the magnitude of war-damages payments undertaken by the State.

[11] Cahill, *1926 Report,* pp. 49–54, 288–290, reproduces interesting figures on the physical side of the reconstruction problem and goes into some detail on the administrative methods. By January 1, 1926, 88 per cent of the 9,300 damaged or destroyed industrial undertakings employing at least ten persons, had been reconstructed and were in operation; 157,500 farm buildings and 364,400 dwellings had been rebuilt or completely repaired, out of the total 800,000 damaged or destroyed: devastated agricultural land had been reclaimed to the extent of eighteen-nineteenths; and the number of livestock rose from 174,000 in November, 1918, to 1,575,000 in January, 1926. *Ibid.,* p. 50.

[12] Laws of March 31, 1919, June 24, 1919. [13] Law of April 17, 1919.

[14] Allix, *Science des Finances,* p. 120. Allix explains its adoption as being due to the feeling of "national solidarity," aroused by sympathy for the sufferers and recognition of the economic necessity of revitalizing the devastated regions.

for optimism as to Germany's ability to pay was running high. The Minister of Finance apparently expected annual payments of 20 billion gold marks for the Allies.[15] It was realized, however, that such payments would come only after several years and France herself would have to advance the funds for immediate reconstruction. The promise to the war-sufferers, furthermore, was in no way made contingent on German payments; the State bound itself to aid them in any case. Such aid was given in two ways: directly by the State, and indirectly through semi-official or private bodies which advanced sums on guarantee of repayment by the State.

The payments made directly to the war-sufferers have taken the form of payments in kind (either from material already in the hands of the Government, or from material delivered by Germany), government securities, cash, and cancellation of taxes.

The payments made indirectly have consisted of money which the war-sufferers have received through loans from the general public. These were floated either by groups of war-sufferers themselves, and secured by damage-claims on the State in the form of annuities; or floated by the *Crédit National* (organized by the law of October 16, 1919),[16] the interest and amortization being directly guaranteed and paid by the State. In the earlier years of reconstruction the *Crédit National* loans played an important part, but since 1924, when one of its issues met with decided failure, this method has been abandoned, and the indirect advances are now made almost wholly through loans floated by the groups of war-sufferers themselves.

The above remarks concern more especially the damages to real property which the State undertook to make good. The other two types of war damage — to persons, and to state property — have been taken care of by pension payments in cash, and by state construction, respectively. How large an amount has been paid out by France to repair the direct ravages of war?

First will be considered the damages to private property. Table 38 shows the nature of the payments for damages to private property up to December 31, 1926.

[15] *Cf.* a history of the reparations problem in *Le Temps Supplément*, May, 1923.

[16] See p. 271.

TABLE 38

PAYMENTS ON ACCOUNT OF WAR DAMAGES TO PRIVATE PROPERTY

To December 31, 1926[a]

(In millions of paper francs)

	1914–1919	1920	1921	1922	1923	1924	1925	1926	AGGREGATE 1914–1926
Cash, through *Crédit National* — Capital	....	1,913	6,901	6,929	5,065	1,943	931	935	24,617
Cash, through *Crédit National* — Interest	....	23	245	880	373	120	52	45	1,738
Annuities	....	....	3,774	2,657	1,711	1,450	361	1,566	11,519
Rentes	....	....	20	445	389	233	122	70	1,279
Treasury payments, including deliveries in kind, and tax cancellations	4,946	7,217	4,212	1,458	1,272	470	689	2,720[b]	31,602[b]
Obligations de la Défense Nationale — Capital	....	....	316	592	2,238	3,134	2,338		
Obligations de la Défense Nationale — Interest	....	....	.....	.....	570	384	324	160	1,438
Total capital payment	4,946	9,130	15,223	12,081	10,675	7,230	4,441	5,291	69,017
Total interest payments on unpaid damage claims	....	23	245	880	943	504	376	205	3,176
Grand total	4,946	9,153	15,468	12,961	11,618	7,734	4,817	5,496	72,193

[a] *Experts' Report*, p. 98, for figures up to 1926. Figures for 1926 taken from 1928 budget *projet, exposé des motifs*, p. 185. The figures for years prior to 1926 as given in the *Experts' Report* and the 1928 *projet* check with each other, with one minor exception (annuities pa-ments for 1922 given as 2,655 million francs in *projet*).

[b] Indications are that these amounts are too small. In the *Palmade Report*, p. 96, it is stated that the sum of 3,077 millions was given to the war sufferers in 1926 in the form of six-year "obligations" (type 1925). On the other hand, the same report gives the total of "obligations" given to the war sufferers in 1923–1925 as 7,086 millions (against 9,896 in the above table) so that the total "obligations" so given to the end of 1926, according to the *Palmade Report*, comes to 10,163 millions — perhaps closely agreeing with what the total in the above table would be, if the figure of 2,720 millions in 1926 could be split down.

The figures for actual payments stop at December 31, 1926. But these may be supplemented by estimates for the years 1927–1928, consisting of the authorizations given by the various laws for such expenditures. These are presented in Table 39, along with similar data for 1926, enabling comparison, for that year, of payments authorized (Table 39) and payments actually made (Table 38).

To find the total payments for damage to private property, made up to the end of 1927, a table may be drawn up as follows (in millions of francs):

Payments on capital value of claims:		
To end of 1926	69,017	
During 1927 (estimate)	6,900	
Total		75,917
Interest payments on unpaid damage claims:		
To end of 1926	3,176	
During 1927 (estimate)	400	
Total		3,576
Total payments on war damages to private property		79,493

Tardieu[17] and Palmade[18] have estimated the payments to the end of 1927 at 73,000 and 75,850 million francs respectively. These figures evidently apply only to payments on the capital value of the claims.

As can readily be seen from Tables 38 and 39, the closing years of the settlement of war-damage claims for private property are marked by greater dependence on the ten-to-thirty-year annuities, and an abandonment of *Crédit National* flotations. The *Crédit National* still exists and plays an important part in the administrative scheme of damage payments; it handles, for instance, the distribution of that part of the cash received from Germany which is turned over to the war-sufferers.

The reliance on annuities has eliminated the use of six-year *obligations* except for payment of interest on the claims. This involves an important step toward amortization of the state debt, as the budget carries, in effect, both interest and amortization

[17] *Le Temps*, February 16, 1928.

[18] *Report*, p. 44.

charges through the payment of annuities, while it carries only the interest charges on the *obligations*.

TABLE 39

AUTHORIZED PAYMENTS ON WAR DAMAGES TO PRIVATE PROPERTY. FISCAL YEARS 1926–1928

(In millions of paper francs)

	1926 [a]	1927 [c]	1928 [d]
Cash, from German reparation receipts (paid *via* the *Crédit National*)	1,000	1,250	1,250
Payments in kind, from German reparation receipts	400	600	600
Six year *Obligations de la Défense Nationale*, given only as interest payments on property damage	....	250	250
Same, given as both capital and interest payments	1,000 [b]	....	....
Same, for both interest and capital payments in Alsace and Lorraine [b]	150	150	150
Ten-year annuities (capitalized value)	1,600	2,500	2,500
Fifteen- and thirty-year annuities, on which groups of war-sufferers float their own loans (capitalized value)	1,000	2,000	2,500
Four-year bonds, non-interest bearing, amortized in half-year installments	1,000	500	....
Rentes	....	50 [e]	50 [e]
Cancellation of taxes	?	?	300 [e]
Total authorized payments on war damages to property	6,150 + [f]	7,300 +	7,600

[a] All the 1926 authorizations appear in articles 10–20 of the law of Feb. 27, 1926. The law decreed that after May 1, 1926, no more six-year "obligations" should be issued for payment in capital of war damages claims. Instead, ten-year annuities were to be given, and the same article (19) set the limit for these, between May 1 and December 31, 1926, at 1,600 million francs. The four-year bonds were first authorized by this law (arts. 17, 18) and were reserved for war-sufferers whose property damage was between 20,000 and 500,000 francs.

[b] Though the text of the law says "interest and capital" it would appear that in fact the six-year "obligations" have been issued only for interest claims, after May 1, 1926. *Cf. Palmade Report*, p. 43.

[c] All the 1927 authorizations appear in articles 105–111 of the law of December 19, 1926.

[d] All the 1928 authorizations appear in articles 171–176 of the law of Dec. 27, 1927.

[e] These figures are "estimates based on estimates." See footnote 9, p. 296.

[f] This total is probably not far from the amount of actual payments made. On February 14, 1928, Tardieu, Minister of Public Works, stated to the Chamber that in 1926 a total of 6 billions was paid; in 1927, 7 billions; in 1928 (to be paid) 7 billions. *Le Temps*, February 16, 1928. Note that Table 38 indicates that not more than 5.5 billions was paid in 1926.

There has been much complaint of inefficiency and even "graft" in the expenditure of the sums set aside for reconstruction, and in the claims originally submitted. In 1924 it reached such a height that a law was passed (May 2) providing for re-examination and reduction of the claims. The complaints still exist, and the subject was debated in the Chamber on February 14, 1928; but M. Tardieu, Minister of Public Works, denied that any widespread basis for such charges existed. The total property-damage claims of 85 billions had been reduced only three-tenths of one per cent up to February, 1928, under the 1924 law's provision. Both Tardieu and Poincaré attacked the insinuation that "graft" had been practiced to any extent. Waste there undoubtedly had been, and mistakes due to ignorance, but there was, they insisted, no basis for widespread scandal.[19]

Having considered payments for damages to private property, we are now in a position to consider the figures available for payments on other damages, and the total payments for all damages. These are presented in Table 40. No estimate appears available for 1927 and 1928, with one exception.

TABLE 40

WAR DAMAGES EXPENDITURES, 1914–1926

(In millions of paper francs)

I. DAMAGES OTHER THAN TO PRIVATE PROPERTY

(Source: 1928 *Budget Projet*, page 185)

	1914–1919	1920	1921	1922	1923	1924	1925	1926	TOTALS TO END OF 1926	1927
Damages to persons (pension payments)	19,112	4,672	4,503	3,194	2,490	2,465	4,070	3,947	44,453	3,821[a]
Damages to state Property: Railroads	434	706	821	145	88	56	28	13	2,291	
Other damages	501	520	536	350	425	315	251	103	3,001	
Miscellaneous expenses[b]	2,974	2,705	949	700	327	208	203	153	8,219	
Totals	23,021	8,603	6,800	4,389	3,330	3,044	4,552	4,216	57,964	

[19] Chamber debates of February 14, 1928. *Le Temps*, February 16, 1928.

II. Private Property Damages, and Grand Totals

Add: Total capital payments for war damages to private property (Table 38)	4,946	9,130	15,223	12,081	10,675	7,230	4,441	5,291	69,017	
Total expenditure on capital value of war damages	27,967	17,733	22,032	16,470	14,005	10,274	8,993	9,507	126,981	
Add: Interest payments on unpaid damage claims (Table 38)	0	23	245	880	943	504	376	205	3,176	
Total expenditure on all war damages	27,967	17,756	22,277	17,350	14,948	10,778	9,369	9,712	130,157	

[a] Derived from figures given for "credits voted for 1927," *Chappedelaine Report* on general budget *projet* for 1928. (*Doc. Parl.*, 1927, *Chambre*, Doc. No. 4870, p. 14 of the *Report*.)

[b] Part of this may belong under the private property damages payments. The full heading is "Autres dépenses (travaux, achats, frais d'administration, etc.)"

The Future Course of Reconstruction and the Foreign Debts. — So much has been paid. How much will the future have to bear?

It is impossible to estimate the future annual burden of the pension payments for "damages to persons," but it seems that it should diminish steadily from year to year, as the recipients die off, although renewed inflation might bring an increase if the pensions were raised to meet a rising cost of living. The present annual charge is not far from 4,000 million francs. The only estimate for the future the writer has been able to find is that made by Lamoureux in his 1924 report [20] on war-damage expenditures, where he evaluated the present value of the pensions remaining to be paid (*valeur actuelle des pensions restant à payer*) at 30,000 millions as of the end of 1924. In the absence of details of the calculations, and in view of the uncertainty surrounding the subject, it seems best to make no estimate, and merely to state that the present budget burden of nearly 4,000 millions per year shows signs of decreasing steadily from now on.

Reconstruction of the damaged state property has apparently been almost finished by now,[21] and it is unlikely that the State faces any future heavy payments on this account.

As to the damages to private property, it has been estimated

[20] *Op. cit.*, p. 14.

[21] *Experts' Report*, p. 97.

that the total capital claims amount to 85,800 million francs.[22] Since 75,917 million francs were paid off by December 31, 1927 (Tables 38 and 39), roughly 9,900 million francs remain to be met. To this must be added whatever interest payments on unpaid claims are necessary; Palmade estimates this at somewhere near 500 millions. Thus one obtains a grand total of 10,400 millions yet to be paid as of January 1, 1928.[23]

In considering these figures concerning private property damages one must realize that, unlike the pension figures, they represent payments which in a sense are not payments — that is, the budget will continue for many years to bear the burden of the interest and amortization charges on the ten-, fifteen-, and thirty-year annuities, on the *rentes* and *Obligations de la Défense Nationale,* which have been given to the war-sufferers. When these have been handed over to the State's claimants, the debt is "paid," and the figures are so entered in Tables 38 and 39; but as long as such payments are not made in the form of cash, or deliveries in kind, the State faces a burden for many years before final liquidation will have been accomplished. Table 41 shows that the annual carrying charges on such "payments" amount to nearly 4 billion francs. Added to the pension payments, this means that nearly 8 billion francs will have to be paid out annually for some years to come in liquidation of the war-damages payments. The pension payments may decrease, but for the next few years the carrying charges on the payments for property damage will increase, as new capital "payments" are made. Not until after 193: will this item diminish.

Though the carrying charges which the budget must bear will not disappear for many years, the capital payments themselves will probably be completed by the end of 1929. Palmade has

[22] *Palmade Report*, p. 44. Palmade, calculating that 75,850 million frans were paid by December 31, 1927, says that 9,950 remain to be paid.

[23] Tardieu estimates it at roughly 12,000 millions, out of a total of 85,000 millions (*Le Temps*, February 16, 1928). It was put even higher — as of October 1, 1927 — by the "balance sheet" of reconstruction submitted by the *Drection Général des Régions Libérées*, headed by Paul Roquère. This showed the total claims to be 85,765 millions, of which 72,592 millions had been paid, leaving an unpaid balance of 13,173 millions. *Le Temps*, December 20, 1927. This report also gives figures on the physical aspect of reconstruction.

TABLE 41

ESTIMATED CHARGE ON 1928 BUDGET FOR INTEREST AND AMORTIZATION PAYMENTS ON ANNUITIES, *RENTES*, AND *OBLIGATIONS* ISSUED SINCE 1919 IN PAYMENT OF WAR DAMAGES TO PRIVATE PROPERTY.

(In millions of francs)

	TOTAL CHARGES CARRIED BY 1928 BUDGET
Rentes, interest only	83.[a]
Obligations de la Défense Nationale, interest only	281.8
Rentes, 6 per cent, 1927 (exchanged for *Obligations de la Défense Nationale*), interest and amortization	353.[b]
Ten-year annuities, interest and amortization	536.5
Crédit National loans, interest, amortization, taxes paid for holders, and administrative expenses	1,625.
Rentes, 6 per cent, 1927 (exchanged for *Crédit National* Bonds), interest and amortization	43.
Thirty-year annuities, interest and amortization	1,066.5
Total burden for 1928, of carrying charges on war-damages payments shown in Tables 38 and 39	3,988.8

[a] Estimated as follows: claims paid to the end of 1926: 1,279; approximate interest charges on this: 77; interest charges on rentes given out in 1927 or to be given out in 1928: 6. Total: 83.

[b] It is assumed here that all the ten-year "obligations" so exchanged were "obligations" that had been given to war-sufferers. The error, if any, is slight, as the interest charge on outstanding "obligations" that had not been given to the war-sufferers was only 5.9 million francs.

calculated that the remaining ten and one-half billions of property damage claims will be settled as follows during 1928 and 1929 (in millions of francs):[24]

Capital payments:	
Cash payments	2,500 to 3,000
Payments in kind direct from Germany	1,000 to 1,200
Ten-year annuities	3,000 to 3,500
Fifteen- to thirty-year annuities	2,000 to 2,500
Rentes	50 to 60
Set off against taxes due	300 to 500
Interest on loss sustained:	
Ten-year annuities and six-year bonds	500
Total	9,350 to 11,760

[24] *Palmade Report*, p. 44.

Part of these capital payments are taken from the reparations payments each year. When the former have been completed, how will the amount of reparations payments available for foreign debts be affected?

If the Dawes payments should continue according to schedule,[25] indications are that France will have an increasing amount available for the payment of foreign debts, if the budget can remain balanced. For the fifth annuity year (September 1, 1928 — October 1, 1929), and those following, Germany will be supposed to pay at least 2,500,000,000 gold marks, of which France will get at least 1,200 million gold marks,[26] probably more. This is about 100 million gold marks, or 600 million francs, more than she is receiving now (1928).

On the expenditures side, it appears that the reparations receipts will be freed, by 1930, from the following payments (in francs) which are a charge on them now (1928):

Payments for reconstruction	1,850,000,000
English war stocks debt (by end of 1928 balance will be about one million pounds sterling)	155,000,000
Argentine loan	226,183,951
Uruguayan loan	79,500,000
Total	2,310,683,951

Since the reparation receipts will have increased by, say, 600 million francs and the expenditures attached thereto will have decreased by 2,311 millions compared with 1928, when 1930 arrives, it might seem at first glance that France would then be able to devote 2,911 millions more to repayment of foreign political debts than she is doing now, without encroaching upon the ordinary budget revenue.

The provisional payments France made during 1927 on her political debt to the United States amounted to 10 million dollars,

[25] This apparently is true even under the Young Plan, which was drawn up while this book was in the hands of the printer.

[26] *Phillippoteaux Report, Doc. Parl., Chambre,* 1926, *Sess. Ord.,* Doc. No. 3405, p. 1992. Under the Spa agreement (July, 1920), modified by the Paris meeting of the finance ministers (January, 1925), France receives 52 per cent of the German payments, after certain prior claims are met. *Cf.* Bergmann, *The History of Reparations,* pp. 39, 290.

or roughly 255 million paper francs; on that of Great Britain, 5 million pounds, or roughly 620 million paper francs — a total of 875 million paper francs. The provisional repayments for 1928 have been planned[27] at $12,132,943 and £7,000,000, or 309 millions and 868 millions of paper francs respectively — a total of 1,177 millions. In the preceding paragraph it was assumed for the moment that by 1930 France would be able to devote 2,911 millions more to repayment of these debts than she is doing in 1928. In brief, by 1930 it might appear that the provisional repayments could proceed almost three times as fast as they are now doing, a total of 4,088 millions being available for that purpose.

Supposing this to be possible, would such an amount suffice to cover the payments called for in 1930 under the Balfour and the Mellon-Bérenger agreements? They call for the payment of £12,500,000 (fiscal year 1930–31) and $35,000,000, or roughly 1,550 million and 892.5 million paper francs respectively at the present exchange rates — a total of 2,442.5 million francs. Compared with the total available above calculated at 4,088 millions, it might seem that France could meet her 1930 political debt payments from the Dawes receipts and have over a billion and a half francs to spare.

But these rough and ready calculations ignore the financial outlook as a whole. There are three reservations that must be made.

First, France will sometime have to start amortizing that part of the huge reconstruction debt outstanding ("paid" as far as the war-sufferers are concerned) for which the budget now provides no amortization — the *Crédit National* bonds, for instance.

Second, even without such added amortization items, a certain part of the budget expenses is certain to grow during the next three years as the final blocks of annuities are given to the war-sufferers and the interest and amortization charges thereon commence. The chances for tax increases seem slight, to say the least; perhaps some of the reparations payments will be called on to meet the increased charges.

[27] *Palmade Report*, p. 53.

Third, entirely aside from a complete revamping of the system of German payments, France may not receive as much added cash as the figures cited above might indicate, for it is probable that she will have to take a larger proportion of the reparations payments in the form of payments in kind, which, even if they can be sold to citizens rather than used for public works, are not productive of much ready cash, for the reason given in a previous paragraph. And indications are that more and more of the reparations payments will take the form of public works. Already the lower Seine has been dredged, and floating docks delivered to Bordeaux and Rouen; new aqueducts, low-rental apartments, canal construction, and electrification of the railways are all in the program,[28] as the effort is made to surmount the difficulty of payments raised by the troublesome question of cash transfers.

These reservations do not lend themselves easily to quantitative expression. But they must always be borne in mind in estimating the surplus France may have to meet foreign debt payments.

[28] Remarks of Seydoux, assistant director of the Bureau of Commercial Relations, cited in the New York *Herald* (Paris Edition), August 6, 1927. See also *Le Matin*, September 4, 1927.

PART THREE

TAXATION AND EXPENDITURE

CHAPTER XVII

NATIONAL TAXATION

The French tax system suggests a huge bouquet gathered from a New England garden. One can make certain general observations about it, such, for instance, that it is old-fashioned and that it is made up of a great many different varieties, some of which are more curious than attractive. If, however, one essays a detailed and accurate description, he is likely to find himself the author of an encyclopedia. No such complete description can be attempted here.[1] It is necessary to be content with a tabulation of its financial results and with the briefest possible outline of the system's features, together with some comments on the manner in which it has functioned under the stress of recent conditions.

This chapter deals with the revenue system of the central government which in 1926 produced approximately 38.1 billion francs. The local revenue system, discussed in the next chapter, produced that year less than one-fifth as much.

In the United States there is a different distribution of governmental functions as between the federal government on the one hand and the state and local governments on the other. This difference is indeed so great that direct comparisons between the French national taxes and the American federal taxes are quite misleading.

Following in the main the French division established for administrative purposes, the French national revenues are grouped in this chapter under three main headings as follows:

	Net yield in the year in billions of paper francs[2]			
	1913	*1919*	*1926*	*1927*
Direct taxes	0.7	3.2	10.5	13.2
Indirect taxes	2.7	6.0	24.5	27.4
Monopolies and miscellaneous	.8	.8	3.1	3.1
Total	4.1	10.0	38.1	43.7

[1] In a separate volume, now in preparation, it is hoped that a more adequate treatment of the French tax system may be presented.

[2] See Table 59, p. 396.

PRELIMINARY CONSIDERATIONS

However, before presenting detailed statistics of revenues it is important that something be said regarding the theory of the financial accounting of the French, particularly regarding their peculiar conception of the financial period, or *exercice,* and of their conception of the Treasury in relation to the budget.

THE *EXERCICE*

Everyone is acquainted with the ordinary accounting distinction between the cash basis and the accrual basis, a distinction which turns upon the manner in which the financial transactions are attached to the successive accounting periods. The French draw a somewhat similar distinction between the *compte de gestion* and the *compte d'exercice.*[3] The *compte de gestion* is our simple and familiar cash account. Entries are made merely of the money taken in and paid out during the accounting period. The *compte d'exercice,* however, although it aims at the same result, is a very different affair from the account on the accrual basis.

The shortcomings of the cash account are obvious. The observations are restricted to finally completed transactions resulting in a payment to or from the cash drawer. Operations under way are ignored, even though they may be the true fruit of the activities of the accounting period under review.

The modern business places its accounts on the accrual basis because the result is a more accurate picture of its financial situation. It is, of course, not a perfect picture because the various operations under way may not turn out precisely as expected. Its accuracy is dependent largely upon the skill with which the various contingencies are evaluated at the end of the accounting period.

The accrual basis, then, is the answer of modern accounting to the problem presented by the inadequacy of the cash basis. The *compte d'exercice* is the answer of French public finance to

[3] The discussion which follows is based upon Allix, *Traité élémentaire de Science des Finances et de Législation financière française,* p. 22 *et seq.*

the same problem and it is a quite different answer. Instead of closing the records of an accounting period promptly on the basis of estimates and valuations, the French method is to "wait and see." Seeking to escape the disadvantages of an accounting which has regard only for the transactions actually terminated at the cash drawer during the period, they go to the opposite extreme and use a system which, in theory at least, has regard only for the transactions initiated during the period. They seek to accomplish this by keeping the accounts open until the transactions actually terminate.

It is then easy to see how the accounting period covered by the *compte d'exercice* almost inevitably becomes personified. Each year sees the creation of a new *exercice* which is duly christened with the name of the year and which lives beyond the end of that year until the day when the last credit or debit arising from an act accomplished during that year has been finally extinguished. The life of the *exercice* then has two stages: first, the financial year (*année financière*) whose operations it records and, second, the complementary period (*période complémentaire*), theoretically without limit, during which it continues to live waiting for the final consummation of all the operations which received a birth certificate (*l'acte de naissance*) during the financial year. The budget is formulated and voted and the accounting is kept and rendered on the basis of the *exercice*.

The *exercice*, a device quite foreign to the public finances of England or the United States, developed very early in France and even before the Revolution had shown itself susceptible of great abuses. At that time, the notion of the artificial personality of the *exercice* was carried to the point where each *exercice* was given its own special functionaries and accountants. Each *exercice* was an air-tight compartment, separate and distinct from every other *exercice*. It was even considered proper for one *exercice* to go bankrupt and deny payment to its creditors while a neighboring *exercice* was in affluent circumstances! Since 1822 there has been a tendency constantly at work to restrict more and more narrowly the term of the *période complémentaire*. At present the law requires that an *exercice* be definitely and completely closed seven months after the end of the *année financière*.[4] The shorter the *période complémentaire*, the more closely, of course, does the account approximate the cash basis.

Narrowly restricted as the *période complémentaire* is under present legislation, the fact remains that for a portion of each year both receipts and expenditures are being made on account of two *exercices* simultaneously, a fact which complicates the compilation of data relating to receipts and expenditures and a fact, by the way, which is often overlooked by those who comment on the financial situation of the French Government. Moreover during the war all the ordinary rules covering dates of closure have been jettisoned and a condition of confusion has arisen which causes even the *fonctionnaires* who have grown gray in the service to wring their hands in despair.

The necessity for a clear conception of the *exercice* in dealing with French financial statistics is obvious. Each *exercice* has its budget which must, before it can be passed, be endowed with revenues judged to be sufficient to meet its obligations, a rule which goes far to explain the various special budgets and special accounts which clutter French finance. The revenues, when collected, belong to the *exercice*, even though not collected until after the end of the *année financière*. The budget is not balanced, as in England or America, on the basis of cash receipts during a twelve-month period and this fact must be borne in mind in dealing with the collection figures.

The French Treasury

In theory, the French Treasury is also personified and stands as a separate entity, distinct from each *exercice* and its budget. It is a function of the Treasury to act as "banker for the budget," advancing it funds as needed until its tax resources materialize

[4] Specific dates are fixed for the various stages of the process of closing the "exercice": thus on March 31 the "exercice" is closed with respect to issuing drafts to the State's creditors (any drafts issued after that must be in the name of the next "exercice"); on April 31 it is closed with respect to payment of drafts and receipt of taxes; on July 31 it is definitely closed for all manner of receipts and payments ordinary or extraordinary.

and providing the funds for large-scale works with a high degree of permanence. The Treasury borrows for both long and short terms, charging to each *exercice* its proper portion of the debt service. Strictly speaking, the Treasury should have no tax revenues, but here again the rules have broken down under the stress of war and post-war conditions and the Treasury has actually received substantial tax collections which accrued directly to its credit rather than to the credit of some budget.

The accounts are so confused that a dependable series of annual deficits cannot be compiled by comparing revenues with expenditures. Consequently the statistics of revenues may be compiled with a view merely to comprehensiveness and avoidance of double counting, without the additional complication of scrupulous assignments to particular *exercices*.

DIRECT TAXES

In recent years the revenues included under the caption of " direct taxes " have produced from one-fourth to one-third of the net revenue of the national Government. For treatment here the " direct taxes " are divided into two groups. The first group, " income and related taxes," includes the tax on the income from securities. The second group, " assimilated taxes," includes the war-profits tax. The Loucheur surtaxes are divided between the two groups.

Income and Related Taxes

The story of the manner in which the old *Quatre Vieilles Contributions* were superseded during the war by the income tax has been described in Part One,[5] where there will also be found an outline of the main characteristics of the new system. Consequently the treatment here may be restricted to the presentation of certain statistics[6] relating to these taxes and a few brief comments.

[5] See pp. 5–23.

[6] Because of the impossibility of allocating refunds in detail, the figures from this point forward are not strictly *net*.

It will be recalled that in contrast to American practice, the French income tax follows the British system of schedular taxes for each separate kind of income, with a surtax or "general income tax" superimposed upon the schedular structure. An attempt is made, in the schedules, to distinguish among income from capital, income from labor, and "mixed" income from both sources. Thus the schedules for income from real estate and securities are classed in the first category, and a higher rate (18 per cent) applies to them than to income from salaries and wages and professional activities (12 per cent). Business profits and agricultural profits are considered "mixed income," though the farmer is shown favor here, as in so many other places throughout the French tax system, by being granted the 12 per cent instead of the 15 per cent rate levied on business profits. These differences in schedular rates indicate somewhat the effort that has been made to distinguish among the sources of revenue, though the absolute amount of the rates means little until taken in connection with initial exemptions, family exemptions, and reduction of the tax payable.

The schedules concerning income from capital are not, with a minor exception (tax on income from non-corporate loans and deposits), a new feature of the tax system. Indeed, they are not considered "schedular" taxes, strictly speaking, in administrative terminology. The real-estate tax has existed since the beginning of the last century, and along with the old *patente* (business tax), the tax on doors and windows, and the *personnelle-mobilière* tax (on presumptive income, based on rentals paid), was part of the *Quatre Vieilles* system from which the State drew its direct tax revenue before 1917. The tax on security income dates from 1872, and even to-day remains, administratively, an "indirect" tax, collected at the source by the registration-taxes administration.

The true schedular taxes, concerning income from labor and "mixed" income, were not established until 1917, when the *patente,* doors-and-windows, and *personnelle-mobilière* taxes were abolished as a source of state revenue.

The surtax, or general income tax imposed in addition to the schedular taxes, makes no distinction as to source of revenue, but is levied upon the individual's, or rather the family's, total income from all sources. Roughly speaking, it is based on the combined income as calculated for the schedular taxes, though there are important exceptions to this rule. It has but one rate, 30 per cent, but is made progressive by exemption of the lower blocks of the income, an exemption that decreases as the income rises. The general income tax is the most "personal" of all, in the sense that it takes account of the taxpayer's total economic situation; corporations and societies of all kinds fall outside its scope. This tax was established in 1914. The salaries and wages tax is almost as personal, and the others shade off into the impersonal until the securities-income tax is reached, where practically no account at all is taken of the individual's status.

Two of the schedular taxes are levied on an estimated (*forfaitaire*) basis, and no attempt is made to ascertain the true income. Thus the real-estate tax and the agricultural-profits tax are levied on an estimate of income derived from the rental value assigned to the real property under the survey, or *cadastre,* made by the State. The other taxes attempt to reach the true income, as revealed through collection at the source (securities income), through information at the source (wages and salaries), or through self-assessment, checked, when possible, by the tax collector (business profits, professional income, general income).

Statistics of Income and Related Taxes.—In Table 42 are presented the national tax levies made annually from 1913 to 1927 of the income taxes as well as of their predecessors, the *Quatre Vieilles.*

It will be noted that the figures in Table 42 as well as those in Table 43 are levies[7] (*rôles émis*), not collections. The levy figures are used because the collection figures are scanty and because an analysis showed that after some delay a very high percentage of the assessments is ultimately collected.[8]

[7] Except for the first three years, for which final collection figures are available from the *Compte Générale.* Space is not available for a full discussion of the various discrepancies which exist among the statistics gathered from the different sources.

[8] This statement is not true of the war-profits tax (see p. 330).

TABLE 42

INCOME AND RELATED TAXES LEVIED FOR THE STATE

1913–1927

(In millions of francs)

Sources: 1913–1915, *Comptes Généraux* for 1914, 1915, and 1916 (collection figures); 1916–1926, *Renseignements statistiques relatifs aux Contributions directes et aux Taxes assimilées* (assessment figures. See text, p. 317).

	1913	1914	1915	1916	1917	1918	1919	1920	1921	1922	1923	1924	1925	1926	1927[h]
Income Taxes (including Alsace and Lorraine from 1922 on)															
1. Tax on income from real estate: Unimproved [a,b]	108	106	64	60	60	75	74	156	168	164	164	196	259	197	516
2. " " " " " " : Improved [a,b]	103	100	109	106	106	133	134	280	296	300	305	369	528	679	1,076
3. Commercial and industrial profits tax [b]	...	...	...	...	...	108	225	457	981	961	1,551	1,875	2,938	2,336	4,348
4. Agricultural profits tax	...	...	...	...	...	1	3	9	28	24	30	47	76	85	269
5. Salaries and wages tax	...	...	...	...	...	36	64	90	296	328	221	267	297	431	656
6. Non-commercial and professional income tax [b]	...	...	...	...	...	3	6	11	43	49	69	87	106	106	154
7. General income tax [b]	...	...	...	32	201	363	571	757	1,472	1,269	1,924	2,665	3,059	3,039	2,247
8. Cost of issuing *rôles*, etc.[c]	1	1	1	13	13	15	16	22	29	39	33	35	38	49	......
9. Tax on income from securities (*valeurs mobilières*) [d]	138	153	157	181	242	253	290	568	926	1,018	1,166	1,684	1,939	2,437	3,385
10. Total income taxes	351	359	331	393	623	988	1,383	2,352	4,239	4,152	5,464	7,225	9,240	9,359	12,651
Old Direct Taxes [e] (not levied in Alsace and Lorraine)															
11. *Personnelle-mobilière* [f]	113	110	108	110	112	5	6	8	9	11	14	16	19	24	
12. Doors-and-windows tax [f]	72	68	66	66	66	3	4	6	8	9	9	10	11		
13. Business tax (*patente*) [f]	173	167	148	171	187	32	18	30	40	43	48	53	63	97	
14. Total old direct taxes (not including real estate taxes)	358	345	322	347	365	41	28	44	57	63	72	79	92	121	222
15. Cost of collection, etc., connected with special Alsace and Lorraine taxes [g]	...	...	...	...	...	.....	.....	.....	.....	46	10	12	13	13	
16. General Total	709	704	653	740	989	1,029	1,411	2,396	4,196	4,262	5,545	7,316	9,345	9,494	12,873

[a] For years previous to 1922 this is the "principal brut," that is, before deduction of the family allowances (charges de famille), which took effect for the first time in 1918. No figures are available for their exact amount previous to 1922. After 1922, the figures in this table are for the "principal net," that is, after deducting the family allowances. These allowances were as follows: (in thousands of francs) 1922, 5,985; 1923, 7,465; 1924, 10,058; 1925, 10,617; 1926, 16,101.

By the law of July 31, 1917 (article 52), a family allowance (charges de famille) was introduced which was deductible from the "rôles" issued (rôles émis) with respect to the real estate tax (impôt foncier, propriétés bâties et propriétés non-bâties). This allowance affected the figures of "rôles émis" for the first time in the year 1918. After 1921, the amounts of these "charges de famille" were stated in the annual volumes of the statistics of the direct taxes (Ministère des Finances, Direction Générale des Contributions Directes, *Renseignements statistiques relatifs aux Contributions directes et Taxes assimilées*). For the years 1918 to 1921, however, the figures were not published, and indeed seem not even to have been tabulated. Officials in the direct tax division, in the division of public accounts and in the budget bureau all testified that the figures were non-existent. Consequently, the "rôles émis" for the four years 1918–1922 are really greater than they should be to the extent of the amount of this item which was uncollectible. However, the deduction was ultimately made in the accounts through the item of refunds (dégrèvements) among the expenditures.

None of the officials interviewed was willing to hazard an estimate of the amount of these "charges de famille" for the years 1919–1921. M. Charra, the chief of the bureau of the budget, stated that they were undoubtedly smaller than in the years succeeding 1921. He pointed out that in these earlier years it was necessary to make a special application to secure the benefit of the allowance and that many taxpayers failed to take advantage of the privilege.

The amount of the "charges de famille" for the year 1922 was 5,985,101 francs, and for 1923 was 7,464,743 francs. The figures for "rôles émis" of direct taxes offer a clue for the two preceding years:

	1920	1921
"Rôles émis" according to the Statistics of Direct Taxes	1,762,362,995	3,284,131,819
"Rôles émis" according to the Monthly Statements of Tax Collections	1,758,212,500	3,279,099,600
Differences	4,150,495	5,032,219

These differences may presumably be ascribed to the "charges de famille." However, to avoid a double deduction, since the allowance is included in the "dégrèvements," the figures from the Statistics of Direct Taxes, used in this table (42), are also used in the aggregate tax table, (Table 59, p. 396) where the refunds (dégrèvements) are taken into account.

The "charges de famille" were applied in Alsace and Lorraine for the first time in 1923.

For certain other tax refunds, apparently not taken into consideration here, see Table 60, p. 398 (Table of Dégrèvements).

[b] The figures indicated in the table above include the Loucheur surtaxes (law of December 4, 1925, art. 2) in 1925–1926, as follows (in thousands of francs):

	1925	1926
Tax on real estate: improved	153,291	4,950
Tax on real estate: unimproved	62,550	1,385
Commerical and industrial profits tax	887,308	88,561
Non-commercial and professional income tax	19,575	1,286
General income tax	458,008	27,556
Total	1,580,732	123,738

It is clear from the figures in Table 42 that the new income tax system is much more productive than the *Quatre Vieilles*. In 1913 the old system yielded only 0.7 billion francs. In 1927 the new yielded 12.9 billion francs. This means that the yield was more than trebled, even when the change in the value of the franc is taken into account.

The figures, however, reveal an interesting situation regarding the impact of the income tax proper. Thus in 1927 more than one-third of the income tax (4.3 billions out of 12.7 billions) came from the tax on commercial and industrial profits. In addition nearly one-half of the old direct taxes levied for the benefit of local government, are taxes on business (*patentes*).[9] Certainly French business bears a surprisingly large share of the direct tax burden.

---

[c] This includes the "centimes d'État" collected for the State on the real estate taxes (except for 1913–1915), and the "frais d'avertissement" concerning the real estate taxes, the other schedular taxes, the old direct taxes, and the special local direct taxes levied in Alsace and Lorraine. For the years 1913–1915 the "centimes d'État" are included in the figures for real estate tax, improved and unimproved.

[d] In the French tax returns this is listed under the registration group of taxes. It has been inserted here because of its close relation to the other income taxes. It includes the tax on income from non-corporate debts, deposits, etc. (créances, depôts, et cautionnements). The true tax return is somewhat smaller than shown here, as these figures apparently include the amount the State pays to itself on the *Crédit National* security issues. The correction has not been made in this table, as the detailed figures are not available. The table of "dégrèvements" (Table 60) shows the estimated total of the taxes paid by the State to itself on these security issues, but the figures apparently include also the indirect transmission tax, if any. The correction on this account has therefore been confined to the aggregate tax table (Table 59) where subtraction of the lump sums can safely be made.

[e] The real estate taxes might have been included here instead of being put in with the income taxes, as they formed the fourth of the famous "Quatre Vieilles" of the French tax system before 1917.

[f] These taxes were not collected for strictly state purposes after 1917, but the State has received a certain amount since then, annually, under the divisions "centimes pour non-valeurs, réimpositions, centimes pour frais de confection des rôles spéciaux, et centimes pour frais de perception des impositions communales." These might be included in the local tax receipts, but they have instead been included here in this table of state receipts, as the official statistics distinguish in their headings between these items and the "centimes départementaux" and "centimes communaux."

[g] The taxes are the "impôt sur le capital, impôt sur les traitements et salaires, impôt sur les professions." The costs of collection, etc., entered in this line were not included in line 8 above. The same remarks as to the propriety of entering such charges under state revenue, as made in footnote *f*, apply here.

[h] Total assessments as of December 31, 1927. *Journal Officiel*, January 17, 1928.

[i] 3000 francs.

[9] See p. 386.

A second interesting conclusion to be drawn from Table 42 is the important rôle played by the tax on the income from securities. This schedule in 1927 produced more than one-fourth of the total income taxes (3.4 billions out of 12.7 billions). It would appear that the strictness of the fiscal control here is in rather striking contrast with that exercised over several of the other schedules.

The lightness of the burden borne by real estate in France is also indicated by these figures. The levies under the real-estate schedules amounted in 1927 to only 1.6 billion francs and the local real-estate taxes bring in only slightly over 1 billion in addition.[10]

The general income tax, which corresponds roughly to the federal surtaxes, yielded in 1927 only 2.2 billion francs, while the remaining three schedules (the taxes on agricultural profits, on non-commercial and professional income and on salaries and wages) yielded only 1.1 billions altogether.

The Income Tax in Operation. — It was an act of considerable boldness for the French to inaugurate their income-tax system with the war in progress. Standards of private accounting in France are notoriously bad. There is a widespread antipathy against " inquisition," which causes an official audit of a private taxpayer's accounts to be bitterly resented. Mobilization made serious inroads upon the trained personnel of the tax officers. There was, and still is, a strong political feeling against the income tax on the ground that it is socialistic in character, a feeling which is carried to the point where one income-tax authority could flatly declare to the writer that " the business men of France will pay the tax to Poincaré but not to Caillaux." Added to all of this is the fundamental fact that the income tax is dependent to a very considerable extent upon valuations of property. Property values in France, with the war costs being met by inflating the currency, have been as unstable as soap bubbles in a hurricane.

The low yield of the real-estate schedules, in spite of the high rate, is explained in part by the concessions which were made at

[10] See p. 379. These statements ignore the effect of the general income tax upon revenue from real estate.

the outset, to secure administrative advantages and to subsidize agriculture. But the low yield is also partly explained by the fact that the rates under this schedule do not apply to the true income derived by the owners of real estate. They apply rather to an artificially determined base which bears only a remote relationship to real income and is in general very far below it.

Thus in the case of unimproved real estate the base is arrived at through the pre-war valuation authorized by the act of 1908, increased 75 per cent by the act of August 3, 1926, with 20 per cent deducted for costs of upkeep. The act of March 29, 1914, had contemplated the revaluation of one-twentieth of the land annually, thus giving a complete revaluation at the end of twenty years, but this procedure brought about such anomalous results during a period of rapidly fluctuating values that it was soon abandoned. In 1924 an attempt was made to secure a general revaluation of unimproved real estate but this likewise was abandoned.

In the case of improved real estate a ten-year revaluation arrangement similar to the twenty-year plan for unimproved land was also cancelled by the act of July 31, 1918, because of the abnormal war conditions. However, a general revaluation was obtained by virtue of the act of March 22, 1924. This new valuation, which came into force in 1926, is based on actual rentals being paid no matter when the leases were drawn, with the result that in the case of old leases the amounts are ridiculously small. The figures, even then, are subject to reductions for upkeep and depreciation (40 per cent in the case of factories and 25 per cent in the case of houses) and additional arbitrary reductions for expenses.[11]

Not only has the process of inflation greatly impaired the validity of the bases used in assessing the real-estate schedules, but the exigencies of the war have also brought about the entire

[11] In this revaluation the 25 per cent reduction for expenses could in no case be less than three times the pre-war reduction. See Allix and Lecerclé, *L'Impôt sur le Revenu,* Vol. 1, pp. 185–249; Allix, *Science des Finances,* pp. 529–549 and Sauzède, *Traité de la Contribution foncière,* pp. 248–261.

elimination of an important portion of the tax base itself. As early as 1890 [12] the French adopted the rule that a new building should be exempt for a period of two years after completion. But the housing shortage after the war prompted an act, passed March 31, 1922, exempting for 15 years all residential buildings completed before January 1, 1930.[13] Another act grants a 12-year exemption to small houses built for the poor.[14]

The agricultural-profits schedule has been subject to much the same influences as the real-estate schedules, for the base normally used is arrived at by applying a coefficient (at present 2.50; until December 27, 1927, 3) to the same cadastral rental value used in establishing the real-estate tax base.

To the taxpayers under the commercial- and industrial-profits schedule also the war brought serious problems. Most of these, however, were solved in a manner which operated to the profit rather than to the injury of the revenue, a fact which has not added to the popularity of the tax. In this schedule valuations are very important — inventory valuations, valuations to determine gain or loss on sale of capital assets and valuations for establishing depreciation allowances. With prices mounting to four, five and six times their normal level, paper profits from sales of stock in trade or capital assets were large, while depreciation allowances, based on old high-value francs, were often ridiculously small. In the case of inventory valuations the administration found it advisable to make concessions. It avoided part of the difficulty by permitting the taxpayer to offset his inventory at the beginning of his taxable year with a similar *quantity* at the end of the year. But this solution, of course, did not prevent the taxation of paper profits in the case of a trader who reduced his inventory during the period of high prices. With respect to capital assets, the gains were subjected to tax, except when arising as the result of the liquidation of a business. Even the mere writing-up of the value of assets on a balance sheet, without a

12 Act of August 8.

13 Such construction was exempted from local taxes as well as the national income tax.

14 Sauzède, *loc. cit.*

definite closing of the transaction, resulted in tax liability, unless the surplus so resulting was credited to a special reserve.[15]

The general income tax, the progressive element in the system, was affected by the abnormal conditions in several ways. In the first place the change in the value of the money completely altered the significance of the exemptions [16] and of the progressive scale. For example, the maximum rate, 60 per cent until 1926 when it was reduced by Poincaré to 30 per cent, applied with full force in normal times only when an income was well in excess of $100,000, which in France is a very large income indeed. The fall of the franc, however, brought the full rate into operation against incomes of less than $25,000. Again, the allowance for a wife, which with the franc at its old par amounted to approximately $600, was cut to less than $120 by the depreciation of the franc. The result was that many people were thrown into the high-rate groups by the mere mechanics of monetary depreciation. They bitterly resented their dilemma and found it easy to justify evasion.

Again, financing the war by borrowing involved flooding the country with government securities the interest on which was to a large extent tax-exempt.[17] Vast quantities of securities whose income was taxable were in effect exchanged for this government paper. Moreover, borrowing to purchase and carry government securities was encouraged and interest paid on such borrowings was deductible under the income tax. Whereas in England the interest on government bonds was taxable and whereas in America, the interest paid on money borrowed to purchase or carry exempt securities was disqualified as a deduction, in France the bond interest was exempt and the loan interest was deductible.

There is no opportunity here to make a detailed comparison of French and American income-tax practice. The differences, however, are numerous and important. For example, the French

[15] *Économiste Européen*, Vol. 72, No. 1865, December 2, 1927. Reports from Paris since the stabilization of the franc indicate that few of the larger firms are restating their accounts in terms of the new franc because of the heavy taxes which will become due when they do so. New York *Journal of Commerce*, August 8, 1928.

[16] This influence was also felt in certain of the other schedules.

[17] See p. 198.

practice is less liberal than the American with respect to the definition of the closed transaction and the taxation of stock dividends. On the other hand, the deduction of the income taxes of the preceding year in computing net income is so liberal an allowance as in itself to invalidate all comparisons of rates.

Assimilated Taxes (*Taxes assimilées*)

The "taxes assimilated with the direct taxes" are numerous, but of little importance as to yield, excepting the war-profits tax. They include levies of diverse natures, and are lumped under direct taxes only by virtue of the fact that, like the income taxes, they are collected through rôles or assessments issued in the name of the taxpayer concerned, and are handled by the direct tax administration.

They may be divided into taxes on the possession of luxuries or semi-luxuries (e.g., on certain carriages), taxes replacing gaps in other parts of the fiscal system (e.g., *taxe des biens de mainmorte*), fees for services (e.g., the numerous inspection fees), and extraordinary taxes levied for only a short period (e.g., war-profits tax and *taxe civique*). Most of them date back to the nineteenth century.

Some of them are levied wholly for the profit of the State; the revenue of others is split between the State and local bodies; and still others are collected entirely for the benefit of the départements, communes, and various local groups. Only the assimilated taxes which aliment the state budget in whole or in part are discussed here; details of the others will be found Chapter XVIII.[18]

Statistics of Assimilated Taxes. — Table 43, corresponding to Table 42, presents the amounts of the assimilated tax levies for the years 1913 to 1927. If one ignores the *taxe civique* and the

18 See pp. 390, 391. Alsace and Lorraine are subject to practically the same state taxes as are the other départements in all branches of the system save that of the "taxes assimilées." Here there is a noticeable distinction: Alsace and Lorraine pay only a few of the "taxes assimilées" — i.e., the "taxe des biens de mainmorte," the "redevances des mines," the weights and measures fee, the pharmacy inspection fee, and the mine inspection fee, and war-profits taxes of a special form (known as the "impôt sur l'accroissement de la fortune" and the "impôt extraordinaire de guerre"). No collections have been made on these latter two since 1924.

war-profits tax, both of which were special taxes which will be discussed separately, it will appear that the yield of the assimilated taxes proper, even in the best year, 1926, failed to yield as much as a half-million francs. A word may be said about a few of the more important of these assimilated taxes.

The *taxe des biens de mainmorte*,[19] which produced 165 millions in 1926, is in reality a part of the inheritance tax. In form it is a supertax, added to the real-estate tax, payable when the real estate is owned by corporations, charitable organizations, etc., the existence of which is not limited by the length of human life and which seldom sell their real estate. The notion is that this tax roughly compensates for the loss of revenue to the State arising from the fact that there is seldom, if ever, an opportunity to impose death and transfer duties on such real estate. It was first established in the year 1849.

The only other tax in this group which produced a substantial revenue in 1926 is the *redevances des mines*.[20] This may be considered a part of the income tax. Mines in France are given special treatment. They were not subject to the *patente* and likewise are not taxed under the commercial- and industrial-profits schedule of the income tax. This tax was designed to fill the gap. It is a combination of an area tax, at a flat rate per *hectare*, and of a percentage tax on the profits from operation. It dates back to the year 1810.

The *taxe civique* was a special supplement to the income tax levied for the year 1926 only. In form it was a poll tax of 40 francs on the poor and a slight additional percentage (2 per cent at the most) on the more fortunate members of the community who had sufficient income to be liable to the general income tax. It was a tax bitterly resented by the Communists who staged a noisy but generally ineffective opposition to its collection.[21]

[19] *Notions elémentaires sur les Impôts directs* (Ministère des Finances), pp. 145–152.

[20] *Ibid.*, pp. 176–187. Rosier, *Tous Nos Impôts*, pp. 347–348.

[21] See Volume IV of this Series: David J. Saposs and A. D. M. Evans, *The Labor Movement in Post-War France* (New York, Columbia University Press, 1930). The "taxe exceptionnelle de guerre" in force from 1916 to 1919, was similar in its general character to the "taxe civique."

War-Profits Tax.[22] — The war-profits tax, established by the law of July 1, 1916, had as its object the taxation of abnormal profits realized during war time (strictly speaking, between August 1, 1914, and June 30, 1920). These were thought of as being in two classes: (1) profits, in excess of those made in pre-war time, coming from the taxpayer's usual business; (2) almost the whole profit made by one who contracted to furnish the Government with supplies, when this was not his usual business (or even if it was, if the taxpayer was an *intermédiare,* dealing in goods not owned by himself). The tax reached corporations and partnerships as well as individuals.

Farmers selling produce from their own lands were exempt; so were those members of the liberal professions not struck by the old business tax, the *patente.*

For the first class of war profits mentioned above, the taxable profit was found by subtracting from the profit of the year in question, the average annual profit for the three years prior to August 1, 1914 (counting deficits as zero) as shown by balance-sheets. The pre-war profit could be estimated if the taxpayer so chose, at 30 times the average annual amount paid to the State in the name of the *patente,* or business tax, during those three years. This opportunity was of course of the most benefit to those virtuous citizens who had made no attempt to keep the *fisc* from getting its due in those times. Finally, as a safeguard against unfairness, the pre-war "normal" profit figure was in any case to be at least 6 per cent [23] of the invested capital, and at least 5,000 francs.[24]

The second class mentioned above (contractors with the Government, not acting in their regular line of business), had of course no pre-war "normal profits" from which to calculate "excess" profits. Practically their entire profits were subject to tax; the law allowed them to claim a nominal fixed sum of 5,000 francs as "pre-war normal profit," and taxed all the rest.

[22] *Cf.* Allix, *Science des Finances,* pp. 456–462; Rosier, *Tous Nos Impôts,* pp. 305–341.

[23] Raised to 8 per cent by the law of December 31, 1917.

[24] Raised to 10,000 francs in calculating taxable profits for the year 1920.

TABLE 43

ASSIMILATED TAXES LEVIED FOR THE STATE, 1913–1927

(In millions of francs)

Sources: 1913–1915 *Comptes Généraux*, for 1914, 1915 and 1916; 1916–1926, *Renseignements statistiques relatifs aux Contributions directes et aux Taxes assimilées*

Assimilated Taxes (not including Alsace and Lorraine):	1913	1914	1915	1916	1917	1918	1919	1920	1921	1922	1923	1924	1925	1926	1927 [c]
1. *Taxe Civique*	....	....	....	....	.....	......	......	......	......	......	......	.....	......	678.7	7.9
2. War profits tax (*contribution extraordinaire sur les bénéfices de guerre*)	....	....	....	....	617.8	1,761.7	1,718.2	5,610.6	2,544.9	3,882.8	1,276.3	607.4	834.7	220.0	269.0
3. Exceptional war levy (*taxe exceptionnelle de guerre*)	....	....	....	....	10.5	18.3	7.3	.3	.1	[y]	[aa]	.....	......	.....	
4. Tax on "*mainmorte*" property (*taxe des biens de mainmorte*)	21.2	20.0	19.7	20.5	21.2	41.2	43.2	47.1	53.2	50.7	59.8	77.5	83.2	165.3	
5. Mine tax (*redevances des mines*). Share of the State [a]	8.5	7.9	3.2	4.7	11.7	13.2	14.8	17.6	30.7	26.4	34.7	50.7	122.7	91.8	
6. Weights and measures fees	6.3	5.8	5.3	5.1	4.9	4.8	10.9	12.2	12.4	13.4	14.0	17.3	17.7	16.0	
7. *Alcoomètres* and *densimètres* inspection fees	[d]	[f]	[i]	[l]	[n]	[q]	[t]	[v]	[x]	.1	.1	.1	.2	.2	
8. Pharmacy inspection fees	.1	[g]	[j]	.1	[o]	[r]	.1	.1	.1	.1	.1	.2	.2	.2	
9. Mineral water inspection fees	[e]	[h]	[k]	[m]	[p]	[s]	[u]	[w]	.1	.2	.2	.3	.3	.4	
10. Tax on carriages, horses and mules. Share of the State	21.9	21.9	19.2	18.8	36.6	34.8	35.8	19.8	19.4	20.0	20.1	23.5	23.2	22.6	
11. Tax on clubs, societies, and meeting places	1.2	1.1	1.0	.8	1.4	1.3	1.3	1.6	2.2	2.5	3.1	4.3	4.7	6.4	
12. Tax for mine inspection (*redevances pour la rétribution des délégués mineurs*)	.5	.3	.2	.3	.3	.5	.8	1.5	2.1	1.9	2.5	3.2	3.5	4.0	
13. Boilers, etc., inspection fees	.3	.2	.1	.1	.1	.2	.3	.4	.4	.4	.8	1.8	1.7	1.5	
14. Oleomargarine inspection fees	.1	.1	.1	.1	.1	.1	.1	.2	.2	.2	.2	.2	.3	.3	
15. Tax to cover inspection for preventing commercial fraud	.7	.6	.5	.5	.5	.5	.5	1.5	1.8	1.8	1.7	2.1	2.1	2.1	
16. Tax on gamekeepers	1.0	.9	.6	.4	.7	.6	.6	.9	1.0	1.1	1.2	1.4	1.5	1.5	
17. Tax on billiard tables	1.1	1.1	1.0	1.0	1.8	1.7	1.7	1.6	1.6	[z]	......	.....	......	......	
18. Tax for development of vocational education (*taxe d'apprentissage*)	....	....	....	....	.....	......	......	......	......	......	......	.....	......	65.8	
19. Cost of issuing rolls concerning carriages and billiard table taxes	.1	.1	.1	.1	.1	.1	.1	.1	.1	.1	......	.....	......	......	
Total Assimilated Taxes, not including Alsace and Lorraine	63.1	60.0	51.0	52.5	713.9	1,879.0	1,835.7	5,715.5	2,670.2	4,010.6	1,415.0	790.1	1,095.9	1,285.7	

	1913	1914	1915	1916	1917	1918	1919	1920	1921	1922	1923	1924	1925	1926	1927
Assimilated Taxes (Alsace and Lorraine only):															
20. Tax on "*mainmorte*" property. — Tax on capital (*impôt sur le capital*)	....	....	....	....	....	......	......	......	......	.2	.2	.5	.4	.5	
21. Tax on "*mainmorte*" property. — Real estate tax (*impôt foncier*)	....	....	....	....	....	......	......	......	......	1.7	1.7	2.1	2.3	2.3	
22. Weights and measures fees	....	....	....	....	....	......	......	......	......	.2	.5	.5	.7	.4	
23. Pharmacy inspection fees	....	....	....	....	....	......	......	......	......	[v]	[w]	[x]	[y]	[z]	
24. Mine tax (*redevances des mines*)[b]	....	....	....	....	....	......	......	......	......	......	11.8	18.9	21.8	39.4	
25. Mine tax (*impôt sur les mines — taxe de superficie*)	....	....	....	....	....	......	......	......	......	8.7	[bb]	[cc]	[aa]	[ee]	
26. Tax for mine inspection	....	....	....	....	....	......	......	......	......	.3	.3	.4	.5	.6	
27. Tax on capital increase (*Impôt sur l'accroissement de la fortune — période* 1914–1916, *et impôt de guerre* 1916)	....	....	....	....	....	......	......	......	......	.3	.5	.....	......	......	
28. War tax of 1918 (*impôt de guerre de* 1918)	....	....	....	....	....	......	......	......	......	1.1	.1	.....	......	......	
29. Tax on capital increase, *période* 1917–1919	....	....	....	....	....	......	......	......	......	2.3	.2	[dd]	......	......	
30. " " " " , *période* 1920–1921	....	....	....	....	....	......	......	......	......	.6	.2	.6	......	......	
31. *Taxe civique*	....	....	....	....	....	......	......	......	......	......	......	.....	......	29.6	
Total Assimilated Taxes, Alsace and Lorraine only	....	....	....	....	....	......	......	......	......	15.5	15.5	23.0	25.7	72.8	
Total Assimilated Taxes, all départements	63.1	60.0	51.0	52.5	713.9	1,879.0	1,835.7	5,715.5	2,670.2	4,026.1	1,430.5	813.1	1,121.6	1,358.5	803.6

[a] Including in 1925–1926 the Loucheur Surtax (law of December 4, 1925, art. 2), as follows: 1925 — 36,565,000 francs, 1926 — 10,129,000 francs.
[b] Including in 1926 Loucheur Surtax (law of December 4, 1926, art. 2) of 10,055,000 francs.
[c] Situation of assessments as of December 31, 1927. *Journal Officiel*, Jan. 17, 1928.

[d] 31,000 francs. [e] 43,000 francs. [f] 23,000 francs. [g] 32,000 francs. [h] 33,000 francs.
[i] 13,000 francs. [j] 46,000 francs. [k] 38,000 francs. [l] 12,000 francs. [m] 43,000 francs.
[n] 16,000 francs. [o] 49,000 francs. [p] 39,000 francs. [q] 20,000 francs. [r] 43,000 francs.
[s] 30,000 francs. [t] 26,000 francs. [u] 43,000 francs. [v] 35,000 francs. [w] 48,000 francs.
[x] 45,000 francs. [y] 47,000 francs. [z] 1,000 francs. [aa] 6,000 francs. [bb] 17,000 francs.
[cc] 14,000 francs. [dd] 25,000 francs. [ee] 13,000 francs.

The rate of the tax at first was fixed at 50 per cent, but was later made progressive by taxing that part of the 1916 excess profits above 500,000 francs, 60 per cent. Still later (law of December 31, 1917) the schedule became as follows:

50 per cent on that part of the taxable profits up to 100,000 francs.
60 per cent on that part of the taxable profits between 100,000 and 250,000 francs.
70 per cent on that part of the taxable profits between 250,000 and 500,000 francs.
80 per cent on that part of the taxable profits above 500,000 francs.

A flat reduction at the base of 5,000 francs was allowed for regular business men (both *patentés*, and mine operators).

The figures shown in Table 43 (line 2) are the annual assessments as set forth in the official "Statistics of Direct Taxes." They differ from the assessment figures published in the monthly statements of collections because of modifications and corrections made in the four months following the close of each year, but the differences amount in the aggregate to less than 1.5 per cent.

There is a very devious history connected with the collection of these levies and the crediting of the proceeds to the various budgets. The collections from this source are shown in Table 44, together with comparisons with the amounts assessed. The collections have been very slow. June 30, 1920, is the date which marks the end of the period during which the profits arising were subject to the tax. Five years later nearly one-fourth of the aggregate net assessments for the entire period of liability were uncollected. The portion which will ultimately be collected is highly uncertain. A part consists simply of bad debts. A considerable sum is tied up in litigation and appeals which may result in the annulment of the assessments. A part will be offset by claims based on "net losses" and upon claims for war damages. On the other hand, a substantial portion is not technically overdue because special privileges of "suspended liability" or of payment by instalments have been granted. Refunds are eliminated from the collections, and the figures as they stand are net.

In the case of the direct taxes the assessments (*rôles émis*) during a given period are dedicated to the budget of a particular

TABLE 44

WAR-PROFITS TAX COLLECTIONS, 1917-1927, AND COMPARISON WITH ASSESSMENTS

Source: Monthly Statements of Collections

	COLLECTIONS (In millions of francs)		PERCENTAGE UNCOLLECTED [b]	
	DURING TWELVE MONTHS PERIOD SPECIFIED [a]	CUMULATIVE TOTAL	OF GROSS ASSESSMENTS	OF NET ASSESSMENTS
1917	192	192	65.8	....
1918	714	906	53.6	....
1919	1,328	2,235	45.5	....
1920	2,031	4,265	56.3	....
1921	3,313	7,578	37.9	....
1922	2,066	9,644	39.9	....
1923	1,334	10,978	36.7	....
1924	1,331	12,309	32.6	27.3
1925	704	13,012	32.0	24.9
1926	586	13,598	29.8	19.8
1927	565	14,163	27.8	14.0

[a] In the table published in the *Inventaire*, p. 112, the figures for three years are different from those shown in this column. The *Inventaire* figures are as follows: 1918, 521,543,000 francs; 1919, 614,357,200 francs; and 1920, 2,937,073,700 francs. The sum of these three figures, 4,072,973,900 francs is, however, the same as the sum of the three corresponding items in the above table. Consequently there is no discrepancy between the figures of total collections.

[b] The assessment figures are from those of the monthly statements of collections.

exercice and the collections arising from each of these groups of assessments are kept separate from the collections of each other group, the proceeds being credited to its particular *exercice*. In the case of the excess-profits tax the situation is quite different. A special, separate account has been set up in the Treasury to receive the excess-profits tax collections and from this fund appropriations are made in support of the successive budgets. The figures in Table 44 represent the total credits of this special fund, minus cash refunds. For example, the aggregate collections available for transfer to the budgets of the various *exercices* amounted to 14.2 billion francs at the end of 1927. The data presented in

Table 45 reveal this highly interesting situation. With collections of only 14.2 billion francs, this fund had already been drawn upon for support of the various budgets to the extent of 18.1 billion francs. In other words, the special account was overdrawn by the difference between these two amounts — that is, to the extent of 3.9 billion francs. Thus, the true budget deficits for the period under review must have been greater by almost four billions than they would appear to be on their face because the Treasury had made good the grants to the various *exercices* from

TABLE 45

WAR-PROFITS TAX — GRANTS TO THE BUDGETS OF THE *EXERCICES*, 1917–1928

(In millions of francs)

Source: 1917–1923, Monthly Statements of Collections; 1923–1928, Budget Laws

Exercice	"Evaluations" for the *Exercices*		Amount of Excess or Deficit when Compared with Cumulative Total Collections[c]	Amount of Excess or Deficit when Compared with Aggregate Total Assessments[d]	
	Annual Grant	Cumulative Total		Gross Assessments	Net Assessments
1917	500	500	− 308	+ 62	.....
1918	580	1,080	− 174	+ 872	.....
1919	650	1,730	+ 505	+ 2,371	.....
1920	4,000	5,730	− 1,465	+ 4,036	.....
1921	4,000[a]	9,730	− 2,152	+ 2,464	.....
1922	3,000[b]	12,730	− 3,086	+ 3,314	.....
1923	2,000	14,730	− 3,752	+ 2,599	.....
1924	2,000	16,730	− 4,421	+ 1,534	+ 206
1925	775	17,505	− 4,493	+ 1,614	− 170
1926	400	17,905	− 4,307	+ 1,452	− 942
1927	200	18,105	− 3,942	+ 1,521	− 1,633
1928	300	18,405	.....	.....	.....

[a] This is the figure given in the monthly statement of collections. The 1921 budget contains also an item of 28,200,000 for Alsace-Lorraine.

[b] This is the figure given in the monthly statement of collections. The 1922 budget gives the item as 3,050,000,000.

[c] As set forth in Table 44.

[d] Assessment figures are from the monthly statement of collections.

some of its resources other than excess-profits tax collections. The source actually utilized was, doubtless, borrowing. The particular budgets to which this deficit of 3.9 billions will finally be charged will presumably be determined in the course of the final adjustment of the accounts of the various budgets. At present it is a floating derelict upon a stormy financial sea, drifting hither and thither without sail or rudder.

It is surprising, when one views this situation from the point of view of sound budgeting, that, in the face of this deficit of 3.9 billions in the special account, the excess-profits tax continues to be counted on as a resource in the current budgets. In the 1928 budget, for example, the excess-profits tax is asked to supply 300 millions. At the beginning of the budget year, the special fund already owed other budgets 3.9 billions. As an asset to offset this liability it had outstanding net assessments of only 2.3 billions, and, as has been pointed out, this asset may be very considerably reduced by bad debts and unfavorable decisions on cases appealed. But, even if every franc of it should prove to be good and collectible, it would be necessary, before the special account would be in a position to advance the sum of 300 million francs to the 1928 budget, to assess and collect during 1928 additional excess-profits taxes to the extent of 1,900 million francs. In the year just closed, 1927, the total new assessments had been only 269 million francs; moreover, abatements had been more than twice as much (760 millions).

This story, however, has still another chapter; for the figures of collections from the excess-profits tax, shown in Table 44, prove to be, for the most part, not cash collections at all as shown in Table 46 (see page 334); and the receipts accepted in lieu of cash were far from being a cash equivalent.

By a series of acts beginning with the law of October 26, 1917, *rentes* issued during and after the war were made acceptable in payment of excess-profits taxes, at not less than the price of emission.[25] This privilege was withdrawn by the law of March

[25] They were acceptable at the average of the official quotations in the market on the day preceding presentation, if that quotation was in excess of the price of emission. — Law of September 19, 1918, art. 7.

TABLE 46

RENTES ACCEPTED IN PAYMENT OF WAR-PROFITS TAXES, 1918–1926

Sources: 1918–1923, *Inventaire*, page 112; 1924–1926, Ministry of Finance

Year	*Rentes* Annual Receipts (In millions of francs)	*Rentes* Cumulative Total (In millions of francs)	Percentage of Total Collections[a] Paid in *Rentes*
1918	168	168	18.5
1919	123	291	13.0
1920	1,861	2,152	50.5
1921	2,507	4,659	61.5
1922	1,398	6,057	62.8
1923	865	6,922	63.1
1924, 1925, 1926	727	7,649	56.3

[a] Cumulative total collections from Table 44.

22, 1924, with certain exceptions,[26] but for the entire period of years ended December 31, 1926, out of the total collections of 13,598,254,200 francs, no less than 7,649,334,700 francs or 56.3 per cent, were paid in bonds. That is to say, enough bonds were turned over in payment of the tax so that if they were calculated as worth what the public paid for them at the time of issue,[27] they paid off 7,649,334,700 francs of the tax. They were so calculated, and did pay off that amount of tax, but the actual market value of

[26] A period of two months was established during which rentes would continue to be acceptable but only in payment of assessments made before the passage of the act. Moreover, rentes deposited as guarantee of payment of assessments appealed or granted delays, were to be acceptable within a limited time after final determination. Even if not actually on deposit, the rentes were acceptable if it could be proved that they had been subscribed to by the taxpayer at the time of issue.

That these exceptions were substantial is shown by the fact that as late as 1927, during the first three months, 10.4 millions of war profits taxes were paid in rentes, as compared with total collections of 116.3 millions.

The law of December 31, 1921 (art. 61) restricted the privilege of payment in rentes to those taxpayers who discharged their liability within two months of the legal due date of the tax.

[27] With the exception given in footnote 25 above, p. 333.

these *rentes* at the times they were turned in to pay the tax would total up to a figure considerably less than this. Until 1921 the market held up well, and the State was getting full cash value for its tax claims. But in 1921 values began to slip, and in 1922 and 1923, when the payments in *rentes* reached their highest, the fall of the *rentes* was accelerated. The difference between the price of emission and the market value reached 23 per cent of the price of emission of the 5 per cent 1915–1916 *rente*, and for the greater part of 1923 the difference hovered around 10 to 15 per cent for all the *rentes*. From 1924 to 1926 new low levels were touched, the 1915–1916 *rente* being at one time off 47 per cent from its emission price.

While the procedure of accepting *rentes* in payment of taxes undoubtedly deprived the State of certain cash resources, the whole process was believed to be justified — regardless of the market value of the citizen's claim on the Government — as a setting-off of debts. The Government gave up the chance to get the full immediate cash value of its tax claims, in return for the chance to get rid of equal [28] (future) claims against it. One might argue that it would be more astute finance to exact cash in payment for the tax and use the proceeds to buy up the depreciated *rentes* on the market. One of the officials of the Ministry of Finance explained, however, that when two parties set off their debts they do not necessarily first try to see what the debts are worth to third parties.

The procedure adopted, however, made the State appear to be getting more than it really was. The cancellation of the claims against it (that is, the giving up of the *rentes*), it treated as revenue, to be entered on the receipts side of the budget. But this required the insertion of an item on the expense side of the budget, as large as the claims given up by the individuals — an item for amortization of these *rentes*, in other words. Otherwise, to carry it to an absurd length, the State might collect all its taxes in government bonds, show revenue enough to balance the current expenditures, have a balanced budget — and yet have no money at

[28] And even greater — where bonds were redeemable at a premium above the emission price.

all with which to meet the current expenses. This, in part, is just what it did in collection of the war-profits tax. Under "revenue from taxes" it included the cancelled claims against it, and only partly offset this by amortization credits on the expenditure side. The former item totals 7,649 million francs; the amortization credits granted come only to 3,510 million francs.[29] Thus there was shown as revenue from taxes, available for meeting current expenditure, a total of 4,139 million francs (7,649 francs minus 3,510 francs) which never really existed. Adding to this the 3.9 billion francs overdraft on the Treasury account,[30] one gets a total of 8 billion francs counted (either in budget laws or tax returns statements) as war-profits tax receipts available to meet current expenditures, which have never, in reality, been available. No estimate of budget surpluses or deficits that the writer has seen has taken these items into account; it appears that when the final accounts are drawn up in the *Compte Général,* the cumulative deficit for the post-war period will be 8 billion francs greater than has hitherto been noted. One may ask how this extra deficit will be apportioned among the preceding *exercices;* that is another knotty problem for the *Cours de Comptes,* not for this work.

[29] The following figures were kindly supplied by the Ministry of Finance and represent (except for 1928) all credits granted for amortization of rentes—thus including supplementary credits, as well as those opened by the annual budget law. The 1928 figure represents credits asked for.

Exercice	Millions of francs
1919	——
1920	200
1921	200
1922	1,500
1923	910
1924	400
1925	110
1926	80
1927	70
1928	40
	3,510

[30] See above, p. 333.

Indirect Taxes

In spite of the enormous increase in the amounts of direct taxes, indirect taxes remain the backbone of the French tax system. As late as 1927, when direct taxes produced 13.2 billion francs, indirect taxes produced 27.4 billion, more than twice as much.

The direct taxes are fairly simple in their main outlines, but often become exceedingly complicated when an attempt is made to apply them to specific cases. The indirect taxes, on the other hand, are usually simple enough when applied to specific cases, but as a body they present a bewildering diversity. Furthermore many of them have several different rates, and though it is not ordinarily difficult to determine what rate should apply in a given case, the variation enhances the appearance of confusion.

They may be conveniently split into five groups. The registration taxes are bound up with legal safeguards involved in litigation; the stamp taxes touch lightly a large section of non-commercial exchanges; the customs duties concern imports and exports; the turnover tax and its offshoots weigh heavily on almost all commercial transactions; and the *contributions indirectes* are levied on certain commodities which have been deemed specially fitted for indirect taxation. This brief characterization is contradicted in many places within the system, but in general it holds good.

Before these divisions are considered separately, it is of interest to note how much of the total indirect tax burden each one has borne throughout the war and post-war period.

In general, the *contributions indirectes,* the registration taxes, and the customs duties shared the burden fairly evenly, until the rise of the turnover tax and the decline of customs revenues altered the picture considerably.

In 1913, the turnover tax did not exist, and if the yield of the other four is totalled, it is found that the *contributions indirectes* contributed 33 per cent of that total, with the registration taxes and customs duties close behind (30.5 per cent and 27.5 per cent respectively). The stamp taxes lagged with only 9 per cent.

By 1919 the proportions had shifted a little, but the general outline remained the same. *Contributions indirectes* had taken over a little more of the total burden (35 per cent now), relieving the customs duties (now a little over 24 per cent), while registration kept its 1913 share. The stamp taxes had diminished in relative importance, but together with the new payments taxes (the forerunners of the turnover tax) accounted for the other 10 per cent.

But by 1927 the entire picture had changed. Most striking was the decline in the relative importance of the customs duties, which now furnished only 9.5 per cent of the total yield, and the rise of the new turnover tax, which carried a larger share of the burden (31 per cent) than any of the other four. *Contributions indirectes* came close behind (29.5 per cent) and registration taxes bore an appreciable share (22 per cent), but both had decreased in relative importance since 1919. The stamp taxes still yielded but a modest share (8 per cent).

The failure of the customs duties to yield more revenue, in the face of a rising price level, is one of the outstanding features of recent French tax history. In 1925 the regular import (and the few export) duties yielded less, even in paper francs, than they had in 1917, 1920, 1922, 1923, and 1924. From 1917 through 1926, the customs receipts in paper francs did not in any year vary more than 22 per cent (above or below) the 1917 figure for receipts. At least two reasons for this failure of the customs revenue to grow may be given: (1) almost all the duties are specific, and though individual rates were increased by administrative decrees after the war, and though the Chamber later raised them 30 per cent at a time, twice, they appear never to have caught up with the rising price level; (2) the duties are protective — revenue is not their sole, or even their chief aim. Much of the heavy imports of raw materials which France works up in her factories enters duty-free.

Considering the " indirect " taxes as a whole, one finds the system exhibiting that characteristic seen even more plainly when the five groups are examined separately — the concentration of most of the yield in comparatively few taxes. There are 62 different taxes listed in these tables, and even that is no fair indicator of the diversity of the system, for many of these taxes are really groups of taxes (e.g., the turnover tax, the "Other Contracts" tax in registration). But only 17 of these 62 are needed to furnish 86 per cent of the total "indirect" tax revenue.[31]

Registration Taxes

Enregistrement. — The yield of the registration taxes during the period under review is summarized in Table 47. It appears that the aggregate yield from this group has increased more than sevenfold since 1913.

The procedure of registration is accomplished by bringing the document in question to a government registration bureau, where an official either copies it, makes an abstract of it, or requires a duplicate to be left. Thus there is kept an accurate record of the date and contents of contracts, judicial decisions, and other written data bearing on property rights or civil status. In general, registration is necessary to establish the date of a document for purposes of litigation. In many cases, registration is free; in others, it involves only a slight fee; in still others, it is made the occasion for a heavy tax on the act the document represents.

To avoid confusion it should be borne in mind that in effect, the agreements of ordinary commercial life usually lie outside this régime. This is because France has a separate set of laws to deal with commercial disputes, and the requirements of formal written proof are not so strict as in the civil law; hence commercial documents are not presented often for registration.

As may readily be seen, the system of registration, while lending safety to titles, at the same time operates as a serious restriction on the alienation of property when it is combined with appreciable tax rates. This is most noticeable in the tax on the transfer of real estate.

The three most important registration taxes were in 1913, and

[31] In the tables that follow, receipts from Alsace and Lorraine are included for 1922 and years following.

TABLE 47

REVENUE FROM REGISTRATION TAXES, 1913–1927

(In millions of francs)

Sources: 1913, 1914, 1915, *Compte Général* for 1914, 1915, and 1916;
1916, *Compte Général* for 1916 (*recouvrements effectués, opérations de l'année* 1916) plus *recettes postérieures* figures from the *Journal Officiel*.
1917–1921, *Projets de Budget* for the years 1919, 1920, 1921, 1922, and 1923;
1922, Twelve-month collections from the *Bulletin de Statistique et de Législation Comparée*, December, 1922, plus *recettes postérieures* figures furnished by the Ministry of Finance;
1923, *Projet de Budget*, 1925;
1924–1925, *Bulletin de Statistique et de Législation Comparée*, May, 1925 and 1926;
1926, *Journal Officiel*, June 17, 1927, p. 6237 *et seq.*;
1927, *Journal Officiel*, January 17, 1928, p. 729 *et seq.*

	1913	1914	1915	1916	1917	1918	1919	1920	1921	1922	1923	1924	1925	1926	1927[c]
Transfers:															
On a valuable consideration:															
Personal property:															
1. Securities	106	112	111	100	101	108	124	211	344	389	467	699	844	983	723
2. Personal debts, annuities, state offices (*créances, rentes, prix d'office*)	5	4	1	1	2	2	10	10	9	12	12	16	16	16	22
3. Businesses (*fonds de commerce*)	15	10	2	3	5	9	40	80	109	141	181	217	238	280	214
4. Material, furniture, etc. (*meubles corporels*)	10	7	6	8	12	17	56	100	77	67	71	94	104	139	111
5. Real property and rights to real property[a]	183	113	22	47	110	199	548	860	757	826	1,002	1,268	1,402	1,871	1,633
Free:															
6. Between living persons (*donations*)	29	21	5	7	21	25	89	136	83	82	92	144	157	162	140
7. Resulting from death (*successions*)	327	226	239	257	340	366	670	792	810	916	991	1,401	1,452	1,653	1,942
8. Non-transferable property (*taxe representative du droit d'accroissement*)	1	1	1	1	2	1	1	1	1	1	1	1	1	2	1
9. Other contracts and civil and administrative documents	107	81	63	84	105	167	275	419	379	380	422	587	701	871	1,062
10. Judicial and extrajudicial documents	23	16	5	6	8	10	21	40	53	52	51	61	67	93	136
11. Mortgages	15	10	3	4	6	10	24	41	43	50	59	77	82	89	71
12. Tax on capital insured by fire insurance companies	5	5	5	5	5	5	7	7	9	11	11	14	17	20	23
13. Fines	4	3	2	2	4	5	10	19	25	26	25	22	30	43	15
14. Miscellaneous receipts	3	2	[d]	1	1	1	2	3	6	8	7	8	11	18	20
Total	834	611	464	525	720	924	1,874	2,718	2,705	2,961	3,392	4,608	5,123	6,239	6,112

[a] Including the "taxe exceptionnelle sur la première mutation" created in 1926. This tax is collected to the credit of the *Caisse d'Amortissement*.
[b] This tax was transferred to the *Caisse d'Amortissement* as of January 1, 1927.
[c] Twelve-month collections not including the "recettes postérieures au 31 Décembre 1927." The "recettes postérieures" are collections made during the first four months of a calendar year, but due to appear in the preceding year's figures (the "exercice"). The 1926 and 1927 figures include receipts by the *Caisse d'Amortissement* from the real-estate transfer taxes and (1927) the death duties.
[d] 423,000 francs.

are today, the taxes on transfer of real estate, on transfer of securities and on transfer resulting from death (inheritance and estate duties).[32] True, from January 1, 1927, the third-named tax has no longer been in the state budget — its proceeds go to the *Caisse d'Amortissement* — but it is still a registration tax, its mode of levy unaltered. No other three taxes in the whole French fiscal system have been the target of such vigorous opposition from the property-owning taxpayers. It is true that there have been protests against the income taxes as a system, but these registration taxes have each been attacked separately, with particular bitterness. This has been so largely because of the high rates of each of the three. Together they supplied 74 per cent of the total yield of registration taxes in 1913, and in 1927, 70 per cent.

Stamp Taxes

The stamp taxes form a system of low, fixed taxes (as a rule), in contrast to the high, percentage taxes of registration. They cover a much wider field than the latter, and are almost always superimposed upon them. Like the registration taxes, they are concerned with judicial or administrative documents, or with the movements of capital in its monetary form. Taxation of commodities is left to the *contributions indirectes*.

The yield from these taxes is presented in Table 48. The increase since 1913 has been nine-fold, even greater than in the case of the registration taxes. No percentage analysis is made of the separate items, as was done with the registration taxes, as two of the largest items each represent an agglomeration of miscellaneous taxes not concerned with any special sort of transaction. It can easily be seen, however, what an important part has been played, especially during the last few years, by the taxes on security issues and commercial bills, and on stock exchange transactions.

[32] Omitting the tax on income from securities, which is discussed under the income tax section, pp. 316, 317, 324.

TABLE 48

REVENUE FROM STAMP TAXES, 1913–1927 (in millions of francs)

Sources: 1913, 1914, 1915, *Compte Général* for 1914, 1915, and 1916;
1916, *Compte Général* for 1916 (*recouvrements effectués, opérations de l'année* 1916) plus *recettes postérieures* figures from the *Journal Officiel.*
1917–1921, *Projets de Budget* for the years 1919, 1920, 1921, 1922, and 1923;
1922, Twelve-month collections from the *Bulletin de Statistique et de Législation Comparée*, December, 1922, plus *recettes postérieures* figures furnished by the Ministry of Finance;
1923, *Projet de Budget*, 1925;
1924–1925, *Bulletin de Statistique et de Législation Comparée*, May, 1925 and 1926;
1926, *Journal Officiel*, June 17, 1927, p. 6237 *et seq.*;
1927, *Journal Officiel*, January 17, 1928, p. 72 *et seq.*

	1913	1914	1915	1916	1917	1918	1919	1920	1921	1922	1923	1924	1925	1926	1927[d]
Non-proportional stamp taxes (fixed taxes, and taxes calculated on size of paper):															
1. Various taxes collected by affixing a standard stamp (*timbre unique*)	...	...	...	...	...	...	...	...	...	...	...	.....	198	757	862
2. Documents subject to the tax calculated on size of paper (*timbre de dimension*)	45	32	18	20	23	33	70	113	130	138	145	161	179	247	264
3. Abstracts from the judicial record (*casier judiciare*)	...	...	...	...	...	...	...	...	[e]	[e]	[e]	[e]	[e]	[e]	1
4. Outdoor advertisements (*affiches*)	5	3	1	2	1	2	4	7	11	11	13	14	13	5	7
5. Insurance contracts	13	12	12	11	11	14	24	28	74	88	94	124	144	188	229
6. Transportation documents	52	36	31	32	29	24	25	28	29	35	41	58	65	85	97
7. Trade marks	[e]	[e]	[e]	[e]	[e]	[e]	[e]	[e]	[e]	[e]	[e]	[e]	[e]	[e]	[e]
8. Passports and visas	[e]	[e]	[e]	[e]	[e]	[e]	[e]	1	2	2	1	2	2	5	4
9. Hunting permits	11	1	[e]	2	8	9	17	18	24	25	26	34	35	35	36
10. Foreigners' identity cards	...	...	...	...	...	...	...	...	...	...	...	.....	11	[c]	29
11. Entry cards to clubs and casinos	...	...	...	...	...	...	...	...	3	2	2	3	2	.....	.....
12. Receipts, checks and intra-bank transfers	32	28	28	30	33	36	41	82	134	146	155	176	116	15	15
Proportional stamp taxes:															
13. Commercial bills, bank notes, etc.	29	19	8	13	18	41	72	151	64	63	76	162	110	11	13
14. Securities	54	66	47	48	48	56	61	86	92	104	142	160	196	278	338
Stamp taxes on bourse operations:															
15. Stock exchange transactions (and fines pertaining thereto)	10[a]	5	1	2	3	3	7	24	19	26	52	92	147	358	321
16. Foreign exchange transactions	...	...	...	...	...	...	...	...	...	...	...	.....	.....	25	23
17. Produce exchange transactions	...	1	[e]	[e]	[e]	[e]	[e]	[e]	[e]	[e]	1	1	2	4	3
18. Stamp tax on occasional sales of *de luxe* objects (*rentes entre non-commerçants*)	...	...	...	...	...	...	...	...	13	20	15	19	20	21	24
19. Fines	1	1	[e]	1	1	1	1	1	2	2	2	2	2	3	4
20. Miscellaneous receipts	[e]	1	[e]	[e]	[e]	[e]	[e]	[e]	[e]	1	[e]	[e]	[e]	[e]	[e]
Total	251	204[b]	146	161	176	219	321	542	597	664	766	1,008	1,240	2,036	2,270

[a] In 1913 this tax is not subdivided into "Impôt sur les opérations traitées dans les bourses de valeurs, impôt sur les opérations traitées dans les bourses de commerce, but is simply entitled: "Impôt sur les opérations de bourse et pénalités."

[b] The total for 1914 includes a tax on "Droits divers et recettes accessoires." As figures are given for only one year, they are not given in the table, but included in the total for the year (72,767).

[c] The total collections (33,722,000) of the "carte d'identité" have been included under the "actes et écrits assujettis au timbre de dimension."

[d] Twelve-month collections, not including the "recettes postérieures au 31 Décembre 1927." The "recettes postérieures" are collections made during the first four months of a calendar year, but due to appear in the preceding year's figures (the "exercice").

[e] Less than one-half million francs.

Customs Duties [33]

As has been pointed out, the French customs duties are protective in character. It is impossible to give the rates here, as they are practically all specific instead of *ad valorem*, and thus are numerous and varied. The increase in the yield, as shown in Table 49, has been insufficient to offset the fall in the value of the franc.

In general, the rates are fixed by law, but the administration has been given power to alter them under certain conditions — in case of mobilization, for reprisal against nations discriminating against French commerce, when making commercial treaties, etc. If a law raising tariff rates is presented by the Government to the Chamber, the Government can raise the tariff rates at once, correspondingly, subject to restitution of the tax, of course, if the law does not pass. Formerly the administration could apply, by decrees, coefficients of increase to the tax due, so that a continual rise in the price level might not make the real burden of the specific rates too light. This process now requires the approval of Parliament before it can be put in operation.

The tariff law itself provides for two rates for every group of articles — a general rate, applied to goods originating in countries which have no trade agreement with France; and a minimum rate, often much lower than the other, which can be granted to countries with which France has concluded commercial treaties. There are also some intermediate rates which may be used on certain occasions.

Sales Taxes

The French encountered difficulties during the inflation period in adjusting the indirect taxes of the classes described above to the changing conditions. In the case of the sales taxes treated in this section, however, they found a type of impost the characteristics of which were eminently suited to the exigencies of a paper

[33] *Décret* of December 28, 1926, *portant codification des textes législatifs concernant les douanes*. *Journal Officiel*, December 31, 1926. Printed separately as *Extrait* No. 126 of the *J. O. Cf.* Rosier, *Tous Nos Impôts*, pp. 789–845.

TABLE 49

REVENUE FROM CUSTOMS, 1913–1927

(In millions of francs)

Sources: 1913, 1914, 1915, *Compte Général* for 1914, 1915. and 1916;
1916, *Compte Général* for 1916 (*recouvrements effectués, opérations de l'année* 1916) plus *recettes postérieures* figures from the *Journal Officiel*.
1917–1921, *Projets de Budget* for the years 1919, 1920, 1921, 1922. and 1923;
1922, Twelve-month collections from the *Bulletin de Statistique et de Législation Comparée*, December, 1922, plus *recettes postérieures* figures furnished by the Ministry of Finance;
1923, *Projet de Budget*, 1925;
1924–1925, *Bulletin de Statistique et de Législation Comparée*, May, 1925 and 1926;
1926, *Journal Officiel*, June 17, 1927, p. 6237 *et seq.*;
1927, *Journal Officiel*, January 17, 1928, p. 729 *et seq.*

	1913	1914	1915	1916	1917	1918	1919	1920	1921	1922	1923	1924	1925	1926	1927[b]
1. Regular import and export taxes[a]	716	549	738	1,367	1,483	1,157	1,437	1,531	1,128	1,536	1,527	1,511	1,390	1,808	2,379
2. Taxes for development of statistics and foreign commerce	17	12	11	13	12	11	19	24	28	35	42	49	54	87	127
3. Navigation taxes	13	11	13	16	12	11	13	15	12	13	15	15	10	16	33
4. Tax on crude mineral oils[c]	2	1	[d]	[d]	[d]	[d]	[d]	[d]	[d]	[d]	[d]	[d]	.....	.....	.....
5. Fines	2	1	1	3	2	3	6	15	17	11	8	7	8	11	11
6. Miscellaneous receipts	6	5	1	1	2	3	3	10	12	17	18	22	25	46	68
Total	756	579	764	1,401	1,511	1,185	1,477	1,596	1,197	1,611	1,610	1,604	1,486	1,968	2,618

[a] For the relatively insignificant drawback on cotton goods allowed, and apparently not taken account of in these figures, see Table 60, p. 398 (Table of *Dégrèvements*).

[b] Twelve-month collections only, not including the "recettes postérieures au 31 Décembre 1927." The "recettes postérieures" are collections made during the first four months of a calendar year, but due to appear in the preceding year's figures (the exercice).

[c] "Taxe de fabrication," collected exclusively by customs.

[d] Less than one-half million francs.

money régime. With gross receipts as the base, a change in prices automatically changed the yield of the tax.[34]

The "sales taxes" now referred to are not those on special kinds of transactions, as found in the registration and *contributions indirectes* sections, but those general ones, striking practically all sales, and not concerned with any particular commodity as such. There is really but one such sales tax — the turnover tax, with its various exfoliations; but the payments taxes which preceded it deserve mention although their brief life (1918–1920) brought them so many troubles that they were scrapped in 1920 in favor of the general turnover tax.[35] There were three distinct taxes: one, a tax of two-tenths of one per cent on all non-commercial payments whenever a receipt was given (and the receipt was not compulsory except when *de luxe* objects were sold, in which case a 10 per cent rate was levied); another, a tax at the same rate on practically all commercial payments for sales at retail or for consumption; and third, a *de luxe* tax of 10 per cent on retail sales of *de luxe* commodities and on the receipts of *de luxe* hotels, restaurants, etc.

The present turnover tax started in 1920 with a fairly simple structure, but it has developed so many branches and different rates by now that the single line "turnover tax" includes in reality a variety of distinct levies. They have this in common: they are all offshoots of the turnover tax itself, evolved either as a supplement and corrective (*de luxe* tax) or as a step toward abandonment of the turnover tax ("production" taxes).

Three tax administrations take a hand in collecting the tax, or taxes. The *contributions indirectes* handles by far the biggest share of the burden, collecting 86 per cent of the receipts in 1926.[36] The customs collected 13 per cent in the same year, and the remaining 1 per cent was garnered by the registration administration, which a few years before had been the most influential of the three in administering the tax.

From the detailed figures available for that part of the tax col-

[34] Assuming a given volume of business.

[35] Allix and Lecerclé, *La Taxe sur le Chiffre d'Affaires*, pp. 15–28.

[36] *Bulletin de Statistique*, August, 1927, p. 249.

lected by the *contributions indirectes* administration, it appears that of the total 1926 yield of 7,479,688,900 francs,[37] about 74 per cent came from the ordinary (now 1.9 per cent)[38] rate, and about 17 per cent from the various *de luxe* rates on retail sales, automobiles and hotel receipts. The 1928 budget *projet* shows that, regarding the 1926 turnover tax collections, 4 per cent of the grand total came from the slaughtering tax, and 2½ per cent from the coal tax. The fertilizer tax gave less than one half of one per cent of the total. The tea and coffee taxes (collected by the customs) accounted for 2 per cent.

Thus it can be seen that the "production taxes," levied in place of the turnover tax, have made appreciable inroads upon the system — they furnish not far from 9 per cent of the total given in the table for the "turnover tax." This percentage will be larger when the new sugar tax comes into operation in October, 1928.

Table 50 summarizes the yield to the State from the sales taxes during the period under review. The turnover tax now produces almost one-fifth of the total state taxes. This fruitfulness is due mainly to its large field of application. With the general exceptions of agricultural and professional revenues, it strikes nearly all sales, wholesale or retail, made in France.[39] It consists really of three taxes: (a) a 2 per cent levy on gross receipts from all [40] commercial sales made within, and all imports into, France; (b) a 2 per cent levy on gross commissions, interest, and other proceeds from what may be termed the sale of commercial services; (c) a special luxury tax, varying from 4 per cent to 13 per cent, on certain *de luxe* sales. In addition there are the various "production taxes" which have been introduced in an effort to replace the turnover tax.

[37] Not including the share of the communes and départements.

[38] Two per cent, including the one-tenth of one per cent for the communes and départements.

[39] *Décret* of December 28, 1926, *portant codification de la législation en matière d'impôt sur le chiffre d'affaires. Journal Officiel*, January 4, 1927. Published separately as *Extrait* No. 132 of the *J. O. Cf.* Allix and Lecerclé, *La Taxe sur le Chiffre d'Affaires.*

[40] With certain exceptions, most of them unimportant from a revenue viewpoint.

The 2 per cent rate, levied on gross receipts, has thus nothing whatever to do with the profit or loss of the business, although deduction of turnover tax paid is allowed in calculating profits subject to the income tax. The tax is almost universal so far as commercial transactions are concerned; the only exemptions allowed here concern, in the main, articles already reached by special taxes of their own, or which are granted special favor as necessary food products, or which are taxed at the stage of production by the recently instituted "production taxes" (coal, meat, fertilizers, coffee, tea and sugar). In 1920 the rate was 1.10 per cent, later raised to 1.30 per cent, and now fixed at 2 per

TABLE 50

REVENUE FROM TURNOVER TAX

(In millions of francs)

Sources: 1918–1921, *Projets de Budget* for the years 1920, 1921, 1922, and 1923;
1922, Twelve-month collections from the *Bulletin de Statistique et de Législation Comparée*, December, 1922, plus *recettes postérieures* figures furnished by the Ministry of Finance;
1923, *Projet de Budget*, 1925;
1924–1925, *Bulletin de Statistique et de Législation Comparée*, May, 1925 and 1926;
1926, *Journal Officiel*, June 17, 1927, p. 6237 *et seq.*;
1927, *Journal Officiel*, January 17, 1928, p. 729 *et seq.*

Year	Payments Taxes 1918–1920	Turnover Tax 1920–1927 [a]	Total
1918	112	.....	112
1919	269	.....	269
1920	314	942	1,256
1921	...	1,897	1,897
1922	...	2,295	2,295
1923	...	3,028	3,028
1924	...	4,101	4,101
1925	...	4,544	4,544
1926	...	7,480	7,480
1927 [b]	..	8,605	8,605

[a] Including regular "taxes de luxe," coal and fertilizer "production" taxes and slaughtering tax.

[b] Twelve-month collections only, not including the "recettes postérieures au 31 Décembre 1927." The "recettes postérieures" are collections made during the first four months of a calendar year, but due to appear in the preceding year's figures (the "exercice").

cent. It must be remembered that sales of agricultural products by the farmer lie entirely outside the field of this tax; they are considered " non-commercial." The same is true of wage-payments.

The same 2 per cent rate is applicable to gross commissions, brokerage fees, interest, agios, and such remunerations which come to those who act as intermediaries in the flow of goods and capital, but who do not actually acquire ownership. The greatest single difficulty in the administration of the tax is the task of distinguishing between the merchant who actually buys the goods to resell them — and hence pays the tax on the total value of the goods — and the merchant who acts only as intermediary, who never really has title to the goods, and hence pays the tax only on his commission.

The luxury tax of 12 per cent strikes all *retail* sales of objects which are classified by the Government as being *de luxe,* either because of their nature or because of the price at which they are sold. There is another branch of the *de luxe* tax, with a rate of 13 per cent, imposed on the gross receipts of certain hotels, restaurants, cafés, etc., which have been classified by governmental commissions as *de luxe* establishments. Some are placed in an intermediate *de luxe* rank and taxed only 4 per cent.

The figure of yield for the turnover tax as given above includes not only the turnover tax proper, as just described, but also the various replacement taxes. These latter are of four kinds:

(1) All sales and imports of coal are exempt from the turnover tax, and in its place is levied a "production" tax of 2.5 per cent on all sales by coal mines (with certain exceptions), and on all imports of coal. Likewise, all sales of fertilizers are exempt from the turnover tax, and producers and importers pay a 3.5 per cent tax on sales and imports (again, with certain exceptions).

(2) A slaughter-house tax (*taxe d'abatage*) is collected on animals slaughtered for meat, and in return, exemption from the turnover tax is granted for sales of the animals or the meat. The rates are specific, are levied on the live weight of the animal to be slaughtered, and vary with the species: calves and sheep, 20 centimes per kilogram; cattle, 12.5 centimes; horses, 10 centimes; hogs, 25 centimes. Imported meats are also taxed at specific rates

(higher, of course, as they are levied on the meat instead of the animal).

(3) Since no tea or coffee is produced in France, a special import tax acts as a production tax. Thus, coffee is taxed 8 per cent on importation (in addition to whatever other import taxes may be in force); tea, 7 per cent. In return, all sales in France are exempt from the turnover tax. The same régime is applied to sulphur, taxable upon importation, after July 1, 1928, at 5 per cent.

(4) Beginning October 1, 1928, sales of sugar will be exempt from the turnover tax, and a replacement "production tax" will come into force. This is a 6 per cent tax (5.7 per cent for the State, 0.3 per cent for the départements and communes) levied on the average price of white sugar No. 3 on sale during the year preceding (September 1 to August 31), as determined by the official Paris Bourse quotations. It is to be collected at the same time as the *droit de consommation*[41] and from the same taxpayer. Certain small chocolate and candy producers will be able to claim from the treasury one-half of the tax already paid on the sugar they use.[42]

The receipts in 1926 from the coal tax were 198,213,000 francs; from the slaughtering and imported meat tax, 311,908,000 francs; from the fertilizer tax, 39,257,000 francs; from the tea and coffee taxes, 151,840,000 francs.

One point should be carefully noted. The rate given above for the 2 per cent turnover tax (1.10 and 1.30 per cent in earlier years) is inclusive of a 0.10 per cent tax levied for the benefit of local finances; the rate of 2.50 per cent for the coal tax likewise includes a 0.15 per cent tax for local finances. But the figures for yield given above do not include the receipts from these taxes for the localities. Thus, the receipts from the turnover tax proper, and the *de luxe* taxes, were 6,672,922,000 francs for 1926, but this is reckoning the turnover tax proper at only 1.90 per cent. Likewise, the coal tax yield figures above are on the basis of a 2.35 per cent tax.

[41] A "contribution indirecte." See p. 351.

[42] Law of December 27, 1927, art. 29.

France's experience with sales taxes undoubtedly constitutes the most interesting chapter in the history of her tax system since the war. So important is it that it has been deemed worthy of exhaustive study, the results of which are presented in a separate volume.[43] Suffice it to say here that it has been regarded chiefly as an emergency tax, the great, if not sole, virtue of which has been to supply the Treasury with large amounts of ready money when the latter's cash assets were scarce. An increase in its rates could be depended upon, as in 1924 and 1926, to give an immediate increased yield, in contrast to the income tax. As inflation progressed and prices rose, its yield increased faster than did that of most other branches of the tax system.

Its faults have been many, however. It has labored under the same disadvantages as the income taxes in causing an immense amount of dispute and litigation over the correct interpretation of the law. In addition, it has been open to attack on the grounds that it observes no laws of fiscal justice, the general impression being that it weighs most heavily on the poor.[44] Parties of the Left have been especially vigorous in their denunciation of the tax, going so far as to make its abolition a campaign promise in 1924 — a promise they were unable to keep simply because of the urgent need for revenue from all possible sources.

Its administration has proved difficult because of the vast number of small taxpayers with whom the fiscal agents must make contact. This caused so much dissatisfaction that a "*forfait*" system has been adopted whereby close to 90 per cent of the turnover-tax payers are assessed on a mere estimate of yearly turnover, free from the necessity of keeping even a record of gross receipts for tax purposes.

There is evidence that the tax has caused a concentration in the ownership of economic goods *en route* to the consumer. Wholesalers have become functional middlemen (commission agents, jobbers, etc.) to avoid holding title to the goods, throw-

[43] See the study of the turnover tax by Carl S. Shoup in the special volume soon to be published by the Columbia University Press.

[44] Note that in Table 63, p. 403, this assumption is not adopted for the tax as a whole.

ing more of the risk of ownership back on producers; the former may in this way escape a tax on the value of the goods and be instead subject only to a tax on their commissions. Vertically integrated concerns have an advantage over the several small units in the chain from producer to consumer, as the goods may then be sold (and hence taxed) only once or twice instead of four or five times.

Despite these considerations, the tax has proven so lucrative that it is assured of a place in the French tax system for some years to come, unless it can be disintegrated by transformation into a series of "production" taxes, which are in effect additions to the *contributions indirectes* system.

Contributions Indirectes

Under this heading French budget practice groups only a part of those taxes which current American usage would call "indirect." Stamp taxes, for instance, come under *enregistrement*, and the general turnover tax has a classification to itself. Nevertheless, the *contributions indirectes* yield far more than the registration or stamp taxes combined, far more than the customs, and come not far behind the turnover tax and the income taxes.

For the most part, these "excise taxes," as they might be called, consist of levies on certain widely used articles of food and drink, and on transportation; alcoholic drinks and rail transport are the chief targets, and of these, strongly alcoholic drinks (as contrasted with wines) yield the bulk of the revenue — indeed, about one-third of the total *contributions indirectes* receipts.

Most of the taxes are specific — so many francs per hectolitre or kilogram or horse power — and their real burden is thus impossible to calculate without precise knowledge of the prices of the articles in question. Two notable examples of the *ad valorem* method, however, are the special 30 per cent tax on *liqueurs*, and the tax on merchandise and passenger transportation.

Many of the taxes were created under the stress of war and post-war finance, but abolishing these would diminish the total revenue of the *contributions indirectes* by only one-fifth. All of these new taxes (excepting the 30 per cent tax on *liqueurs*) illustrate a characteristic feature of *contributions indirectes,* namely, the presence of a large number of small taxes which even in the aggregate make up a comparatively unimportant part of the total yield. Twenty-eight taxes (including the sugar tax) are listed in the budget under the above heading, and if twenty-two of these were abolished, the revenue would decrease by little more than one-ninth.

The details of the yield of the *contributions indirectes* are given in Table 51 (page 354). Since 1913, the revenue from this group of taxes has increased ninefold.

From 1913 through to 1925 the liquor taxes accounted, each year, for not far from half of the total *contributions indirectes* yield. Their share in the yield declined steadily, however, from 1913 (53 per cent) to 1917 (45 per cent), and would have become still less had it not been for the imposition of the *ad valorem* tax on spirits, established in 1918. This brought it up so that by 1921 the share had reached 52 per cent; but then it started a decline again, dropping to 48 per cent in 1925, and abruptly to 30 per cent in 1927.

What is taking up the slack? There is no one tax to which the burden is being shifted, but the levies on railroad revenue (the share of which increased from 15 per cent to 18 per cent from 1925 to 1926 and to 21 per cent in 1927) are taking up some of it, and the rest is divided mainly among the automobile, sugar and gasoline taxes.

Thus, to the rescue, while the share of the liquor taxes (and, before 1927, that of the sugar tax) decreased appreciably, came chiefly the new taxes established since 1913, and the tax on railroad revenue.

Among the new taxes, the two most important are those on gasoline and oils, and on automobiles. The latter is not a "new" tax, strictly speaking; it was transformed in 1920 from a direct tax into an indirect one. In 1927 it yielded 7.5 per cent of the total *contributions indirectes* receipts. The gasoline and oils tax gave 10.5 per cent, and another new tax, on certain colonial products (largely a customs duty, but classed here for administrative purposes), 5 per cent.

The revenue from railroads has seen its proportion to the total *contributions indirectes* nearly double since 1913. In that year the proportion was only 10 per cent; by 1915 it had sunk to 7 per cent; but by 1927, as has been noted, it had risen to 21 per cent. The rates of this tax are admittedly very high, and there has been more than one complaint voiced about the burden passengers and shippers must bear thereby.[45] Perhaps even more of the burden than the legislator intended has been shifted to railroad traffic. There have been other changes, of course, but they are of minor importance compared to the ones mentioned above.

MONOPOLIES AND MISCELLANEOUS TAXES

In addition to the revenues arising from the direct and indirect taxes discussed above, the State is in receipt of certain other items which deserve to be included in any comprehensive tabulation of tax revenues. In amount this group of miscellaneous revenues is small. In 1927 they yielded only 3.1 billions out of a total of 43.7 billions.

One item which, after consideration, was excluded from the general revenue table [46] is that of receipts from the state domain. It may be noted, however, that the accounts for 1926 show the receipt of 332 million francs from the sale of wood cut from the state forests, but a large part of this represents a mere bookkeeping entry, the sales having been made to the forest service.[47] There was also a credit of 166 million francs arising from a miscellany of items, among which may be noted the sale of real estate, of old material (including, after 1922, sale of war stocks),[48] the State's right to the property of one who dies intestate without leaving near relations, its right to unclaimed bank deposits, etc., and certain charges for the use of state property.

[45] See, for example, *Le Temps*, December 14, 1927.

[46] See p. 396.

[47] *Projet du Budget*, 1928, p. 94.

[48] *Projet du Budget*, 1923, p. 251.

TABLE 51

REVENUE FROM OTHER INDIRECT TAXES (*CONTRIBUTIONS INDIRECTES*) 1913-1926

(In millions of francs)

Sources: 1913, 1914, 1915, *Compte Général* for 1914, 1915, and 1916;
1916, *Compte Général* for 1916 (*recouvrements effectués, opérations de l'année 1916*) plus *recettes postérieures* figures from the *Journal Officiel;*
1917–1921, *Projets de Budget* for the years 1919, 1920, 1921, 1922, and 1923;
1922, Twelve-month collections from the *Bulletin de Statistique et de Législation Comparée*, December, 1922, plus *recettes postérieures* figures furnished by the Ministry of Finance;
1923, *Projet de Budget*, 1925;
1924–1925, *Bulletin de Statistique et de Législation Comparée*, May 1925 and 1926;
1926, *Journal Officiel*, June 17, 1927, p. 6237 *et seq.;*
1927, *Journal Officiel*, January 17, 1928, p. 729 *et seq.*

	1913	1914	1915	1916	1917	1918	1919	1920	1921	1922	1923	1924	1925	1926	1927 [a]
1. *Ad valorem* tax on certain spirits	...	...	...	...	.....	98	361	491	463	527	570	724	780	885	924
Specific taxes on drinks:															
2. Consumption tax on spirits collected by Corsican customs	1	[d]	[d]	[d]	[d]	[d]	[d]	[d]	[d]	?	[d]	[d]	[d]	[d]	?
3. Wines, cider, perry, and hydromel	66	59	77	60	114	193	356	459	580	481	560	584	598	833	520
4. Beer	16	11	7	10	17	19	38	51	69	76	87	93	89	109	96
5. Spirits	399	335	278	289	320	241	315	467	594	715	788	867	959	1,019	955
6. Mineral waters	...	...	...	...	4	3	5	8	14	15	19	24	28	38	25
7. Patent medicines	...	...	...	...	10	14	20	24	23	26	27	28	29	46	44
8. Perfumery	...	...	...	...	.....	.....	.....	.....	.....	.....	.....	.....	.....	46	83
9. Candles and stearine (*droit de fabrication*)	4	4	5	5	5	3	3	3	3	4	4	5	5	7	10
10. Vinegar and acetic acid (*droit de consummation*)	3	2	2	2	2	4	8	9	10	8	8	9	11	12	16
11. Railroad passenger and freight revenue	91	70	52	65	69	186	377	476	479	545	589	686	736	1,296	1,747
12. Revenue from horse-drawn vehicles (*autres voitures que les chemins de fer*)	5	4	2	2	2	2	3	5	4	4	4	4	4	4	3
13. Amusements	...	...	...	...	11	14	25	41	51	55	59	75	86	99	106
14. Billiard tables	...	...	...	...	.....	.....	.....	.....	.....	1	2	2	2	2	5
15. Games of chance in clubs (*jeux de hasard dans les cercles*)	...	...	...	...	.....	.....	.....	.....	.....	.....	.....	12	16	21	24
16. Bicycles, etc.	11	11	6	6	6	7	10	14	15	28	31	35	43	45	119

	1913	1914	1915	1916	1917	1918	1919	1920	1921	1922	1923	1924	1925	1926	1927
17. Automobiles	...	...	...	...	...	...	...	60	102	124	149	206	313	465	620
18. Gambling token-machines (*distributeurs automatiques*)	1	1	[d]	[d]	[d]	[d]	[d]	1	[d]	[d]	[d]	[d]	[d]	[d]	1
19. Licenses (liquor dealers, carriage owners, etc.)	38	35	29	27	26	33	47	54	53	56	57	66	69	73	136
20. Guarantee stamp on gold, platinum, and silver articles	9	5	2	4	6	6	14	15	12	13	12	15	15	24	29
21. Playing cards	3	2	2	2	2	2	2	2	2	4	3	4	4	6	8
22. Freight transport on internal waterways	...	...	...	...	...	...	...	...	...	...	...	...	...	7	27
Colonial products, coffee substitutes, vanilla, etc.:															
23. Collected by the customs	...	...	...	...	60	52	79	112	148	154	156	177	186	215	343
24. Collected by indirect tax administration	...	...	...	...	20	16	24	30	30	29	30	32	36	52	68
Salt [b]:															
25. Collected by the customs	22	24	22	21	28	21	22	19	20	19	16	17	18	47	89
26. Collected by indirect tax administration	13	10	10	10	9	11	9	14	13	17	19	21	22	70	128
Sugar, saccharine and molasses:															
27. Collected by the customs	26	36	138	145	193	59	315	349	198	410	342	280	106	234	192
28. Collected by indirect tax administration	165	123	75	43	73	125	60	94	167	188	202	263	354	487	808
Gasoline and oils:															
29. Collected by the customs	...	...	...	...	...	...	...	76	165	228	271	348	418	608	832
30. Collected by indirect tax administration	...	...	...	...	...	...	...	12	1	6	6	7	6	11	14
Heavy mineral oils:															
31. Collected by the customs	...	...	...	...	...	...	...	...	...	...	...	...	...	59	66
32. Collected by indirect tax administration	...	...	...	...	...	...	...	...	...	...	...	...	...	12	9
Benzol and similar coal products:															
33. Collected by the customs	...	...	...	...	...	...	...	[d]	8	7	6	5	5	3	3
34. Collected by indirect tax administration	...	...	...	...	...	...	...	1	5	5	7	12	11	18	23
35. Fines	5	4	4	5	6	8	10	17	15	13	13	11	12	16	19
36. Miscellaneous receipts	33	27	18	17	19	18	22	124	39	29	30	44	76	322	111
Total [c]	911	763	730	712	1,001	1,134	2,128	3,027	3,283	3,790	4,066	4,657	5,037	7,193	8,222

[a] Twelve-month collections only, not including the "recettes postérieures au 31 Décembre 1927." The "recettes postérieures" are collections made during the first four months of a calendar year, but due to appear in the preceding year's figures (the exercice).

[b] These figures of total collections apparently do not allow for certain tax refunds, which however are relatively insignificant. See Table 60, p. 398.

[c] The figures in this table occasionally differ slightly from those given in the annual reports of the Contributions Indirectes administration, published in the *Bulletin de Statistique et de Legislation Comparée*. These reports discuss in some detail the yield of each tax.

[d] Less than one-half million francs.

Monopolies

A substantial revenue arises from the operation of state monopolies and, in so far as the collections from this source are in excess of the costs involved, it has seemed desirable to include them with taxes in the general table.[49]

The most important fiscal monopolies in France are those concerned with tobacco, matches (including lighters), and powder.

The tobacco monopoly, established in 1674, abolished in 1791, and reëstablished in 1810, gives the largest yield of the three. By the law of August 7, 1927, its management and its revenues were turned over to the autonomous *Caisse d'Amortissement*, which applies the net receipts against the interest of the *Bons de la Défense Nationale* and the bonds of the *Caisse* itself.

The State allows tobacco to be cultivated only in certain départements, upon express permission. The crop must be sold to the State, which has the sole right of manufacture, and which disposes of the finished product either directly to consumers, or to retailers, who must sell at prices fixed by the Government. They are allowed to keep 8 per cent of the gross sales receipts as their "profit," or rather commission. With minor exceptions, no tobacco may be imported except by the State.[50]

The match monopoly was established and farmed out in 1872 (law of August 2, decrees of October 7 and 12), but has been managed directly by the State since 1889 (decree of December 30).

The State has a complete monopoly of the manufacture and sale of matches of all kinds. It supplements its manufacture by large purchases abroad.[51] The prices at which they are sold (to wholesalers, by wholesalers to retailers, and by retailers to the

[49] See p. 396.

[50] Rosier, *Tous Nos Impôts*, pp. 769–772. Hourcade, *Manuel encyclopédique des Contributions indirectes*, p. 818 *et seq*.

[51] *Doc. Parl., Chambre*, 1927, *Sess. Ord.*, No. 4872. *Palmade Report*, 1928 budget, pp. 216, 221 of the *Report*. In November, 1927 it was announced that the Government would retire its $70,000,000 of 8 per cent bonds outstanding in the American market through the sale of $75,000,000 of 5 per cent bonds to the Swedish Match Company, which in turn was to raise money through the sale of its own bonds. The relatively high price paid by the Match Company for French bonds

public) are fixed by decree.[52] In Alsace and Lorraine, the State's monopoly extends only to wholesale purchases and sales. Manufacturing is left to private enterprise.[53]

Briquets, or portable lighters which in effect replace matches (e.g., cigar and cigarette lighters) are not a state monopoly, strictly speaking, but they can be manufactured only under special permit, and their retail sale is strictly regulated. They are subject to a fixed tax of from 5 to 240 francs (not collected if the *briquets* are exported). The state monopoly was formed in 1871 (law of September 4), and its present status was established in 1910 (law of December 28).[54]

The powder monopoly is not as complete as the tobacco and match monopolies. With but few exceptions, however (e.g., explosives of a nitro-glycerine base), no explosives may be manufactured or sold except by the State. Those which can be manufactured by private interests are taxed at various rates, fixed by decree. Imports are likewise taxed, and exports are exempt.[55] Powder that does not come under the monopoly is taxed at varying rates.[56]

In addition to the tobacco, match and powder monopolies, the State operates several other branches of business, all of which, excepting the railroads and the postal, telegraph and telephone monopoly, are comparatively insignificant. Unlike the match monopoly, these state establishments have their own budgets. Some of them are attached to the general budget and consequently must be passed on by Parliament; others, such as the state railroads budget, are entirely autonomous, and enter the general budget only to deposit therein a surplus or to draw therefrom enough to make up a deficit.

---

was in consideration for certain privileges granted it for supplying the Government monopoly with machinery, raw materials and matches.—*New York Times*, November 6 and 11, 1927.

[52] Rosier, *Tous Nos Impôts*, pp. 773–774. Hourcade, *op. cit.*, p. 799 *et seq.*

[53] *Doc. Parl.*, *Chambre*, 1926, *Sess. Ord.*, p. 2032 (*Rapport*, *Annexe* No. 3409).

[54] Codification. *Extrait* No. 132, arts. 117–121. Hourcade, *op. cit.*, p. 809 *et seq.*

[55] Hourcade, *op. cit.*, p. 839 *et seq.*

[56] For rates on "explosifs à l'oxygène liquide," for example, see *Bulletin de Statistique*, April, 1927, p. 801. For further details on the powder monopoly, see pp. 358, 360 below.

These annexed budgets always appear in perfect balance, but this is either because the surplus is entered in the expenditures side, to be paid to the general budget, or to a special reserve; or because the deficit is made up by an entry in the receipts side of a sum coming from the general budget, or from a surplus built up in former years. The estimated surplus (1928) for the postal, telegraph and telephone monopoly, for instance, is entered on the expense side of its *budget annexe* as "excess of receipts over expenses," and one finds the item again in the general budget, entered under "miscellaneous receipts" (*produits divers*) as "excess . . . of receipts over expenses of the *budget annexe* of the postal, telegraph and telephone monopoly." The surplus of the mint is likewise transferred to the general budget, but instead of appearing under "*produits divers,*" it is entered under the heading "*diverses exploitations.*"

The notable example of the second class, where Parliament is given no hand in determining the individual expense items, is the state railroad system. Its details of revenue and expenditure are nowhere to be found in the budget.[57] The same appears to be true of the Saar and Alsatian mines.

The method of arriving at the net profit figures incorporated in the general table is fully explained in the footnotes to that table.[58] The figures are in several cases mere estimates. For the most important monopoly, however, that dealing with tobacco, definite figures for practically the entire period are available from the *Inventaire* and the *Experts' Report,* although the data from these two sources do not entirely agree. Table 52 presents these figures, while Table 53 gives the *Inventaire* figures for the match monopoly, both gross and net.

The Ministry of War manufactures the powder, and sells it not to the public but to the War Department, the Navy Department, and the Indirect Taxes Administration.[59] This latter ad-

[57] For a criticism of the illogical way in which certain establishments are given their separate "budgets annexes," while others have their receipts and expenditures mingled in the general budget, see Allix, *Science des Finances,* pp. 75–78.

[58] See pp. 396, 397.

[59] *Doc. Parl., Chambre,* 1926, *Sess., Ord.,* p. 2037 (*Rapport* by M. Valière, Doc. No. 3411).

TABLE 52

YIELD OF TOBACCO MONOPOLY, 1913–1925

(In millions of francs)

Year	According to *Inventaire* (p. 135)			According to Experts' Report (p. 161)		
	Gross receipts	Expenses	Net yield	Gross receipts	Expenses	Net yield
1913	545	109	436	545	115	430
1914	530	111	418	531	112	419
1915	535	133	401	535	134	401
1916	594	163	430	600	164	436
1917	695	231	465	709	228	480
1918	684	310	374	694	296	398
1919	952	411	540	966	422	544
1920	1,452	638	814	1,454	712	742
1921	1,600	565	1,035	1,605	564	1,040
1922	1,664	466	1,198	1,667	498	1,169
1923	1,807	524	1,282	1,808	543	1,266
1924	.....	...	.....	1,998	624	1,374
1925	.....	...	.....	2,295	652	1,643

TABLE 53

YIELD OF MATCH MONOPOLY, 1913–1923

(In millions of francs)

Source: *Inventaire*, page 136

Years	Gross receipts	Expenses	Net Yield
1913	45	13	32
1914	41	11	29
1915	45	18	27
1916	50	21	28
1917	55	22	33
1918	65	28	36
1919	87	42	45
1920	105	49	57
1921	110	51	58
1922	120	51	69
1923	127	56	72

ministration resells its share to the public, and the gross receipts it receives from this source are entered in the budget under "proceeds from the sale of gunpowder" (*produit de la vente des poudres à feu*). To get the profit accruing from this operation, all that is necessary, it would seem, is to find the amount paid by the Indirect Taxes Administration to the War Department for the powder, if one is willing to omit the incidental costs of handling the commodity. In the absence of published figures as to the amount actually paid, however, the estimates as indicated in the credits opened in the annual budget laws have been used in arriving at the "tax" figures in the aggregate table (Table 59, p. 396). Estimated by this method, the yield in 1926, net, was 66,594,000 francs.

One of the *budgets annexes* is headed "*Service des Poudres.*" It gives the receipts and expenditures of the War Department resulting from its manufacture of powder. The receipts, as intimated above, come wholly from other governmental administrations, as the War Department does not sell directly to the public. This situation has led to some dissatisfaction, as it seems the War Department simply supplied the amounts demanded and then set a price high enough to cover the expenses it had incurred. This was hardly an incentive to efficient management, and the law of April 29, 1926,[60] put the operation on a more strictly business basis. It required that a reserve fund for profits and losses be established, and devised a system for amortizing capital expenditures over a period of years instead of making the current year's receipts cover them (a procedure that had sometimes raised the price of powder high enough to bring considerable complaint). The profit for 1926 has been estimated at 20 million francs, but as it has not been possible to get accurate data on profit from inter-administration sales, this point has not been considered in making up Table 59.[61]

Up to 1915, the operation of the posts, telegraph and telephone apparently resulted in a profit.[62] For 1916–1919, there

[60] Articles 58–61.

[61] *Cf. Doc. Parl.*, 1926, No. 3411, *loc. cit.*, and *Doc. Parl., Sénat*, 1926, *Sess Extraord.*, Doc. No. 667, p. 275. *Rapport* by M. Gardey.

[62] Allix, *Science des Finances*, p. 153.

appeared to be no figures available, but for 1920–1926 the following may be cited: [63]

		Francs
1920	Deficit	186,198,047
1921	Deficit	250,197,573
1922	Deficit	112,005,529
1923	Deficit (*Inventaire*)	3,082,824
	Surplus (*Rapport*)	10,403,539
1924	Surplus	127,672,866
1925	Surplus	98,787,432
1926	Surplus	304,180,025

Until 1923, the receipts and expenses were scattered under a number of heads through the general budget, but starting with that year, they were grouped together under a *budget annexe*, where they appear today.

The 1923 law [64] required that a reserve account of 150,000,000 francs be built up before any surplus could be turned over to the general budget. Apparently such a reserve has not yet been constituted. None of the *projets de loi* provide for this, and the *Dezarnaulds Report* states that the surpluses left from operations from 1923 to 1925 were used to cover interest and depreciation charges on the capital equipment existing on December 31, 1922, as provided by the 1923 law. Thus, even supposing the reserve to have been built up, no surplus has yet developed that can be given to the general budget.

Capital expenditures up to 1927 had been entirely covered by advances from the Treasury, in the absence of a favorable situation for floating loans to the public. These advances bear interest, and the interest charges have apparently been taken into account in arriving at the net results given above. In 1927 it was planned to devote part of the surplus from operations to capital expenditures, the rest to go to provide higher salaries.[65]

From all this it can be seen that the estimated items in the

[63] For 1920–1923, the figures have been taken from the *Inventaire*, pp. 100–101. For 1923–1926, they are from *Doc. Parl.*, *Chambre*, 1926, *Sess. Ord.*, p. 2044 (*Rapport* by M. Dezarnaulds, Doc. No. 3413). So far as can be judged, in no case are expenses for capital outlays considered in arriving at the final figures as given above.

[64] Law of June 30, 1923, art. 72.

[65] *Cf. Dezarnaulds Report, loc. cit.*, p. 2053.

budget *projets* (*budget annexe des P.T.T.*) are likely to mislead, as they show an estimated " excess of ordinary receipts over ordinary expenditures " of 296,363,651 francs for 1925, of 664,440,483 francs for 1926, of 795,440,173 francs for 1927, and of 311,190,430 francs for 1928. For 1925, 1927 and 1928[66] these items are carried, as estimated receipts, to the general budget, under " Miscellaneous receipts " (*produits divers*), and labelled " provisional surplus " (*excédent provisiore*). In 1926 the estimated surplus was carried, also as a receipt, to the general budget under " Bookkeeping items " (*recettes d'ordre*), and labelled " Repayment of advances made by the general budget."

What advances the general budget has made to the P.T.T. *budget annexe* since 1923 are not known to the writer. Only two such items have appeared in the budget *projets'* estimates, and one (361,214,974 francs for 1926) was an advance to cover capital outlay. The *projet* for 1923 estimated that the Treasury would have to advance 92,102,786 francs to cover a deficit from operation.

Miscellaneous Taxes

Certain taxes on gambling feed " hidden " budgets. These are (a) the tax on gambling in casinos, (b) the tax on gambling in clubs (*cercles*), (c) the " tax " on the state-operated *pari-mutuel*. The larger part of the yield of these taxes is destined for various " good works." For the most part, the proceeds so destined do not appear in the state budget, but can be found in the statements of the *Caisse des Dépôts et Consignations*, which receives the money and then distributes it.

The provisions governing the imposition of these taxes and the distribution of the yield are so very complicated and have been subject to such frequent change,[67] that a discussion of them would require more space than is available. Their yield, however, is summarized in Table 54.

[66] Only 306,866,308 francs in 1927. The other 488,573,865 francs was to be used to cover all capital outlays for that year.

[67] *Rapport par la Commission de Surveillance de la Caisse d'Amortissement et de la Caisse des Dépôts et Consignations sur les Operations de l'Année 1925*, p. 23 *et seq.*

TABLE 54

SPECIAL TAXES ON GAMBLING DEDICATED TO VARIOUS "GOOD WORKS"—CREDITS ON THE BOOKS OF THE *CAISSE DES DÉPÔTS ET CONSIGNATIONS* (INCLUDES INTEREST ON BALANCES IN THE *CAISSE*)

(In millions of francs)

Source: Annual reports, *Commission de Surveillance de la Caisse d'Amortissement et de la Caisse des Dépôts et Consignations.*

	1913	1914	1915	1916	1917	1918	1919	1920	1921	1922	1923	1924	1925	1926
1. Levy made on the gross product of gambling in clubs and casinos	8.3	4.3	0.3	0.3	0.2	0.2	5.1	19.8	39.7	33.5	51.0	70.7	95.1	144.5
2. Part of the levy on the gross product of gambling destined for the support of organizations and works of reforestation, improvement of pastures, fish culture, and hunting	....	....	....	....	....	....	....	....	2.9	9.2	5.8	9.3	13.0	16.6
3. Levy made on the *pari-mutuel* in favor of local organizations of charity	8.2	5.4	0.2	0.2	0.2	0.2	11.9	26.8	24.2	23.3	24.1	25.5	27.3	32.8
4. Levy made on the *pari-mutuel* and on the product of gambling for the support of communal works for supplying drinking water	3.8	5.5	0.2	0.1	0.1	0.1	5.8	12.8	13.1	16.5	14.9	17.7	25.8	25.7
5. Supplementary levy made on the *pari-mutuel* in support of local organizations of charity interested in the regions devastated by the war	....	....	....	....	....	....	....	15.6	11.0	10.2	10.8	11.3	11.9	14.3
6. Supplementary levy made on the *pari-mutuel* for the support of communal works for supplying drinking water in the regions devastated by the war	....	....	....	....	....	....	....	15.6	11.0	10.2	10.9	11.4	12.0	19.4
Total	20.3	15.3	0.6	0.6	0.6	0.6	22.8	90.6	101.9	102.9	117.4	145.9	185.1	253.4

CHAPTER XVIII

LOCAL TAXATION

THIS chapter sketches the local revenue system of France and analyzes the fiscal results from its operation since 1913.

There is a current impression that local taxes in France have increased enormously and that they now greatly exceed the sums collected before the war. In terms of depreciated paper money, this is true. However, if one takes into account the change in the value of the franc, the total collections today, according to the writer's best estimates, are not in excess of those of 1913.

An important shift has occurred in the sources of local taxes. Real estate taxes have declined sharply in relative importance [1] and the local business taxes (*patentes*) have expanded to take up the slack. The *octrois* have also declined sharply and the doors-and-windows tax has been abolished, their burden being assumed to a large extent by the new *fonds communs* (fed by taxes on automobiles, beverages, *cartes d'identité* and business turnover) and by an expansion of municipal fees. In the general readjustment, business taxes have increased and the policy of pricing governmental services has received a marked stimulus.

France is subdivided into 90 départements and 37,963 communes. The finances of the départements, the communes and the national government are closely intertwined. In the first place an important part of the local revenues flows from the so-called *centimes additionnels*, which are taxes levied upon a basis originally established for national purposes. A second important part of the local revenues finds its source in grants and subventions from the national Treasury to départements and communes.

[1] Since real estate values in France appear to have been less unfavorably affected by the inflation process than almost any other class of property, this fact is of particular interest. As to the value accruing to the owner, reservation must of course be made for the cases of long-term leases.

Then, in contrast with these payments flowing from larger divisions to the smaller, the départements receive large payments from the communes and the national Government receives small payments from both.[2]

STATISTICS OF LOCAL REVENUES

It is evident, therefore, that in dealing with the financial statistics for these various governmental subdivisions, there is serious danger of double counting. Indeed, because of the crudeness of the financial reports, it is impossible to present figures with confidence that this danger has been entirely avoided.

Sources of Data

There are four possible sources of information with regard to the finances of the local governmental bodies. First, one might conceivably examine the local records of each département and commune. This, however, would be a very large task indeed. A restricted inquiry was made into the records of the département of the Seine and of the city of Paris (which is classed as a commune), but, because of lack of time, it was impossible to attempt an analysis of the local records of the other subdivisions.

The second source of information consists of the reports published by the Ministry of the Interior. For the départements the Ministry issues each year a document entitled: *Situation financière des Départements*. The latest available volume in this series was published in 1925 and presents data for the year 1923. The Ministry, however, kindly supplied the investigator with unpublished aggregate figures for the years 1924 and 1925. There is a corresponding document for the communes, entitled: *Situation financière des Communes*. Here, also, the latest document was published in 1925 and presents data for the year 1923. In contrast with the series for the départements, this series for the communes is very incomplete, reports having been issued only for the years

[2] These latter appear in the accounts of the state under the heading: "Recettes d'ordre et produits divers."

1913, 1914, 1920 and 1923.[3] During the other years the data were not even compiled, so that it was impossible for the Ministry of the Interior to supply any information at all with regard to the finances of the communes for the ten years for which no documents were published.

The third source of information is found in a publication of the Direct Tax Division of the Ministry of Finance (*Direction Générale des Contributions Directes. Renseignements statistiques relatifs aux contributions directes et aux taxes assimilées*). This volume, which has appeared annually without interruption, presents the amounts of the *centimes* and other " direct " taxes levied to the credit of the départements and communes.

A fourth source consists of tables published occasionally in the *Bulletin de Statistique et de Législation Comparée* which give the local revenues from certain specified sources either more promptly than they appear in the financial documents of the Ministry of the Interior or for years for which no such financial documents are published. The revenues dealt with in these tables include the *octrois*, the tax on beverages, etc.[4]

To one who is seeking to assemble a definite statement of the revenues of France, subdivided so as to make significant comparisons regarding the character of the sources, the data available from the reports mentioned above have serious shortcomings. The data in Table 55 dealing with the départements and Table 56 dealing with the communes have been assembled from the various sources described above and have been arranged so as to present the available facts in a form which facilitates the compilation of estimates of the revenues of these administrative subdivisions.

Estimated Tax Revenues of the Départements

Turning then to Table 55 dealing with the départements, it will be noted that it is possible to present aggregate figures from

[3] It is the announced intention to issue these reports every third year.

[4] In addition to the above sources some data were found available in the *Experts' Report*. Certain of the information published is reprinted annually in the *Annuaire Statistique*. Scattered figures also appear from time to time in the newspapers.

the publications of the Ministry of the Interior showing the income of the départements, subdivided into *centimes départementaux* and "other receipts," for each year from 1914 to 1925.

Considering first the *centimes départementaux*, it will be seen that, in addition to the figures from the Ministry of the Interior, it is possible from the Finance Ministry's volume of "Statistics of Direct Taxes" to present detailed figures showing the subdivision of these *centimes*, according to the character of the base, for each year from 1913 to 1926. It will be noted that these figures from the Ministry of Finance do not check precisely with the figures of the Ministry of the Interior. The explanation given for this discrepancy is twofold. First, the figures from the former represent levies, and those from the latter, collections. Second, there are certain differences in the fiscal periods covered by the statistics.[6] The discrepancy, however, is small and the data for the *centimes départementaux* are, on the whole, satisfactory.

The difficulties multiply when one comes to consider figures included under the heading of "other receipts." No subdivisions of the aggregate figures for the two main divisions of *centimes départementaux* and "other receipts" are attempted in the reports of the Ministry of Interior. The officials state, however, that there are included in these figures the net proceeds from loans during the period under consideration, and, since these figures are stated in another section of the report, it is possible to set them down and to eliminate them in seeking an estimate of tax revenue.

Another non-tax item included among "other receipts" is subventions. It seems to be quite impossible to gather the necessary data for the entire elimination of this item. The reports of the Ministry of the Interior show the amounts of subventions received "*par les divers services d'assistance*," included under "other receipts," and these can be subtracted. But in addition there is a substantial amount of other subventions. So far as the subventions of the national Government to the local bodies are concerned, the amounts are scattered so widely throughout the budget, and are merged with other items in such a manner that,

[6] The complete agreement between the figures from the two sources in the case of Alsace and Lorraine casts doubt upon the accuracy of this explanation.

TABLE 55

REVENUES OF DÉPARTEMENTS, WITH ESTIMATES OF TOTAL REVENUE FROM TAXATION, 1913–1926

(In millions of paper francs, each total and each constituent item evened off to nearest million. Estimates in italics)

		1913	1914	1915	1916	1917	1918	1919	1920	1921	1922		
											Old Départements	Alsace and Lorraine	Total All Départements
	Centimes départementaux:												
1.	According to data from Ministry of Interior [a]	?	295	283	294	299	315	343	513	760	923	?	923+
2.	According to data from Ministry of Finance [b]	283 [e]	300 [g]	284 [h]	296	301	317	341	508	760	928	42	970
3.	Real estate — improved	57	60	65	69	71	78	86	121	178	217	4	221
4.	Real estate — unimproved	90	95	83	81	78	77	80	110	151	172	3	174
5.	*Personnelle-mobilière* [m]	59	62	60	62	63	67	71	97	140	166	..	166
6.	Doors and windows	25	27	26	26	26	28	31	49	74	91	..	91
7.	*Patentes* [m]	52	56	50	58	62	67	73	132	217	282	..	282
8.	Tax on capital in Alsace and Lorraine	...	...	...	...	...	...	.....	.....	.....	.....	3	3
9.	Tax on salaries and wages in Alsace and Lorraine	...	...	...	...	...	...	.....	.....	.....	.....	15	15
10.	Tax on professions in Alsace and Lorraine	...	...	...	...	...	...	.....	.....	.....	.....	17	17
11.	Mine tax. ("*Redevances des mines*" in old départements and "*taxe de superficie*" in Alsace and Lorraine)	...	...	...	...	...	...	.....	.....	.....	.....	0.1	0.1
12.	Other receipts: [c]	?	267	268	283	422	400	745	1,090	1,411	1,699	?	1,699+
13.	Non-tax items included in "other receipts" (line 12)	242+	150+	151+	161+	321+	216+	362+	523+	969+	1,272+	?	1,272+
14.	Loans (Annual increase in "*réalisations effectuées*")	*89* [f]	2	1	...	158	...	72	170	546	631 [i]	?	631+
15.	Subventions for "*les divers services d'assistance*"	154	148	150	161	162	216	290	353	423	641	?	641+
16.	Other subventions	?	?	?	?	?	?	?	?	?	?	?	?
17.	Taxes included in "other receipts" (line 12)	...	...	...	...	...	...	.....	29	73	?	?	86
18.	*Fonds communs* [d]: Automobile circulation tax	...	...	...	...	...	...	.....	9	14	?	?	18
19.	*Fonds communs* [d]: Turnover tax	...	...	...	...	...	...	.....	20	59	?	?	67
20.	*Fonds communs* [d]: *Carte d'identité*	...	...	...	...	...	...	.....	.....	.....	.....	..	......
21.	Total receipts "*propres à l'exercice,*" line 1 + line 12)	613	563	551	577	721	715	1,088	1,602	2,170	2,622	?	2,622+
	Limits for estimating total receipts from taxation:												
22.	Lower limit	283	295	283	294	299	315	341	537	833	923+	42+	1,051
23.	Upper limit	370	412	400	416	400	500	726	1,079	1,201	1,350	?	1,350+
24.	Estimate of total receipts from taxation	*290*	*300*	*285*	*300*	*305*	*320*	*350*	*550*	*850*	*1,030*	*50*	*1,080*

[a, c] 1913–1923, from *Situation financière des Départements en 1923;* 1924–1925, from unpublished records of the Ministry of the Interior.
[b] Except as otherwise specified, 1913–1925, from *Renseignements statistiques relatifs aux contributions directes et aux taxes assimilées.*
[d] 1920–1925, from *Rapport du Comité des Experts*, p. 106; 1925–1926, from unpublished records of the Ministry of Finance.
[e] *Compte Général*, 1913, pp. 742–745.
[f] In the absence of a published report for 1912, this figure was estimated on the basis of the 1911 figures.
[g] *Compte Général*, 1914, pp. 760–763. [h] *Ibid.*, 1915, pp. 776–779.
[i] This figure includes $25,000,000 and £3,000,000 borrowed by the département of the Seine, translated into francs at the average of the monthly averages of exchange rates for 1922 (12.32 francs per dollar and 54.56 francs per pound).
[j] According to the *Compte Général* for the département of the Seine for 1923, the "other subventions" amounted to 13,808,495 francs. The estimate given above is based on the assumption that a similar ratio to "subventions d'assistance" obtained in the other départements. [k] Provisional figure. [l] Less than 100,000 francs.

	1923			1924			1925			1926		
	Old Dé-partements	Alsace and Lorraine	Total All Dé-partements	Old Dé-partements	Alsace and Lorraine	Total All Dé-partements	Old Dé-partements	Alsace and Lorraine	Total All Dé-partements	Old Dé-partements	Alsace and Lorraine	Total All Dé-partements
Centimes Départementaux:												
1. According to data from Ministry of Interior [a]	976	43	1,019	1,045	48	1,093	1,194	54	1,247	?	?	?
2. According to data from Ministry of Finance [b]	978	43	1,020	1,049	48	1,097	1,193	54	1,246	1,646	60	1,705
3. Real estate — improved	228	4	232	246	4	250	271	4	275	344	6	350
4. Real estate — unimproved	175	2	177	181	2	184	198	2	201	243	4	247
5. *Personnelle-mobilière* [m]	171	....	171	180	....	180	198	..	198	350	..	350
6. Doors and windows	94	....	94	100	..	100	110	..	110	.....	..	.....
7. *Patentes* [m]	309	....	309	343	..	343	416	..	416	709 [l]	..	709 [l]
8. Tax on capital in Alsace and Lorraine	.....	3	3	.....	4	4	.....	4	4	.....	4	4
9. Tax on salaries and wages in Alsace and Lorraine	.....	15	15	.....	17	17	.....	20	20	.....	18	18
10. Tax on professions in Alsace and Lorraine	.....	18	18	.....	20	20	.....	23	23	.....	28	28
11. Mine tax. ("*Redevances des mines*" in old départements and "*taxe de superficie*" in Alsace and Lorraine)	.....	0.1	0.1	.....	.. [l]	..... [l]	.....	.. [l]	..... [l]	..... [l]	.. [l]	..... [l]
12. Other receipts: [c]	1,336	22	1,358	1,453	27	1,480	1,286	22	1,308	?	?	?
13. Non-tax items included in "other receipts" (line 12)	821	?	821 +	849+	?	849+	77+	?	77+	?	?	?
14. Loans (Annual increase in "*réalisations effectuées*")	213	?	213 +	271	?	271+	77	?	77+	?	?	?
15. Subventions for "*les divers services d'assistance*"	543	?	543 +	578	?	578+	?	?	?	?	?	?
16. Other subventions	65 [i]	?	65 +	?	?	?	?	?	?	?	?	?
17. Taxes included in "other receipts" (line 12)	?	?	103	?	?	124	?	?	134	?	?	170
18. *Fonds communs* [d] { Automobile circulation tax	?	?	21	?	?	24	?	?	35	?	?	51
19. Turnover tax	?	?	82	?	?	99	?	?	98	?	?	115
20. *Carte d'identité*	.....	....	......	.....	..	.....	?	?	1	?	?	4 [k]
21. Total receipts "*propres à l'exercice*" (line 1 + line 12)	2,313	65	2,378	2,497	76	2,573	2,480	76	2,556	?	?	
Limits for estimating total receipts from taxation:											?	
22. Lower limit	976+	43 +	1,123	1,045+	48+	1,217	1,193+	54+	1,380	1,646+	60+	1,875
23. Upper limit	1,492	65	1,557	1,648	76	1,724	2,403	76	2,478	?	?	?
24. Estimate of total receipts from taxation	*1,100*	*50*	*1,150*	*1,200*	*60*	*1,260*	*1,370*	*66*	*1,436*	*1,872*	*68*	*1,940*

[m] For the years 1919–1925, there should be deducted from these items a certain amount as tax refunds to men called to the colors. The same applies to the "patente" and "personelle-mobilière" items in the communal tax table. The figures for the combined tax refund, that is, for communes and départements, are available, and reproduced in Table 60, p. 398 (*dégrèvement* table). But how this amount should be split up, is not indicated. The existence of this refund was discovered only after all the tables, charts and text of the local revenues had been made up, and in view of its comparative insignificance except for the years 1919–1921, the tables, etc., have not been altered. In 1920, when the refund reached its highest point (71,801,000 francs) it equalled 11 per cent of the total departmental and communal revenue from the two taxes, and not quite 3 per cent of the total departmental and communal revenue as estimated without considering the refund. In the other years these percentages were sharply lower. The refunds are taken into account in the aggregate tax table (Table 59, p. 396).

Furthermore, it is not certain that these *dégrèvements* were not already taken into account by the bureau that compiled the local "patente" and "personelle-mobilière" returns.

	1919	1920	1921	1922	1923	1924	1925
The *dégèevements* were as follows: (from Table 60, p. 398) (in francs)	23,940,300	71,801,000	56,519,200	17,000,000	6,000,000	3,544,860	390,545

according to the testimony of the budget officials, it is practically impossible to identify and segregate them. The analysis of the accounts of the département of the Seine yielded the fact that in this département alone in the year 1923 there were other subventions than for the "*divers services d'assistance*" amounting, in the aggregate, to 13,808,495 francs which is approximately between 11 and 12 per cent as much as the subventions "*d'assistance.*"

In addition to these major items which should be subtracted from the "other receipts" to arrive at a figure of tax revenue, it was possible from different sources to glean data regarding certain minor items which were also included under this general heading and which should be subtracted. One such item is the revenue from the public domain. It was found that in the département of the Seine such receipts amounted in the year 1923 to 28,647,037 francs (*propriété départementale*), approximately 5 per cent of the total receipts of the département of the Seine for that year. There is no clue as to what this item amounts to in the other départements.[6]

The last line in Table 55, shown in italics, presents the estimates of the investigator as to the total taxes of the départements for each year. The possible margin of error in making these estimates will be apparent from an examination of the figures in the body of the table.

Estimated Tax Revenues of the Communes

The problem of arriving at an estimate of tax revenues of the communes is attacked in Table 56 in the same general fashion as the problem of the départements in Table 55, but here the data are less satisfactory and complete. In the first place it has been pointed out that aggregate figures are available from the Minis-

[6] Included among the revenues of the départements are certain taxes "sur les bois de l'État" which are paid by the State to those départements which have state forests within their borders. These items appear among the expenses of the public domain in the accounts of the State. Double counting is avoided if the net receipts rather than the gross receipts of the public domain are used. In a purely tax table, however, there is a small element of double counting because of this item.

try of the Interior for only four years of the period under consideration. It is true that full data are available from the Direct Tax Division of the Ministry of Finance for each year, but the revenues from the so-called " direct taxes " make up even a smaller percentage of the aggregate receipts of the communes than they do in the case of the départements. For example, in 1923 the percentage is only 21 for the communes as compared with 42 for the départements.[7]

There are set forth in Table 56 all of the data regarding tax yields in the communes which it was possible to gather from the various available sources. However, as will be seen, information regarding the revenues not derived from taxes are very scanty indeed even in those years for which reports have been issued by the Ministry of the Interior. Because of the relative difficulty of establishing an " upper limit " of tax revenue, the margin of error in the estimates is larger than in the case of the départements.

It is also true that the detailed analysis which was made of the financial reports of the city of Paris yielded information which was decidedly discouraging regarding the value of the aggregate figures for the communes as published by the reports of the Ministry of the Interior. For example, although inquiry at the Ministry of the Interior elicited the statement that no receipts from loans were included in the statistics of the receipts of the communes, the local officials in Paris testified that, at least in so far as Paris figures were concerned, the aggregate shown in the reports of the Ministry of the Interior did include such receipts. Moreover, they contended that their local figures had been incorrectly interpreted by the officials of the Ministry of the Interior with a result that, in the year 1923, for example, at least 37 per cent of the figure given for the total communal revenue represented merely double counting.[8]

[7] Old départements only. See also Diagrams VI and VII, pp. 380, 381.

[8] The figure of 8,157,176,937 francs is given in the *Situation financière des Communes* for 1923 (p. viii) as " le total des recettes et des restes à recouvrer," whereas: (a) it is meaningless to add the " restes à recouvrer " (1,245,032,430 francs) to the total receipts of 6,912,144,507 francs, for the latter sum already includes these same " restes à recouvrer," (at least it includes the city of Paris " restes à recouvrer " item; there is reason to believe the same is true of the other

TABLE

REVENUES OF COMMUNES, WITH ESTIMATES OF

(In millions of paper francs.

		1913	1914	1915	1916	1917
	Centimes Communaux:					
1.	According to data from Ministry of Interior[a]	277	296	?	?	?
2.	Ordinary and special *centimes*	132	146	?	?	?
3.	Extraordinary *centimes*	144	150	?	?	?
4.	According to data from Ministry of Finance[b]	302	306	294	316	329
5.	Real estate, improved	58	59	65	70	74
6.	Real estate, unimproved	74	75	68	67	66
7.	*Personnelle-mobilière*[v]	57	58	57	60	61
8.	Doors and windows	35	35	33	35	35
9.	*Patentes*[x]	78	79	70	85	93
10.	Tax on capital in Alsace and Lorraine	....	....	....	....	....
11.	Tax on salaries and wages in Alsace and Lorraine	....	....	....	....	....
12.	Tax on professions in Alsace and Lorraine	....	....	....	....	....
13.	Mine tax in Alsace and Lorraine (*taxe de superficie*)	....	....	....	....	....
	Fonds Communs:					
14.	According to data from Ministry of Interior[c]	....	....	....	....	....
15.	Tax on beverages (*boissons*)	....	....	....	....	....
16.	Turnover tax	....	....	....	....	....
17.	According to sources from Ministry of Finance[g]	....	....	....	....	....
18.	Tax on beverages	....	....	....	....	....
19.	Turnover tax	....	....	....	....	....
20.	Identity card tax	....	....	....	....	....
21.	*Taxes Assimilées:*[d]	2	2	1	2	3
22.	Mine tax (*redevances des mines*)	1	1	....[r]	1	2
23.	Tax on carriages, horses, and mules	1	1	1	1	2
24.	Tax for the payment of the *délégués mineurs*	....	....	....[t]	....	....
25.	Other "Direct" Municipal Taxes (*taxes municipales*)[e]:	138	141	132	123	120
26.	Suburban road tax (*taxe des prestations—chemins vicinaux*)	34	33	29	24	23
27.	Rural road tax (*taxe des prestations—chemins ruraux*)	1	1	....[r]	....[r]	....[r]
28.	*Centime* road tax (*taxe vicinale*)	29	32	30	27	26
29.	Dog tax	11	12	10	9	8
30.	Taxes in substitution for the *octrois* and *boissons hygiéniques*	63	64	62	63	63
31.	Special tax in Alsace and Lorraine for *chambres de métier*	....	....	....	....	....
32.	Tax on large stores (*grands magasins*) in Alsace and Lorraine	....	....	....	....	....
	Octrois:					
33.	According to data from Ministry of Interior[f]	316	326	?	?	?
34.	According to data from Ministry of Finance[g]	334	268	233	225	231
35.	Total Ordinary and Extraordinary Receipts[j]	1,071[h]	1,128[i]	?	?	?
	Limits for Estimating Total Receipts from Taxation:					
36.	Lower limit	*871*	*858*	*795*	*811*	*835*
37.	Total taxes giving preference to data of Ministry of Interior (Sum of lines 1, 14, 21, 25, and 33)	733	765	?	?	?
38.	Total taxes giving preference to data of Ministry of Finance (Sum of lines 4, 17, 21, 25, and 34)	776	717	660	666	684
39.	To be added: other local fees, poor taxes (*droits des pauvres*), and miscellaneous local taxes[m]	*139*	*141*	*135*	*145*	*151*
40.	Upper limit	922[q]	?	?	?	?
41.	Total receipts	1,071	1,128	?	?	?
	To be subtracted:					
42.	Surplus brought forward from previous exercices	?	?	?	?	?
43.	Levies revalidated (*restes à recouvrer sur produits constatés aux comptes des exercices antérieurs*)	?	?	?	?	?
44.	Subventions	37+?	?	?	?	?
45.	Loans	?	?	?	?	?
46.	Receipts from public utilities	65+?	?	?	?	?
47.	Miscellaneous deductions[k]	48+?	?	?	?	?
48.	Estimate of Total Receipts from Taxation	*880*	*865*	*800*	*820*	*850*

Footnotes to this table will

56

TOTAL REVENUE FROM TAXATION, 1913–1926

Estimates in italics)

1918	1919	1920	1921	1922 Communes in old départements	1922 Communes in Alsace and Lorraine	1922 Total — Communes in all départements	1923 Communes in old départements	1923 Communes in Alsace and Lorraine	1923 Total — Communes in all départements
?	?	662	?	?	?	?	992	?	992+
?	?	288	?	?	?	?	446	?	446+
?	?	374	?	?	?	?	546	?	546+
388	442	719	880	954	88	1,042	1,043	89	1,132
93	110	173	206	222	9	231	236	9	245
65	60	73	100	89	7	96	89	7	96
76	87	138	162	171	....	171	180	....	180
41	47	79	95	102	....	102	106	....	106
113	138	256	317	370	....	370	432	....	432
....	....	....	....	....	7	7	....	7	7
....	....	....	....	....	29	29	....	29	29
....	....	....	....	....	36	36	....	38	38
....	....	....	....	....	....[r]	....[r]	....	....[r]	....[r]
?	?	?	?	?	?	?	633	?	633+
?	?	?	?	?	?	?	476	?	476+
....	....	?	?	?	?	?	157	?	157+
153	263	414	561	439+	16+	590	481+	17+	662
153	263	374	444	439	16	455	481	17	498
....	....	41	118	?	?	135	?	?	164
....	....	....	....	....	....	....	....	....	....
4	4	5	9	8	....	8	12	....	12
2	2	4	8	7	....	7	11	....	11
2	2	1	1	1	....	1	1	....	1
....	....	....	....	....	....	....	....	....	....
120	125	221	331	393	....[r]	393	423	1	424
22	24	51	94	106	....	106	108	....	108
....[r]	....[r]	1	2	2	....	2	2	....	2
25	27	51	104	135	....	135	151	....	151
8	7	8	15	17	....	17	19	....	19
65	67	110	115	134	....	134	143	....	143
....	....	....	....	....	....	....	....	....[r]	....[r]
....	....	....	....	....	....[r]	....[r]	....	....[r]	....[r]
?	?	449	?	?	?	?	528	?	528+
174	228	379	450	500	5	506	529	6	535
?	?	7,358	?	?	?	?	6,912	?	6,912+
1,018	*1,265*	*2,069*	*2,634*	*2,732+*	*150+*	*3,017*	*3,066*	*219*	*3,285*
?	?	?	?	?	?	?	2,587	?	2,587+
839	1,052	1,739	2,231	2,294+	110+	2,539	2,488 +	113+	2,765
178	*203*	*330*	*404*	*438*	*41*	*478*	*479*	*41*	*520*
?	?	?	?	?	?	?	3,671[p]	?	3,671+
?	?	7,358	?	?	?	?	6,912	?	6,912+
?	?	?	?	?	?	?	1,050+?	?	?
?	?	?	?	?	?	?	781+?	?	?
?	?	?	?	?	?	?	87+?	?	?
?	?	?	?	?	?	?	?	?	?
?	?	?	?	?	?	?	150+?	?	?
?	?	?	?	?	?	?	373+?	?	?
1,030	*1,280*	*2,090*	*2,660*	*2,891*	*159*	*3,050*[a]	*3,100*	*225*	*3,325*

be found on page 376.

TABLE 56

REVENUES OF COMMUNES, WITH ESTIMATES OF

(In millions of paper francs.

		1924		
		Communes in old départements	Communes in Alsace and Lorraine	Total — Communes in all départements
	Centimes Communaux:			
1.	According to data from Ministry of Interior [a]	?	?	?
2.	Ordinary and special *centimes*	?	?	?
3.	Extraordinary *centimes*	?	?	?
4.	According to data from Ministry of Finance [b]	1,112	96	1,208
5.	Real estate, improved	249	8	257
6.	Real estate, unimproved	90	7	97
7.	*Personnelle-mobilière* [v]	187	....	187
8.	Doors and windows	110	....	110
9.	*Patentes* [t]	477	....	477
10.	Tax on capital in Alsace and Lorraine	....	8	8
11.	Tax on salaries and wages in Alsace and Lorraine	....	31	31
12.	Tax on professions in Alsace and Lorraine	....	42	42
13.	Mine tax in Alsace and Lorraine (*taxe de superficie*)	....	.... [r]	.... [r]
	Fonds Communs:			
14.	According to data from Ministry of Interior [c]	?	?	?
15.	Tax on beverages (*boissons*)	?	?	?
16.	Turnover tax	?	?	?
17.	According to sources from Ministry of Finance	480+	17+	696
18.	Tax on beverages (from *Bulletin de Statistique et de Législation Comparée*)	480	17	497
19.	Turnover tax	?	?	199
20.	Identity card tax	....	....	....
21.	*Taxes Assimilées:* [d]	14	....	14
22.	Mine tax (*Redevances des mines*)	13	....	13
23.	Tax on carriages, horses and mules	1	....	1
24.	Tax for the payment of the *délégues mineurs*	....	....	....
25.	Other "Direct" Municipal Taxes (*taxes municipales*) [e]	446	7	453
26.	Suburban road tax (*taxe des prestations—chemins vicinaux*)	109	4	114
27.	Rural road tax (*taxe des prestations—chemins ruraux*)	2	1	3
28.	*Centime* road tax (*taxe vicinale*)	164	....	164
29.	Dog tax	20	2	22
30.	Taxes in substitution for the *octrois* and *boissons hygiéniques*	150	....	150
31.	Special tax in Alsace and Lorraine for *chambres de métier*	....	.... [s]	....
32.	Tax on large stores (*grands magasins*) in Alsace and Lorraine	....	.... [r]	.... [r]
	Octrois:			
33.	According to data from Ministry of Interior [f]	?	?	?
34.	According to data from Ministry of Finance [g]	552	7	559
35.	Total Ordinary and Extraordinary Receipts [i]	?	?	?
	Limits for Estimating Total Receipts from Taxation:			
36.	Lower limit	*3,177+*	*177+*	*3,553*
37.	Total taxes giving preference to data of Ministry of Interior (Sum of lines 1, 14, 21, 25, and 33)	?	?	?
38.	Total taxes giving preference to data of Ministry of Finance (Sum of lines 4, 17, 21, 25, and 34)	2,604+	127+	2,930
39.	To be added: other local fees, poor taxes (*droits des pauvres*), and miscellaneous local taxes [m]	*574*	*50*	*623*
40.	Upper limit	?	?	?
41.	Total receipts	?	?	?
	To be subtracted:			
42.	Surplus brought forward from previous exercices	?	?	?
43.	Levies revalidated (*restes à recouvrer sur produits constatés aux comptes des exercices antérieurs*)	?	?	?
44.	Subventions	?	?	?
45.	Loans	?	?	?
46.	Receipts from public utilities	?	?	?
47.	Miscellaneous deductions [k]	?	?	?
48.	Estimate of Total Receipts from Taxation	*3,410*	*190*	*3,600*

Footnotes to this table will

(Continued)

TOTAL REVENUE FROM TAXATION, 1913–1926

Estimates in italics)

1925			1926		
Communes in old départements	Communes in Alsace and Lorraine	Total — Communes in all départements	Communes in old départements	Communes in Alsace and Lorraine	Total — Communes in all départements
?	?	?	?	?	?
?	?	?	?	?	?
?	?	?	?	?	?
1,216	107	1,322	1,520	120	1,640
267	8	275	314	11	325
98	7	106	114	10	124
200	....	200	318	....	318
118	....	118	....[r]	....	....[r]
532	....	532	774	....	774
....	8	8	....	9	9
....	35	35	....	33	33
....	49	49	....	57	57
....	....[r]	....[r]	....	....[r]	....[r]
?	?	?	?	?	?
?	?	?	?	?	?
?	?	?	?	?	?
495+	17+	711	?	?	733
495	17	512	?	?	496
?	?	196	?	?	229
?	?	3	?	?	8[t]
21	....	21	22	....	22
20	....	20	21	....	21
1	....	1	1	....	1
....	....	....	....	....	...
491	7	499	728	8	736
121	4	125	143	4	148
3	1	4	4	1	5
187	....	187	226	....	226
21	2	23	24	2	26
159	....	159	331	....	331
....	....[w]	....	....	....[z]	....
....	1	1	....	1	1
?	?	?	?	?	?
606	8	614	711	8	719
?	?	?	?	?	?
3,498+	*198*+	*3,894*	*4,339*+	*242*+	*5,314*
?	?	?	?	?	?
2,830+	139+	3,167	2,982+	136+	3,850
669	*59*	*727*	*1,357*	*107*	*1,464*
?	?	?	?	?	?
?	?	?	?	?	?
?	?	?	?	?	?
?	?	?	?	?	?
?	?	?	?	?	?
?	?	?	?	?	?
?	?	?	?	?	?
?	?	?	?	?	?
3,740	*210*	*3,950*	*5,210*	*290*	*5,500* [a]

be found on page 376.

The footnotes to Table 56 supply detailed information regarding the procedure used in arriving at the estimates of the tax revenues of communes. On the whole, it is felt that these estimates closely approximate the actual figures. Unfortunately, there is

---

communes); (b) even in this latter sum, there is an item of 1,049,962,979 francs for the city of Paris which is merely a surplus carried forward from previous years; (c) and another item of 781,097,893 francs for the city of Paris as levies revalidated. At least the three items above, totalling 3,076,093,302 francs, must be subtracted from the total of 8,157,176,937 francs, if an idea is to be had of the amount of communal revenue originating during the year.

FOOTNOTES TO TABLE 56

[a, c, f, i] *Situation financière des Communes*, 1913, 1914, 1920, and 1923.

[b, d, e] *Renseignements statistiques relatifs aux contributions directes et aux taxes assimilées*. The data for the "centimes communaux" and "taxes assimilées" for the years 1913–1916 inclusive are from the *Compte Général*.

[g] *Annuaire Statistique* and *Bulletin de Statistique et de Législation Comparée*.

[h, j] The figures for these two years are headed merely "recettes ordinaires." No data are given regarding the "recettes extraordinaires" for these two years. See *Situation financière des Communes*, 1920, pp. ix and x. Moreover the 1913 total, unlike those given for 1920 and 1923, apparently does not include (1) surplus from previous exercices, (2) levies revalidated, (3) loans. Also, it is based on budget evaluations, and not (as are the 1920 and 1923 totals) on the definitive accounts. Presumably this is also true for 1914.

[k] These figures include certain inter-fund transfers, receipts from sale of capital assests, interest on investments, repayments of advances, etc.

[l] Provisional figure.

[m] In 1923, the local fees and miscellaneous local taxes in Paris were approximately 100,000,000 francs. The "droits des pauvres" in Paris were 32,915,884 francs. Altogether these items produced 45.9 per cent as much as "centimes." If one assumes that this same relationship existed in the other communes, the figures entered on line 39 result.

For the years 1913 to 1922, the estimates given on line 39 assume that the receipts from these sources for the old départements varied in the same manner as the receipts from communal centimes in the old départements. The estimate for 1913 which results from this procedure produces a figure which appears to be more reliable than that produced by the method of calculating the revenue from the communes outside of Paris by assuming that the percentage was the same as in Paris for that year. The centimes in Paris for 1913 appear to be unduly low and the estimate based upon them results in a figure in excess of the maximum limit.

The figures for 1925 are arrived at by the same method as that used for the 1923 figures. Between 1923 and 1925, in spite of an increase in their absolute amount, the relative importance of the centimes in Paris declined (local fees, etc. were 45.9 per cent as great as the centimes in 1923 and 55.0 per cent in 1925). This seems to have been caused, in large part at least, by the growth of the poor taxes. The 1924 figures assume that this change had been one-half accomplished in 1924.

The 1922 figures for Alsace and Lorraine are based on the 1923 relationship.

[p] This figure is arrived at by subtracting from the total receipts (line 41), which, to avoid double counting, is presented in a form which does not include the item of "restes à recouvrer" (see *Situation financière des Communes*, 1923, p. viii), the known Paris figures for non-tax receipts (lines 42 to 47). The figures given on lines 42 to 47 inclusive are for Paris only.

[q] Arrived at by subtracting the sum of lines 44, 46, and 47 from line 41.

[r] Less than one-half million francs.

[s, u] The subdivision of the proceeds of the turnover tax between the old départements on the one hand and Alsace and Lorraine on the other is made on the basis of the 1923 figures for the turnover tax, five per cent being credited to Alsace and Lorraine.

[t] The only year in which a figure is given for this item is 1915 when the receipts amounted to 200.99 francs.

[v, w, x] In the years following 1923, the figures for this tax are merged with the yield of the "Tax on professions in Alsace and Lorraine" (line 12). The figures are (in thousands of francs): 1924, 425; 1925, 539; 1926, 540.

[y, z] For the years 1919–1925, there should be deducted from these items a certain amount as tax refunds to men called to the colors. The same applies to the "patente" and "personnelle-mobilière" items in the départemental tax table. The figures for the combined tax refund, that is, for communes and départements, are available, and are reproduced in Table 60, p. 398. But how this amount should be split up, is not indicated. The existence of this refund was discovered only after all the tables, charts, and text of the local revenues had been made up, and in view of its comparative insignificance except for the years 1919–1921, the tables, etc., have not been altered. In 1920, when the refund reached its highest point (71,801,000 francs) it equalled 11 percent of the total départemental and communal revenue from the two taxes, and not quite three per cent of the total départemental and communal revenue as estimated without considering the refund. In the other years these percentages were sharply lower. The refunds are taken into account in the aggregate tax table (Table 59, p. 396.)

no prospect, as there is in the case of the figures for the state revenues, that future official publications, such as the *Compte Général*, will supply a more full and accurate basis for estimates.

Analysis of Aggregate Local Tax Revenues

The estimates of total tax revenues of the départements and communes are consolidated and deflated in Table 57 and the results illustrated in Diagram V on page 378.

TABLE 57

ESTIMATES OF TOTAL REVENUE FROM TAXATION, DÉPARTEMENTS AND COMMUNES,

1913–1926

(In millions of francs)

Source: Tables 55 and 56

	Old Départements	Alsace and Lorraine	Total — All Départements	
	In paper francs	In paper francs	In paper francs	In pre-war francs [a]
1913	1,170	—	1,170	1,170
1914	1,165	—	1,165	1,146
1915	1,085	—	1,085	776
1916	1,120	—	1,120	595
1917	1,155	—	1,155	441
1918	1,350	—	1,350	398
1919	1,630	—	1,630	458
1920	2,640	—	2,640	518
1921	3,510	—	3,510	1,018
1922	3,921	209	4,130	1,264
1923	4,200	275	4,475	1,068
1924	4,610	250	4,860	995
1925	5,110	276	5,386	980
1926	7,082 [b]	358	7,440	1,059

[a] Deflated according to index of wholesale prices, 1913 = 100. See p. 448. The figures resulting from the use of the French price index of the Federal Reserve Board are as follows: 1920, 516; 1921, 1,020; 1922, 1,295; 1923, 1,136; 1924, 1,090; 1925, 1,124; 1926, 1,200.

[b] It is of interest to note that late in 1927, M. L. Dausset (*Le Matin*, December 26, 1927) estimated the taxes imposed by the communes and départements for the year 1927 at 6 to 7 billion francs.

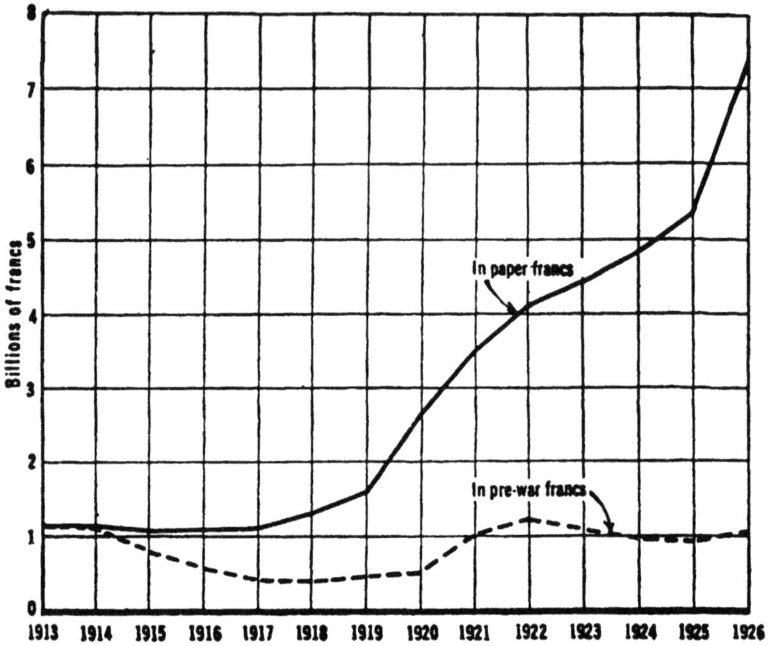

Diagram V
Total Local Tax Revenues, Départements and Communes, 1913–1926

It appears that the outbreak of the war caused a slight decline in local tax collections in paper francs. Indeed not until 1918, the year of the Armistice, did the collections, even in paper, reach once more the level of 1913. By 1921 the paper collections had trebled and by 1926 had reached a point more than six times as high as that of 1913.

But when the paper francs are translated into francs of pre-war value, these increases are reduced to the vanishing point. Rapid as it was, the increase in paper collections after the war failed to keep pace with the depreciation of the value of the money. Measured in terms of pre-war francs, the 1918 collections were only about one-third of the 1913 collections. The 1922 collections were slightly larger and the 1926 collections were slightly smaller than those of 1913. Moreover the situation is, in reality, worse than this, for both the 1922 and the 1926 figures include Alsace and Lorraine while the 1913 figures do not.

In the aggregate then, the collections were practically the same as in 1913, measured in francs of the same value. But during this period there were important changes in the sources utilized in obtaining this money. Table 58 and Diagrams VI and VII on pages 380 and 381 show what these changes have been.

The marked decline in the relative importance of the local *centimes* on real estate is worthy of special mention. In 1913 the départements secured approximately one-half of their taxes from this source. In 1926 they secured from it less than one-third. In the communes, also, this tax shows a severe decline, although here the real estate tax has never been so important a source as in the départements.

TABLE 58

TAX REVENUES OF DÉPARTEMENTS AND COMMUNES, CLASSIFIED ACCORDING TO SOURCE, WITH PERCENTAGE DISTRIBUTION, 1913, 1919, AND 1926

Source: Tables 55 and 56. Estimates in italics

Sources of Tax Revenue	Amounts (In millions of paper francs)			Percentage Distribution		
	1913	1919	1926[a]	1913	1919	1926[a]
Real estate, improved and unimproved, *centimes départementaux et communaux*	279	336	1,046	23.9	20.6	14.1
Personnelle-mobilière, centimes départementaux et communaux	116	158	668	9.9	9.7	9.0
Patentes, centimes départementaux et communaux	130	211	1,483	11.1	13.0	19.9
Doors and windows, *centimes départementaux et communaux*	60	78	.....	5.1	4.8	.....
Fonds communs	.....	263	903	.....	16.1	12.1
Octrois	334	228	719	28.5	14.0	9.6
Miscellaneous municipal fees, poor taxes, etc.	*139*	*203*	*1,464*	*11.9*	*12.5*	*19.7*
Other taxes	*112*	*153*	*1,157*	*9.6*	*9.3*	*15.6*
Total tax revenues of départements and communes	*1,170*	*1,630*	*7,440*	100.0	100.0	100.0

[a] Includes Alsace and Lorraine.

The second of the local *centimes* taxes, the *personnelle-mobilière,* bears a slightly smaller percentage of the total local tax burden than in 1913. It has contributed nothing to offset the decline in the real estate taxes.

It is the third local *centimes* tax, the *patentes,* which has come to the rescue as the real-estate tax has fallen off. Since 1913 its

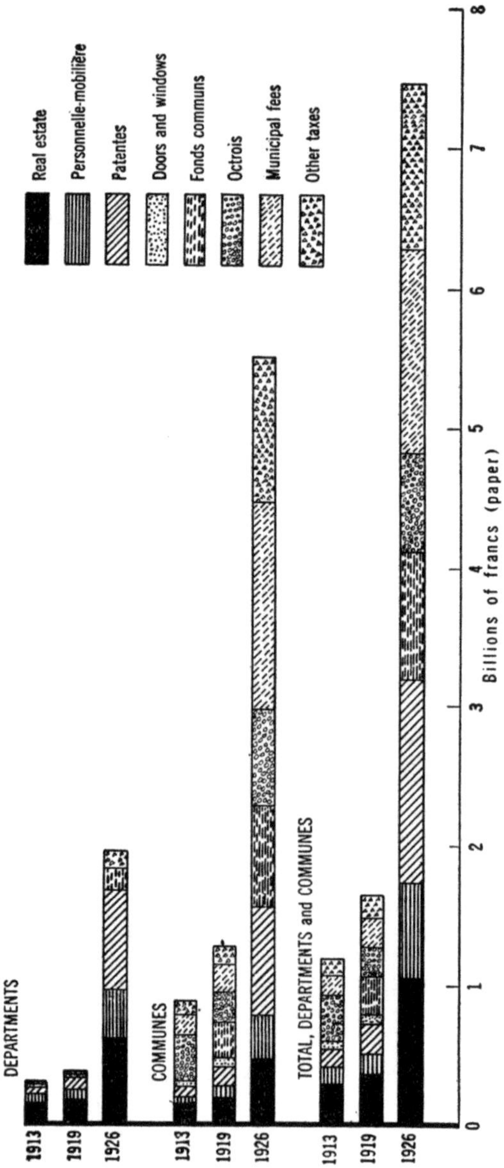

DIAGRAM VI

Subdivision of Local Tax Revenues, by Nature of Taxes, 1913, 1919, 1926

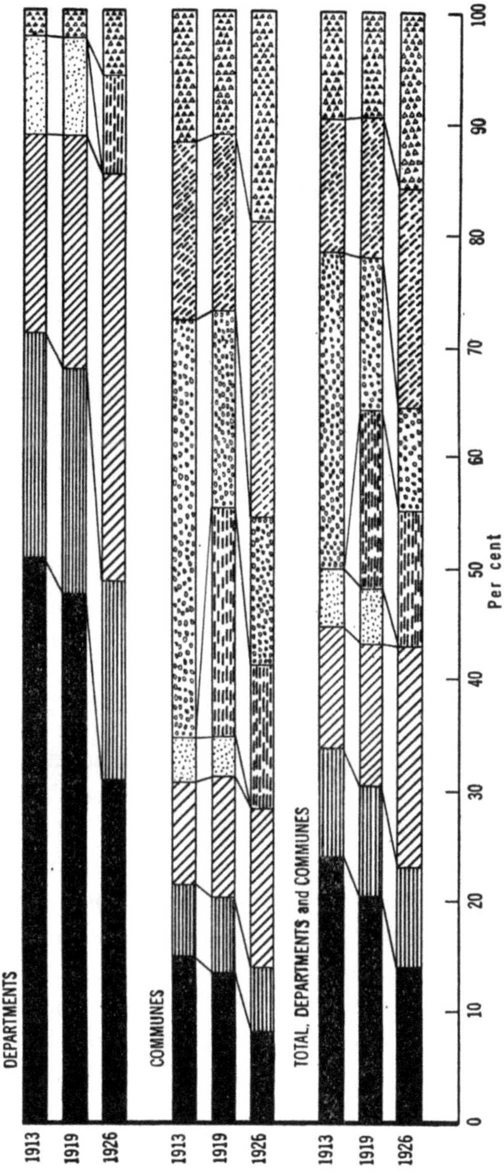

DIAGRAM VII

Percentage Distribution of Local Tax Revenues, by Nature of Taxes, 1913, 1919, 1926
(Key to various taxes in Diagram VI)

importance has doubled in the revenue system of the départements and has increased nearly as much in the communes. In the aggregate its gain has practically blotted out the loss in the real-estate tax and the *personnelle-mobilière* tax, so that the three *centimes* taxes are today almost as important as they were in 1913.

The fourth local *centimes* tax, that on doors and windows, which brought in about one franc in twenty of the local taxes in 1913, has been abolished during the period. On the other hand, an entirely new source has been developed in the *fonds communs*, a central fund apportioned among the localities and alimented by the automobile circulation tax, taxes on beverages, turnover and *cartes d'identité*. This new *fonds communs* was a source of revenue three times as important in 1926 as the doors and windows tax had been in 1913. Its proceeds, together with moderate increases in miscellaneous municipal fees and taxes, have offset the important decline in the yield of the *octrois*, which during the period under review have retired from a commanding position in the communal tax system, supplying 38 per cent of the revenue, to a decidedly minor place, supplying only 13 per cent.

THE LOCAL TAX SYSTEM [9]

Although the départements and the communes are the bodies which levy the great bulk of the local taxes, small levies are also made by various official or semi-official bodies such as *bourses*, chambers of commerce, hospitals and other institutions which impose small local taxes to cover certain of their expenses, the proceeds of which are merged with the statistics for the départements and communes given in the preceding pages.

As has been seen, the commune is far more important than the département as to total amount of taxes collected. Its taxing system is also more complicated than that of the département. For the sake of clearness the revenues collected from the départements will be described first.

[9] The chief sources drawn upon for this description were: Rosier, *Tous Nos Impôts* and *Législation financière;* Allix, *Législation financière; Doc. Parl., Chambre*, 1924, annexes 402 and 403.

Taxation in the Départements

The départements depend almost wholly upon taxes collected for their account by the State. These fall into two groups, the *centimes additionnels* or *centimes départementaux,* and the *fonds communs.*

Centimes Départementaux. — (Yield in 1926, 1,656,000,000 francs). These are, in effect, taxes on local real estate, assessed on a rental basis, and on local business, the *personnelle-mobilière* in its present form being a tax on rentals. The term "*centimes additionnels,*" usually applied to them, comes from the fact that the State formerly levied the same kind of taxes for its own benefit, and the départements then collected an additional tax on the same basis. This additional tax was expressed as a fraction of the amount collected by the State. Thus, if the State collected 500,000 francs (this was called the "*principal*") from one of these taxes, and the départements levied 8 *centimes additionnels,* the tax collected by the départements amounted to 8 per cent of 500,000 francs, or 40,000 francs, and the total tax collected by both the State and the départements from this amounted to 540,000 francs.

At present, however, the State no longer levies these taxes (the "*Quatre Vieilles*"). It abandoned the old tax on "*propriété bâtie*" [10] in 1890 (or rather transformed it from an apportioned into a percentage tax, thus destroying the "*principal*"), did the same for the tax on unimproved real estate ("*propriété non-bâtie*") in 1914, and no longer collected any revenue from the *patente* (business tax), the *contribution personnelle-mobilière* and the tax on doors and windows, after 1917. In the finances of the State these old taxes find their successors in certain schedules of the income tax. The départements, however, have not yet de-

[10] The term "propriété bâtie," translated in this book as "real estate — improved," is a technical term which has a meaning somewhat more restricted than the American term "improved real estate." Indeed, for a period between 1881 and 1914, the legal definition excluded land entirely and confined the term to "improvements" on land. However, by the law of March 29, 1914 (article 3), the definition was extended to include the land actually covered by a structure together with such other land as is immediately adjacent and indispensable to the use of the structure, such as passages, entry strips, etc. Allix and Lecerclé, *L'Impôt sur le Revenu,* pp. 196–197, 205–208; Sauzède, *Traité de la Contribution foncière,* p. 187.

veloped other taxes to take their place. The question then arises: Since the State no longer employs these taxes, upon what can the *centimes départementaux* be based? There is no longer any real "*principal*," or state levy, upon which they can be calculated. The difficulty has been overcome by using what is known as the "*principal fictif*," the character of which is explained below.

The three taxes collected on the basis of the "*principal fictif*" are: (1) the tax on real estate, improved and unimproved; (2) the *personnelle-mobilière* tax, levied on the rental value of the room or house occupied by the taxpayer; and (3) the *patente*, or profession and business tax, levied on a variety of bases, to be described later. Until recently there was a fourth (whence the name "*Quatre Vieilles*") — a tax on doors and windows — but this was completely suppressed on January 1, 1926. The second tax noted above, the *personnelle-mobilière*, was formerly, in part, a capitation tax, calculated on the basis of the value of three days' labor, but this element disappeared in 1917 and the tax is now in theory based on rentals.

The old real-estate tax (*contribution foncière*) was an apportioned tax (*impôt de répartition*): the total amount to be collected for a given calendar year was decided by Parliament in midsummer of the preceding year, and was then split up among the départements and communes. Thus to fix definitely and well in advance the total amount of the tax was, of course, a great convenience to the départements as it enabled them to make accurate estimates of their probable resources for the coming year. When the départements fixed their number of *centimes additionnels*, they knew exactly how much revenue they could expect. When the State changed the form of its real-estate tax and, instead of apportioning a fixed amount, simply imposed a certain percentage of the rental value of the property from each owner, it became impossible to know with precision in advance what the state collections would amount to. As the départements did not want to abandon the system of *centimes additionnels*, they resorted to the device of retaining as their base the last apportioned *principal* which the State had collected under the old system. This occurred in 1890 for the tax on improved real estate and in 1914 for the tax on unimproved real estate. Thus there are now (1) the actual tax collections by the State, levied by the percentage method, (2) the *principal fictif*, or the last state collections under the old system, modified by subsequent changes in property, and (3) the *centimes additionnels*, levied by the départements, and calculated on the *principal fictif*.

In the second place, the new percentage tax on real estate is collected, as a part of the income tax, from the owner of the real property at his place of residence, no matter where his property may be located. The old *principal*, on the other hand, was apportioned with regard to the location of the property itself. This is another reason why the départements could not abandon the old *principal* as a basis for calculating their *centimes*. If they tried to calculate them on the yield of the State's new percentage tax, those départements which contain much real property but very few residents would be poor, while those, such as Seine (in which Paris is located), where there reside many wealthy men owning real estate located in other départements, would suddenly become rich.

All that has been said above about the *centimes départementaux* applies as well to the communes, which also get part of their revenue from such *centimes*.

A complete description of the three taxes which comprise *centimes additionnels* would take too much space here, for the bases of imposition are complicated. The real property tax (*contribution foncière*) was originally supposed to be a tax on both rental value and agricultural profits, as far as unimproved real estate ("*propriété non-bâtie*") was concerned. However, in practice, the tax came to be levied only on rental value, long before such a method was legally adopted in 1914. At present, it is difficult to say to what extent the *centimes* are levied on pure rent, since they are based on a *principal fictif* which has lost much touch with reality (since 1890 for the improved real estate and since 1914 for the unimproved). The *principal fictif*, it is true, is changed slightly from year to year as new lands are brought into cultivation, or as new buildings are erected, or old ones demolished, but, on the whole, the *principal* has remained nearly constant since the State abandoned it.

The *patente,* or business tax, attempts to reach profits through external signs. Practically all commercial and industrial establishments, no matter how small, and many of the liberal professions (those of lawyers, doctors, architects, etc.) are subject to the tax. All except the liberal professions are reached by a fixed tax which varies with the classifications which the administration has drawn up for the various kinds of business. In some cases this " fixed " tax also varies with the number of employees of the business, with the population of the place in which it is located, with the amount of machinery or other means of production employed, or with still some other factor. The proportional tax, which is added to the fixed, to get the total of the *patente* due, is based on the rental value of the house of the taxpayer, plus the rental value of his factory or shop. This system is so complex that it is impossible to give rates here which would have any significance. The *principal fictif,* the tax the State would have collected under the former régime, is calculated, and the *centimes additionnels* for the départements and communes are then levied on this *principal.* In 1926 the départements and communes had levied approximately one and one-half billion francs under the *patente* — approximately two-thirds of what the State demanded from business men by the commercial and industrial profits schedule of the income tax for the same year (2,247 million francs).

The *personnelle-mobilière* tax is levied theoretically on the rental value (unfurnished) of the furnished rooms or house occupied by any resident, foreigner or stranger. However, in practice, the assessments often bear only a remote relationship to actual rentals. Thus, the law allows certain flat deductions from the tax base and gives favors to large families. Moreover, fiscal agents long ago took it upon themselves to modify the tax in accordance with any general signs of wealth they perceived.[11] As with the patente and the *contribution foncière,* the *principal fictif* of the State is first calculated, and the *centimes additionnels* of the

[11] Allix, *Législation financière,* pp. 623–627.

départements and communes are based on this. The départements imposed 350 million francs and the communes 318 million francs, through this tax, in 1926.

Fonds Communs. — (Yield in 1926, 170,000,000 francs.) The only considerable source of tax revenue for the départements outside of the *centimes* is a share in the *fonds communs*, which is fed by taxes. These are as follows, the percentages representing the approximate share of the départements in the total collections: (1) the turnover tax proper [12] (1.66 per cent) and the coal-extraction tax [13] (2 per cent); (2) the circulation tax on automobiles [14] (10 per cent); and (3) the charge for *cartes d'identité* for foreigners [15] (5 per cent of the 100-franc tax; 7.50 per cent of the 20-franc tax).[16] The total revenue of the départements from those sources was approximately 170 million francs for 1926 — less than 9 per cent of the total tax revenue.

Other Départemental Taxes. — (Estimated yield in 1926, 114,000,000 francs.) The départements have no taxes which they levy and collect themselves, with the exception of a few court fees and other miscellaneous items, which supply an insignificant sum. The rest of their receipts come from subventions granted them by the State, by the communes, and by individuals, and from loans.

Taxation in the Communes

The total communal tax revenues are approximately two and one-half times as great as those from the départements. In addition to the sources utilized by the départements, they avail themselves of many other revenues, including the *octrois* and a number of important local direct taxes and fees.

Centimes Communaux. — (Yield in 1926, 1,541,000,000 francs.) Although the absolute amounts collected are about the

[12] See p. 349.

[13] See p. 349.

[14] See p. 352.

[15] See p. 342.

[16] There may be added here the small amount received by the départements from the taxation of oil concessions.

After October, 1928, the départements and communes together receive five per cent of the total yield of the new tax on sugar, levied to replace the turnover tax on that commodity.

same as for the départements, the communes draw only about 28 per cent of their total tax revenues from *centimes additionnels*. These are levied on the same *principaux fictifs* utilized by the départements. The treatment of the *centimes départementaux*[17] makes unnecessary additional discussion at this point.

Fonds Communs. — (Yield in 1926, 733,000,000 francs.) The communes receive about 13 per cent of their tax revenues from this source, more than four times as much as the départements. The manner in which they share in this fund of state-collected taxes[18] is radically different. The arrangement, with the approximate share of the communes in the collections, is as follows: (1) the turnover tax proper (3.33 per cent) and the coal-extraction tax (4 per cent);[19] (2) the charge for *cartes d'identité* for foreigners (10 per cent of the 100-franc tax and 12½ per cent of the 20-franc tax);[20] and (3) the tax on beverages — wine, cider, perry, hydromel (26⅔ per cent); diluted wine (*piquette*) (66⅔ per cent); beer (25 per cent); alcohol (specific tax) 19 per cent.[21]

Octrois. — (Yield in 1926, 719,000,000 francs.) Although the relative importance of the *octrois* has declined greatly since 1913,[22] this source, in 1926, still ranked with the *patentes* and the *fonds communs* as one of the major elements in the communal tax system, having supplied 13.1 per cent in 1926.

It is a common impression that the *octrois* are merely a series of local customs duties. In theory, at least, this is not exact. They are really taxes on certain products consumed within the town, and are levied on the articles whether they are produced within the town or are brought in from elsewhere. Since most of the *octrois*, however, are collected on food, fuel, and building materials, which are usually brought in from the surrounding coun-

[17] See p. 383.

[18] Other state-collected taxes, the proceeds of which are shared with the communes, include the proportional tax on mine profits (22 per cent) and the tax on carriages and horses. The statistics of these revenues are included under the heading of "taxes assimilées."

[19] See p. 349.

[20] See p. 342.

[21] See pp. 354, 355.

[22] See p. 379.

try, in practice they resolve themselves almost entirely into taxes on entry into the commune.

The *octrois* are unpopular and are rapidly being abandoned. In 1924, only 1,113 communes, less than 3 per cent of the total number, utilized them. During 1925 and 1926, 21 additional communes abolished them.[23] But among those which retain them is Paris itself and Paris alone now accounts for half of the total *octrois* collections in France.

The unpopularity rests on a wide foundation. All agree that the tax is antiquated and inconvenient and that the expenses of collection are high (18.9 per cent in 1926).[24] In Paris the city has shifted far beyond the old municipal limits, many of the factories are located in the suburbs, and the *octrois* impose a serious obstacle to the local movement of goods. Finally, there is considerable objection, particularly from the Communists, on the ground that it increases unduly the cost of living of the poor. Proposals to substitute some other source of revenue have frequently been urged but no decisive action has been taken. The Conseil Municipal of Paris on December 31, 1926, voted a sharp increase in the rates, but the yield during the early months of 1927 was disappointing. This has once more brought to the fore the question of abolishing the *octrois*. In April, 1927, the Paris billboards flamed forth with protests against the new " illegal and scandalous " rates, against the *octrois* in general as " the abettor (*fauteur*) of the high cost of living " and the " fleecer (*écorcheur*) of the poor " and against the Conseil Municipal because it could find no better way to balance its budget than " to starve the worker and the unemployed by madly turning the screw, pitilessly and without end, of this most cunning of the indirect taxes." *L'Humanité*[25] charged that the rates were weighted heavily against the poor and concluded a violent article with the following sardonic exclamation: " The city of Paris needs the money. . . . She intends to take it from the pockets of the workers and the consumers . . . at least as long as they will permit it! "

In Paris the task of finding a substitute source which will pro-

[23] *Bulletin de Statistique*, July, 1927, p. 90. [24] *Ibid.*, p. 92.

[25] April 23, 1927.

duce more than 400 million francs is, however, not a simple one. When Rouen abolished its *octrois,* it made up its loss by a surcharge on gas and electricity. Saint-Nazaire imposed a new tax on the real estate of industrial and commercial establishments. In Paris the proposals which are receiving most serious attention are an increase, for local benefit, in the rate of the turnover tax and a special tax on transportation by land and water.[26]

Miscellaneous Municipal Fees, Poor Taxes, etc. — (Estimated yield in 1926, 1,464,000,000 francs.) This large and increasing source produced nearly one-fifth of all the communal tax revenue in 1926.

An important part of this group of revenues consists of a series of specific charges (*taxes*) made for services rendered, the exact yield of which is unascertainable. They fall into six main groups.

(1) Fees levied for the privilege of cutting wood in the communal forests, of pasturing on the common land, etc. (*taxes d'affouage, de pâturage, de tourbage*).

(2) Assessments for paving, sweeping, and special assessments (*taxe des plus-values*) collected on increase in value of real estate due to local improvements.[27] In Paris the sweeping tax alone produces about 16 million francs.

(3) Fees for parking privileges (e.g., paid by taxicabs in Paris), for use of market places, for use of municipal warehouses (*entrepôts — taxe de magasinage*), etc. It may be of interest to American cities, struggling with the problem of parked automobiles, to learn that Paris collects about 50 million francs annually from taxicabs and business vehicles for permits to park their cars in the public streets.

(4) Municipal slaughter-house fees, to pay cost of inspection and upkeep (not to be confounded with the state *taxe d'abatage*). The yield in Paris is about 8 million francs.

[26] *Le Matin,* September 15, 19, 1927. See also *Le Temps,* November 24, 1927. The proposal to substitute special transportation taxes was introduced as a bill in the Chamber of Deputies early in December, 1927. *Le Temps,* December 9, 1927.

[27] Here are found the revenues from such special assessments as are levied in France. It is necessary to bear in mind the fact that special assessments are included in the French figures, when comparisons are made with the United States, where they produce so substantial a share of local revenues.

(5) Sanitation fees of various kinds (*taxes de désinfection, taxes funéraires*).

(6) *Subventions industrielles* — payments to cover certain costs of compulsory inspection, and for other purposes.

The above list must not be taken as all-inclusive, for no two communes seem to collect the same service charges.

A second important element in this category of communal receipts is a series of so-called "indirect" taxes of which several deserve special mention.

(1) The *taxe de séjour,* levied on visitors at watering places and other health resorts.

(2) The surtax on railroad revenue, usually levied only to pay for an improvement connected with rail transport.

(3) The surtax on mineral waters (part of which, in some cases, goes to the départements).

(4) Tax on found articles deposited with the police.

Included also under this heading are various taxes which are levied for the support of certain semi-official institutions [28] and charities, among which are the poor tax (*droits des pauvres*) and various other taxes dedicated to the support of *associations syndicales,* the *Caisse des Monuments Historiques, Office National de la Propriété Industrielle,* etc.

The *droits des pauvres* are taxes on amusements, collected in substantially the same manner as the state tax on amusements.[29] The proceeds go to the public charitable institutions (*bureaux de bienfaisance*). Maximum rates on gross receipts are fixed as follows: theaters, 9.09 per cent; balls, concerts and *fêtes,* 25 per cent; and 5 per cent on certain specified types of "artists' concerts." The actual rates levied are fixed, within these limits, according to the needs of the institutions. In Paris, in 1926, the *droits des pauvres* produced nearly 54 million francs.[30]

Other Communal Taxes. — (Estimated yield in 1926,

[28] It should be noted that the special centimes added to the "patentes" to defray the expenses of local bourses and chambers of commerce are included under this heading.

[29] See p. 354.

[30] In all the communes except Paris the proceeds are credited directly to the communal budgets. In Paris they are credited to the autonomous budget of the *Administration Générale de l'Assistance Publique.*

1,043,000,000 francs.) The taxes included under this heading contribute about one-fifth (18.9 per cent) of the communal revenues.

There are, first of all, the road taxes which produced nearly 379 million francs in 1926. The most important of these, the *centimes* road tax (*taxe vicinale*) is nothing but the *centimes additionnels* under another name, for the revenue is raised by additions to the tax on real estate and to the *contribution mobilière*. This tax was instituted in 1903 for the use of those communes which desired to abandon the *taxe des prestations*, next to be described. Its purpose is to provide for road building and maintenance. The *taxe des prestations* is still in force in many communes, despite the development of the *taxe vicinale*. It is levied according to the number of men and draft animals the head of any household or establishment has working for him. This is supposed to be some measure of the wear and tear on the roads caused by the taxpayer. The tax can be paid off by furnishing three days labor on the roads, for each taxable subject, but it can also be paid in money, and this latter method is now the one almost universally used. The yield of the tax is now about two-thirds as great as that of its younger brother, the *taxe vicinale*.

Almost equally important financially are the taxes in substitution for the *octrois* on *boissons hygiéniques* (*taxes en remplacement*), yielding, in 1926, about 331 million francs. These taxes take many different forms. Before the reform of August 1926, they could be levied only in place of the *octrois* which had been suppressed by the commune, and certain of them could not be levied at all unless special authorization for the commune was given by law of Parliament. Examples of the latter were: a tax on net revenue of real estate; on the market value of real estate; on pianos, domestic help, umbrellas, and a further miscellany too complicated to describe here. Since the 1926 reform of local finance, however, all of the taxes mentioned above need only the approval of the *préfet* of the département to become effective after having been passed by the commune.[31] *Taxes de remplacement*

[31] For details of reform of local taxation, see law of August 13, 1926, and decree of December 11, 1926.

which did not need parliamentary approval even before August, 1926, include: liquor licenses, taxes on horses, on automobiles, on theater receipts, and others.

Among the remaining imposts, the dog tax, producing about 26 million francs in 1926, is of special interest as an illustration of the degree of refinement with which the French elaborate even their simplest taxes. This tax is a compulsory one. Every commune must impose it. But the law sets only maximum limits. In fixing these limits the law divides the communes into three classes, on the basis of size. It also divides the dogs into three classes, according to use. A pleasure dog (*chien d'agrément*) pays a higher tax than a hunting dog. A hunting dog in turn pays a higher tax than a watch dog. A pleasure dog in a large commune pays a tax of 40 francs, at a maximum. A watch dog in a small commune pays, at the most, a tax of five francs.

Taxation in Alsace and Lorraine

What has been written above applies to all France except Alsace and Lorraine, which has been under a special fiscal régime since rejoining France. Several provisions may be specially noted.

Neither the *patente* nor the *personnelle-mobilière* is levied in Alsace and Lorraine; instead, special taxes on capital, on salaries and wages, and on " professions " are imposed. No local revenue is procured from the *redevances des mines* or the tax on carriages and horses; instead, a special *impôt sur les mines*, based on area, is levied for the départements and communes. Alsace and Lorraine have a special tax on large stores, but no *taxe vicinale* or *taxes de remplacement*.

CONCLUSION

An American, studying the French system of local taxation, is impressed both by its relative unimportance in the finances of the country as a whole and by the absence of anything really comparable with the American local property or real-estate taxes. He is amazed at the French ingenuity in developing complicated devices for apportioning their local expenses, but he is not overwhelmed with admiration for the net result.[32] The system of *centimes additionnels,* with its roots in an obsolete and abandoned national tax, appear to have lost almost all touch with reality and to be failing completely to fulfill its function. The *octrois* are frankly medieval and deserve the peace of the grave into which they are stumbling. The French themselves are alive to the need for radical reform and recognize that the need promises to become yearly more acute. The changes in French taxation during the next decade will almost certainly be predominately in this field of local finance. The readjustment when it comes promises to take the form (1) of a further development of the trend, already apparent, in the direction of municipal fees and prices; (2) of a reorganization of the local business taxes, with perhaps greater weight given to net profits and less to external signs, and (3) of a reform of the real-estate tax. To the foreigner, the French seem not to realize the possibilities of the real-estate tax, which in England on the rental basis and in America on the capital basis, plays so great a rôle in local finance. Instead of considering it, as they now do, essentially a part of the income tax, they may come to regard it, as it is regarded elsewhere, as an attractive method of apportioning the costs of a great mass of local functions, whose benefits are too general to trace accurately and recover through prices and fees, but nevertheless sufficiently specific to permit localization by areas.

[32] Past proposals for changes in local sources of revenue, and a new plan, are to be found in *Réforme des Finances locales,* by J. P. Boissonet, a contrôleur of the direct taxes department (Paris, Rousseau, 1926; vii, 188 pp.). This book sketches briefly the sources of local revenue as they existed in 1926 and mentions some of the reform proposals of the last forty years — especially the Caillaux *projet de loi* resulting from the report of the special commission appointed in 1908, headed by Caillaux himself, which report recommended levying local income taxes on the same basis the State would use. Alterations suggested by Malvy, of the Chamber Finance Committee, are noted. The author then outlines a somewhat similar plan of his own, by which additional centimes are to be levied on the present state income taxes (with many of the present deductions at the base eliminated), the instability of the revenues from year to year being counterbalanced by equalization funds, allowing the local units to borrow from one another.

CHAPTER XIX

THE BURDEN OF TAXATION

It is now possible to consolidate the detailed tables of the two preceding chapters, to eliminate certain items the inclusion of which would lead to double counting, and to compare the resulting aggregate figures of taxes with such standards as are available for testing the weight of the tax burden.

Aggregate State and Local Taxes

The construction of an aggregate tax table for both state and local taxes (Table 59) is not merely the addition of the tax figures shown in other tables in the book. Certain deductions that should be made, but which were not made in the other tables largely because they could not be properly allocated, are cared for here. Other items (e.g., tax and fee items in *recettes d'ordre* and *produits divers*) have not been entered in separate tables.

Supplementing Table 59 is a tabulation (Table 60) showing the deductions, or *dégrèvements,* that have had to be considered in constructing the aggregate table.

A summarized statement of the aggregate taxes is presented in Table 61 showing the percentage distribution among the groups of state taxes, and among state, département and commune taxes.

Finally, the annual state revenue from taxation has been deflated in Table 62, in terms of 1913 francs. This reveals the fact that although the State is receiving over ten times as much in paper francs as it did in 1913, it is receiving not quite twice as much in actual purchasing power. Furthermore, nearly all this increase came in 1927; in 1926 its tax revenue, measured in purchasing power, had increased only 35 per cent over 1913. As for the communes and départements, Table 57 (p. 377) shows that they are receiving a little less in tax revenue than in 1913 measured in purchasing power. State and local taxation together, which was 5,236 million francs in 1913, was in 1926 only 6,478 million francs of the same purchasing power.

TABLE 59

AGGREGATE STATE AND LOCAL TAXES, 1913–1927[a]

(In millions of paper francs) Sources: Tables 42, 43, 47–56, 60. See also footnotes.)

	1913	1914	1915	1916	1917	1918	1919	1920	1921	1922	1923	1924	1925	1926	1927
State direct and assimilated taxes (including income taxes on securities)	**745**	**741**	**679**	**752**	**1,662**	**2,868**	**3,192**	**8,035**	**6,824**	**8,031**	**6,759**	**7,797**	**10,179**	**10,528**	**13,207**
Direct and assimilated taxes. Net	607	589	521	570	1,419	2,615	2,902	7,467	5,898	7,013	5,593	6,113	8,238	8,091	9,822
Direct tax assessments.[b] Gross	634	611	547	611	1,460	2,655	2,956	7,544	6,040	7,270	5,810	6,445	8,527	8,415	10,292
Income taxes and other direct taxes, including assimilated taxes	634	611	547	611	842	893	1,238	1,934	3,495	3,387	4,534	5,838	6,075	8,052	10,023
War-profits tax (1917–1927)	....	....	....	....	618	1,762	1,718	5,611	2,545	3,883	1,276	607	2,452	363	269
Deduct: Refunds of direct and assimilated taxes[c]	*−27*	*−23*	*−26*	*−41*	*−41*	*−40*	*−54*	*−77*	*−142*	*−257*	*−217*	*−332*	*−290*	*−324*	*−470*
Tax on income from securities	138	153	157	181	242	253	290	568	926	1,018	1,166	1,684	1,939	2,437	3,385
State indirect taxes. Net	**2,744**	**2,149**	**2,095**	**2,788**	**3,407**	**3,568**	**6,046**	**9,107**	**9,536**	**11,149**	**12,496**	**15,580**	**17,002**	**24,474**	**27,380**
Indirect taxes. Gross	2,752	2,157	2,105	2,798	3,408	3,575	6,069	9,139	9,680	11,321	12,862	15,979	17,430	24,915	27,828
Registration taxes	834	611	464	525	720	924	1,874	2,718	2,705	2,961	3,392	4,608	5,123	6,239	6,112
Stamp taxes	251	204	146	161	176	219	321	542	597	664	766	1,008	1,240	2,036	2,270
Customs tax	756	579	764	1,401	1,511	1,185	1,477	1,596	1,197	1,611	1,610	1,604	1,486	1,968	2,618
Turnover tax	....	....	....	....	....	112	269	1,256	1,897	2,295	3,028	4,101	4,544	7,480	8,605
Contributions Indirectes	911	763	730	712	1,001	1,134	2,128	3,027	3,283	3,790	4,066	4,657	5,037	7,193	8,222
Deduct: Refund of indirect taxes	*−8*	*−8*	*−9*	*−10*	*−1*	*−7*	*−23*	*−11*	*−50*	*−43*	*−70*	*−74*	*−73*	*−105*	*−74*
Deduct: Taxes on Crédit National issues, paid by the State[d]	....	....	....	....	....	....	....	*−21*	*−94*	*−129*	*−296*[k]	*−325*[k]	*−350*	*−337*	*−374*
State monopolies. Net yield[e]	**486**	**450**	**429**	**468**	**507**	**420**	**596**	**879**	**1,107**	**1,287**	**1,366**	**1,488**	**1,779**	**2,193**	**2,744**
Tobacco monopoly[f]	436	418	401	430	465	374	540	814	1,035	1,198	1,266	1,374	1,643	2,019	2,533
Match monopoly[g]	32	29	27	28	33	36	45	57	58	69	72	71	78	106	132
Powder monopoly[h]	18	1	—	8	9[k]	9[k]	8	7	12	18	26	41[k]	55	67	76
Tax on *briquets*[i]	....	1	1	1	1	2	2	1	1	2	2	2	3	3	3
State miscellaneous taxes. Net	**91**	**83**	**89**	**87**	**87**	**96**	**155**	**271**	**371**	**380**	**297**	**510**	**812**	**879**	**370**
Miscellaneous taxes: Gross	91	83	89	87	87	96	155	271	371	380	298	510	813	879	370
Taxes and fees included under *recettes d'ordre et produits divers*[j]	71	68	88	86	86	95	132	180	269	277	181	364	628	626	117+
Taxes on gambling. Portion excluded from state budget	20	15	1	1	1	1	23	91	102	103	117	146	185	253	253+
Deduct: Miscellaneous refunds, Alsace and Lorraine	....	....	....	....	....	....	....	....	....	....	*−1*	....	*−1*	....	....

Local taxes. Estimates. [l] **Net**	**1,170**	**1,165**	**1,085**	**1,120**	**1,155**	**1,350**	**1,606**	**2,568**	**3,453**	**4,113**	**4,469**	**4,856**	**5,386**	**7,440**	?
Local taxes. Gross	1,170	1,165	1,085	1,120	1,155	1,350	1,630	2,640	3,510	4,130	4,475	4,860	5,386	7,440	.....
Départements	290	300	285	300	305	320	350	550	850	1,080	1,150	1,260	1,436	1,940	.....
Communes	880	865	800	820	850	1,030	1,280	2,090	2,660	3,050	3,325	3,600	3,950	5,500	.....
Deduct: Refunds of patente and personnelle-mobilière [m]	....	....	....	....	....	....	−24	−72	−57	−17	−6	−4	.....	.....	.....
Total revenue from State and local taxes	**5,236**	**4,587**	**4,377**	**5,214**	**6,817**	**8,302**	**11,595**	**20,859**	**21,293**	**24,961**	**25,388**	**30,232**	**35,156**	**45,514**	**43,701 +**

[a] From 1922 on, this table includes figures for Alsace and Lorraine.

[b] The reasons for using assessments rather than collections are explained on p. 317.

[c] For use in the above table the figures of refunds (as they appear in Table 60) have been reduced by the "charges de famille" figures (see footnote (*a*), Table 42) for the years 1922–1927, the "charges de famille" reductions having already been taken into account in arriving at the total of direct and assimilated taxes for those years, as given above. No figures for the "charges de famille" are available for the earlier years, but according to information received from the Direct Tax Administration these reductions were included in the "dégrèvements" (refunds) figures. It is here assumed that the same method has been followed for the subsequent years.

[d] The budget of the Ministry of Finance carries each year as an expense item the security taxes on the Crédit National issues which the State undertakes to pay to itself, relieving the security holders of this obligation. How much of this belongs under the direct tax group and how much under the indirect tax group is unknown to the writer.

[e] No "surplus" from the post, telegraph, and telephone monopoly has been included, for it appears that there has been none which might fairly be called such since 1920 after all expenses including overhead. For 1913–1919 no figures are available. There is an indication that up to 1915 this monopoly did yield some real surplus. See p. 360.

[f] For 1913–1922 the figures are taken from the *Inventaire*, p. 135; for 1923–1925 from the *Experts' Report;* for 1926 and 1927 the figures are estimates, 68 per cent of the gross receipts as given in monthly tax returns (this percentage during 1913–1925 as calculated from the figures in the *Inventaire* and the *Experts' Report* range from a low of 54.64 per cent (1918) to a high of 71.99 per cent (1922)). The *Inventaire* figures for 1913–1922 are used in preference to the *Experts' Report* figures because the gross receipts in the former come nearer to checking with the gross receipts as given in the monthly tax returns. In any case the net results figures can probably be taken only as approximations.

[g] For 1913–1923 the figures are taken from the *Inventaire*, p. 136. For 1924–1927 the figures are estimates, 55 per cent of the gross receipts as given in monthly tax returns (this percentage during 1913–1923 as calculated from the figures in the *Inventaire* ranged from a low of 51.82 per cent (1919) to a high of 57.50 per cent (1922)).

[h] These figures are only rough approximations, arrived at by deducting, from the gross receipts as given in monthly tax returns, the credits granted to the indirect tax administration by the budget laws of each year for the purchase of the powder from the War Department. For some years, where figures of credits granted were not available, an estimate had to be made from gross receipts alone. See pp. 358, 360.

[i] Not strictly a monopoly, but placed here in French tax returns. See p. 357.

[j] This item is subject to a wide margin of error. From calculations made with several of the budget law estimates, the writer concludes that from 20 to 30 per cent of the total collections under these heads comes from taxes and fees, and so 25 per cent of the collections listed under this head in the fiscal reports is entered above as a roughly approximate figure.

[k] Estimate.

[l] For details see special chapter on local revenues, pp. 368, 369, 372-376.

[m] For explanation of this deduction from the estimates, see footnote *m*, p. 369, and footnote *y*, p. 376.

TABLE 60

REFUNDS AND DRAWBACKS (*DÉGRÈVEMENTS*), 1913–1927[a] TO BE DEDUCTED FROM *RÔLES ÉMIS* OR TAX COLLECTIONS TO ARRIVE AT NET AMOUNT PAID BY TAXPAYERS

(In thousands of paper francs. Source: Ministry of Finance)

	1913	1914	1915	1916	1917	1918	1919	1920	1921	1922	1923	1924	1925	1926	1927
Direct and assimilated taxes:															
Miscellaneous tax refunds[b]	26,830	22,722	25,664	40,969	34,752	38,526	41,653	62,993	97,000	230,700	220,000	339,994	300,000	340,000	470,000[c]
Refunds to owners of rented real estate (art. 5 of law of June 29, 1917, art. 31 of law of March 9, 1918), whose leases are revised downward	......	......	......	......	6,234	985	12,772	13,970	45,000	31,963	4,353	2,158	123	......	......
Refunds of the *personnelle-mobilière* and *patente* tax to men called to the colors (art. 15 of law of March 31, 1919)	......	......	......	......	......	......	23,940	71,801	56,519	17,000	6,000	3,545	391	......	......
	26,830	22,722	25,664	40,969	40,986	39,511	78,365	148,764	198,519	279,663	230,353	345,697	300,514	340,000	470,000
Indirect taxes:															
Miscellaneous tax refunds	6,580	7,256	8,691	9,418	70	6,376	22,834	10,557	45,945[d]	38,861[d]	66,657	70,589	69,177	101,740	70,001
Refund of salt tax on exported salt and other exempt salt	52	48	23	19	23	11	17	7	8	16	12	15	12	30	230
Drawback on exported cotton goods (art. 10 of law of January 11, 1892)	1,000	928	625	524	791	317	414	582	4,093	3,873	3,131	3,500	3,372	3,500	3,300
	7,632	8,231	9,339	9,962	885	6,706	23,265	11,145	50,045	42,749	69,801	74,103	72,561	105,270	73,531
Miscellaneous (Alsace and Lorraine)	......	......	......	......	......	......	......	......	......	[e]	1	[f]	1	......	......
Grand total	34,462	30,953	35,004	50,931	41,871	46,217	101,631	159,910	248,564	322,413	300,154	419,801	373,075	445,270	543,531

[a] For the years 1913–1926 the "ordonnances délivrées" figures have been used. For 1927 the only figures available were for the "crédits ouverts." From 1922 on the figures in this table include Alsace and Lorraine.

[b] "Dégrèvements et non-valeurs sur contributions directes et taxes y assimilées, y compris les taxes additionnelles pour fonds de garantie."

[c] This figure is 170 million francs higher than the "crédits ouverts" figure; according to information received from the Ministry of Finance a "crédit supplémentaire" of this amount will be necessary before the fiscal year ends.

[d] This amount includes refunds made in the Territoire de la Sarre.

[e] 291 francs.

[f] 156 francs.

TABLE 61

TAX REVENUES OF THE STATE, CLASSIFIED ACCORDING TO SOURCES AND POLITICAL DIVISIONS, WITH PERCENTAGE DISTRIBUTION, 1913, 1919 AND 1926

Source: Table 59

	Amounts (In millions of paper francs)			Percentage of State Taxation		
	1913	1919	1926	1913	1919	1926
Total direct taxes (net) (including tax on income from securities)	745	3,192	10,528	18.3	32.0	27.6
Total indirect taxes (net)	2,744	6,046	24,474	67.5	60.5	64.3
Net return from monopolies	486	596	2,193	12.0	6.0	5.8
Tax and fee items in *recettes d'ordre et produits divers*.	71	132	626	1.7	1.3	1.6
Taxes on gambling (that part of the yield which does not appear in the state budget)	20	23	253	0.5	0.2	0.7
Total net revenues of the State from taxation	4,066	9,989	38,074	100.0	100.0	100.0
				Percentage of Total Taxation (State and Local)		
Départements — Estimates of total receipts from taxation	290	350*	1,940	5.5	3.0*	4.3
Communes — Estimates of total receipts from taxation	880	1,280*	5,500	16.8	11.0*	12.1
State — Total net revenues from taxation	4,066	9,989	38,074	77.7	86.0	83.6
Total receipts from state and local taxes	5,236	11,619	45,514	100.0	100.0	100.0

* These figures and percentages are before deduction of refund on "patente" and "personnelle-mobilière" allowed that year to men called to the colors. This total refund figure is available (see Table 60) but it is not divided between départements and communes. It is so small that its inclusion here would not alter the percentage figures as much as one-fourth of one per cent one way or the other.

Relation to Population, Income and Wealth

The writer's contribution to the tangled problem of the burden of taxation in France is primarily the estimates of aggregate taxes presented above. It is, of course, a simple matter to relate these figures to population, but only the simple-minded attach much significance to the results thus obtained. The taxes paid per person means little to one who seeks a measure of burden unless he knows the capacity of the person to bear burdens. This capacity may be expressed either in terms of wealth or in terms of income, but the statistics of wealth and income in France in the present disturbed condition of the country are unreliable. Again,

TABLE 62

TOTAL STATE REVENUE FROM TAXATION, 1913–1927

(In millions of francs)

Source: Table 59

	In Paper Francs	In Pre-War Francs [a]
1913	4,066	4,066
1914	3,422	3,366
1915	3,292	2,355
1916	4,094	2,175
1917	5,662	2,164
1918	6,952	2,050
1919	9,989	2,804
1920	18,291	3,590
1921	17,839	5,171
1922	20,848	6,382
1923	20,919	4,993
1924	25,375	5,195
1925	29,771	5,415
1926	38,074	5,419
1927	43,702 [b]	7,040 [c]

[a] Deflated according to index of wholesale prices, 1913 = 100. See p. 448.
[b] Twelve-month collections only, not including the "recettes postérieures."
[c] Deflated by 620.8, the average for 8 months only.

while aggregate tax collections are useful if one desires to form a judgment regarding the strain being placed on the taxing machinery, they tell little about the placing of the economic strain upon the individual members of the community. To secure a conception of this economic strain, one needs to know the manner in which taxes are distributed among the members of the community, not merely in their initial impact but also in their ultimate incidence and repercussions. Again, the purposes for which the proceeds of the taxes are used should also be brought into the picture. More than 40 per cent of the French taxes go to meet debt service. But debt service on a foreign debt implies a different degree of burden from debt service on a widely distributed domestic debt. Certainly bare comparisons of tax rates, without taking into account significant differences in the composition of tax bases, can lead to nothing but confusion.

The provisional results of the March, 1926, census give

France a total population of 40,922,385.[1] Applying this to the aggregate tax total of 45.5 billion francs for the year 1926,[2] one gets the per capita taxation of France, state and local, as 1,112 francs. With francs at 25.25 to the dollar, the rate of exchange for December, 1926, this means about $44 per capita.

Much more significant would be the relation of taxation to national income, or even to national wealth. Unfortunately, the estimates for these quantities give the appearance of being none too reliable and the writer is not in a position to improve them. Dr. Gini,[3] after reviewing various estimates which would give a national income of from 156 billions to 235 billions, decides it is desirable to consider as an approximate figure 150 billions, as of 1925. Applying to this the 1925 aggregate tax total of 35,156,439,000 one arrives at the estimate that 23.4 per cent of the national income was taken in taxation in 1925.[4] If the same estimate of national income be taken for 1926, and the aggregate tax total of 45,514,387,000 is applied thereto, it appears that 30 per cent of the national income went for taxes. But this latter figure is undoubtedly too high, as the price level was higher in 1926 than in 1925; furthermore, Dr. Gini's estimate of national income is, as noted, lower than that of others. Further refinement of this discussion seems useless here, as the writer believes that the data available for national income figures are of very doubtful validity.

Dr. Gini estimates the wealth of France, as of 1925, to be approximately 1,000 billions. Thus the 1925 tax revenue would represent 3.5 per cent of the national wealth; the 1926 revenue 4.6 per cent, again not allowing for the price level increase.

[1] *Annuaire Général*, 1927, p. 598 *et seq.*

[2] See Table 59.

[3] *A Comparison of the Wealth and National Income of Several Important Nations*, p. 11 *et seq.* See also Professor Boldrini's monograph, *International Comparisons on the Burden of Taxation.*

[4] The League of Nations' *Memorandum on Public Finance, 1922–1926* estimates (p. 17) the national income of France in 1924 at 140 to 170 billion francs, the total taxation at 30,293 million francs (as compared with 30,232 millions in Table 59), and the percentage of income taken in taxes as 17–20 per cent.

Taxes on the Rich versus Taxes on the Poor

Table 63 is an attempt to portray in what proportions the French tax system seems to be specially constructed to bear more heavily on the rich than on the poor, on the poor more heavily than on the rich, and indiscriminately on both.

Such a classification is bound to be rough, and parts seem at first sight to be incongruous. Thus the tax on wages and salaries is listed as " weighted against the rich "; the turnover tax proper is put in the third category instead of being labelled as " weighted against the poor," as its opponents would certainly demand; the *octroi*, closely akin to the turnover tax in a sense, is listed in the second category. The reason for such treatment lies in the attempt, not merely to see whether a tax on the whole burdens the poor more than the rich, but to note especially whether it is so constructed that the rich are called on to bear more than a merely proportionate share as compared with the poor. The salaries and wages tax has exemptions at the base that lessen the tax considerably for the small wage earner; the turnover tax proper has no such provision, while the *octroi*, limited as it is largely to the necessaries of life, is by its nature a tax on the poor rather than on the rich. Similarly, taxes that are limited to articles consumed by the rich or the well-to-do are listed as " weighted against the rich."

The figures are compiled from tables printed elsewhere in the book showing tax returns for the State, départements, and communes. The totals arrived at are not the same as those in the aggregate tax tables, as certain refunds, and the tax and fee items in *recettes d'ordre* and *produits divers* have been omitted in this classification table because of the impossibility of splitting them up into the proper classes.

The table suggests that, in spite of its high proportion of indirect taxes, the French tax system is so devised as to spare, to a remarkable extent, the poorer elements in its population. Moreover, even with the new turnover tax in full effect, the system, judged by this test, is more " democratic " to-day than it was at the outbreak of the war.

TABLE 63

PROPORTION OF TAXES WEIGHTED AGAINST THE RICH AND AGAINST THE POOR, 1913, 1919, 1925, AND 1926*

Source: Tables 42, 43, 47–51, 54–56, 59.

	1913		1919	
	Amount (In millions of paper francs)	Percentage	Amount (In millions of paper francs)	Percentage
Taxes weighted against rich	2,493	46.5	7,367	61.4
Taxes weighted against poor	2,058	38.4	3,741	31.2
Taxes with no definite weighting	814	15.2	888	7.4
Total	5,365	100.0	11,996	100.0

	1925		1926	
	Amount (In millions of paper francs)	Percentage	Amount (In millions of paper francs)	Percentage
Taxes weighted against rich	24,526	66.0	27,348	59.5
Taxes weighted against poor	6,429	17.3	7,832	17.1
Taxes with no definite weighting	6,190	16.7	10,766	23.4
Total	37,145	100.0	45,946	100.0

* The classification of the taxes is as follows:

(1) Taxes weighted against rich:

State taxes:

Income taxes; assimilated taxes and other direct taxes, except those listed under (3); war profits tax; registration taxes; stamp taxes, all except that listed under (2).

"Contributions indirectes:"

Tax of 30 per cent on spirits; consumption taxes on alcohol, mineral waters, perfumery, railway, boat and carriage revenue, amusements, billiard tables, gambling, automobiles, gasoline, oils, precious metals, and playing cards; license taxes;

Turnover tax on sale of luxury articles, including "de luxe" taxes on restaurants and hotels.

Département and commune taxes:

Direct and assimilated taxes (except those specified under (2) and (3)).

"Contributions indirectes:"

Automobile tax; "carte d'identité" tax; tax on drinks.

Classification of taxes continued (Table 63):

"Municipal taxes:"
"Taxe vicinale" (road tax); dog tax; tax on department stores in Alsace and Lorraine.

(2) Taxes weighted against poor:
State taxes:
Stamp taxes:
Tax on extracts from court records; customs duties (all except those listed under (3)).
"Contributions indirectes:" Taxes on wine, beer, patent medicines, candles, vinegar, bicycles, slot (gambling) machines, coffee and other colonial products, salt and sugar.
Turnover tax: Special "production" taxes on coal, meat, tea and coffee.
Monopolies: Gross yield from tobacco, matches and lighters.
Département and commune taxes:
Direct and assimilated taxes; tax on doors and windows.
"Municipal taxes:"
"Taxes des prestations" (road taxes); "octroi."

(3) Taxes with no definite weighting:
State taxes:
Assimilated taxes:
Fees for weights and measures, for "alcoömètres" and "densimètres" for pharmacy, mineral water, mine, boiler, and oleomargarine inspection; "taxe civique;" "taxe d'apprentissage;" tax for fraud prevention.
Customs duties: "Droits de statistique, droits de navigation," etc.
Administrative fees and costs concerned with the levy of direct taxes.
"Contributions indirectes:" All except those listed under (1) and (2).
Monopolies: Explosives and miscellaneous.
Turnover tax: All except those levies listed under (1) and (2).
Département and commune taxes:
Direct and assimilated taxes: Business tax (patente).
Turnover tax.
"Municipal" and other local taxes: Taxes established in replacement of "octroi" on drinks; local fees, "droits de pauvres," and miscellaneous taxes.

Comparisons with American Income Tax

A number of detailed comparisons were made of the manner in which the French income taxes apply to certain given sets of facts as compared with the manner in which the United States income tax applies to the same sets of facts. The primary object was to secure a detailed demonstration of the French procedure, and the material is used for this purpose in a separate study.[5] In addition, however, it was hoped that the comparisons would show

[5] In a volume dealing with French taxation which is in preparation, in collaboration with Carl S. Shoup.

how the differences in definitions of income and methods of computation invalidate mere comparisons of rates. Finally it was thought that the computations would throw some light on the relative severity of the French tax. The results of the comparisons will be briefly summarized here. The computations were made with the assistance of the Paris office of Price, Waterhouse and Company and of M. Jean Marlin, *Contrôleur Principal des Contributions Directes,* each working independently.

Preliminary Considerations. — An accurate comparison of the burden of French income taxation with the American would involve exact knowledge of the extent of evasion, to which the writer lays no claim. The hypothetical cases show merely the theoretical operation of the tax, although they probably give an approximation of the burden really borne, especially since Poincaré's reform of the system of control.

The schedular tax on income from real estate would appear very heavy from its rate (18 per cent) and from the absence of any deductions at the base. But as it is levied on the cadastral values, which are much lower than the true values for most of the land and for a large part of the built property, its real burden is probably not heavy compared with such a tax as that on income from securities, which has the same rate. In a specific instance of which the writer happens to know, a house, with the land underneath and the garden adjoining, paid a total of 1,079 francs for state and local real estate taxes, whereas the owner estimated the selling value of the property to be about 400,000 francs. Supposing the income to be 6 per cent of this, or 24,000 francs, the state and local taxes together took only 4.5 per cent of the income, whereas the rate of the state tax alone is 18 per cent of the cadastral value. In a second case, where the details were made available, a piece of real estate with a capital value of 300,000 francs paid a tax of 652.7 francs. This would mean about 3.6 per cent of the income.

The tax on income from securities is probably the most severe of the income taxes, and the calculations worked out in the comparisons probably represent more nearly the actual burden than in any of the other income taxes. The tax is deducted at the source, and no allowances whatever are made for the family situation of the security holder. The problem of taxing the income from securities under the general income tax is a totally different matter. Here evasion has long been complained of. But in the separate tax on security income alone, it would seem that little or no evasion is possible. Strictly speaking, this is not a "schedular" tax; administratively, it is indirect, and is collected, not by the administration of direct taxes, but by the registration taxes administration. Nevertheless, it is so clearly allied to the schedular income taxes in nature that it has been included in the examples given.

A somewhat similar tax is the one on revenue from private debts, from deposits, etc., created in 1917, and collected by the registration taxes administration.

The tax on salaries and wages is an example of how the rate fails to give a true idea of the burden, even if no part of the tax is evaded. The full effect of the rate is in many cases largely counteracted by the deductions allowed for family charges,[6] the exemption of part of the income even after this allowance has been made,[7] and the reduction of the tax itself for family charges.[8] Since employers must declare to the fisc the wages they pay, evasion is difficult.

The tax on professional income (the same schedule is rather a catch-all for taxable income not specifically reached by the other taxes) appears to offer a wide field for evasion, as by its nature it is largely self-assessed.

The tax on business profits has given more occasion for legal dispute than any of the other income taxes. It would be difficult to estimate how much evasion can, or does, take place, and before 1927 the situation was further complicated by the taxation of certain forms of business on an estimated basis (*forfaitaire*) which was reached by applying a percentage (varying for different businesses) to the gross turnover (*chiffre d'affaires*).

[6] The general income tax is the only other one to have this feature.

[7] All income taxes except those on securities, real estate, and business profits, have a similar provision.

[8] This is a reduction which is present in all the income taxes save that on securities.

The tax on agricultural profits makes little attempt to reach the actual profits of the farmer, but contents itself with applying the rate (12 per cent) to the cadastral rental value, multiplied by a coefficient. Thus the wheat farmer's profit is at present supposed to be equal to twice the cadastral estimate of the land's rental value.

The general income tax rate of 30 per cent means less on its face than the rate of any other tax in the French system. Deductions from the base for family allowances, exemption of a large part of the income above that (decreasing as the income increases) and reduction of the tax for family charges, all tend to make the 30 per cent rate applicable only to those portions of the taxpayer's income well above 550,000 francs. When there is added to this the fact that all the income taxes paid during the previous year may be deducted in arriving at the taxable income, it can be seen that the rate alone means little. The actual burden must — at least in the past — have been considerably reduced by the possibilities of evasion, especially as regards the income from securities.[9]

In calculating the several schedular income taxes, the tax paid the previous year can be deducted from the net income. This affects the significance of all the schedular rates noted above.

Case One.[10] *A Professional Man.* — The first of the comparisons is based on the actual accounts of a professional man in comfortable circumstances. His income and expenses may be summarized as follows:

Income

Salary	$5,850.00	
Fees (net)	8,641.23	
Royalties	546.00	
Dividends	492.57	
Interest	3.12	
Rents (net before taxes)	1,053.00	
Total income		$16,585.92

[9] See pp. 85–87.

[10] These cases are based on the laws in force in 1927. In 1928 the federal income tax was considerably reduced.

Deductions

Interest	$1,217.58	
Taxes	58.50	
Miscellaneous	4.87	
Total deductions		1,280.95
Net income		$15,304.97

The taxpayer is married and has five dependents, two of whom are disqualified under the United States law because over eighteen years of age.

In America this man's income tax is $265.13. In France his income tax comes to $2,409.19.[11] In other words the French income tax is nine times as heavy as the American in this particular case.

Even if to the federal income tax one should add the local real-estate tax this man would pay to New York City and the income tax he would pay to New York State, his total direct tax bill in America would be less than half the French income tax alone. No account is taken of the various indirect taxes, but such taxes in France are many times as heavy as the corresponding taxes in America.

Case Two. A Small Investor.—The second comparison, which again is based on actual accounts, is that of a man with a moderate income, most of which arises from investments. The following are the facts:

Income

Salary	$1,579.50	
Fees	652.08	
Interest	920.79	
Dividends ($2,496.97 in liquidation) ..	4,951.04	
Rents	73.12	
Total income		$8,176.53

Deductions

Interest	$368.55	
Charitable contributions	97.50	
Total deductions		466.05
Net income		$7,710.48

[11] This, moreover, is the second-year figure. In France a new taxpayer with such a statement would pay $3,345.22.

This is a married man with one dependent child.

His federal income tax is $3.35. The French income tax comes to $1552.18.[12]

Case Three. A Small Newspaper Publisher. — The facts regarding the third case, a hypothetical one, of a married newspaper publisher with three dependents, are as follows:

Income

Net profit from publication of newspaper	$2,535.00	
Salary of wife	546.00	
Salary of son (unemancipated)	390.00	
Rents	585.00	
Compensation for personal injuries	390.00	
Total income		$4,446.00

Deductions

Life insurance premiums	$58.50	
Taxes	75.27	
Total deductions		133.77
Net income		$4,312.23

This man's federal income tax would be nothing at all, but the French income tax would be $486.49.[13]

Case Four. A Moderate-sized Manufacturing Corporation. — The next comparison is based on the accounts of a corporation engaged in the refining of sugar:

Income

Net profits from business operations	$78,000.00	
Mortgage interest	117.00	
Dividends (cash)	4,756.00	
Stock dividends (market value when received)	47,561.00	
Profit from redemption of bonds	195.00	
Profit from sale of bonds	195.00	
Total income		$130,824.00

Deductions

Interest paid	$390.00	
Total deductions		390.00
Net income		$130,434.00

[12] During the first year the tax would be $1,660.68.

[13] In his first year as a taxpayer his tax would be $597.95.

In the United States this corporation would pay an income tax of $10,545.80. In France it would pay more than twice this amount, $21,097.17.[14]

Case Five. A Partnership Engaged in Manufacturing.—The fifth comparison utilizes the same figures as the fourth but it is assumed that the sugar refinery, instead of being owned by a corporation, is owned by a partnership consisting of two single men without dependents, and without income other than that accruing from this partnership. In the United States the income-tax liability of these two partners arising from their interests in the profits of the firm would have been $18,856.04. In France the combined income taxes on the partnership and the partners would have been $39,514.61.[15]

Case Six. A Small Hotel Keeper.—The last of the examples to be presented is of a different character. It is essentially a tabulation of the receipts for the taxes paid for the year 1927 by a widow, the propietor of a small country inn in Normandy. In America she would have paid no income tax. Had she been located in New York State her entire direct taxes, including her tax on real estate, would scarcely have exceeded $200. Her receipts showed that she had paid taxes amounting to $357.55, classified as follows:

	Francs	*Dollars*
Real estate tax (*impôt foncier*):		
General:		
Built-on property (*bâties*)	551	21.49
Garden (*non-bâties*)	25	.98
Local tax (*taxe vicinale*):		
Built-on property	73	2.84
Garden	3	.12
Total	652	25.43
Personnelle-mobilière:		
General	97	3.78
Local tax	29	1.13
Total	126	4.91

14 In the first year it would pay $22,670.87.

15 The first-year tax would have been $54,046.

Patente	*Francs*	*Dollars*
General	535	20.87
Local	163	6.36
Chamber of Commerce	29	1.13
Taxe des poids (on kitchen scales)	3	.12
Tax for suppression of frauds	4	.16
Total	734	28.63
Dog tax (*taxe sur le chien*)	8	.31
Industrial and commercial profits tax	1,500	58.50
General income tax (*impôt général sur le revenu*)	145	5.66
Turnover tax (*chiffre d'affaires*)	6,000	234.00
Frais d'avertissement, etc.	3	.12
Grand total	9,168	$357.55

The real estate included in the foregoing computation has a market value of approximately 300,000 francs or $11,700. The *bénéfice industriel et commercial* was assessed on the assumption that the business fell in the class with a profit range of from 10,001 to 15,000 francs. The *impôt général sur le revenu* was assessed on the basis of an 18,000-franc income with a *majoration célibataire* of 10 per cent.

During the year in question the widow sold a separate piece of real estate for $4,800 and the purchaser presumably paid a special tax of 25 per cent of the purchase price.

This case, which is probably typical, serves to emphasize both the relative insignificance of the ordinary taxes on real estate in France and the relatively high degree of dependence on business taxes, especially on the turnover tax. The elimination of the turnover tax in this case would reduce the total tax bill by more than two-thirds.

Conclusions

Even though it be granted that France has paid her bill for the war almost entirely by watering her money, it is clear her taxes to-day are appreciably heavier than they were before the war, at which time they were generally conceded to be heavy. It is clear also that the French income, real-estate and business taxes, considered as a group, are much heavier than the corresponding group of taxes in America. The miscellaneous indirect taxes are, of course, enormously more heavy in France. These statements almost undoubtedly hold true, even taking into account the degree of evasion which exists. Until recently evasion of the income tax was widespread, but testimony is unanimous that since the advent of Poincaré the control, while not yet so efficient as in England or the United States, is greatly improved.

CHAPTER XX

EXPENDITURES

Expenditure figures are usually drawn up with one of two main purposes in mind. One is to find the total gross expenditures of the State in all its branches, to determine the size of the Government's operations. The other is to find a total of expenditures exclusive of those connected with state business ventures, etc. Such expenditures do not involve corresponding receipts and must therefore be met out of loans or taxes. The total of these expenditures, applied against the total of taxes collected, would show the surplus or the deficit for the fiscal year in question.

Neither of these aims has been accomplished here. The discussion in the following pages will outline the obstacles and warn against figures rather than furnish definitive answers to the questions: " How much did France spend? " and " How much of the expenditure involved corresponding receipts? "

Difficulty of Obtaining Satisfactory Figures

To find the total expenditures of the State from 1913 to 1927, one must search in five directions: the general state budget, the budgets " annexed " to the state budgets (*budgets annexes*),[1] the special Treasury accounts, the autonomous budgets such as those of the *Caisse d'Amortissement* and the state railroads, and various " hidden budgets "[2] such, for instance, as those fed by the gambling taxes. With sufficient time and labor a fairly accurate estimate of the total expenditures from the above sources might conceivably be compiled from the published figures. But the difficulty of unraveling bookkeeping entries that lead to double counting, and the uncertainty of finding every one of the " hidden

[1] Only the net credit or debit balances of these " budgets annexes " appear in the general state budget.

[2] *Cf.* p. 362.

budgets " make this task such a large one that it has been found impracticable of accomplishment here.

The most important source of double counting is the system of special Treasury accounts in their relation to the state budget. The theory of the Treasury accounts, or *services,* is that they care for expenditures which are met, either before or after, by corresponding receipts.[3] Certain state employees, for instance, must deposit money with the Government as a bond for good conduct, the money to be returned to them when they quit the service. Or the State may loan money to certain groups of citizens, which is to be repaid. To have such receipts and expenditures appear in the budget would give a false picture of the State's true financial experience during the current fiscal year or *exercice,* since such items are neither permanent receipts nor charges, and especially since the operations are often drawn out over several fiscal years.

On the other hand, some of these receipts and expenditures (connected, e.g., with the purchase and sale of bread, noted below) may be of great significance. It is in dealing with such items that double counting is apt to arise. Suppose, for instance, the receipts do not arrive after all, and the special Treasury account is balanced by a " receipt " drawn from the state budget. The item then appears in the state budget as an expense, to be covered by loans or taxes as the case may be. But it has already appeared as an expense in the Treasury account in some previous year. To add the total expenses of Treasury accounts and total expenses of the state budget, without analyzing the receipts side of the ledger, would clearly involve double counting. Such a call on the state budget has occurred so often and in such large amounts that it cannot be ignored. Thus the state budget paid the Treasury 1,304,250,000 francs in 1920 to make up the deficit of the special account opened to care for sale of bread to the public.

Another source of double counting lies in the state budget figures. No complete figures for actual budgetary expenditure are available after 1916, and the best that can be done is to use the figures for expenditures authorized (credits opened) for the fiscal year. But some of the credits opened may never be used, and may

[3] *Cf.* Allix, *Science des Finances,* p. 89 *et seq.*

be annulled at the end of the *exercice,* while double counting arises from the fact that some of the credits opened may be passed on from *exercice* to *exercice,* the same item appearing in one, two, three and even four final statements for fiscal years, while the actual expenditure, of course, occurs only in the last year. This passing-on can arise from at least two circumstances. The credits have not even been drawn upon by the ministry concerned, and are " reported " to the next *exercice.* Or the ministry may have become indebted to a private contractor, but may not yet have given him a draft in payment; in such case, the authorized credits against which these debts were contracted are transferred to the new fiscal year under the item " *dépenses d'exercices clos* " which appears in each ministry (the budget law gives no figure for the item, merely putting "*pour mémoire,*" as at the time it is not known what the amount is to be). In these cases the same credit may appear in two or more final budgetary statements. It may not be impossible to segregate completely these double-counting items, but it has not been attempted here.

Statistics of Credits Opened

In the following pages an attempt is made to arrive, not at total state expenditures, but at net expenditures involving no corresponding receipts and which must be met by taxes and loans, by giving the most reliable figures attainable on credits opened (with an attempt in one place to eliminate the double counting due to the " *dépenses d'exercices clos* "), and by giving the figures for the net deficit of the Treasury's special accounts.[4]

These figures come from two sources: (1) the *Compte Général,* 1913–1916, the *Bulletin de Statistique et de Législation Comparée,* and the *Journal Officiel;* (2) parliamentary documents, more especially, the budget *projets* for the fiscal years 1923 and 1928, and the *Inventaire* of 1924 (Annex to the *Projet de Budget*

[4] See p. 414. The best estimates of the net deficits which had to be covered by loans is, the writer believes, the statement of Treasury deficits as compiled from loan figures (see Table 1). For the rest, one must await the definitive statements of the *Compte Général.* The last one of these to appear to date is that dealing with the fiscal year 1916.

of 1925). The figures from the different sources do not, in general, check with one another, but it is worth while to show what data are available. This is done in the tables below and is followed by the differing estimates.

Figures from 1923 Projet. — A detailed statement of expenditures (credits opened) for the years 1913–1922, taken from the 1923 *projet,* is set forth in Table 64. A brief description of the different headings will make the figures more comprehensible. The first class, expenditures of the general budget, can be better understood if one first considers what the other two classes — recoverable expenditures and special services — include.

The recoverable expenditures were taken out of the general budget by the law of July 31, 1920, and from then up to, but not including, 1925 formed the debit side of a separate budget. "Recoverable" indicated that all such outlays were sometime or other to be recouped from Germany under provisions of the Treaty of Versailles, and it covered, in general, all the work of reconstruction and the civil and military pensions granted to war-sufferers. The French Government had promised its citizens that it would repay them for damages to their person and property resulting from the invasion.[5] Though it did not make such payment conditional on receipt of reparations from Germany, it was generally understood that such would be the source of the necessary funds. Germany did not pay; the expenditures were none the less made, and the State covered them by loans. Indeed, it covered even the interest on these loans by more loans, and it was not until 1922 that a part of such interest charges [6] were taken out of the loan-fed recoverable-expenditure budget and put in the general budget, to be met, theoretically, by taxes.

Thus the figures designated as "*dépenses recouvrables*" cover a miscellany of expenditures, including even interest on

[5] Law of December 26, 1914; law of June 27, 1917, establishing state adoption of war orphans (pupilles de la nation); law of March 31, 1919, extending pension rights of war-wounded; law of April 17, 1919, concerning damage to property; law of June 24, 1919, extending the law of March 31, 1919 to civilians. Allix, *op. cit.*, p. 119.

[6] See p. 80. Those concerning loans issued from the Armistice up to January 1, 1922, to cover reconstruction charges.

loans, but, on the whole, directly or indirectly connected with reconstruction and war-sufferers.

The first items under this heading, " Maintenance of the Army of Occupation," are concerned with the expenses of the army kept on the Rhine after the Armistice and peace treaty. These expenses exist yet, of course, and are now met from part of the payments under the Dawes Plan. The second item, " Military (army and navy) Services," is composed largely of the payments made to families of mobilized men, and to civil victims of the war; it also includes the cost of keeping prisoners in war-time, the bureau for the assistance of disabled veterans (*L'Office National des Mutilés et Reformés*), and the repair of damaged military establishments. The third item, " Public Debt," includes payments for military and civil pensions to war-sufferers and charges on loans floated by the *Crédit National*[7] and by groups of the war-sufferers themselves to secure the funds for reconstruction. The fourth item, " Civil Services," includes mainly the payments made by the Ministry of Liberated Regions for reconstruction purposes and the capital value of loans floated by the *Crédit National* and the war-sufferers groups to obtain money for reconstruction purposes.[8]

While it would not be exact to say that these figures of recoverable expenditures cover the whole of the reconstruction and war-sufferers' indemnity payments, the amounts given are probably a fair approximation. There seems to be an element of double counting, however, in so far as certain annual payments entered herein cover not only interest charges on loans floated by the *Crédit National* and the war-sufferers' groups (the estimated capital value of such loans is also included in the table) but also amortization payments. This apparently applies only to the years 1921 and 1922.

The recoverable expenditures are carried back beyond 1920, though the separate budget was not established until that year. This was done, says the budget *projet* from which these figures

[7] See p. 271.

[8] These details are drawn from the *Exposé des Motifs* of the 1923 budget *Projet*, p. 30 *et seq.*

were taken, by regrouping the items formerly mixed together in the general budget.

At present the reconstruction and war-sufferers' charges (of which ten billion francs remained to be paid at the beginning of 1928 [9]) are covered by the extra-budgetary item of Dawes Plan payments (cash and deliveries in kind) or else their interest and amortization charges are included in the budget (*Crédit National* "*emprunts*," ten- and thirty-year annuities [10]). Exception must be made for nearly eleven billions of outstanding ten- and six-year *Obligations de la Défense Nationale* given to the war-sufferers, for which the budget provides interest payments, but no amortization.[11] This type of loan is now resorted to for reconstruction purposes only to an insignificant degree, however (only 400 millions are to be issued in 1928), so that the present policy is, in general, not to include in the budget the capital value of the reconstruction and war-sufferers' payments made by the State each year, but to include the interest and amortization charges on these amounts, or else to meet the outlay from the Dawes Plan payments.[12]

The theory of the special Treasury accounts was briefly outlined above.[13] The figures given in Table 64 show, not the gross expenditures, but the total net debit balances of all these accounts. They must not be taken as an indication of how well or how poorly the accounts balanced their receipts and expenditures, as the debit balances would be larger had they not been diminished by grants from the state budget. Even as additions to make to the state budget expenditures, to show the amounts to be covered by loans and taxes, they are probably wide of the truth. Let the Finance Minister of the time (M. de Lasteyrie, 1923) speak: [14]

The figures which we are giving below represent the net results of

[9] Estimated by M. Palmade in his report on the Finance Ministry, Budget for 1928, p. 99 (*Doc. Parl., Chambre*, 1927, *Sess. Ord.*, Doc. No. 4872).

[10] The capital value of the "titres d'annuités" which may be issued each year is fixed by the annual budget law (*Cf.*, for example, arts. 175, 176 of law of December 27, 1927).

[11] *Palmade Report*, pp. 96–97.

[12] For more details, see pp. 293–303.

[13] See p. 414.

[14] 1923 budget *Projet, Exposé des Motifs*, p. 33.

TABLE 64

FUNCTIONAL ANALYSIS OF EXPENDITURES, AS INDICATED BY FINAL CREDITS GRANTED (*CRÉDITS DÉFINITIFS*), INCLUDING GENERAL BUDGET (*BUDGET GÉNÉRAL*), RECOVERABLE EXPENDITURES (*DÉPENSES RECOUVRABLES*), AND DEBIT BALANCES OF SPECIAL TREASURY SERVICES (*SOLDES DÉBITEURS DES SERVICES SPÉCIAUX DU TRÉSOR*), 1913–1922

(In millions of francs. Source: 1923 Budget *Projet*, *Exposé des Motifs*, p. 10 *et seq.*)

	A. Ordinary and Extraordinary Expenditures of the General Budget (*Dépenses Ordinaires et Dépenses Extraordinaires du Budget Général*)				B. Recoverable Expenditures (*Dépenses Recouvrables*)					C. Total Debit Balances of the Special Services. (*Soldes Débiteurs Globaux des Services Spéciaux*)
	"Civil Services" (*Services Civils*)	Public Debt (*Dette Publique*)	Military Expenses (*Charges Militaires*)	Total	Maintenance of the Army of Occupation. Special Account. (*Entretien des Troupes d'Occupation. Compte Spécial*)	Military Services, Army and Navy (*Services Militaires Guerre et Marine*)	Public Debt (*Dette Publique*)	"Civil Services" (*Services Civils*)	Total	
1913	1,904	1,355	1,807	5,066	......	.....	.....	......	......	6
1914	2,005	1,360	6,526	9,891	......	368	.....	4	372	108
1915	2,479	1,818	14,712	19,009	......	1,882	17	15	1,914	1,197
1916	2,817	3,327	23,853	29,997	......	2,495	107	345	2,947	3,904
1917	4,119	4,816	28,662	37,597	......	3,233	149	699	4,081	2,983
1918	5,443	7,021	36,120	48,584	......	5,250	168	534	5,952	2,113
1919	9,257	7,903	18,185	35,345	1,790	3,400	186	10,105	15,481	3,387
1920	11,377	11,747	7,648	30,772	644	1,994	3,454	16,187	22,279	5,092
1921	9,938	11,636	6,312	27,886	786	1,604	4,364	14,669[b]	21,423	2,714
1922	7,035	13,191	4,910[a]	25,136	527	453	4,973	17,131[c]	23,084	500

GRAND TOTALS (A + B + C)

	AMOUNTS					PERCENTAGES				
	"Civil Services" (*Services Civils*)	Public Debt (*Dette Publique*)	Military Expenses (*Charges Militaires*)	Special Services (*Services Spéciaux*)	Total	"Civil Services" (*Services Civils*)	Public Debt (*Dette Publique*)	Military Expenses (*Charges Militaires*)	Special Services (*Services Spéciaux*)	Total
1913	1,904	1,355	1,807	6	5,072	37.5	26.7	35.6	00.1	100
1914	2,009	1,360	6,894	108	10,371	19.4	13.1	66.5	00.1	100
1915	2,494	1,835	16,594	1,197	22,120	11.3	8.3	75.0	5.4	100
1916	3,162	3,434	26,348	3,904	36,848	8.6	9.3	71.5	10.6	100
1917	4,818	4,965	31,895	2,983	44,661	10.8	11.1	71.4	6.7	100
1918	5,977	7,189	41,370	2,113	56,649	10.6	12.7	73.0	3.72	100
1919	19,362	8,089	23,375	3,387	54,213	35.7	14.9	43.1	6.2	100
1920	27,564	15,201	10,286	5,092	58,143	47.4	26.1	17.7	8.8	100
1921	24,607	16,000	8,702	2,714	52,023	47.3	30.8	16.7	5.2	100
1922	24,166	18,164	5,890	500	48,720	49.6	37.3	12.1	1.0	100

[a] Not including supplementary credits of 180 millions for military expenses in the Near East (see p. 19 of the *Exposé des Motifs*).

[b] Including 3,769 millions as the capitalized value of the thirty-year annuities granted to groups of war-sufferers, on the basis of which they might float loans on their own account.

[c] Including 4,000 millions as the capitalized value of annuities, as above, and 8,000 millions as capital value of the loans which the *Crédit National* was authorized to float.

TABLE 65

BUDGETARY EXPENDITURE AUTHORIZED, AUGUST 1, 1914–APRIL 8, 1927

(Source: 1928 Budget *Projet, Exposé des Motifs*, pp. 67–75)

I. CREDITS GRANTED FROM AUGUST 1, 1914, THROUGH THE 1919 FISCAL YEAR

	Ordinary Civil Expenses		Military Expenses and Exceptional War Expenses	Total	Percentage of Military Expenses
	Debt	Other expenses			
Various laws (Exercice 1914. Period of the war)	59,626,763	128,881,725	6,400,925,761	6,589,434,249	97.13
Various laws (Exercice 1915)	1,899,393,673	2,449,686,102	18,455,406,750	22,804,486,525	80.92
Various laws (Exercice 1916)	3,333,015,879	2,371,725,031	27,240,404,259	32,945,145,169	82.68
Various laws (Exercice 1917)	4,863,686,400	2,750,104,103	34,065,809,126	41,679,599,629	81.73
Various laws (Exercice 1918)	7,087,677,888	3,401,679,123	44,047,748,089	54,537,105,100	80.76
Various laws (Exercice 1919)	7,986,823,151	5,228,374,327	35,823,476,970	49,038,674,448	73.05
Total of Exercices from 1914 to 1919	25,230,223,754	16,330,450,411	166,033,770,955	207,594,445,120	79.97

TABLE 65 (continued)

BUDGETARY EXPENDITURE AUTHORIZED, AUGUST 1, 1914–APRIL 8, 1927

(Source: 1928 Budget *Projet*, *Exposé des Motifs*, pp. 67–75)

II. Credits Granted, 1920–1925, and Credits Granted or Asked for, 1926–1927

	Ordinary Budget			Extraordinary Budget			Total Ordinary and Extraordinary Budget	Special Budget of Recoverable Expenditure	Grand Total	Total of Military Expenses	Percentage of Military Expenses
	Debt	Military Expenses	Other Expenses	Debt	Military Expenses	Other Expenses					
Exercice 1920	11,825,580,176	4,283,651,647	7,447,867,055	200,000,000	2,409,260,074	4,988,657,703	31,155,016,655	21,254,304,021	52,409,320,676	6,692,911,721	12.77
Exercice 1921	11,885,876,880	4,063,508,957	7,714,621,107	200,000,000	1,641,597,230	2,013,355,643	27,518,959,817	16,259,055,532	43,778,015,349	5,705,106,187	13.031
Exercice 1922	13,194,559,550	4,019,905,402	7,398,685,034	....	853,383,365	906,801,001	26,373,334,352	11,054,562,448	37,427,896,800	4,873,288,767	13.02
Exercice 1923	12,644,549,246	4,276,878,342	5,962,908,436	165,200,000	566,545,125	546,325,958	24,162,407,107	13,781,972,873	37,944,379,980	4,843,423,467	12.764
Exercice 1924	12,930,459,273	5,232,438,945	6,411,761,406	143,210,000	713,199,993	4,002,942,386	29,434,012,003	11,780,045,115	41,214,057,118	5,945,638,938	14.426
Exercice 1925	19,389,946,302	5,582,118,851	7,199,475,059	90,750,000	406,961,181	454,210,105	33,123,461,498	1,062,608,156	34,186,069,654	5,989,080,032	17.519
Exercice 1926	22,875,726,058	7,120,045,117	9,075,825,927	93,650,000	620,178,991	78,935,672	39,864,361,765	1,066,811,171[a]	40,931,172,936[c]	7,740,224,108	18.91
Exercice 1927	22,540,502,971	7,513,157,410	9,281,625,559	83,250,000	3,193,287,112	168,339,003	42,780,162,055	1,222,569,758[b]	44,002,731,813[d]	10,706,444,422	24.33
Total of Exercices from 1920 to 1927	127,287,200,456	42,091,704,671	60,492,769,583	976,060,000	10,404,413,071	13,159,567,471	254,411,715,252	77,481,929,074	331,893,644,326	52,496,117,642	15.817
Total of Exercices from 1914 to 1919	....	....	....	....	....	....	....	....	207,594,445,120	....	....
Total of Exercices from 1914 to 1927	....	....	....	....	....	....	....	....	539,488,089,446	....	....

[a], [b] For these two years the heading changes from "Special budget of recoverable expenditure" to "Non-recurring expenses concerned with reconstruction (reparations des dommages de guerre)," though it appears the change should include 1925 too, as the separate recoverable expenditures budget was abolished in that year.

[c], [d] Unlike those of former years, these totals, it would seem, do not include the expenses of the state railways, which since 1925 have been given an autonomous budget, not under Parliamentary control.

transactions which have been entered on the books for each respective year. It must be pointed out that some of the charge entries do not correspond to actual cash payments by the Treasury, for instance, in the case of advances to foreign governments (advances to Russia secured by bonds, advances in the form of opening of credits which have not been availed of). Equally, some of the credits do not show actual receipts in cash. On the other hand, numerous purchases made outside of France have been paid for by the Treasury from the balances which it had built up abroad, and these transactions are not yet all included in the Special Accounts, since they have not been definitively settled [*liquidés*]. Besides, in a general way and in particular for those branches of *services* which have put through numerous transactions abroad (food supplies,[15] gasoline and oils, merchant marine), the entries on the books of expenses and receipts have been made with considerable delay. The following statement does not therefore always show with exactness the charge actually borne by the Treasury in each of the years under consideration.

The expenditures included under recoverable expenses and special services have been broadly outlined. No analysis need be made here of the remaining items — the ordinary and extraordinary expenses of the general budget. They include the usual administrative, military and debt service charges of any budget, except as these have been accorded special treatment. The distinction between "ordinary" and "extraordinary" is discussed elsewhere.[16]

Figures from 1928 Projet. — The figures just given (Table 64) do not go beyond 1922. Estimates for expenditures beyond that point may be taken, first, from the *Projet* for the 1928 budget, where there is given a list of credits granted or asked for ("*ouverts ou demandés*") from August 1, 1914 to April 8, 1927, for each fiscal year. This is reproduced in Table 65, pages 420 and 421. Note that this table does not include estimates of the debit balances of the special Treasury "*services.*"

Figures from Inventaire. — Another source for figures beyond 1922 (but only up to 1924) is the *Inventaire*. It is not as detailed as the other sources, but it gives figures for the debit balances of the special Treasury "*services.*" The figures are reproduced in Table 66.

[15] "Ravitaillement."

[16] See p. 51.

TABLE 66

FUNCTIONAL ANALYSIS OF EXPENDITURES, AS INDICATED BY FINAL CREDITS GRANTED (*CRÉDITS DÉFINITIFS*), INCLUDING GENERAL BUDGET (*BUDGET GÉNÉRAL*), RECOVERABLE EXPENDITURES (*DÉPENSES RECOUVRABLES*), AND DEBIT BALANCES OF SPECIAL TREASURY SERVICES (*SOLDES DÉBITEURS DES SERVICES SPÉCIAUX DU TRÉSOR*), 1919–1924

(In billions of francs. Source: *Inventaire*, p. 21)

Year	A. Ordinary and Extraordinary Expenditures of the General Budget. (*Dépenses Ordinaires et Dépenses Extraordinaires du Budget Général*)				B. Recoverable Expenditures (*Dépenses Recouvrables*)	C. Total Debit Balances of the Special Services (*Soldes Débiteurs Globaux des Services Spéciaux*)	Grand Total
	"civil services" (*Dépenses des Services Civils*)	public debt (*Charges de la Dette Publique*)	military expenses (*Charges Militaires*)	total			
1919	9.2	7.9	18.2	35.3	15.5	3.4	54.2
1920	11.4	11.7	7.6	30.7	22.3	5.1	58.1
1921	9.9	11.1	6.0	27.0	21.4	2.7	51.1
1922	7.7	13.6	5.0	26.3	22.1	0.5	48.9
1923	6.5	12.8	4.8	24.1	21.7	....	45.8
1924	?	?	?	?	?	....	40.2

Figures Compiled from Monthly Statements. — Finally there are available certain data drawn from the *Compte Général* for 1913–1916, and from the *Bulletin de Statistique et de Législation Comparée* (checked, where inconsistencies have appeared, with its source, the *Journal Officiel*) for 1917–1926. These data are briefly summarized in Tables 67, 68, and 69. As originally compiled, with the figures classified by ministries and various discrepancies noted, the figures were too voluminous to justify reproduction here in full. The headings of the columns in Table 67 require some explanation. The first column for each year, the total of credits opened by Parliament, is the only one in the table that gives an adequate idea of probable expenditures, and even it is apparently not as reliable as those taken from the summaries presented in the 1923 — and perhaps the 1928 — budget *projets*, as they take no account of any supplementary credits opened for the *exercice* after the summary, usually compiled in the spring just at the theoretical close of the fiscal year, was made. They have one advantage, however; they permit allowance to be made for the double counting caused by the "*dépenses*

TABLE 67

DISTRIBUTION OF CREDITS GRANTED AMONG VARIOUS BUDGETS

(Sources: See text, p. 423.)

"*Exercices Clos*" and "*Fonds de Concours*" items are included in "Total Credits" column unless otherwise noted.

	Total Credits Opened	Expenditures of the "*exercices clos et périmés*"	Credits from the "*fonds de concours et des dons et legs*"	Total "*émissions*"	Total Credits Opened	Expenditures of the "*exercices clos et périmés*"	Credits from the "*fonds de concours et des dons et legs*"	Total "*émissions*"
	1918				1919			
Ordinary budget of civil "*services*"	6,327,323,740.13	[a]21,807,127.34	....	5,895,870,667.10	11,820,689,546.40	....	....	8,648,842,150.43
Budget of the military expenditures and exceptional expenditures of the civil "*services*"	46,933,069,589.29	....	[b]846,100,000.00	36,511,258,980.36	37,830,923,785.23	....	[a]83,000,000.00	29,661,921,226.01
Total	53,260,393,329.42	21,807,127.34	846,100,000.00	42,407,129,647.46	49,651,613,331.63	....	83,000,000.00	38,310,763,376.44
	1920				1921			
Ordinary budget	25,197,529,212.16	1,940,332,596.08	[d]199,924,881.90	19,806,975,425.76	26,391,278,981.97	2,221,556,212.45	145,767,114.59	20,031,761,342.57
Extraordinary budget	6,329,936,494.11	[a]29,578,080.71	18,451,645.44	4,871,167,230.76	4,183,693,318.58	153,428,778.60	4,472,270.41	2,976,430,113.55
Special budget of recoverable expenditures	21,265,420,934.81	....	275,859.81	11,106,124,521.56	16,617,399,814.44	5,456,050.50	2,104,005.94	4,404,577,699.44
Special Treasury account: Maintenance of troops of occupation abroad	....	....	....	....	785,609,128.35	....	365.35	471,621,742.10
Total	52,792,886,641.08	1,969,910,676.79	218,652,387.15	35,784,267,178.08	47,977,981,243.34	2,380,441,041.55	152,343,756.29	27,884,390,897.66
	1922				1923			
General budget	29,276,621,338.23	[f]2,690,505,440.27	290,387,957.07	19,460,409,145.03	26,881,492,059.74	2,760,721,445.74	156,801,908.52	17,497,917,222.06
Special budget of recoverable expenditures	20,331,975,684.86	9,609,625,530.03	1,487,344.63	16,197,194,233.33	14,779,443,182.57	890,541,037.99	5,983,310,401.44	9,849,025,733.40

	1922				1923			
Special Treasury account: Maintenance of troops of occupation abroad	537,335,495.00	....	....	362,347,629.50	1,040,927,496.36	....	....	792,904,363.54
Total	50,145,932,518.09	12,300,130,970.30	291,875,301.70	36,019,951,007.86	42,701,862,738.67	3,651,262,483.73	6,140,112,309.96	28,139,847,319.00
	1924				1925			
General budget	27,828,634,111.41	[e,h] 2,631,961,820.14	[i] 189,720,951.12	19,747,361,353.63	[f] 34,669,806,817.61	569,294,655.47	192,457,036.60	25,272,939,904.59
Special budget of recoverable expenditures	13,240,032,053.04	1,457,031,841.07	490,802.65	10,232,043,277.70	....	....	....	....
Special Treasury account: Maintenance of troops of occupation abroad	818,754,144.79	12,845,573.79	....	656,191,491.95	680,721,530.60	30,356,687.60	....	573,942,442.44
Total	41,887,420,309.24	4,101,839,235.00	190,211,753.77	30,635,596,123.28	35,350,528,348.21	599,651,343.07	192,457,036.60	25,846,882,347.03
	1926							
General budget	42,780,770,371.55	292,410,380.22	167,999,405.79	24,485,017,075.56				
Special Treasury account: Maintenance of troops of occupation abroad	550,450,566.07	25,207,831.07	....	524,637,666.75				
Total	43,331,220,937.62	317,618,211.29	167,999,405.79	25,009,654,742.31				

[a] Included in the "émissions," as "mandaté au titre d'exercices clos," not in "credits opened."

[b] Expenditures made for the account of various departments on sums furnished by them. Included in the "émissions," not in "credits opened."

[c] Expenditures made for the account of the war department on sums furnished by it. Included in the "émissions," not in "credits opened."

[d] Part of this amount is included in the "émissions," not in "credits opened," as follows:

69,499.84 — credits from the "fonds de concours."
1,200,000.00 — expenditures made for the account of the war department on sums furnished by it.
31,053,300.00 — expenditures made for the account of the war department on sums furnished by it.
4,713,600.00 — expenditures made for the account of the marine department on sums furnished by it.

[e] Part of this amount (2,482,214.15) is included in the "émissions," not in "credits opened."

[f] Including 1,638,665.99 — credits from "exercices périmés." Included in the "credits opened."

[g] Including 252,307,861.70 "dépenses d'exercices périmés" and 15,502,916.65 "dépenses d'exercices clos et périmés." Included in the "credits opened."

[h] Part of this amount (129,315,818.19) is included in the "émissions," not in "credits opened."

[i] Part of this amount (26,940,000.00) is included in the "émissions," not in "credits opened."

[j] Including 2,652,910,011.82 — "ordonnances émises sur chapitre R-18." Included in the "credits opened."

d'exercices clos." This is not done in this table, but is deferred to Table 68.

The column headed "*fonds de concours*" gives figures for sums paid to the State from outside sources for a special purpose and sent through the budget on their way to being spent. They first appear in two of the Treasury's special accounts as receipts, then as expenses as the Treasury accounts turn the money over to the budget, where they appear as "*recettes d'ordre,*" then as expenses in the budget as they are actually spent. This, by the way, is another example of double counting involved in adding the total expenditures of the Treasury accounts to those of the budget.

The last column, headed "*émissions,*" shows the drafts, or "*ordonnances*" given to the State's creditors — that is, the amount actually spent against budgetary credits (save as the State's creditors fail to present their drafts for payment: unless they do so within five years, their claims become invalid). But these figures are in no sense indicative of the total expenditures even of the state budget alone, for many of the expenditures are made without first issuing *ordonnances,* and later (after the figures in Table 67 are compiled) are covered by blanket *ordonnances.* The holders of the *rentes,* for instance, get their interest payments by merely presenting their "*titres de rente*" or coupons, which payments are later "regularized" by blanket *ordonnances.*[17] Another important instance of *ordonnances* issued after the figures in Table 67 are drawn up, occurs when it is found that at the end of the fiscal year some minister has gone beyond his parliamentary grants, despite the elaborate administrative checks devised to prevent this. Parliament must open a supplementary credit, after which follows the *ordonnance.* There are still other examples of *ordonnances* issued after the figures in Table 67 are compiled.[18] Further summaries of the figures are given in Table 68. This table, derived directly from Table 67, shows the total credits after allowance has been made for "*dépenses d'exercices clos.*"

[17] Girault, *Législation financière, Première Partie, les Budgets et le Trésor,* p. 120. Allix, *op. cit.*, p. 259.

[18] *Cf.* Allix, *op. cit.*, chapter xxiii, especially p. 240.

TABLE 68

CREDITS OPENED BY END OF FISCAL YEAR, 1920–1926, AFTER DEDUCTION OF CREDITS OPENED FOR "*DÉPENSES D'EXERCICES CLOS*"

(In millions of francs. Source: Table 67)

	1920	1921	1922	1923	1924	1925	1926
General budget..........	29,560	28,200	26,586	24,121	25,326	34,101	42,488
Budget of recoverable expenditures............	21,265	16,612	10,722	13,889	11,783	.....	.....
Total..........	50,825	44,812	37,308	38,010	37,109	34,101	42,488
Special Treasury account..	.....	786	537	1,041	806	650	525
Grand Total.....	50,825	45,598	37,846	39,051	37,915	34,751	43,014

Comparison of Various Figures of Credits Opened. — Comparison may now be made of the statistics given for at least a part of the state expenditure. Table 69 presents such a comparison of budgetary credits opened, with some data on deficits from the Treasury special "*services.*"

Columns 3, 4 and 5, and columns 7 and 10 in Table 69 are the ones that can be best compared. The figures for the earlier years — especially 1913 and 1917–1919, show a close correspondence, but beyond 1919 the variations are wide. So far as the writer knows, there is no way to reconcile them until the *Comptes Généraux* appear.

The only sources of estimates that include the debit balances of the special Treasury "*services*" remain the 1923 budget *projet* and the *Inventaire,* the figures from which are given in columns 5 to 10 of the table.

It must be borne in mind that none of these figures pretends to give the total gross expenditures by the State, nor are they strictly comparable from year to year. This situation arises mainly from the following causes:

(a) The figures for budgetary grants do not include the expenditures of the annexed budgets, for only the credit or debit balances of these annexed budgets are carried into the main budget. Thus, before 1923 the total expenditures by the postal, telegraph, and telephone monopoly appeared in the main body of the budget, and are apparently included in the tables presented here (scattered throughout various ministries — Ministry of Public Works, Ministry of Finance, etc.[19]); but for 1923 and the following years these expenses — which for 1928 exceed 3.5 billion francs — have disappeared from the main body of credits granted and the figures in Table 69 are correspondingly diminished. The expenses of the state railroad were carried in a *budget annexe* before the war, and now do not even appear there, as the railroad has an autonomous budget. Since October 1926 the expenses of the state tobacco monopoly are not included in the budget, as they are accounted for in the books of the *Caisse d'Amortissement*, and interest and amortization of *Bons de la Défense Nationale* and of the monopoly's own bonds are likewise cared for here, outside the state budget. All this is not to say that the figures given in these tables cannot be refined so that the various years can be made more comparable with one another; but it is to warn the reader that the present work has not attempted the task, and that the figures as they appear even in official publications require extensive interpretation before they can be compared, or before one can assert he knows how much the State spends.

(b) The gross expenditures from various special Treasury "*services*" or accounts — with the exception of the one for maintenance of troops abroad, for which Parliament must grant credits — are not included. At best, only the net debit balances are shown.

(c) There are certain "hidden" budgets, not budgets at all properly speaking, the expenditures of which do not appear in either the general budget, the annexed budgets, or the Treasury accounts. They are of relatively minor importance. A certain amount is taken from the proceeds of the state horse-race betting monopoly, the *pari-mutuel,* and is turned over to the *Caisse des Dépots et Consignations,* which in turn expends it in the manner authorized by law, without either the receipts or expenditures appearing in any budget. The Ministry of the Interior receives a

[19] Allix, *op. cit.*, p. 152.

part of the tax on gambling in casinos, to be paid to certain health and other establishments, in the same manner.[20]

TABLE 69

COMPARISON OF STATISTICS ON BUDGETARY CREDITS GRANTED (WITH SOME DATA ON TREASURY "*SERVICES*" DEFICITS), 1913–1926

(In millions of francs)

	Various Sources [a]			1928 Budget *Projet*	1923 Budget *Projet*			*Inventaire*		
	1 Budgetary Credits Granted against Budget Revenue [b]	2 Budgetary Credits Granted for Special Treasury Account [c]	3 Total Budgetary Credits Granted	4 Budgetary Credits Granted [d]	5 Budgetary Credits Granted [e]	6 Debit Balance of Special Treasury "*Services*"	7 Total of Estimated Expenditures	8 Budgetary Credits Granted [f]	9 Debit Balance of Special Treasury "*Services*"	10 Total of Estimated Expenditures
1913	5,067	......	5,067	......	5,066	6	5,072	......	......	......
1914	10,065	......	10,065	......	10,263	108	10,371	......	......	10,400
1915	20,925	......	20,925	22,804	20,923	1,197	22,120	......	......	22,100
1916	30,916	......	30,916	32,945	32,944	3,904	36,848	......	......	36,800
1917	41,919	......	41,919	41,680	41,678	2,983	44,661	......	......	44,600
1918	53,260	......	53,260	54,537	54,536	2,113	56,649	......	......	56,600
1919	49,651	......	49,651	49,039	50,826	3,387	54,213	50,800	3,400	54,200
1920	50,825	......	50,825	52,409	53,051	5,092	58,143	53,000	5,100	58,100
1921	44,812	786	45,598	43,778 [g]	49,309	2,714	52,023	48,400	2,700	51,100
1922	37,308	537	37,845	37,428 [g′]	48,220	500	48,720	48,400	500	48,900
1923	38,010	1,041	39,051	37,944	......	......	......	45,800	......	45,800
1924	37,109	806	37,915	41,214	......	......	......	40,200	......	40,200
1925	34,101	650	34,751	34,186	......	......	......	......	......	......
1926	42,488	525	43,013	40,931 [h]	......	......	......	......	......	......
1927	......	......	......	44,003 [i]	......	......	......	......	......	......

[a] 1913–1916, *Comptes Généraux;* 1917–1926, *Bulletin de Statistique et de Législation Comparée*, and *Journal Officiel*. See also Table 67 for 1918–1926.

[b] After subtraction of any "dépenses d'exercices clos" items originally included in the total of credits granted.

[c] This is the account dealing with maintenance of the army of occupation in Germany. The other sources of figures for "budgetary credits granted" do not say whether or not these Treasury-account credits are included in their totals, but it seems probable that they are.

[d, e, f] The *projets* and the *Inventaire* do not indicate whether or not allowance has been made for the "dépenses d'exercices clos" to avoid double counting.

[g, g′] The enormous discrepancy in budgetary credits granted, between the 1928 *projet's* figures and those of the 1923 *projet* and the *Inventaire* appears to come from the inclusion in the latter two of the *capital value* of annuities and bonds given to the war sufferers instead of merely the carrying charges on these loans. See footnotes (*b*) and (*c*) to Table 64.

[h, i] Unlike the rest of the figures in this column, these are only for credits asked for in the budget *projet*, instead of the credits actually granted by law.

[20] Allix, *op. cit.*, pp. 107–108, notes. See also p. 362.

Comparison of Expenditure Figures from Secondary Sources

Finally it is of interest to compare expenditure figures given in several of the published studies of French finance. They are shown in Table 70.

The *Gold and Silver Inquiry Report* figures do not check with any of the figures presented here. A study of the detailed table presented in the *Inquiry Report* shows that the recoverable expenditures figures are the same as reprinted here from the 1923 budget *projet*. The other figures that go to make up the total were taken, says the *Inquiry*, from the *Bulletin de Statistique*, the Senate report on the 1920 budget, and the budgets for 1923 and 1925. Germain-Martin's figures are apparently taken from the *Inventaire*.

TABLE 70

COMPARISON OF STATISTICS OF TOTAL EXPENDITURES SHOWN IN VARIOUS PUBLISHED WORKS, 1913–1925

(In billions of francs)

	Gold and Silver Inquiry, Senate Document, 1925, Serial 9, Vol. I, p. 493	Germain-Martin, *Les Finances publiques*, etc., pp. 131–132 [a]	Cahill, *Report on the Economic and Industrial Conditions*, 1926, p. 36	Moulton, *The French Debt Problem*, pp. 52, 59, 85 [b]	*Le Temps*, December 4, 1924	Fisk, *French Public Finance*, p. 22 [c]
1913	5.067		5.072	5.072	5.046	
1914	10.065	10.4	10.371	10.371		10.371
1915	20.889	22.1	21.400	22.120		22.120
1916	36.848	36.8	36.848	36.848		36.848
1917	44.661	44.7	44.661	44.661		44.661
1918	56.649	56.7	56.649	56.649		56.649
1919	54.213	54.2	54.253	54.2	35.345	54.213
1920	58.143	58.1	58.163	58.1	39.523	58.143
1921	52.023	51.1	52.023	51.1	35.603	52.023
1922	49.719 [d]	48.9	48.220	48.9	34.386	
1923	42.635 [d]	45.8	41.701	45.8	32.583	
1924	36.911 [d]	40.2	41.882	45.5	31.891 [f]	
1925	33.990 [e]		38.094		33.195 [f]	
1926			39.658 [f]			
1927			39.960 [f]			

[a] Source is apparently the *Inventaire*.
[b] In part from budget *projet*, 1923, pp. 10–33.
[c] Source: Ministry of Finance.
[d] Credits granted.
[e] Credits asked for. Estimate in budget *projet*.
[f] Provisional figure.

Cahill's figures are the same as those in the 1923 *projet*, with the exception of four individual items, which exceptions make four of the totals differ slightly from those in Table 64.

The figures from *Le Temps* do not agree with any of the sources quoted here.

Fisk's figures for 1914–1918 agree with those in the *Inventaire*, though they are carried out further. For 1919–1921 they check rather closely with those in the 1923 *projet*.

Comparison of Deficits Calculated by Two Methods

As has been noted, the writer believes that in determining the amount of the deficits since 1913, it is better to use the analysis of Treasury operations than to set off the figures of receipts against those of expenditures. The latter task has been attempted in a rough way, however, so that the results may be compared with those arrived at by using Treasury statistics. Table 71, on page 432, shows the results of such comparison.

Conclusions

After wading through the morass of figures in expenditure the reader will find himself almost at the point from which he started. The journey will probably have not been in vain, however, if it convinces him that any confident statement on how much France spent during and after the war — and even how much she is spending to-day — must be looked at with a cold and suspicious eye. Apparently nobody yet knows, and it seems quite probable that no one ever will know exactly.

In summary, the main points that any compiler of state expenditures from 1913 to 1927 will have to bear in mind are:

(a) The necessity of collecting figures from the general budget (and for 1920–1924, from the recoverable expenditures budget), the annexed budgets, the autonomous budgets, the special Treasury accounts, and the " hidden budgets," if an estimate of total expenditures is to be made.

TABLE 71
COMPARISON OF ESTIMATES OF DEFICITS BASED ON ANALYSIS OF RECEIPTS AND EXPENDITURES AND ON ANALYSIS OF TREASURY OPERATIONS

Sources: 1913–1918: Budget *Projet*, 1923, p. 10 *et seq.*; 1920–1924: *Inventaire*, p. 21; *Experts' Report*, pp. 148–9. Also see footnotes.

(In billions of francs)

Year	As Arrived at by Comparison of Receipts and Expenditures				As Arrived at by Analysis of Treasury Operations			
	Receipts	Expenditures	Deficits	Cumulative Total	Borrowings	Reimbursements	Deficits	Cumulative Total
1913	4.907	5.072	.165	.165	.091	.000	.091	.091
1914	4.196	10.371	6.175	6.340	6.299	.042	6.257	6.348
1915	4.130	22.120	17.990	24.330	20.708	.402	20.306	26.654
1916	4.932	36.848	31.916	56.246	29.583	.347	29.236	55.890
1917	6.186	44.661	38.475	94.721	35.633	.512	35.121	91.011
1918	6.791	56.649	49.858	144.579	37.668	.442	37.226	128.237
1919	11.586	54.213	42.627	187.206	51.331	2.676	48.655	176.892
1920	20.100	58.100	38.000	225.206	42.822	5.136	37.686	214.578
1921	23.100	51.100	28.000	253.206	31.208[a]	5.066	26.054	240.632
1922	24.200	48.900	24.700	277.906	20.248[a]	2.088	17.947	258.579
1923	27.700	45.800	18.100	296.006	18.089[a]	1.451	16.638	275.217
1924	31.100	40.200	9.100	305.106	11.298[a]	3.680	7.618	282.835
1925		35.351[c]			18.755[a]	13.407	5.348	288.183
1926		43.331[d]			6.602[a]	6.081	.521	288.704[b]

[a] Includes "contrevaleur des émissions de jetons métalliques".
[b] Not including the operations of the "Caisse d'Amortissement" established August, 1926.
[c] Total credits opened, *Journal Officiel*, September 15, 1926.
[d] Total credits opened, *Bulletin de Statistique*, May, 1927, p. 1059.

(b) The danger of double counting caused by transfers of sums both ways between the Treasury accounts and the budgets.

(c) The danger of incompleteness and of double counting in the use of figures for credits opened, as long as complete figures for amounts actually spent are unavailable.

If a summary of the entire nation's expenditures were to be undertaken, allowance would have to be made for double counting as between state and local figures.

The foregoing analysis has been concerned with the nature of the statistics rather than with what they reveal. No study of the distribution of expenditures is made here, but there may be cited the calculation worked out in the *Chéron Report* in the Senate on the 1928 budget.[21] Out of every 100 francs spent by the State, said M. Chéron, the following distribution is made:

	Francs
Public debt (including amortization)	41.50
Retirement pensions, war pensions and care of war victims	16.44
Civil and military personnel	16.44
National defense	15.61
Pouvoirs publics	.15
Charity and other aid	1.85
" International " expenses	.06
Other " civil expenses "	7.95
Total	100.00

[21] *Le Temps*, December 18, 1927.

APPENDICES

APPENDIX A

LIST OF FRENCH PRIME MINISTERS AND MINISTERS OF FINANCE

1914 — 1929

(Source: *Annuaire Générale Larousse*)

Date of formation of cabinet		Date of resignation of cabinet	*Prime Minister*	*Minister of Finance*
Dec. 9, 1913	—	June 6, 1914	Doumergue	Caillaux
June 9, 1914	—	June 12, 1914	Ribot	Clémentel
June 13, 1914	—	Aug. 26, 1914	Viviani	Noulens
Aug. 27, 1914	—	Oct. 29, 1915	Viviani	Ribot
Oct. 29, 1915	—	Dec. 8, 1916	Briand	Ribot
Dec. 12, 1916	—	Mar. 17, 1917	Briand	Ribot
Mar. 20, 1917	—	Sep. 12, 1917	Ribot	Thierry
Sep. 13, 1917	—	Nov. 15, 1917	Painlevé	Klotz
Nov. 16, 1917	—	Jan. 17, 1920	Clemenceau	Klotz
Jan. 20, 1920	—	Sep. 23, 1920	Millerand	François-Marsal
Sep. 24, 1920	—	Jan. 12, 1921	Leygues	François-Marsal
Jan. 16, 1921	—	Jan. 12, 1922	Briand	Doumer
Jan. 15, 1922	—	Mar. 26, 1924	Poincaré	De Lasteyrie
Mar. 30, 1924	—	June 1, 1924	Poincaré	François-Marsal
June 9, 1924	—	June 13, 1924	François-Marsal	François-Marsal
June 16, 1924	—	Apr. 10, 1925	Herriot	Clémentel De Monzie
Apr. 17, 1925	—	Oct. 27, 1925	Painlevé	Caillaux
Oct. 29, 1925	—	Nov. 22, 1925	Painlevé	Painlevé
Nov. 28, 1925	—	Mar. 6, 1926	Briand	Loucheur Doumer
Mar. 9, 1926	—	June 15, 1926	Briand	Péret
June 23, 1926	—	July 17, 1926	Briand	Caillaux
July 19, 1926	—	July 21, 1926	Herriot	De Monzie
July 23, 1926	—	Nov. 6, 1928	Poincaré	Poincaré
Nov. 11, 1928	—	July 26, 1929	Poincaré	Chéron
July 30, 1929	—	Oct. 22, 1929	Briand	Chéron

APPENDIX B

NOTE ON STABILIZATION LAW OF JUNE 25, 1928

TEXT OF MONETARY LAW [1]

The Senate and the Chamber of Deputies have adopted, the President of the Republic promulgates, the law of which the text follows:

Art. 1. The provisions of article 3 of the law of August 5, 1914, which establish, temporarily, inconvertibility (*le cours forcé*) of the notes of the Bank of France and of the Bank of Algeria are abrogated.

Art. 2. The franc, the French monetary unit, contains 65.5 milligrams of gold, nine-tenths fine.[2]

The present [new] definition does not apply to international payments which, before the promulgation of the present law, were validly stipulated to be in gold francs.

Art. 3. The Bank of France must guarantee, to the bearer and at sight, the convertibility of its notes in gold. It has the power of guaranteeing this convertibility, either in redeeming its notes in gold coins, which are legal tender, or in exchanging for them gold at the rate of 65.5 milligrams of gold nine-tenths fine, per franc.

It has the power of making no such redemptions or exchanges except at its central office and for minimum amounts which shall be fixed by agreement between the Minister of Finance and the Bank of France.

[1] *Journal Officiel, Lois et Décrets,* June 25, 1928.

[2] This makes the dollar worth 25.52 of the new francs; the pound sterling, 124.21 francs. It appears that the smallest coined piece of gold will be the 100-franc piece, worth approximately $3.92. *Cf. L'Economiste Français,* July 7, 1928, p. 2.

[There follows a similar section, relative to the Bank of Algeria.]

The Bank of France must buy gold at the windows of its central office and such branches as it may choose, at the rate of one franc per 65.5 milligrams of gold, nine-tenths fine, and without deduction of interest. It will have the power to recover from the seller the costs of mintage at the rate of the Paris mint. The costs of assaying will be defrayed by the seller.

Art. 4. The Bank of France must keep a reserve in gold bullion and coin equal to at least 35 per cent of the total of the notes in circulation and the current deposits.[3]

Previous legal provisions fixing a maximum for the amount of Bank of France notes in circulation are abrogated.

Art. 5. There shall be made by the mint gold pieces of 100 francs, nine-tenths fine.

The limit of tolerance of quality (of the gold) is fixed at one one-thousandth either way. The limit of tolerance of weight is fixed at two one-thousandths either way.

These coins shall be legal tender up to any amount.

Art. 6. A decree by the Council of Ministers shall fix the date after which the mint shall resume the free coinage of gold for private persons. This decree shall fix the conditions under which the gold shall be admitted for mintage on the basis fixed in article 2, and shall fix the cost of mintage.

Until the publication of this decree, the mintage of gold coins can be executed by the mint only for the account of the Bank of France, and the cost of mintage shall be 40 francs per kilogram of gold, nine-tenths fine.

Art. 7. To replace the five,- ten,- and twenty-franc notes of the Bank of France, which shall be retired from circulation be-

[3] Before the war no such legal ratio requirement existed; instead, the total amount of notes the Bank could issue was fixed by law. The latter provision is now done away with, the legal ratio requirement being introduced instead.

fore December 31, 1932, after which date they shall cease to be legal tender, the mint shall produce, for the account of the State, silver coins of a face value of 10 and 20 francs, sixty-eight one-hundredths fine, up to but not exceeding a total of three billions (*milliards*) of francs.

The weights of the silver coins are fixed as follows:

Ten grams for each ten-franc piece.

Twenty grams for each twenty-franc piece.

The limit of tolerance shall be five one-thousandths both for the weight and the quality.

One-third of the profit resulting from the mintage of the silver coins shall be paid, at the end of each fiscal year, to a reserve fund destined for the maintenance of the monetary circulation; the other two-thirds shall be put to the use noted in article 6 of the convention entered into June 23, 1928 between the President of the Council, Minister of Finance, and the Governor of the Bank of France.

In transactions between private persons, the silver coins need be accepted only up to a maximum of 250 francs.[4]

The types of the new coins, gold and silver, shall be fixed under conditions laid down by decree.

Art. 8. The tokens of the Chambers of Commerce,[5] at the same rate as they are withdrawn from circulation, shall be replaced, kind for kind, by coins minted by the State.

In transactions between private persons, the bronze-aluminum coins need be accepted only up to a total of 50 francs, the nickel and bronze coins only up to a total of 10 francs.

Art. 9. After the promulgation of the present law, all gold and silver coins minted before this date shall cease to be legal tender as between private persons, and shall not be received by the public Treasury.

[4] This marks the definite abandonment, by France, of the bimetallic standard. Up to 1914 the five-franc silver pieces remaining in circulation were legal tender up to any amount.

[5] Small coins issued during the war period.

Art. 10. The gold and silver reserves at present held by banks which have received from the State the privilege of note issuance in the colonies and protectorates where the franc is legal tender, shall be revalued on the basis of the new monetary par.

The Minister of Finance is authorized to conclude with the above banks of issue conventions fixing the conditions under which the State shall receive the total of the surpluses [arising from the revaluation].

Art. 11. The deposit accounts at the Treasury, opened at the central office of the Treasury as per the *arrêté* of the Minister of Finance of December 17, 1920, are abolished.

Article 104 of the law of April 19, 1926, is abrogated save as concerns the deposits made by groups forced or authorized to deposit their free funds with the Treasury.

The above provisions shall take effect July 1, 1928.

Art. 12. The law of 17 *germinal, an* XI on the mintage and testing of coins is abrogated.[6]

There are, and shall remain, abrogated:

The law of November 15, 1915, prohibiting the export of gold bullion, gold coins and silver coins.

The law of April 12, 1916, prohibiting the export of silver bullion.

The decrees of April 1, 1915 and December 2, 1921, prohibiting the export of nickel and token coins, as well as bronze-aluminum coins.

The laws of February 12, 1916 and October 16, 1919, regulating dealings in national money.

The law of October 20, 1919, forbidding the melting and demonetization of national coins.

[6] This law first defined the franc in terms of silver (5 grams, 9/10 fine) and then stated that one kilogram of gold, 9/10 fine, should be equivalent to 155 pieces of 20 francs each This made the franc equal to .3225774 + grams of gold, 9/10 fine. *Cf. L'Economiste Européen*, June 29, 1928, p. 404.

The provisions of the law of April 3, 1918 and subsequent laws concerning prohibition of export of French bank notes above a certain amount.

The law of August 7, 1926, concerning operations with a view toward stabilizing the money, as well as all other laws the provisions of which run counter to the present text.

Art. 13. There are approved:

1. The convention passed June 23, 1928, between the President of the Council, Minister of Finance, and the Governor of the Bank of France;

2. The convention passed June 23, 1928, between the President of the Council, Minister of Finance, and the presidents of the council of administration and of the financial committee of the *Caisse Autonome* for the handling of the *Bons de la Défense Nationale* and for the amortization of the public debt;

3. The convention passed June 23, 1928 between the presidents of the council of administration and of the financial committee of the *Caisse Autonome* [etc.] and the Governor of the Bank of France.

These conventions are exempt from the stamp and registration taxes.

The present law, deliberated upon and adopted by the Senate and by the Chamber of Deputies, will be executed as law by the State.

Done at Paris, the 25th of June, 1928.

Gaston Doumergue

By the President of the Republic:
The President of the Council,
Minister of Finance,
Raymond Poincaré.

TABLE 72

COMPARATIVE BALANCE SHEETS OF THE BANK OF FRANCE, BEFORE AND AFTER STABILIZATION [*]

(In thousands of francs)

ASSETS

June 21, 1928		June 25, 1928	
Bank reserves:		Gold reserves	
Gold: In France	3,678,542	(coin and bullion)	28,934,885 [a]
Free, and gold resources abroad	462,771		
Abroad, but not available	1,401,549		
Total	5,542,863	Silver coins and token money	233
Silver	342,944		
	5,885,807		
Resources and assets abroad: Claim against the State Bank of Russia	*mémoire*		
Resources abroad	63,291	Resources abroad (sight claims)	15,984,601
Purchases of gold, silver and exchange	2,963,040	Foreign exchange loaned	9,777,768 [b]
Bills matured yesterday, to be paid today	10,834	Advances on bullion and gold coin	37,259
Current postal accounts	467,018	Current postal accounts	699,823
Carried forward	9,389,990		55,434,569

[a] The enormous increase in the gold reserve is due to (1) the revaluation of the gold on the basis of the new franc (the June 21 statement treated gold in terms of pre-war francs); (2) the inclusion here of some gold which had heretofore been counted under the headings "Purchases of gold, silver, and exchange," and "Divers." This figure does not include the gold "abroad, but not available" which has been "amortized," or written off the books — 1,350 millions of it through the surplus resulting from revaluation of the rest of the gold (Convention of June 23) and the rest through the resources of the Bank itself. Exchange formerly entered under "Free, and gold resources abroad" is now entered instead under "Divers." (*Cf.* statement of Bank of France, *L'Économiste Français*, July 7, 1928, pp. 8–9.)

[b] Foreign exchange loaned did not appear in the former Bank statements. This new item is counterbalanced on the liability side by a similar entry.

[*] The totals given are the true totals, to the nearest thousand francs.

Brought forward	9,389,990		55,434,569
June 21, 1928		June 25, 1928	
Paris Portfolio: Bills on Paris	535,452	Commercial bills discounted: On France	2,955,454
Foreign bills	14,705	Foreign bills	16,969
Treasury paper	6,130		
Portfolio of the branches:		Negotiable bills:	
Local bills	1,145,256	Bought in France	....
Treasury paper	12,030	Bought abroad	10,544,906
Advances on securities:		Total advances on securities	1,846,774
At Paris	220,555		
At branches	1,676,808		
Advances to the State ("permanent")	200,000	Loans to the State without interest	3,200,000 [c]
Advances to the State ("temporary")	17,900,000 [d]		
French Treasury bonds discounted for advances by the State to foreign governments (Russian loan)	5,930,000	Negotiable bonds of the *Caisse d'Amortissement*	5,930,000 [e]
Rentes for the reserve	12,981	*Rentes* set aside for special use	112,981
Disposable *rentes*	212,423		
"Immobilised" *rentes*	100,000		
Building and furniture	4,000	Real estate	219,327
Real estate of branches	215,267		
Administrative expenses	87,522	Demonetized silver coins, to be remelted	784,825
Special reserve	8,156		
Divers	31,305,167	*Divers*	1,239,423 [f]
	68,976,442		82,285,227

[c] The new item of 3,000,000,000 is repayable when the Bank's charter expires—i.e., December 31, 1945. It was created that the Treasury might have adequate "working capital." It bears no interest.

[d] These advances were wiped out through the surplus coming from revaluation of the Bank's gold stock.

[e] The French Treasury Bonds deposited with the Bank to secure the Russian Loan (see page 220) were turned over to the *Caisse*, which has the task of amortizing them; in return, the *Caisse* gave its own (negotiable) three-months' bonds to the Bank, which the Bank may sell and repurchase as it wishes — a species of "open-market operation." As the Treasury bonds are amortized, the *Caisse* bonds will likewise be redeemed.

[f] Foreign exchange bought by the Bank is transferred from "Divers" to (*a*) Resources abroad (sight claims), (*b*) Negotiable bills — bought abroad.

LIABILITIES

June 21, 1928		June 25, 1928	
Capital	182,500	Capital	182,500 [g]
Profits to be added to capital	272,696	Profits to be added to capital	272,696
Legal *réserves mobilières:*			
Law of May 17, 1834	10,000		
Former départemental banks	2,981		
Law of June 9, 1857	9,125	Legal reserves	22,106
Réserve immobilière	4,000	*Réserve immobilière*	4,000
Special reserve	8,407		(no item) [h]
Amortization account (Laws of Dec. 26, 1914 and of Dec. 20, 1918):			
Amortization guarantee (Convention of Oct. 26, 1927, art. 3)	*mémoire*		(no item) [h]
Surplus employed toward amortization of advances to the State	492,300		(no item) [h]
Supplementary account of interest of the amortization account (Law of Dec. 20, 1918)	19,412		(no item) [h]
Note circulation	58,881,795	Note circulation	58,772,461
Interest on securities transferred or deposited	89,210		(no item)
Bills and notes payable at Paris and in the branches	209		(no item)
Current account of the Treasury	9,058	Current account of the Treasury	5,078,689 [i]
Current accounts and other deposits at Paris	5,741,283	Current account of the *Caisse d'Amortissement*	1,934,117
Carried forward	65,722,976		66,266,569

[g] Doubts have arisen whether this sum is now large enough for the Bank, as it is but one-fifth the pre-war capital (measured in gold). (*Cf. L'Économiste Français*, July 14, 1928, p. 35.)

[h] These accounts are now closed (Convention of June 23, 1928).

[i] This increase is due largely to the provision (Convention of June 23, 1928) that the surplus resulting from the revaluation of the gold, silver, and foreign exchange should be credited to the Treasury's current account — that is, all of the surplus that remained after wiping out the State's debt to the bank, and most of the item "gold abroad, but not available."

Brought forward	65,722,976		66,266,569
June 21, 1928		June 25, 1928	
Same, at branches	1,630,031	Current accounts and other deposits	5,471,053
Dividends payable	2,870	Other sight obligations	273,390
Divers discounts and interest, at Paris and the branches	97,694	Obligations arising from loan of foreign exchange	9,777,768
Rediscount of the last half year at Paris and the branches	9,159		
Divers	1,513,711	*Divers*	496,448
	68,976,442		82,285,227

APPENDIX C

NOTE ON INDICES USED FOR DEFLATING PURPOSES

The data upon which chief dependence has been placed as a basis for reducing paper franc values to a pre-war basis are the wholesale price indices of the *Statistique Général* (Table 73). These, however, have been transferred to the base of 1913 as one hundred. For full discussion of the limitations of these figures the reader is referred to Volume II of this series, *The Process of Inflation in France*, 1914–1927, by Professor J. H. Rogers.

The series of exchange rates which were used for the purpose of deflating the paper franc figures are shown in Table 74. This table was prepared by Professor J. H. Rogers.

TABLE 73

FRENCH WHOLESALE PRICE INDEX

BASE 1913=100. 1913 FROM 1901–1910 INDEX=115.6

(Source: *League of Nations Bulletin*)

Year	Jan.	Feb.	March	April	May	June	July	Aug.	Sept.	Oct.	Nov.	Dec.	Yearly Average
1913	100.78	100.26	100.52	101.12	100.43	101.38	99.13	99.05	100.43	98.96	99.22	98.53	100.00
1914	99.0	99.9	99.5	98.7	99.6	99.3	97.9	102.2	102.9	103.8	106.7	110.5	101.67
1915	119.5	124.5	129.5	133.0	135.2	137.4	139.8	140.7	144.5	151.3	158.9	163.2	139.79
1916	172.7	177.9	185.9	190.9	190.4	188.4	184.5	186.0	188.7	192.9	197.4	203.5	188.27
1917	215.6	225.6	228.9	248.0	256.0	266.2	268.0	270.0	279.9	283.6	293.2	304.3	261.61
1918	312.8	319.4	327.1	333.4	335.5	328.7	337.3	350.0	355.1	359.9	357.9	352.8	339.16
1919	347.6	340.4	335.7	332.2	325.1	328.7	348.6	347.5	360.0	381.8	405.0	422.7	356.275
1920	486.8	521.9	554.5	587.5	550.1	492.7	495.6	501.3	525.7	501.7	460.7	434.8	509.44
1921	406.6	377.4	359.9	347.1	329.4	325.0	330.1	331.3	344.0	331.3	331.8	325.7	344.96
1922	313.8	306.4	307.4	313.7	316.8	325.0	325.1	331.2	329.3	337.4	352.1	361.9	326.67
1923	386.9	421.8	424.0	414.7	406.5	408.6	406.7	413.1	423.6	420.5	442.9	458.6	418.99
1924	494.0	543.7	499.3	450.0	458.5	465.3	481.0	476.6	485.6	497.1	503.5	507.2	488.48
1925	514.4	515.0	513.5	512.8	519.8	542.6	556.8	557.2	555.7	572.3	605.5	632.4	549.83
1926	633.5	635.6	631.8	650.1	687.9	738.4	836.2	769.5	786.9	751.5	683.8	626.5	702.64
1927	621.8	631.6	641.4	636.5	628.6	622.6	619.9	617.9	600.3	587.5	.....	.....	......

TABLE 74

DOLLAR EXCHANGE IN PARIS

(END-OF-MONTH DAILY RATES (1914–1918) AND AVERAGES OF DAILY RATES FOR FINAL WEEKS OF EACH MONTH (1919–1927); FRANCS PER DOLLAR)*

	1914	1915	1916	1917	1918	1919	1920
January....	5.18 [a]	5.18	5.87	5.84	5.70	5.45	13.07
February...	5.18	5.28	5.87	5.84	5.70	5.45	14.25
March......	5.18	5.31	5.97	5.84	5.70	5.92	14.50
April.......	5.15	5.33	5.94	5.70	5.70	6.05	16.77
May.......	5.15	5.42	5.93	5.70	5.70	6.43	13.15
June.......	5.15	5.50	5.91	5.70	5.70	6.45	12.06
July.......	5.15	5.68	5.91	5.70	5.70	7.12	12.95
August.....	5.12 [b]	5.95	5.89	5.70	5.50	8.03	14.37
September..	....	5.75	5.85	5.70	5.47	8.52	14.68
October.....	5.18 [c]	5.97	5.84	5.70	5.47	8.67	15.67
November..	5.10	5.91	5.84	5.70	5.47	9.68	16.40
December...	5.17	5.85	5.84	5.70	5.45	10.52	17.04

	1921	1922	1923	1924	1925	1926	1927
January....	14.04	12.31	15.57	21.74	18.49	26.77	25.32
February...	13.92	11.00	16.45	25.57	19.38	27.49	25.55
March......	14.30	11.12	15.23	18.32	19.06	28.65	25.54
April.......	13.22	10.82	14.84	15.45	19 20	30.15	25.53
May.......	11.79	11.07	15.15	18.80	19.83	30.60	25.53
June.......	12.40	11.99	16.32	18.88	21.56	34.93	25.54
July.......	12.98	11.96	16.84	19.86	21.11	41.15	25.56
August.....	12.96	13.02	17.65	18.48	21.30	35.12	25.51
September..	14.00	13.15	16.15	18.96	21.12	35.66	25.48
October.....	13.74	14.19	17.19	19.13	23.92	32.52	25.47
November..	14.23	14.38	18.51	18.82	26.09	28.11	25.43
December...	12.40	13.74	19.59	18.56	26.90	25.25	25.40

[a] January 22 [b] August 8 [c] November 18

* The rates given in the table are, for the years 1914–1918 inclusive, daily rates for the last Thursday of each month as given by *L'Économiste Français;* and for the years 1919–1927 inclusive, arithmetic averages of daily rates for the last week of each month during which there were at least four quotation days. For 1919 the average rates were computed from the daily rates published in the *Journal Officiel;* for the years 1920–1926 from material furnished by the *Statistique Général de la France* and compiled by it; for the period 1920–February 1924, from the daily rates given by the *Journal Officiel,* and for the period February 1924–1926, from those published in the *Cote des Agents de Change;* and for 1927 from the rates in the *Cote des Agents de Change.* The daily rates given in the table or used in computing the average rates represent averages of highest and lowest quotations during official exchange hours, except those taken from the *Journal Officiel,* which are single prevailing daily rates.

BIBLIOGRAPHY

BIBLIOGRAPHY

The following bibliography is not comprehensive; the amount of material on public finance that has appeared in France during and since the war is so large that much more space would be required. Furthermore, much of it is either polemic or superficial, and by far the largest number of books on taxation are handy manuals, brief and apt to mislead one who does not already know the tax system as a whole. There has, of course, been a large amount of argument and some description in the periodicals and newspapers, but most of the material for this book has been drawn from official sources — conversations at the Ministry of Finance, and inspection of official publications and unpublished records — and from a few exceptionally well informed books.

Public Documents

Bérenger Memorandum (to the American Debt Funding Commission).
Reprinted in *France and Her Capacity to Pay* (Paris, Reference Service on International Affairs of the American Library in Paris, 1926).

Bulletin de Statistique et de Législation Comparée (Imprimerie Nationale).
Monthly publication, reprinting practically all the information appearing in *Lois et Décrets* which concerns the Ministry of Finance, and in addition, certain material not easily available elsewhere — e.g., annual collection reports of Indirect Taxes Administration, etc. It also contains current fiscal information concerning other countries, new tax laws, tax returns, etc.

Compte Général de l'Administration des Finances (Imprimerie Nationale).
Annual publication containing definitive statement of receipts and expenses for the *exercice*. The last one to appear, to date, was that for the year 1916, published in 1925.

Compte Général des Recettes et Dépenses de la Ville de Paris (Paris, Imprimerie Paul Dupont).
Annual volume, containing definitive statement of receipts and expenditures of City of Paris.

Compte Général du Département de la Seine.
Same as above, for the département of the Seine.

Inventaire de la Situation Financière de la France au Début de la Treizième Législature. Présenté par M. Clémentel, Ministre des Finances (Imprimerie Nationale, 1924), 273 pp.

A *document parlementaire,* annexed to the 1925 budget *projet,* giving summary of French financial situation as of 1924, and French fiscal history since 1914.

Journal Officiel.

1. *Lois et Décrets:* Issued five or six times a week, gives the text of laws, decrees, and *arrêtés* promulgated; also, monthly statements of revenue and expenditure; occasional official interpretations of the tax law, and other official information issued by the various ministries.

2. *Documents Parlementaires.* Each document is first printed separately, and at the end of the year all are printed together in volume form. They include:

(a) *Projets de lois* as submitted by the ministers to Parliament — i.e., the text of the proposed law with, usually, explanations of its purposes and details (*exposé des motifs*);

(b) *Propositions de lois,* or *propositions de résolutions,* proposed laws and resolutions, drawn up by members of the Chamber or Senate and sent to the appropriate commission for study;

(c) Reports by the Chamber and Senate commissions on (a) and (b) above, usually with lengthy discussion and analysis — the most important part of the *Journal Officiel* for such purposes, and

(d) Reports of various administrative commissions, savings banks reports, etc., collected and published annually, usually having little to do with taxation.

3. *Débats.* Transcript of Senate and Chamber debates, appearing the day following such debates.

Loi de Finances de. . . . (Imprimerie Nationale).

Annual volume compiled by same bureau that edits the *Bulletin de Statistique.* A collection of the fiscal laws passed during the year (tax laws, budget laws, supplementary credits, provisional credits).

Notions Élémentaires sur les Impôts Directs (Paris, Ministry of Finance, Imprimerie Nationale, 1926), viii, 509 pp.

Official interpretation of administration of income taxes, *taxes assimilées,* and local direct taxes.

Projets de Budget Général.

Proposed annual budget law as submitted to Chamber by Minister of Finance. Most of the first volume appears in the *Documents Parlementaires,* but this and succeeding volumes are published separately, available as soon as the law has been submitted. The first volume contains, among other things, the text of the law, summary of receipts and expenditures, statement of public debt and of Treasury accounts, and reference list of previous tax laws. Other volumes contain detailed analysis of estimated expenses of the general ministries.

Among these *projets*, that for the 1923 budget (No. 4220) presented by M. de Lasteyrie, is especially valuable for a detailed survey of war and post-war finances.

Rapport du Comité des Experts (Imprimerie Nationale, 1926), 171 pp.

Report of Experts' Commission created by decree of May 31, 1926, to study the entire fiscal situation and make recommendations.

Renseignements Statistiques relatifs aux Contributions Directes et aux Taxes Assimilées (Imprimerie Nationale).

Annual volume published by Direct Tax Administration, giving detailed analysis of returns for income taxes, *taxes assimilées*, local *centimes additionnels*, and the war-profits tax.

Situation Financière des Départements en. . . . (Melun, Imprimerie Administrative).

Annual report to the Minister of the Interior, summarizing département tax receipts from *centimes additionnels*, département total receipts, expenses, indebtedness, and the larger part of subventions received. The last volume published, to date, is that for the year 1923.

Situation Financière des Communes de France et d'Algérie en. . . . (Melun, Imprimerie Administrative).

Triennial report to the Minister of the Interior, summarizing total population, area, receipts, expenditures, indebtedness, and number of *centimes additionnels* of each commune. The last volume published, to date, is that for the year 1923.

Tax Manuals

A. *All Taxes*

Benjamin Monteux et André Sauzède, *Nos Impôts en 1926* (Paris, Librairie du Barreau, 1926), 298 pp. + addenda of 8 pp.

Camille Rosier, *Traité théorique et pratique de Législation fiscale*, (Paris, Librairie Générale de Droit et de Jurisprudence, 1926), Vol. I, *L'Histoire des Impôts; Les Impôts directs actuels;* 447 pp.; Vol. II, *Les Impôts indirects et les Impôts locaux actuels; Les Réformes envisagées*, 602 pp.

——, *Tous Nos Impôts* (Paris, Société des Annales Commerciales, Judiciaries et Fiscales, 1926), lviii + 1021 pp. The most complete manual covering all French taxes.

——, *Les Lois fiscales de 1926* (Paris, Société des Annales Commerciales, Judiciaires et Fiscales, 1927), 230 pp. Brings *Tous Nos Impôts* up to date.

B. *Income Taxes and Other Direct Taxes*

Edgard Allix and Marcel Lecerclé, *L'Impôt sur le Revenu* (Paris, Rousseau, 1926), Vol. I, vii + 443 pp.; Vol. II, 466 + xi pp. *Complément* (*Commentaire des Lois du 4 Décembre 1925, du 4 Avril et du 29 Avril 1926*), 124 pp. Much more than a mere tax manual, this work outlines the history of the direct taxes, and adds a chapter on local *centimes additionnels.*

Lucien Bocquet, *L'Impôt sur le Revenu. Troisième Édition* (Paris, Sirey, 1926), viii + 1112 pp. *Supplément* (*Lois de 4 et 9 Avril, du 3 Août, du 19 Décembre 1926, avec la Codification*), 1927, 285 pp. Somewhat narrower in scope than Allix and Lecerclé, and more fully documented.

André Sauzède, *Traité de la Contribution foncière* (Paris, Sirey, 1926), 351 pp.

Albert Wahl, *Juris-Classeur fiscal* (Paris, Administration des Juris-Classeurs), Vol. I, Industrial and Commercial Profits Tax, Non-Commercial Revenues Tax; Vol. II, Salaries Tax, Tax on Income from *Capitaux Mobiliers,* Agricultural Profits Tax, Real Estate Tax; Vol. III, General Income Tax, Local Taxes. Detailed legal analysis, kept up to date by loose-leaf system. Excellent reference for legal development of tax and current legal interpretation.

C. *Registration and Stamp Taxes*

Code de l'Enregistrement et du Timbre (Paris, Dalloz, 1924–1925), vii + 103 + 881 + 75 pp. Compilation of laws and decrees (without comment) from 1738 to 1925.

Édouard Maguéro, Édouard Tassain, et Étienne Molas, *Supplément à la 2ème Édition dû Traité alphabétique des Droits de l'Enregistrement, de Timbre et d'Hypothèques* (Paris, La Revue de l'Enregistrement, 1926), 1113 pp. Exhaustive legal treatise, in dictionary form, supplementing earlier work published in 1911.

Manuel des Successions (Paris, Dalloz, 1925), vii + 311 pp.

Georges Vincent, *Traité technique et pratique des Droits d'Enregistrement, de Timbre et d'Hypothèques* (Paris, Rivière, 1927), x + 504 pp.

D. *Turnover Tax*

Edgard Allix and Marcel Lecerclé, *La Taxe sur le Chiffre d'Affaires* (Paris, Rousseau, 1927), viii + 440 pp. Analytic and critical as well as an excellent tax manual.

Maurice Gardes, *L'Impôt sur le Chiffre d'Affaires* (Poitiers, Oudin, 1924), two volumes; vii + 94 pp., viii + 356 pp. One of the two best manuals on this subject. New edition about to appear.

Albert Wahl, *Juris-Classeur fiscal*, Vol. IV, *Impôt sur le Chiffre d'Affaires*.

E. *Indirect Taxes*

L. Hourcade, *Manuel encyclopédique des Contributions indirectes et des Octrois* (Poitiers, Oudin, 1925), xiii + 1275 pp. + addenda. Exhaustive manual designed especially for tax collectors.

F. *War-Profits Taxes*

Emmanuel Besson, *Traité pratique de la Contribution extraordinaire des Bénéfices de Guerre et de l'Impôt cédulaire sur les Bénéfices commerciaux et industriels. Troisième Édition* (Paris, Dalloz, 1919), xv + 375 pp. Almost all the book devoted to technical description of war-profits tax, containing many references to legal decisions. *Supplément* to the above, concerning the laws of June 25 and June 31, 1920 (Paris, Dalloz, 1921), 62 pp.

Maurice Palmade, *Traité pratique de la Contribution sur les Bénéfices de Guerre* (Paris, Sirey, 1922), 157 pp.

General Treatises Dealing in Whole or in Large Part with French Public Finance

Edgard Allix, *Traité élémentaire de Science des Finances et de Législation financière française. Cinquième Édition* (Paris, Rousseau, 1927), xxix + 1053 pp. Comprehensive, accurate, and up-to-date survey of French fiscal problems. By far the best of its kind.

J. R. Cahill, *Report on the Economic and Industrial Conditions in France. Revised to July, 1925* (Report to British Department of Overseas Trade, London, His Majesty's Stationery Office, 1925), 301 pp.

——, Same as above, for 1925–1926 (London, H.M. Stationery Office, 1926), 300 pp.

Arthur Girault, *Manuel de Législation financière* (Paris, Sirey), three volumes; Vol. I, *Les Budgets et le Trésor* (1924), viii + 306 pp., Vol. II, *Les Ressources publiques; L'Impôt* (1925), xii + 398 pp., Vol. III, *Les Dépenses publiques; L'Emprunt* (1927), vi + 256 pp.

Germain-Martin, Les Finances publiques de la France et la Fortune privée (1914–1925) (Paris, Payot, 1925), 444 pp, A running account of French fiscal changes during and after the war.

Félix Moreau, *Manuel élémentaire de Législation et Science financières* (Paris, de Boccard, 1925), 636 pp.

Budget and Public Debt

Gaston Jèze, *Cours de Science des Finances et de Législation financière. Sixième Édition* (Paris, Giard, 1922), Vol. I, *Théorie générale du Budget*, xx + 286 pp.; Vol. II, *Dépenses publiques — Théorie générale du Crédit public*, xxviii + 507 pp.

Georges Lachapelle, *L'Évolution de la Circulation, des Changes, des Prix et de l'Émission des Valeurs à court terme du Trésor de 1914 à 1926* (Paris, Société d'Études et d'Informations Économiques, 1926).

Theodoric Legrand, *Répertoire de la Comptabilité publique. Principes généraux. Lois et Règlements* (Paris, Direction des Publications Administratives et Bibliothèque Municipale et Rurale, 1924), 688 pp. Quotations from laws, decrees and administrative interpretation, without comment, concerning methods of collection and disbursement of public revenues.

Raymond Levrault, *Les Caisses d'Amortissement de la Dette publique d'après Guerre* (Paris, Sagot, 1926), viii + 109 pp.

F. François-Marsal, *Les Dettes interalliées* (Paris, La Renaissance du Livre), 176 pp.

Harold G. Moulton and Cleona Lewis, *The French Debt Problem* (New York, Macmillan, 1925), xii + 459 pp.

War Finances

Gaston Jèze, *Les Dépenses de Guerre de la France.* (Paris, Les Presses Universitaires de France, 1925), xii + 229 pp.

——, *Les Finances de Guerre de la France: La Politique financière du Gouvernement pendant les Années 1915 et 1916* (Paris, Giard et Brière, 1918), 205 pp.

——, *La Politique financière pendant les Années 1917 et 1918* (Paris, Giard et Brière, 1919), 138 pp.

——, *La Liquidation financière de la Guerre, 1918–1920* (Paris, Giard et Brière, 1920), 245 pp.

Gaston Jèze, J. Barthélemy, C. Rist, L. Rolland, *Problèmes de Politique et Finances de Guerre* (Paris, Alcan, 1915), vii + 227 pp.

G. Olphe-Galliard, *Histoire économique et financière de la Guerre (1914–1918)* (Paris, Rivière, 1925), 504 pp.

Henri Truchy, *Les Finances de Guerre de la France* (Paris, Les Presses Universitaires de France), xii, 171 pp.

Miscellaneous

B. M. Anderson, *The Progress of French Finance* (New York, Chase National Bank, February 18, 1927), Chase Economic Bulletin, Vol. vii, No. 1.

J. B. Boissonnet, *Réforme des Finances locales* (Paris, Rousseau, 1926), vii + 188 pp.

Marcello Boldrini, *International Comparisons on the Burden of Taxation* (Rome, Provveditorato Generale dello Stato Libreria, 1925), 16 pp. + graphs.

L. Chatin-Ollier, *La Politique douanière et la Stabilité dans les Relations commerciales* (Paris, 1925), x + 241 pp. Describes efforts of France and other countries to allow the customs duties to advance with the price level.

Corrado Gini, *A Comparison of the Wealth and National Income of Several Important Nations (Italy, France, Belgium, United Kingdom and United States) before and after the War* (Rome, Provveditorato Generale dello Stato Libreria, 1925), 16 pp. + graphs.

Sisley Huddleston, *France* (London, Benn, 1926), 613 pp.

Bertrand Nogaro, *Finances et Politique* (Paris, Giard, 1927), viii + 223 pp.

George Peel, *The Financial Crisis of France* (London, Macmillan, 1926), xi + 323 pp.

Periodicals

I. *Weekly Publications:*

L'Économiste Européen (Paris). One of the best weeklies for general summary of French and foreign finance.

L'Économiste Français (Paris). Old and well known weekly, with important leading articles.

Journal des Contributions Indirectes (Poitiers, P. Oudin). A journal for the tax collector, occasionally containing interesting special articles.

II. *Important Monthly and Irregular Publications:*

Bulletin de la Chambre de Commerce de Paris. Presents viewpoint of this representative business group.

Journal des Économistes (Paris).

Revue Bibliographique des Ouvrages de Droit, de Jurisprudence et d'Économie Politique (Paris, Giard).

Revue d'Économie Politique (Paris). Edited by Charles Gide.

Revue des Impôts sur le Commerce et l'Industrie (Paris, E. Maguéro). Prints laws, court decisions, etc., concerning taxes affecting business.

Revue de Science et de Législation Financières (Paris). Edited by Gaston Jèze.

Revue Politique et Parlementaire (Paris).

BIBLIOGRAPHY, DICTIONARIES, ETC.

Dalloz, *Répertoire pratique de Législation, de Doctrine, et de Jurisprudence.* Annual volume, giving laws passed, significant extracts from official documents, debates, etc., pertaining thereto, and court decisions. Excellent source for a preliminary, and yet detailed study of any fiscal question.

A. Grandin, *Bibliographie générale des Sciences juridiques, politiques, économiques et sociales de 1810 à 1925–1926.* Three volumes. Exhaustive bibliography of works in French. Covers financial field thoroughly.

T. Thaller, *Traité élémentaire de Droit commercial. Septième Édition* (Paris, Rosseau, 1925), 1340 pp. One of the best elementary treatises on commercial law.

INDEX

Bei Fragen zur Produktsicherheit wenden Sie sich bitte an:
If you have any questions regarding product safety,
please contact:

Walter de Gruyter GmbH
Genthiner Straße 13
10785 Berlin
productsafety@degruyterbrill.com